Impulsivity and Aggression

We would like to dedicate this book to our wives, Beth Fein and Heather Zar, for all their support and understanding.

Impulsivity and Aggression

Edited by

E. HOLLANDER
Mount Sinai School of Medicine, New York, USA

D. J. STEIN
University of Stellenbosch, Tygerberg, South Africa

JOHN WILEY & SONS

Chichester • New York • Brisbane • Toronto • Singapore

Other Wiley Editorial Offices

John Wiley & Sons, Inc., 605 Third Avenue,
New York, NY 10158-0012, USA

Jacaranda Wiley Ltd, 33 Park Road, Milton,
Queensland 4064, Australia

John Wiley & Sons (Canada) Ltd, 22 Worcester Road,
Rexdale, Ontario M9W 1L1, Canada

John Wiley & Sons (SEA) Pte Ltd, 37 Jalan Pemimpin #05-04,
Block B, Union Industrial Building, Singapore 2057

Library of Congress Cataloging-in-Publication Data

Impulsivity and aggression/edited by E. Hollander and D.J. Stein.
    p. cm.
  Includes bibliographical references and index.
  ISBN 0 471 95328 8
  1. Aggressiveness (Psychology)   2. Impulse control disorders.
I. Hollander, Eric, 1957– . II. Stein, Dan J.
  [DNLM: 1. Impulsive Behavior—psychology. 2. Aggression—psychology. BF 685 I34 1994]
RC569.5.A34I47 1994
155.2'32—dc20
DNLM/DLC
for Library of Congress   94-27712
                                                                              CIP

British Library Cataloguing in Publication Data

A catalogue record for this book is available from the British Library

ISBN 0 471 95328 8

Typeset in 10/12pt Times by Keytec Typesetting Ltd, Bridport, Dorset.
Printed and bound in Great Britain by Bookcraft (Bath) Ltd, Midsomer Norton, Avon

Contents

Contributors

Dr Per Bech
Professor of Psychiatry, Psychiatric Institute, Frederiksborg General Hospital, Dyrehavevj 48, DK 3400, Hillerød, Denmark

Dr José Luis Carrasco
Psychiatrist, Department of Psychiatry, San Carlos Hospital, Complutense University, Madrid 28040, Spain

Dr Emil F Coccaro
Associate Professor of Psychiatry and Director, Clinical Neuroscience Research Unit, Department of Psychiatry, Medical College of Pennsylvania at Eastern Pennsylvania Psychiatric Institute, 3200 Henry Avenue, Philadelphia, PA 19129, USA

Dr Burr Eichelman
Professor & Chairman, Department of Psychiatry, Temple University School of Medicine, 3401 North Broad St, Philadelphia, PA 19140, USA

Dr Armando R Favazza
Professor, Department of Psychiatry, University of Missouri-Columbia, Three Hospital Drive, Columbia, MO 65201, USA

Dr Eric Hollander
Associate Professor and Vice-Chairman of Psychiatry, Director–Clinical Psychopharmacology and Clinical Director–Seaver Center for the Research and Treatment of Autism, Mount Sinai School of Medicine, 1 Gustave L. Levy Place, New York, NY 10029, USA

Dr James I Hudson
Chief of Neurophysiology Laboratory, Laboratories for Psychiatric Research, McLean Hospital, Belmont, MA, and Associate Professor of Psychiatry, Harvard Medical School, Boston, MA 02178, USA

Dr Martin P Kafka
Attending Psychiatrist, McLean Hospital, 115 Mill St, Belmont, MA 02178, USA and Clinical Instructor in Psychiatry, Harvard Medical School, Boston, MA, USA

Dr Paul E Keck Jr
Co-Director, Biological Psychiatry Program, University of Cincinatti College of Medicine, 231 Bethesda Avenue ML 559, Cincinatti, OH 45267-0559, USA

Dr Paul de Koning
Clinical Director, Serenics Program, CNS Pharmacology, Solvay Duphar BV, PO Box 900, NL-1300, DAAWeesp, The Netherlands

Dr Juan José López-Ibor Jr
Professor of Psychiatry, The Lopez-Ibor Clinic, Neuva Zelande 44, 28035 Madrid, Spain

Dr Marianne Mak
Clinical Director, Serenics Program, Solvay Duphar BV, PO Box 900, NL-1380, DA Weesp, The Netherlands

Dr Paul Markovitz
Assistant Clinical Professor of Psychiatry, Mood & Anxiety Research Center, Case Western Reserve University, 2101 Richmond Road, Beachwood, Ohio, OH 44122 USA

Philip I Markowitz
Research Psychiatrist, Clinical Neurosciences Research Unit, Department of Psychiatry, Medical College of Pennsylvania at Eastern Pennsylvania Institute, 3200 Henry Avenue, Philadelphia, PA 19129, USA

Dr Susan L McElroy
Co-Director, Biological Psychiatry Program, University of Cincinatti College of Medicine, 231 Bethesda Avenue ML 559, Cincinatti, OH 45267-0559, USA

Dr Jan Mos
Research Project Manager, Anxiety Disorders, CNS Pharmacology, Solvay Duphar BV, PO Box 900, NL-1380, DA Weesp, The Netherlands

Antonia S New
WPIC, Room 1175, 3811 O'Hara Street, Pittsburgh, PA 15213, USA

Dr Berend Olivier
Head of CNS Pharmacology, Solvay Duphar BV, C J van Houtenlaan 36, 1381 CP Weesp, The Netherlands

Dr Robert Plutchik
Director of Program Evaluation, Division of Substance Abuse, Professor of Psychiatry, Albert Einstein College of Medicine, Bronx Municipal Hospital Center, Pelham Parkway South & Eastchester Road, Bronx, New York 10461, USA

Dr Harrison G Pope
Chief of Biological Psychiatry Laboratory, Laboratories for Psychiatric Research, McLean Hospital, Belmont, MA, and Associate Professor of Psychiatry, Harvard Medical School, Boston, MA 02178, USA

Dr William H Reid
Medical Director (TXMHMR), Professor of Psychiatry, University of Texas System, PO Box 12668, Austin, TX 78711-2668, USA

Dr Lee N Robins
Professor of Social Science in Psychiatry, Department of Psychiatry, Washington University School of Medicine, 4940 Children's Place, St Louis, MO 63110, USA

Dr Larry J Siever
Professor of Psychiatry, Veterans Affairs Medical Center, Kingsbridge Road, Bronx, New York, USA and Department of Psychiatry, Mount Sinai School of Medicine, Queens Hospital Center, 82-68 164th Street, Jamaica, NY 11432, USA

Dr Jonathan Silver
Director of Neuropsychiatry, Columbia-Presbyterian Medical Center, Associate Professor of Clinical Psychiatry, College of Physicians and Surgeons, Columbia University, Morningside Heights, New York, NY 10027, USA

Dr Daphne Simeon
Assistant Professor, Department of Psychiatry, Mount Sinai School of Medicine, Queens Hospital Center, 82-68 164th Street, Jamaica, NY 11432, USA

Dr Robert I Simon
Clinical Professor of Psychiatry, Georgetown University School of Medicine, Washington DC. 7921 D. Glenbrook Road, Bethesda, MD 20814, USA

Dr Dan J Stein
Director of Research, Department of Psychiatry, Faculty of Medicine, University of Stellenbosch, PO Box 19063, 7505 Tygerberg, South Africa

Dr David Stoff
Chief, Perpetrators and Violence Research Program, Violence and Trauma Stress Research Branch, Division of Epidemiology and Services Research, National Institute of Mental Health, 5600 Fisher Lane, Room 10C-26, Rockville, MD 20857, USA

Dr Michael H Stone
Professor of Clinical Psychiatry, Columbia College of Physicians & Surgeons, Apt# 114, 225 Central Park West, New York City, NY 10024, USA

Dr James Towey
Research Scientist, Department of Biopsychology, New York State Psychiatric Institute, 722 W 168th St, Unit 50, New York, NY 100032, USA

Robert L Trestman
*Assistant Professor of Psychiatry, Veterans Affairs Medical Center,
Kingsbridge Road, Bronx, New York, USA, and Department of Psychiatry,
Mount Sinai School of Medicine, Queens Hospital Center, 82-68 164th Street,
Jamaica, NY 11432, USA*

Dr Herman van Praag
*Professor and Chairman of Psychiatry, Academic Psychiatric Center,
University of Limburg, P-Debyelaan 25, Postbus 5800, 6202 AZ Maastricht,
The Netherlands*

Dr Benedetto Vitiello
*Head, Pediatric Psychopharmacology Program, Child and Adolescent
Disorders Research Branch, Division of Clinical Research, National Institute
of Mental Health, 5600 Fishers Lane, Room 10c-26, Rockville, MD 20857,
USA*

Dr Stuart C Yudofsky
*Professor & Chairman, Department of Psychiatry and Behavioral Sciences,
Baylor College of Medicine, One Baylor Plaza, Rm 115-D Houston, TX
77030-3498, USA*

1 Introduction

ERIC HOLLANDER* AND DAN J STEIN‡
*Department of Psychiatry, Mount Sinai School of Medicine, NY, USA
‡Department of Psychiatry, University of Stellenbosch, Tygerberg, South Africa

A man inexplicably opens fire with a semiautomatic weapon on a crowded commuter railway, killing and injuring a large number of people in only a few moments of panic and disarray. A high-level government official who has experienced unflattering reports in the media suddenly shoots and kills himself. Taxi cab drivers in New York City are reported to have the most dangerous profession in America. The homicide rate in the USA is seven times higher than that of the second most violent country. How can we understand or make sense of such tragic occurrences, and such discouraging statistics? What role does impulsivity and aggression play in these events?

Impulsivity and aggression are phenomena that are present in all species and are manifest as affects, emotions, and observable behaviors. In recent years, intense scrutiny of these phenomena has generated important developments in a number of related fields and disciplines, such as sociology, criminal justice, epidemiology, neurobiology, animal models, functional imaging, and psychopharmacology.

In addition, impulsivity and aggression contribute to major public health problems such as crime, violence, homicide, suicide, substance abuse, and sexual dyscontrol. As such, they impinge on the public's attention via media coverage of so-called random acts of violence; influence the national condition by impacting on the economy via health-care and prison costs, lost productivity, post-traumatic stress symptoms, and disability claims; and are reflected in the national fear of crime. Nothing effects the psyche of the individual and society more than random acts of violence and suicide, which seem to be ever more frequent, and are reported in the media with ever increasing and lurid detail. Next to the economy, crime is the second greatest concern to the average US citizen. Of particular concern, a greater percentage of the aggression in our society is associated with the young, and half of all homicides currently are committed by those under the age of 25.

Clearly, the causes of impulsivity and aggression are highly complex and multifaceted. Sociological explanations suggest that poverty, lack of education, the breakdown of the nuclear family, substance abuse and alcohol abuse, lack of jobs and opportunity, racism, despair, and the widespread availability of guns and automatic weapons are contributing factors. Thus, targeted approaches to these important environmental or sociological factors may modify the expression of impulsive aggressive behavior in our society. An alternate approach focuses on the biological underpinnings in the mediation and modification of these impulsive and aggressive phenomena (see later). This book focuses on the phenomenology, neurobiology, and treatment of impulsivity and aggression, as well as on specific disorders of impulse control and related disorders.

Diagnostic and phenomenological approaches to impulsivity are outlined by Drs Plutchik and van Praag in this book, who suggest that impulsivity is a multidimensional concept and involves sexual and aggressive emotions and the ability to delay gratification. Impulsivity is seen as only one trait system among a complex balance of forces within the individual. Dr Bech describes progress and difficulties in the measurement of aggression, including the use of self-rating and clinician-administered psychometric scales.

Epidemiological approaches to violence are described by Dr Robins, who notes the importance of childhood predisposition, as well as the impact of historical moments and circumstances in the expression of these predispositions in adult life. Potential causes of the rapid upward trajectory of violence in America are described. This violence has implications for social policy, as well as for the testing of causal roles for violence.

The biological approach suggests that specific biological and neurological dysfunction may mediate symptoms of impulsivity and aggression, and that these observable behaviors and their biological pathways may be reliably observed in different species. While there are likely to be complex interactions between these biological and environmental conditions, targeted approaches at the biological level may lead to a clearer understanding of these behaviors, with the hope of leading to specific treatments. Dr Eichelman reviews animal and evolutionary models of impulsive aggression. The importance of biological (and especially serotonergic) influences on impulsive and aggressive behavior is documented in chapters by Dr Linnoila, Drs Stein, Hollander and Towey, and Drs PI Markowitz and Coccaro, who report on the role of challenge studies in elucidating the biology of impulsive aggression. One example of this serotonergic link is documented in our recent report that core symptoms of borderline personality disorder, such as fear, anger, and impulsivity, and well as neuroendocrine sensitivity, were altered in response to the partial serotonin agonist *meta*-chlorophenylpiperazine (mCPP), in comparison with healthy controls (Hollander et al., 1994).

A categorical approach may reveal specific disorders in which impulsive and aggressive symptoms predominate. These may include personality disorder (i.e. borderline and antisocial personality disorder), disorders of impulsive control (i.e. intermittent explosive disorder, kleptomania, pyromania, trichotillomania), neurological disorders with aggressive/disinhibited behavior (i.e. frontal lobe damage, epilepsy), substance use disorders, and sexual disorders [i.e. pedophilia, nonparaphilic coercive disorder (rape), promiscuous sexual behaviors].

Drs McElroy and colleagues describe the history and definitions, prevalence and course, comorbidity and family studies, biology and treatment response of disorders of impulse control. The consistent structure of the irresistible impulse along with its response to pharmacological treatments suggest the validity of this group of disorders. Drs López-Ibor and Carrasco focus on pathological gambling from diagnostic, demographic, pathogenic, and treatment perspectives.

Drs New, Trestman and Siever describe difficulties in finding specific criteria that differentiate borderline personality disorder from other diagnostic categories, and suggest that a dimensional approach has yielded greater clarity in searching for biological markers and guiding pharmacological treatments. Family and electrophysiological studies, neuroimaging, and measures of central and peripheral serotonergic and noradrenergic function highlight the impulsive aspect of borderline personality disorder. Dr Reid assesses impulsivity and aggression in antisocial personality disorder, and highlights issues such as predatory aggression, substance abuse and criminality, and responsibility and culpability.

As noted above, the dimensional approach to impulsivity and aggression has been championed in recent years, and has been supported by, and facilitated additional studies in, phenomenology, neurochemistry, psychology, psychiatry, neuroanatomy, imaging, and neuropsychopharmacology.

Drs Favazza and Simeon describe the fascinating literature regarding self-mutilation. Dr Kafka describes the epidemiology, etiology, and treatment of sexual impulsivity, paraphilias, rape, and related disorders. Drs Vitiello and Stoff describe the biology of impulsivity and aggression in childhood psychiatric populations, and Drs Silver and Yudofsky describe the evaluation and treatment of aggression in brain damaged populations.

In the last section of this book, treatment strategies for impulsive and aggressive behavior are highlighted. Dr P Markowitz highlights the use of serotonin reuptake inhibitors, and Drs Mak, de Koning, Mos, and Olivier explore the use of selective serotonin (5-hydroxytryptamine) agonists in the treatment of aggression. To date, complex regulatory guidelines have limited industrial development of agents with putative anti-aggressive properties. Trials that focus on the specific personality disorders and disorders of impulse control appear a more promising approach. Dr Stone describes the role of psychological treatments in the management of impulsivity and aggression. Finally, Dr Simon reviews legal and ethical issues, and comments on the role of psychiatrists in providing expert advice and testimony concerning violent behavior.

In summary, this book has attempted to gather together information regarding recent developments in a number of related disciplines, and to present the most up-to-date data on the phenomenology, epidemiology, biology (preclinical peripheral markers, serotonin function, and biological challenges), and neurology of the specific personality disorders, and disorders of impulse control. Chapters on treatment focus on serotonin reuptake inhibitors, other novel serotonergic agents, psychological approaches, and inpatient management, and legal and societal implications are discussed as well.

Remaining problems in the field of impulsivity and aggression include the lack of integration of biological and sociological models, the need for better definition of both dimensional and categorical variables, and the need for better treatment strategies, better animal models, more neuroimaging studies, and more collaboration by people in different fields. Nevertheless, it is important to keep in mind that aggression may be part of life itself, and thus should not always be viewed as pathological.

While studies in this field continue to make important strides, the hope is that this book will provide a state-of-the-art summary and will have an impact on and orient future developments in the field.

ACKNOWLEDGEMENTS

This work was supported in part by Research Scientist Development Award MH-00750 from the National Institute of Mental Health to Dr Hollander, and a NARSAD Young Investigator Award to Dr Stein.

REFERENCES

Hollander, E., Stein, D.J., DeCaria, C.M., et al. (1994). Serotonergic sensitivity in borderline personality disorder: Preliminary finding. *Am. J. Psychiatry*, 151, 277–280.

Part I

PHENOMENOLOGY

2 The Nature of Impulsivity: Definitions, Ontology, Genetics, AND Relations to Aggression

ROBERT PLUTCHIK* AND HERMAN M VAN PRAAG‡
*Albert Einstein College of Medicine, New York, USA
‡Academic Psychiatric Center, University of Limburg, Maastricht, The Netherlands

INTRODUCTION

The concept of impulsivity plays a major role in clinical psychiatry as well as in everyday life. Impulsivity is part of the defining characteristics of a number of psychiatric diagnoses, for example borderline and antisocial personality disorders (Stein et al., 1993), as well as several neurological disorders (Woodcock, 1986). It is believed to be part of the hyperactive syndrome in children, and has been reported to be associated with alcoholism (von Knorring et al., 1987), substance abuse (van Knorring et al., 1987), brain damage (Caplan and Schechter, 1990), and anorexia nervosa and bulimia (Sohlberg et al., 1989). Impulsivity has also been found to be a significant correlate of suicidal and violent behavior (Plutchik and van Praag, 1990). Neurological soft signs have also been correlated with impulsivity (Vitiello et al., 1990).

Although impulsivity has sometimes been confused with aggression or violence, the differences, from both a theoretical and a practical standpoint, are important. The focus of the present chapter, however, will be on impulsivity rather than aggression. It will examine a number of issues connected with the concept of impulsivity. It will consider the question of whether impulsivity has components, how one can measure the concept, its relation to other emotions and states including aggression, its ontogenetic development, whether it has a genetic source, and how one may conceptualize it theoretically. But first, let us look at some definitions that have been proposed.

Impulsivity and Aggression. Edited by E. Hollander and D.J. Stein
© 1995 John Wiley & Sons Ltd

DEFINITIONS OF IMPULSIVITY

In 1938, Murray described impulsivity as the tendency to respond quickly and without reflection. Impulsive individuals have difficulty in restraining their own behavior. They may also be spontaneous. In 1972, Douglas described impulsivity as largely related to the inability to sustain attention. Monroe (1970) has characterized impulsivity in terms of the affects of rage and aggression expressed by homicidal, suicidal, or sexually aggressive behavior. Eysenck (1983) described an impulsivity scale as part of the dimension of extroversion. Barrett and Patton (1983) have defined impulsivity as acting without adequate reflection, spur of the moment reactions, taking risks and trying to get things done quickly. Dickman (1990) has described dysfunctional impulsivity as the tendency to engage in rapid, error-prone information processing. Lorr and Wunderlich (1985) concluded that there are two major bipolar components to the dimension of impulsivity: (1) resisting urges versus giving in to urges, and (2) responding immediately to a stimulus versus planning before making a move.

These definitions have come largely from the research and speculations of psychologists. In contrast, psychiatrists have tended to consider impulsivity in a somewhat broader way. Stein et al. (1993), following the earlier work of Frosch and Wortis (1954) as well as the current DSM-III-R schemas, describe kleptomania, pyromania, addictions, perversions, some sexual disorders, and bulimia as impulse disorders. Also included among the impulse disorders are suicidal threats or acts as well as self-mutilating behavior. By implication, some personality disorders, such as antisocial personality and borderline personality, reflect disorders of impulse control. These examples clearly reflect the psychiatrist's concern with impulsivity as an aspect of behavioral disorders of various kinds.

These ideas have several implications. One is that impulsivity has a number of possible components or subfactors; for example, risk taking and lack of control over affects. Second, most of the literature tends to treat impulsivity as a trait rather than a state; that is, impulsivity is seen more as a personality trait than a transient event in an individual's life. Third, to the extent that impulsivity is a trait, efforts have been made to determine possible underlying brain mechanisms and genetic sources.

MEASURING IMPULSIVITY

Because of the obvious importance of impulsivity as a concept, a number of attempts have been made to measure it. Most such attempts rely on self-report questionnaires of one sort or another, but some laboratory-type tests (for reaction time, for example) have also been tried. Unfortunately the self-report tests and the laboratory tests generally do not correlate very well (Barrett and Patton, 1983), so that most impulsivity measures have been based upon self-report items. The problems connected with the measurement of aggression are considered elsewhere in this volume (see Chapter 3).

Examples of self-report impulsivity scales may be found in the Barrett Impulsiveness Scale (Barrett, 1965), the Thurstone Temperament Schedule (Thurstone, 1953), the Guilford Zimmerman Temperament Survey (Guilford and Zimmerman, 1949), the Sixteen Personality Factor Questionnaire (16PF) (Cattell et al., 1957), the Personality Research Form (Jackson, 1974), the Eysenck Extroversion Scale (Eysenck and Eysenck, 1978), the Monroe Scale (1978), the Zuckerman Sensation Seeking Scale (Zuckerman, 1974), the Emotions Profile Index (Plutchik and Kellerman, 1974), the Karolinska Scales of Personality (KSP) Impulsiveness Scale (Schalling et al., 1983), the Impulse Control Scale (Plutchik and van Praag, 1989), and the Interpersonal Style Inventory (Lorr and Youniss, 1985). This range of tests attempting to measure impulsivity further attests to the importance of the concept.

Some of these scales have conceptualized impulsivity as a single dimension, while others have attempted to measure different components. An illustration of the latter approach may be seen in the report by Dickman (1990), who distinguishes between *dysfunctional* and *functional* impulsivity. Examples of functional impulsivity are the following items:

People have admired me because I can think quickly.
I would enjoy working at a job that required me to make a lot of split-second decisions.
I like to take part in really fast-paced conversations, where you don't have much time to think before you speak.

Examples of dysfunctional impulsivity are the following items:

I often say and do things without considering the consequences.
Often, I don't spend enough time thinking over a situation before I act.
I will often say whatever comes into my head without thinking first.

Another example of a scale with several components is the one developed by Asberg and her colleagues (Schalling et al., 1983).
Examples of impulsivity items are:

I often throw myself too hastily into things.
I usually "talk before I think."
I consider myself an impulsive person.

Examples of "monotony avoidance items" are:

I have an unusually great need for change.

I like doing things just for the thrill of it.
I try to get to places where things really happen.

The various scales that conceptualize impulsivity as a unidimensional trait tend to show great overlap and generally have items that look like Dickman's dysfunctional scale. Examples are as follows:

I have trouble controlling my impulses to do things without thinking.
I am inclined to jump quickly from one interest to another.
I must admit I am a person who is somewhat disorderly and disorganized [Lorr and Youniss, 1985].

The scale developed by Monroe designed to identify the episodic dyscontrol syndrome has the following kinds of items:

I have acted on a whim.
I have had sudden changes in mood.
I have been surprised by my actions.
I have frightened other people with my temper [Plutchik, 1976].

The Impulse Control Scale contains items of the following type:

Do you find it difficult to control your emotions?
Are you easily distracted?
Do you find it hard to control your sexual feelings?
Do you spend money impulsively? [Plutchik and van Praag, 1989.]

This brief overview suggests that impulsivity is an important concept for personality theorists, that many personality tests have included it as a basic dimension, and that it is believed to be measurable by relatively short scales. Also of interest is the fact that psychiatrists are typically most interested in impulsivity as a dysfunctional condition (Stein et al., 1993) rather than as a normal personality trait.

THE INTERACTION OF IMPULSIVITY WITH OTHER PERSONALITY TRAITS

The fact that an impulsivity scale may be found in many tests of personality suggests that there may be some systematic relations among the various scales of the tests; that is, that impulsivity interacts with other personality dimensions. The most explicit statement of this idea has been presented by Plutchik (1980, 1989, 1990) in his theoretical model of the emotions, which he calls a psychoevolutionary theory. Very briefly, the theory assumes the existence of eight basic emotion dimensions that are systematically related to eight clusters or families of personality traits. The relations among the emotions and among the personality traits can be best described by means of a circular or circumplex model. Such a model implies a similarity structure among traits and a set of bipolar dimensions. These ideas are partly expressed in Table 1.

An important aspect of the theory is that personality traits may be conceptualized as derivatives of emotions. It also assumes that extreme manifestations of personality traits lead to a new derivative domain, that of personality disorders. Thus, for example, extreme and persistent forms of gloominess may be called depressive personality disorder, extreme and persistent forms of sociability may be called hypomania or mania, and extreme and persistent forms of impulsivity may be part of antisocial or borderline personality disorder.

A personality test developed on the basis of the theory is the Emotions Profile Index (EPI; Plutchik and Kellerman, 1974), which has been widely used in clinical research. The test presents the patient or client with pairs of trait words such as shy vs gloomy, sociable vs impulsive, and resentful vs brooding. Each time the patient chooses one of the two traits in a pair as most descriptive of him or herself, a score is obtained on the underlying emotion dimensions for that trait. Thus, if someone chooses shy over gloomy, a score is obtained on the fear dimension; if he or she chooses impulsive over sociable, a score is obtained on the surprise or dyscontrol dimension; and if brooding is chosen over resentful, a score is obtained on the sadness dimension. Based on such choices and extensive norms, a circular profile is obtained for each subject. This is illustrated in Figure 1.

The profile shown in Figure 1 was obtained from a 35-year-old woman who sought therapy because of depression associated with the breakup of her marriage. On the EPI, impulsivity is measured by the dyscontrol dimension. This woman, whom we shall call Ann, was extremely high on dyscontrol (impulsivity) and extremely low on timidity (or fear). This was consistent with a lifestyle oriented toward getting involved in foolhardy adventures, and travel. She was extremely impatient with her husband and her two children, often losing control and screaming at them for apparently minor provocations. She was often restless and dissatisfied with her relationships with close family members, including her parents. She was also high on aggressive on the EPI as well as on distrust, suggesting a somewhat antisocial style of interacting. Conflicts with her husband were more understandable when his EPI profile revealed a pattern that was almost opposite on each dimension.

One important implication of these ideas is that impulsivity should not be considered in isolation from other traits that an individual possesses. A person who is high on impulsivity (or dyscontrol) and low on control would be expected to show erratic and impulsive behavior, while another indiv-

Table 1 Three languages that may be used to describe emotional states

Subjective language	Behavioral language	Trait language
Fearful, terrified	Escaping, avoiding	Timid, shy
Angry, furious	Attacking, biting	Quarrelsome, irritable
Joyful, ecstatic	Cooperating, mating	Sociable, friendly
Sad, griefstricken	Crying for help, distress signals	Gloomy, pensive
Accepting, open	Affiliating, grooming	Trusting, gullible
Disgusted, loathful	Rejecting, vomiting	Distrustful, hostile
Anticipating, expectant	Exploring, mapping	Controlling, manipulative
Surprised, astonished	Losing control, disorienting	Dyscontrolled, impulsive

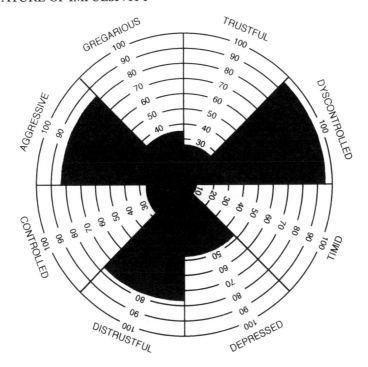

Figure 1 A personality profile based on the Emotion Profile Index, showing a very high dyscontrol or impulsivity score interacting with other personality dimensions.

idual who is high on *both* impulsivity and control would be expected to show high levels of conflict that is not often expressed in overt behavior. Similarly, a person high on impulsivity and high on fear (or timidity) would probably appear much more inhibited and conflicted than one who is high on impulsivity and low on fear (as shown in the case of Ann). Since fear is an inhibitor of action, the second person might be expected to express the impulsivity in a more overt and persistent form. These ideas lead to the concept of the interaction of traits or what we have called a model of countervailing forces.

THE CONCEPT OF COUNTERVAILING FORCES

The concept of countervailing forces stems from a series of studies that we have carried out that is concerned with the interaction of risk and protective factors in suicide and violence. We have reviewed a large number of empirical findings on the nature of suicide and violence and have seen that there is unequivocal evidence of a relationship between them. The relationship is not a simple one. The old psychoanalytical idea that suicide is violence turned inward has some validity, but it does not help us understand why some violent people are suicidal and why others are not. In order to answer such questions, we need to identify the variables that influence both violence and suicide risk in individuals. And we need to examine these questions from the broadest perspective we can find.

The conceptual approach that we have found most helpful is a broad ethological–evolutionary one that looks for general principles and common elements across species. One such general principle is the universality of aggression (which refers to complex patterns of behavior connected with fight and defense in all species). The ethologists have pointed out that aggressive behavior serves to increase the probability of access to resources, helps deal with conflicts among individuals, and increases the chances of successful courtship and mating. The overall function of aggression is that it increases the chance of individual survival as well as increasing inclusive fitness, i.e. the likelihood of gene representation in future generations.

In addition, neurophysiological research over many decades has established the existence of brain structures that organize patterns of aggressive behavior (e.g. lateral hypothalamus, ventral tegmental areas, midbrain central gray area, and the central and anterior portions of the septum). Recent research has also shown that various neurotransmitter systems are involved in the expression of aggression. For example, animals fed a tryptophan-free diet became increasingly aggressive, implying that low serotonin (5-hydroxytryptamine, 5-HT) levels are associated with a risk of violent behavior (Gibbons et al., 1979).

Finally, the recent literature on behavioral genetics has revealed that many, if not most, emotional characteristics are heritable. Aggressivity has been shown to be heritable in mice and dogs (Fuller, 1986), and human studies of personality and temperament have also indicated significant genetic components in assertiveness, extraversion and dominance (Loehlin and Nichols, 1976; Loehlin et al., 1981; Wimer and Wimer, 1985).

A recent review of the literature on predation within species (i.e. cannibalism) has demonstrated that the killing and eating of an individual of one's own species is very widespread. It has been observed in about 1300 species, including humans (Polis, 1981). It appears to have a strong genetic component, although its frequency can be affected by the availability of food supplies. In some species, cannibalism has a major influence on population size. It has been observed in at least 14 species of carnivorous mammals. In most such cases, adults preyed on immature animals and cubs. Cannibalism has also been reported in 60 human cultures (Schankman, 1969).

This brief overview suggests that aggressive behavior has fundamental importance for survival and for regulation of populations in humans and lower animals. The evidence clearly indicates that there are neurological structures and biochemical processes that are intimately connected with aggressive behavior, and that there are genetic contributions to the individual differences seen in aggressive traits.

Ethological research has further indicated what classes of events tend to trigger aggressive impulses. Generally speaking, threats, challenges, changes in hierarchical status, and various losses tend to increase aggressive impulses (Blanchard and Blanchard, 1984). However, we need to distinguish between aggressive impulses and aggressive behavior (or violence). Whether or not the aggressive impulse is expressed in the form of overt action, i.e. violent behavior, depends on the presence of a large number of forces, some of which act as amplifiers of the aggressive impulse and some act to attenuate the impulse. Examples of amplifiers are extensive school problems in the history of the individual, a history of assaultive acts, pervasive feelings of distrust, easy access to weapons, and a tolerant attitude toward the expression of violence. Examples of attenuators are a timid personality style, close family ties, and appeasement from others. These variables interact in complex ways and determine the probability that the aggressive impulse will be expressed in overt violent behavior. We call these factors Stage I countervailing forces.

Overt action, however, requires a goal object toward which it is directed. The model assumes that a separate set of variables determines whether the goal of aggressive actions will be other people or oneself. The set of variables that determine the goal of the aggressive impulse we refer to as Stage II countervailing forces. The presence and interaction of these various countervailing forces determine both the strength of aggressive behavior and the final goal of the aggressive behavior. Needless to say, impulsivity is one of the key variables involved in this complex set of interactions. The general model is shown in Figure 2.

STUDIES OF IMPULSIVITY IN RELATION TO SUICIDE AND VIOLENCE

Using the model described above, a number of studies have been carried out that attempted to measure impulsivity and to determine its relation to suicidal and violent behavior. Some of the results will be briefly described.

In the first study, 100 psychiatric inpatients were interviewed using standard scales designed to measure a large number of variables. Examples of the variables studied included impulsivity (as measured by the Impulse Control Scale), depression, hopelessness, life problems, family violence, social network, and coping styles. These variables were considered to be possible predictor variables that might be able to correlate with two outcome measures: a self-report measure of suicide risk and a self-report measure of violence risk. These measures had been independently determined to be related to a history of suicide attempts or to a history of acting-out behavior (Plutchik et al., 1989).

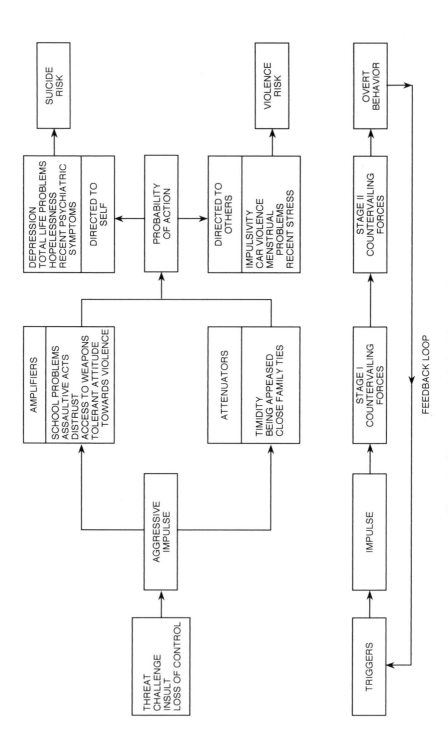

Figure 2 Two-stage model of suicide and violence.

The results of the study revealed that many variables correlated with both the suicide and violence risk measures. However, through the use of partial statistics, it was determined that the primary correlates of suicide risk alone are depression, feelings of hopelessness, a large number of life problems, and recent psychiatric symptoms. In contrast, the primary correlates of violence risk seemed to be impulsivity, problems with the law, menstrual problems in women, and recent life stresses.

In this study, impulsivity correlated with suicide risk ($+0.43$) and with violence risk ($+0.63$). When partial correlations were obtained holding the relationship between suicide risk and violence risk constant, impulsivity correlated with suicide risk ($+0.22$) and with violence risk ($+0.53$). It was also found that the extent of one's social network acted as a countervailing force attenuating the risk of both suicide and violence.

A second study was concerned with the measurement of ego defenses as possible correlates of suicide or violence risk (Apter et al., 1989). In this investigation, 30 patients admitted to a psychiatric hospital subsequent to a suicide attempt, were compared with matched psychiatric inpatients who were admitted for other reasons. Ego defenses were measured with the Life Style Index (Plutchik et al., 1979; Plutchik and Conte, 1989; Conte and Plutchik, 1994) and were correlated with measures of suicide risk and violence risk. Impulsivity was measured with the Impulse Control Scale.

Analyses of the data revealed that suicidal patients were significantly higher on the impulsivity measure than were the nonsuicidal control patients. In addition, a subgroup of patients were identified who were considered to be violent on the basis of behavior on the ward, need for seclusion, and past history. The violent patients were also found to be significantly higher on the impulsivity measure than were patients without a history of violence. Impulsivity was also found to correlate significantly with measures of state anxiety ($+0.33$), trait anxiety ($+0.48$), anger ($+0.43$), and confusion ("confused", "indecisive", and "surprised") ($+0.33$) (Apter et al., 1990).

When the ego defense measures were correlated with suicide and violence risk, regression and displacement were found to be significantly correlated with both the suicide and violence risk measures. From a theoretical point of view, displacement is a way of dealing with conflicts by transforming angry impulses to new targets, while regression is a way of dealing with conflicts by acting in more childish ways; that is, by losing control, and allowing impulsive behavior to dominate. It thus appears that derivatives of impulsivity are related to the risk of suicidal or violent behavior.

In a further study using the Impulse Control Scale, impulsivity was again found to be significantly correlated with a suicide risk measure, in both a group of violent inpatients in a facility for violent, mentally ill patients ($+0.59$) and in a group of nonviolent patients in a psychiatric hospital ($+0.32$) (Apter et al., 1991).

Another recent study looking at coping styles in relation to suicide and violence also found that suicidal patients had significantly higher scores on the Impulse Control Scale than did nonsuicidal patients (Kotler et al., 1993). In addition, it was found that impulsivity correlated significantly with anger (+0.64), blame (+0.37) and both suicide risk (+0.50) and violence risk (+0.48). In one additional study, not yet published, it was found that psychiatric inpatients with personality disorders had significantly higher impulsivity scores than did patients without personality disorders (Botsis et al., 1993).

These various studies have been quite consistent in showing that impulsivity is found at significantly higher levels in both suicidal and violent patients. These disorders are considered to be disorders of impulsive and emotion, and the empirical data support these concepts. It has also been found that certain ego defenses related to loss of control (displacement and regression) are correlated with suicide and violence risk (and by implication with impulsivity). In addition, patients with personality disorders have higher levels of impulsivity than those without. These results provide some degree of construct validation for the measure of impulsivity (the Impulse Control Scale) used in these studies. They also imply the ubiquity of impulsivity as a trait in many psychiatric patients.

In a number of earlier studies using prisoners as well as psychiatric patients, impulsivity was measured with the Monroe Scale (Plutchik et al., 1976). It was found that the mean correlation between impulsivity (episodic dyscontrol) and violence risk in seven different groups was +0.61, a very significant correlation. In the same series of studies it was found that impulsivity as measured by the Monroe Scale correlated significantly in many groups with the schizophrenia scale of the Minnesota Multiphasic Personality Inventory (MMPI; +0.42), with the total number of life problems an individual has (+0.58), with a history of violence in one's family (+0.56), with the psychopathic deviate scale of the MMPI (+0.52), with a measure of sexual drive (+0.53), with social deviance (+0.48), and with depression (+0.58). Overall, the studies revealed that individuals who show repeated acts of violence against other individuals have a life history and lifestyle that can be described in terms of a number of dimensions. Probably the most important of these are a history of episodic dyscontrol (impulsivity), a history of family violence, a large number of life adjustment problems, behavior problems in family members, and certain psychopathic tendencies.

THE GENETICS OF IMPULSIVITY

Genetic studies comparing monozygotic and dizygotic twins, cross-adoption studies and other methods have revealed hereditary contributions to impulsive behavior. This has been reported by Goldsmith (1983) and Scarr (1969), and is implied by the work of Freedman (1974) and Rose et al. (1981), dealing with reactivity to stimulation and with psychopathic deviate behavior, respectively. The work of Roy (1983) also suggests that the trait of constraint is subject to strong genetic influence.

Three other genetic studies also support the heritability of impulsiveness. Gottesman (1966) compared monozygotic and dizygotic twins on the MMPI. He found that monozygotic twins are significantly more similar to each other than dizygotic twins on Self-control as well as several other MMPI scales. Another study of twin pairs revealed that impatience, risk-taking and lack of planning had significant genetic components (Eaves et al., 1977). Eysenck (1983) also reported strong genetic heritability for impulsivity, based on twin studies, as did Plomin (1974).

In an interesting neuropharmacological model, King (1986) described a number of studies that suggest that mesolimbic dopamine lowers the response threshold to certain cues, thereby initiating action. Evidence was presented for genetically based differences in mesolimbic cell numbers as well as the extent of release of dopamine into the limbic striatum. King then used this model to postulate that such variation is the underlying basis for the personality traits of impulsiveness vs inhibition.

Finally, after a review of the literature on the role of serotonin, Depue and Spoont (1986) presented the hypothesis that there are two general behavioral systems, a "behavioral facilitation system" and a "behavioral inhibition system" that interact with each other. The behavioral facilitation system is activated by stimulus contexts that produce goal-oriented behavior. Neurobiologically, such behavior is assumed to be integrated in the mesolimbic dopaminergic pathways. Depue and Spoont (1986) assumed that the neurobiological foundation of the behavioral inhibition system is the septal–hippocampal system. Data cited also suggest that low levels of serotonin are associated with increases in the behavioral facilitation system behavior (sexual, social, and aggressive). High levels of serotonin tend to inhibit such activities.

One implication of this model is that it may represent a neurobiological basis for the behavioral bipolar traits of impulsivity/constraint. It may even provide a partial explanation of borderline personality disorder, which is characterized by impulsivity, unstable moods, variable and often inappropriate anger, and various ego disturbances.

THEORIES OF IMPULSIVITY

The neurobiology of impulsivity has been summarized most fully by Stein et al. (1993). Most studies have used suicidal or aggressive behavior toward others as indices of impulsivity. This is reasonable as a first approximation, but it should be noted that "pure" impulsivity measures correlate about

+0.5 or +0.6 with "pure" aggression measures. Thus, about 30% of the variance in aggressive behavior is accounted for by impulsivity as an independent variable.

Soubrie and Bizot (1990) suggest that a decrease in serotonergic transmission leads to an inability to adopt passive or waiting attitudes. However, differences among the various disorders listed above indicate that the underlying mechanism is probably more complex. This conclusion is also supported by the fact that medications, such as anxiolytics and anticonvulsants, that do not act on the serotonin system decrease suicidal and personality disorder symptoms.

Buss (1988) has considered impulsivity from a broad evolutionary framework. He points out that some animals (such as dogs and monkeys) are often described as impulsive, whereas some (such as cats) are more controlled. If such species differences exist, they must surely be based on neurobiological and genetic foundations.

If we consider any one species, such as humans, we recognize wide individual differences in impulsivity (or self-control). Some people can diet, stop smoking or drinking coffee, and avoid drugs, while others appear helpless in their addictions. Some children and adults are hyperactive and others are calm. Such differences presumably reflect the interaction of a number of variables, including impulsivity and its countervailing forces (such as anxiety). If this assumption is correct, then the ability to cope with addictions is related to the strength of one's impulsivity, the strength of one's anxiety, or both. Variations (due to medication, life experiences, illness, etc.) in either one may have a major effect on the expression of addictive behavior.

Buss (1988) also emphasizes that traits such as impulsivity do not occur in isolation but can inhibit or amplify each other. For example, the interaction of fearfulness and impulsivity may lead to uncontrolled anxiety. The combination of impulsivity and sociability creates extraversion, while impulsivity and nurturance may lead to spontaneous altruistic actions. When impulsivity combines with aggressiveness, the outcome may very well be psychopathic or criminal behavior.

In this latter context, an early study by Marohn et al. (1971) of juvenile delinquents revealed that they were usually able to describe accurately their own impulsive behaviors, and that the subjective experience of being unable to control their own impulses led to feelings of helplessness about the future. Most were believed to show impulsivity as a result of a defect in ego development (that is, a limited ability to delay gratification).

Another theoretical approach to impulsivity has been proposed by Soubrie and Bizot (1990). Assuming that impulsivity could be measured in lower animals in terms of waiting capacity or tolerance to delay of reward, experiments were carried out with rats to study the effect of various drugs on these parameters.

Using this general model, they found that both serotonin (5-HT) uptake blockers, which enhanced serotonin transmission, and noradrenaline uptake blockers and β-stimulants, which enhanced noradrenergic transmission, decreased impulsivity. Drugs that reduced serotonin transmission, such as 5-HT$_{1A}$ agonists and benzodiazepines, increased impulsivity. In general, it was found that all antidepressant drugs studied enhanced waiting capacity (or reduced impulsivity). These findings help account for the beneficial effects of antidepressants on impulse-control disorders such as bulimia and obsessive compulsive symptoms.

Soubrie and Bizot (1990) proposed that serotonin-containing neurons are involved in the control of response emission and in the speed of information processing. They believe that "serotonergic neurons do not directly govern a single behavior nor even a set of behaviors, but that, in contrast, they govern any kind of behavior (aggression, exploration, pressing for food, approach or avoidance) when that behavior enters into the waiting dimension" (their p. 266). The evidence also implies that both noradrenergic and serotonergic systems interact to influence waiting capacity.

SUMMARY

Impulsivity appears to reflect a multidimensional concept that has something to do with restraint of one's own behavior, handling of different emotions, particularly sexual and aggressive ones, rapid processing of information, novelty seeking, and ability to delay gratification. A number of self-report scales have been published which are designed to measure this construct.

Research has demonstrated that impulsivity is moderately related to expressions of aggression but is also related to a number of other variables. Some refer to family experiences and some to life stresses. Others are probably related to genetics, since large scale studies of twins and adopted children have revealed genetic components in impulsive expression.

Psychiatrists have tended to focus on brain neurotransmitter systems. Evidence now exists that impulsivity is, at least in part, probably related to a decrease in serotonergically mediated behavioral inhibition. However, it is also important to emphasize that impulsivity is only one trait system among many others, and that a complex balance of forces exist in any one person. Some variables are likely to enhance impulsivity while others inhibit it. The precise balance of countervailing forces determines the form and intensity of the resulting behavior.

REFERENCES

Apter, A., Plutchik, R., Sevy, S., Korn, M., Brown, S., and van Praag, H.M. (1989). Defense mechanisms in risk of suicide and risk of violence. *Am. J. Psychiatry*, 146, 1027–1031.
Apter, A., van Praag, H.M., Plutchik, R., Sevy, S., Korn, M., and Brown, S.

(1990). Interrelationships among anxiety, aggression, impulsivity, and mood: A serotonergically linked cluster? *Psychiatry Res.*, 148, 191–199.

Apter, A., Kotler, M., Sevy, S., et al. (1991). Correlates of risk of suicide in violent and nonviolent psychiatric patients. *Am. J. Psychiatry*, 148, 883–887.

Barrett, E.S. (1965). Factor analysis of some psychometric measures of impulsiveness and anxiety. *Psychol. Rep.*, 16, 547–544.

Barrett, E.S., and Patton, J.H. (1983). Impulsivity: Cognitive, behavioral, and psychophysiological correlates. In: *Biological Bases of Sensation Seeking, Impulsivity and Anxiety* (ed. M. Zuckerman) pp. 77–116. Erlbaum, Hillsdale, NJ.

Blanchard, D.C., and Blanchard, R.J. (1984). Affect and aggression: An animal model applied to human behavior. In: *Advances in the Study of Aggression*, vol. 1, (eds R.J. Blanchard and D.C. Blanchard). Academic Press, New York.

Buss, A.H. (1988). *Personality: Evolutionary Heritage and Human Distinctiveness.* Lawrence Erlbaum, Hillsdale, NJ.

Cattell, R., Saunders, D., and Stize, E. (1957). *Handbook for the Sixteen Personality Factor Questionnaire.* Institute for Personality and Ability Testing, Champaign, IL.

Conte, H.R., and Plutchik, R. (1994). The measurement of ego defenses in clinical research. In: *The Concept of Defense Mechanisms in Contemporary Psychology: Theoretical, Research and Clinical Perspectives* (eds U. Hentschel, G. Smith, W. Ehlers, and J.G. Draguns). Springer, New York.

Depue, R.A., and Spoont, M.A. (1986). Conceptualizing a serotonin trait: A behavioral dimension of constraint. In: *Psychobiology of Suicidal Behavior* (eds J. Nemm and N. Stanley) pp. 47–62. Annals of the New York Academy of Sciences, New York.

Dickman, S.J. (1990). Functional and dysfunctional impulsivity: personality and cognitive correlates. *J. Personal. Soc. Psychol.*, 58, 95–102.

Douglas, V. (1972). Stop, look, and listen: The problem of sustained attention and impulse control in hyperactive and normal children. *Can. J. Behav. Sci.*, 4, 259–282.

Eaves, L.J., Martin, N.G., and Eysenck, S.B.G. (1977). An application of the analysis of covariance structures to the psychogenetic study of impulsiveness. *Br. J. Math. Statistics Psychol.*, 30, 185–197.

Eysenck, H.J. (1983). A biometrical–genetical analysis of impulsive and sensation-seeking behavior. In: *Biological Bases of Sensation Seeking, Impulsivity and Anxiety* (ed. M. Zuckerman) pp. 1–27. Erlbaum, Hillsdale, NJ.

Eysenck, S.B.G., and Eysenck, H.J. (1978). Impulsiveness and venturesomeness: Their position in a dimensional system of personality description. *Psychol. Rep.*, 43, 1247–1255.

Freedman, D.G. (1979). *Human Infancy: An Evolutionary Perspective.* Erlbaum, Hillsdale, NJ.

Frosch, J., and Wortis, S. (1954). A contribution to the nosology of the impulse disorders. *Am. J. Psychiatry*, 111, 131–138.

Fuller, J.L. (1986). Genetics and emotions. In: *The Biological Foundations of Emotions* (eds R. Plutchik and H. Kellerman). Academic Press, New York.

Gibbons, J.L., Barr, G.A., Bridger, W.H., and Leibowitz, S.F. (1979). Manipulation of dietary tryptophan: Effects on mouse killing and brain serotonin in the rat. *Brain Res.*, 169, 139–153.

Goldsmith, H.H. (1983). Genetic influences on personality from infancy to adulthood. *Child Dev.*, 54, 331–335.

Gottesman, I.I. (1966). Genetic variance in adaptive personality traits. *J. Child Psychol. & Psychiatry*, 7, 199–208.

Guilford, J.P., and Zimmerman, W. (1949). *The Guilford–Zimmerman Temperament Survey* [Manual]. Sheridan Supply Co, Beverly Hills, CA.

Jackson, D.N. (1974). *Personality Research Form*, revised edn. Research Psychologists Press, Port Huron, MI.

King, R. (1986). Motivational diversity and mesolimbic dopamine: a hypothesis concerning temperament. In: *Biological Foundations of Emotion* (eds R. Plutchik and H. Kellerman) pp. 363–380. Academic Press, New York.

Kotler, M., Finkelstein, G., Molcho, A., et al. (1993). Correlates of suicide and violence risk in an inpatient population: coping styles and social support. *Psychiatry Res.*, 47, 281–290.

Loehlin, J.C., and Nichols, B.C. (1976). *Heredity, Environment and Personality: A study of 850 Twins*. University of Austin Press, Austin, TX.

Lorr, M., and Wunderlich, R.A. (1985). A measure of impulsiveness and its relation to extroversion. *Educ. Psychol. Meas.*, 45, 251–257.

Lorr, M., and Youniss, R.P. (1985). Manual of the *Interpersonal Style Inventory*. Western Psychological Services, Los Angeles, CA.

Marohn, R.C., Offer, D., and Ostrov, E. (1971). Juvenile delinquents view their impulsivity. *Am. J. Psychiatry*, 128, 418–423.

Monroe, R.R. (1970). *Episodic Behavioral Disorders*. Harvard University Press, Cambridge, MA.

Monroe, R.R. (1978). *Brain dysfunction in aggressive animals*. Heath; Lexington, MA.

Murray, H. (1938). *Explorations in Personality*. Oxford University Press, New York.

Plomin, R. (1976). Extroversion: Sociability and impulsivity? *J. Pers. Assess.*, 40, 24–30.

Plutchik, R., Climent, C., and Ervin, F. (1976). Research strategies for the study of human violence. In: *Issues in Brain/Behavior Control* (eds W.L. Smith and A. Kling). Spectrum, New York.

Plutchik, R. (1980). *Emotion: A Psychoevolutionary Synthesis*. Harper & Row, New York.

Plutchik, R. (1989). Measuring emotions and their derivatives. In: *The Measurement of Emotions* (eds R. Plutchik and H. Kellerman) pp. 1–36. Academic Press, San Diego.

Plutchik, R. (1990). Emotions and psychotherapy: A psychoevolutionary perspective. In: *Emotion, Psychopathology and Psychotherapy* (eds R. Plutchik and H. Kellerman) pp. 3–42, Academic Press, San Diego.

Plutchik, R., and Conte, H.R. (1989). Measuring emotions and their derivatives: Personality traits, ego defenses, and coping styles. In: *Contemporary Approaches to Psychological Assessment* (eds S. Wetzler and M. Katz). Brunner/Mazel, New York.

Plutchik, R., and Kellerman, H. (1974). Manual of the *Emotions Profile Index*. Western Psychological Services, Los Angeles.

Plutchik, R., and van Praag, H.M. (1989). The measurement of suicidality, aggressivity and impulsivity. *Prog. Neuropsychopharmacol. Biol. Psychiatry*, 13, 523–534.

Plutchik, R., Climent, C., and Ervin, R. (1976). In: *Issues in Brain/Behavior Control* (eds W.L. Smith and A. Kling). Spectrum, New York.

Plutchik, R., Kellerman, H., and Conte, H.R. (1979). A structural theory of ego defenses and emotions. In: *Emotions in Personality and Psychopathology* (ed. C.E. Izard). Plenum, New York.

Plutchik, R., van Praag, H.M., and Conte, H.R. (1989). Correlates of suicide and violence risk III. A two-stage model of countervailing forces. *Psychiatry Res.*, 28, 215–225.

Polis, G.A. (1981). The evolution and dynamics of intraspecific predation. *Rev. Ecol. Systematics*, 12, 225–252.

Rose, R.J., Miller, J.Z., Pogue-Gelle, M.F., and Cardwell, G.F. (1981). Twin-family studies of common fears and phobias. *Progr. Clin. Biol. Res.*, 69B, 169–174.

Roy, A. (1983). Family history of suicide. *Arch. Gen. Psychiatry*, 40, 971–974.

Scarr, S. (1969). Social intraversion–extraversion as a heritable response. *Child Dev.*, 40, 823–833.

Schankman, P. (1969). Le roti et le bouilli: Levi-Strauss' theory of cannibalism. *Am. Anthropol.*, 71, 54–69.

Schalling, D., Edman, G., and Asbert, M. (1983). Impulsive cognitive style and inability to tolerate boredom: psychobiological studies of temperamental vulnerability. In: *Biological Bases of Sensation Seeking Impulsivity and Anxiety* (ed. M. Zuckerman) pp. 123–150. Erlbaum, Hillsdale, NJ.

Sohlberg, S., Norring, C., Holmgren, S., and Rosemark, B. (1989). Impulsivity and long-term prognosis of psychiatric patients with anorexia nervosa/bulimia nervosa. *J. Nerv. Ment. Dis.*, 177, 249–258.

Soubrie, P., and Bizot, J.C. (1990). Monoaminergic control of waiting capacity (impulsivity) in animals. In: *Violence and Suicidality* (eds H.M. van Praag, R. Plutchik and A. Apter). Brunner/Mazel, New York.

Stein, D.J., Hollander, E., and Liebowitz, M.R. (1993). Neurobiology of impulsivity and the impulse control disorders. *J. Neuropsychiatry Clin. Neurosci.*, 5, 9–17.

Thurstone, L. (1953). *Examiners Manual for the Thurstone Temperament Schedule*. Science Research Associates, Chicago.

von Knorring, L., Oreland, L., and von Knorring, A.L. (1987). Personality traits and platelet MAO activities in alcohol and drug abusing teenage boys. *Acta Psychiatr. Scand.*, 75, 307–314.

Vitiello, B., Stoff, D., Atkins, M., and Mahoney, A. (1990). Soft neurological signs and impulsivity in children. *J. Dev. Behav. Pediatr.*, 11, 112–115.

Wimer, R.E., and Wimer, C.C. (1985). Animal behavior genetics: A search for the biological foundation of behavior. *Ann. Rev. Psychol.*, 36, 171–218.

Woodcock, J.H. (1986). A neuropsychiatric approach to impulse disorders. *Psychiatric Clinics of North America*, 2, 341–352.

Zuckerman, M. (1974). The sensation seeking motive. In: *Progress in Experimental Personality Research* (ed. B. Maher). Academic Press, New York.

3 Measurements of Impulsivity and Aggression

PER BECH* AND MARIANNE MAK†
*Psychiatric Institute, Frederiksborg General Hospital, Hillerød, Denmark
†Solvay Duphar BV, Weesp, The Netherlands

INTRODUCTION

Aggressive behavior, including impulsive reactions, causes much distress for many patients, their relatives, and their care-givers. Thus, the multi-axis system of the *Diagnostic and Statistical Manual of Mental Disorders, third revised version* (DSM-III-R; American Psychiatric Association, 1987) has placed aggressive behavior as an indicator for severe maladaptive social functioning (Axis V). In DSM-III-R, the "danger of hurting self or others" exceeds other indicators of "inability to function socially in almost all areas".

Scales measuring aggressive or impulsive behavior have been developed, covering both personality dimensions and clinical syndromes. These scales have been used both prognostically (e.g. to indicate when specific care or treatment are needed) and as tools for measuring the outcome of interventions.

This chapter attempts to provide a framework for the choice of scales rather than to describe all the different aggression scales systematically.

DEFINITIONS OF IMPULSIVITY AND AGGRESSION

Basic emotions such as fear and anger are often defined as impulsive emotions, i.e. emotions leading to impulsive reactions that are difficult to resist and may be harmful to oneself or others. In impulse control disorders, for example kleptomania, pathological gambling, and pyromania, the impulsive emotions are characterized by a sense of pleasure when gratified (Kaplan and Sadock, 1990). On the other hand, obsessive compulsive disorder is defined by recurrent impulses that produce anxiety if resisted. Thus, an aggressive obsession is the fear of harming self or others. People with such obsessions make attempts to ignore or suppress these thoughts, which they themselves consider senseless or ego-dystonic. In fact, obsessive people are anti-aggressive. It was part of Sjöbring's personality theory (Sjöbring, 1973) that impulsive people are "subsolid" (hysterical) and

Impulsivity and Aggression. Edited by E. Hollander and D.J. Stein

obsessive people are reflective "supersolid". In the Marke–Nyman Temperament Scale (Bech et al., 1978) an example of a subsolid item is: "Do you follow momentary whims and start things which later give you trouble?" An example of a supersolid item is: "Do you often 'sleep' on a problem before making a decision?" Psychopathologically, obsessions are connected with guilt feelings (inward aggression) and hysterical and impulsive behavior with outward aggression, as shown by Kiloh and Garside (1977).

As discussed by Plutchik and van Praag (1989), the most distinct factor of impulsivity has been identified by Lorr and Wunderlich (1985), who concluded that the two components of impulsivity are not resisting urges and responding immediately to a stimulus.

In terms of Eysenck's personality theory obsessive people are introverted, and impulsive persons are extroverted (Eysenck and Eysenck, 1977). However, impulsivity in its narrow sense seems only to be weakly correlated with extroversion (Eysenck and Eysenck, 1977) and seems closer to Barratt's concept of impulsive reactions "to act on the spur of the moment" (Barratt, 1990). Studies using the Special Hospital Assessment of Personality and Socialization (SHAPS; Blackburn, 1993) have shown that primary psychopaths are impulsive, aggressive, hostile, and extroverted. Likewise, the Psychopathy Checklist developed by Hare (1980) is based on the theory that the psychopath is extremely impulsive, irresponsible, selfish, and intolerant of frustration. Kernberg (1992) has emphasized that patients with antisocial personality disorder have some degree of super-ego pathology, including the incapacity to experience self-reflective sadness, deep mood swings, and a predominance of shame as contrasted to guilt in their intrapsychic regulation of social behavior. In the aggressive type of antisocial personality disorder the super-ego pathology is more serious (Kernberg, 1992), with a clear incapacity for feeling guilt and remorse. The extreme and persistent forms of impulsivity, in relation to antisocial and borderline personality disorder, have been discussed by Plutchik and van Praag in Chapter 2. Likewise, scales measuring impulsivity, for example the Emotions Profile Index (EPI), are described in Chapter 2. In the present chapter, we will focus mainly on aggression.

Aggressive behavior has been defined by Bond (1992) as "behavior directed by one individual against another individual (or object or self) with the aim of causing harm". Accordingly, aggression can be divided into outward aggression (against others) and inward aggression (against self). Most rating scales for aggression have been devoted to the measurement of outward aggression because inward aggression is associated with depression and guilt, implying that scales for depression are recommended for measuring inward aggression. Furthermore, as discussed elsewhere, self-mutilation might be considered to be an indicator of borderline symptomatology rather than of inward aggression (ERAG, 1992).

Among the items found in the various scales measuring impulsivity and aggression are yelling or screaming, demanding behavior, sexually provocative behavior, tearing off clothes, refusal of food, irritability, negativism or uncooperative behavior, dangerous behavior, and suicidal impulses or behavior.

This broad range of mood and behavior raises the question whether use of the term "aggressive behavior" should be restricted to episodes or acts that have a clear intention to hurt and may, eventually, cause physical damage. This approach, however, has the disadvantage that it separates the current act from the underlying emotions and impulses, whereas aggression often is a complex syndrome that is only indirectly intentional. Thus, the psychopathic aggression is a co-axial syndrome [fluctuating between Axis II (personality diagnosis) and Axis I (clinical syndromes) of the DSM-III-R]. In elderly patients and dementia patients, Patel and Hope (1992) have suggested to define aggression as: ". . . an overt act, involving delivery of noxious stimuli to (but not necessarily aimed at) another organism, object or self, which is clearly not accidental".

A broad definition of aggression (e.g. "social dysfunction" or "problem behavior") is valid when the objective of a study is to classify patients with an optimal condition of care, i.e. taking the total psychopathology into consideration. In other words, it is important to define the objectives of a study on aggression in order to select the most appropriate rating instrument.

It should be emphasized that impulsivity (not resisting urges, as well as responding immediately to stimuli) has associations with pathological gambling, pyromania, and suicidal behavior, as discussed in Chapter 2. However, outward aggression as measured by the Freiburg Personality Inventory (Bech, 1993) has the same level of correlation with suicidal behavior as impulsivity (Angst and Clayton, 1986). Thus, there is a gray zone between impulsivity and aggression, often referred to as irritability or dysphoria.

BASIC ISSUES FOR THE SELECTION OF SCALES

The different ways of obtaining information for the scoring of aggression scales and the different time frames to be covered (current symptomatology versus lifelong traits) vary from scale to scale. The psychometric properties of scale items (dichotomous answer categories versus different quantifiers) also have implications for the selection of the right scale for the study being undertaken. In the following, some of these issues will be discussed briefly.

SOURCES OF INFORMATION AND THEIR VALIDITY

Rating scales measuring aggression can, according to their administration or sources of information, be arranged into self-rating scales (self-reports by the patients), nursing staff observer scales (observational reports by the ward staff), and psychiatrists' observer scales (observational interviews by the treating psychiatrist).

The measurement of severe aggressive behavior (e.g. physical aggression) is limited to observer scales because data based on the patient's own reports are likely to be biased by the effect of social desirability (Bech, 1993). Few patients will faithfully report their own aggressive behavior. Also, in patients with reduced or no verbal capacity (e.g. dementia or mental handicap), the use of self-reporting is obviously limited.

Conversely, observer scales have their main application in moderate to severe aggression, i.e. in hospitalized or institutionalized patients. Within the observer scales it is important to differentiate between items based on direct observations made during the interview and items based on reports by the care-giver or family. The use of reports by close relatives to the patient is most relevant in patients who have dementia or mental handicaps and are living at home. Scales designed especially for relatives to measure aggression are still lacking. Furthermore, using such scales, especially if the rater is the spouse, there may be problems in obtaining unbiased observations.

The most commonly used aggression questionnaire is the Buss–Durkee Hostility Inventory (Buss and Durkee, 1957). In a recent overview, Buss and Perry (1992) concluded that this scale covers four components: verbal and physical aggression, anger, and hostility. However, the items of anger seem very close to the concept of impulsivity (see Chapter 2). Likewise, hostility in the Buss–Durkee scale seems close to Eysenck's concept of psychoticism (Eysenck and Eysenck, 1976), which again is only a weak predictor of delusional symptomatology.

In conclusion, the components of the different aggression scales are not transferable from self-rating to observer rating scales. The various components can only be compared at the most general level: hostility is an attitude, anger is an emotion like irritability, an impulse is a drive to react, and aggression, then, is the end product of the whole process. The various forms of rating scales for aggression measure various aspects of the aggressive process.

TRAIT VERSUS STATES OF AGGRESSION; EPISODES VERSUS BASELINE LEVEL OF AGGRESSION

Analogous to anxiety (in which it has been found clinically meaningful to differentiate between trait and state anxiety; Bech, 1993), it has been shown that aggression can be measured in trait versus states (Spielberger et al., 1980, 1985) as well as in peak episodes versus general aggression (ERAG, 1992).

It has been demonstrated (ERAG, 1992) that episodes of aggressive behavior (often lasting minutes), either verbal or physical, are interspersed with longer duration of generalized (day-to-day) aggression. These findings raise at least the following two questions. First, what is the agreement between the patient and his or her environment when comparing the distressfulness of episodes and the distressfulness of generalized aggression (it is, as discussed later, important to supplement ratings of behavior with ratings of distress)? Second, is there a correlation between generalized aggression seen in the psychiatric patient population and the trait of aggression found in college students (i.e. the population in which both the Spielberger scales and the Buss–Durkee scale have been developed)? In other words, is there a basic disposition for aggression and mental disorder, in terms of the DSM-III-R a co-axial association between personality diagnoses (Axis II) and clinical syndromes (Axis I)?

Concerning the prediction of severe aggressive behavior, the psychiatric diagnosis seems to have only limited validity. Previous violence is still the best predictor of future violence (Palmstierna and Wistedt, 1989).

Most empirical studies of aggression trait have been carried out in psychosomatic medicine, for example type A behavior (including impulsivity and sociability) and cardiovascular disorders (Jenkins et al., 1979). Type A behavior can also be considered as a non-neurotic defense mechanism with high arousal as its main component (Bech, 1993). The displacement and regression factors of the Life Style Index Questionnaire (Plutchik et al., 1979) have importance when correlating impulsive behavior and violence risk (see Chapter 2). In a recent study using the Life Style Index Questionnaire, displacement and regression covaried (Olff and Endresen, 1990).

RATING SCALES FOR GENERAL PSYCHOPATHOLOGICAL AND AGGRESSIVE SYMPTOMS

Studies using comprehensive psychopathological rating scales, especially the Association for Methodology and Documentation in Psychiatry (AMDP) System (Ban and Guy, 1982) have shown that, to some extent, the items of aggression cluster with other psychopathological symptoms (such as suspiciousness and lack of insight; Pietzcker et al., 1983). A less comprehensive observer scale such as the Brief Psychiatric Rating Scale (BPRS; Overall and Gorham, 1962), which is the most frequently used scale of this type, includes two aggression items (uncooperativeness and hostility) which cluster with core symptoms of schizophrenia (Andersen et al., 1989). The BPRS hostility item has also been included in the Positive and Negative Syndrome Scale (PANSS; Kay et al., 1987) as an indicator of the positive syndrome of schizophrenia. Likewise, the Mania Scale (MAS; Bech et al., 1979) has included a verbal and physical aggression item.

The most widely used self-rating scale for measuring general psychopathology is the Hopkins Symptom Checklist (SCL-90; Guy, 1976). Factor analysis of this scale has identified an anger–hostility syndrome, which includes such items as impulsivity, irritability, and aggression, but no hostility item (i.e. no attitudinal aggression item). While the SCL-90 is mainly applicable to populations of neurotic patients, the AMDP and BPRS have mostly been used in psychotic patients. The BPRS hostility item refers to animosity, contempt, belligerence, and disdain for others. In contrast to this, the SCL-90 hostility factor is a measure of anger and impulsivity.

Examination of the aggression subscales of general psychopathological rating scales shows both that the same term (e.g. hostility) refers to different aspects of aggression and that the subscales are too short to cover the clinical picture of aggression. On the other hand, it might be important in some studies to measure the current psychopathological states of patients, especially of manic patients (Verdoux and Bourgeois, 1993). In these cases, both a specific aggression scale and a psychopathological rating scale are recommended.

THE PSYCHOMETRIC SCORING OF AGGRESSION SCALES

Table 1 shows the different quantifiers of items to be considered in aggression scales. There is, however, no "standard" quantifier, because this depends on the frame of reference. The following issues should be taken into account:

1. It is essential to select the most appropriate quantifier for the study under performance, avoiding an unsystematic mixture of quantifiers, for example an unspecified use of frequency and intensity ratings.
2. The distance between the levels of a quantifier (e.g. such answer categories as mild, moderate, and severe) is not always the same (equidistant). This has consequences for the statistical analysis and interpretation of a "mean" change in aggression scores.
3. Scales with dichotomous answer categories (e.g. true versus false, or present versus absent) has no "mean" score. Thus, it might be difficult to answer the Buss–Durkee hostility item "I am always patient with

Table 1   Options of item scoring in aggression scales

Type of quantifier	Range of quantifier
Frequency	Never, sometimes, rarely, often, always 0–4 (exact number per time period)
Severity	None, mild, moderate, severe (very severe) 0–10 points (unspecified); 0–100 mm, visual analogue
Degree of problem	None, mild, moderate, severe
Agree with statement	Yes/no or true/false Not at all, somewhat, moderately so, very much so

others" as either true or false (a score in between might be preferable). In general, scales with dichotomous answers are not very sensitive to change in aggressive states.

In scoring "degee of problem" (Table 1), there is a major risk that the answers will be too dependent on the situation or the rater. However, the quantifier of problems in some studies is useful as a supplement to the more naturalistic quantifiers such as frequency and intensity.

TYPES OF AGGRESSION SCALES

Conventionally, rating scales are divided into diagnostic scales and scales measuring the severity of symptoms or syndromes. Symptom rating scales are most frequently used to measure outcome of treatment. However, as discussed elsewhere (Bech, 1981, 1993), symptom rating scales can also indicate when a diagnosis is required. Scales measuring severity of aggressive states can, thus, be used both to indicate when a diagnosis or an intervention is required and to monitor outcome of treatment. As discussed earlier, a high level of aggression is often associated with mania and schizophrenia.

SCALES INDICATING WHEN SPECIFIC CARE AND TREATMENT ARE NEEDED

There have been only a few attempts to develop a comprehensive diagnostic scale for aggression. Among these is the Carolina Nosology of Destructive Behaviors (CNBD) developed by Eichelman and Hartwig (1990). This system consists of two parts of which one is descriptive, with codes for the type of aggressive behavior displayed, and the other contains four axes by which the aggressive behavior can be related and explained: Axis A, the medical diagnosis; Axis B, the psychological dimensions; Axis C, the biological findings; and Axis D, the moral and cultural background of the patient. The CNBD system seems very logical and promising, but its validity still remains to be shown.

Scales to indicate when interventions are needed (e.g. better supervision of the patient, closer observation, immediate medication, and isolation without or with seclusion) for the aggressive patient have been designed. In principle, these scales are symptom scales and can also be used as outcome measures.

The most frequently used scale in this context is the Nurses' Observation Scale for Inpatient Evaluation (NOSIE; Honigfeld et al., 1966). The scale consists of 30 items (NOSIE-30), and seven factors have been identified which are used as subscales to describe the profile: (a) social competence,

(b) social interests, (c) personal neatness, (d) irritability, · (e) manifest psychosis, (f) retardation, and (g) depression. It should be emphasized that the irritability factor includes no items of verbal or physical aggression. The profile consists, then, of negative behavior (irritability, manifest psychosis, retardation, and depression) and positive behavior (social competence, personal neatness, and social interest).

Figure 1 illustrates the relevance of using a broad spectrum of symptoms (including nonspecific aggression items) in a group of aggressive patients with mental handicaps.

In patients with mental handicaps the most widely used scale is the Handicaps, Behavior and Skills Scale (HBS) developed by Wing (1980). Although the psychometric structure of the scale has been found adequate by Lund (1989), the standardization of the scale in terms of interventions is still limited. Another scale, the Disability Assessment Schedule (DAS) was developed on the basis of the HBS (Holmes et al., 1982) but has not been frequently used in Europe.

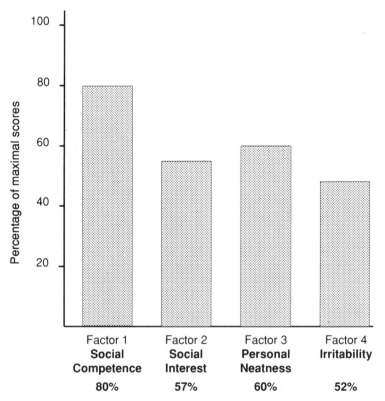

Figure 1   NOSIE, Profile of aggressive mentally retarded patient group.

SCALES MEASURING OUTCOME OF INTERVENTION

Observer scales

Scales measuring outcome of anti-aggressive interventions should include the target symptom or syndrome of the aggressive spectrum.

The most basic scales for measuring aggressive behavior in the sense of episodes, peaks or acts are the Overt Aggression Scale (OAS; Yudofsky et al., 1986), the Staff Observation Aggression Scale (SOAS; Palmstierna and Wistedt, 1987), and the Scale for Assessment of Agitated and Aggressive Behavior (SAAB; Brizer et al., 1987).

The principle of these scales is a description of separate aggressive "events", i.e. episodes of either verbal or physical aggression. There are some differences between the scales which, to some extent, are related to the populations in which they were developed (e.g. the SOAS elderly patients, the OAS with children and adult patients in intensive wards, and the SAAB with severely aggressive delinquents).

Table 2 compares the three scales. Although all three give the impression of being simple and reliable instruments for the measurement of verbal and physical aggression, they have many limitations. Thus, in severely aggressive patients with several "events" or episodes per day the completion of the forms per event poses a heavy burden on the nursing staff, so the episodes are often under-reported. More importantly, the interobserver reliability of the three scales has not been high even when administered by trained and skilled staff. This is especially the case for verbal aggression. Finally, the scoring systems of the scales, especially the OAS, is problematic. Thus, whether to use a total score, a weighted score, or a profile score has not

Table 2   Main features of event scales: Overt Aggression Scale (OAS), Staff Observation Aggression Scale (SOAS), and Scale for Assessment of Agitated and Aggressive Behavior (SAAB)*

Scale components	OAS	SOAS	SAAB
Provocation			
Events	−	+	−
Verbal	+	+	+
Physical			
Objects	+	+	+
Others	+	+	+
Self	+	−	+
Instruments used	−	+	−
Result/injuring	±	+	(±)
Action taken by staff	+	+	+
Circumstances onward	−	−	+
Paradigm for overall score	+	+	−

*+, Included; −, excluded.

been clarified. The authors and users of the OAS have realized these difficulties, and have modified the scale. A modification using retrospective scores per week (instead of perspective scores per episode) has been suggested (Silver and Yudofsky, 1991; Sorgi, 1991). Another modification of OAS for rating the severity of episodes has been suggested by Kay et al. (1988). Recently, Coccaro et al. (1991) have enlarged the OAS to cover irritability and suicidal ideation, resulting in the OAS—Modified for Out-patients (OAS-M). Preliminary findings with the OAS-M indicate that it is sensitive to measuring improvement during pharmacotherapy (Coccaro et al., 1991).

The concurrent validity of OAS using a Global Aggression Scales (GAS) score as an index of validity (ERAG, 1992) has been found to be only modest.

The within-patient variation in aggression over time is large (Figure 2). Such data are very useful in understanding the nature of aggression when correlated to time of the day, day of the week, season, and staff availability.

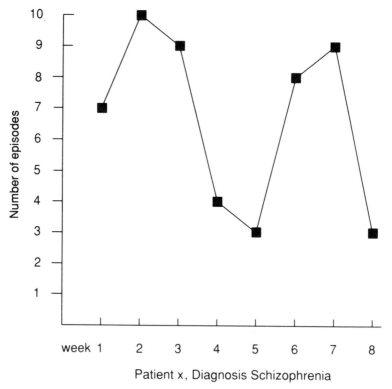

Patient x, Diagnosis Schizophrenia

Figure 2 Episodic nature of aggressive behavior. Number of episodes per week, Overt Aggression Scale.

They may be useful in discussing strategies in the ward and the duty schedules of the clinical staff (Silver and Yudofsky, 1988).

The Social Dysfunction and Aggression Scale (SDAS; Wistedt et al., 1990; ERAG, 1992) has recently been developed to overcome some of the problems found in connection with the use of OAS and other short scales used by nursing staff to measure episodes of severe aggressive behavior. The SDAS is a psychiatrist-administered scale like the BPRS, relying on observations made during an interview and on information from the nursing staff, other care-givers, or relatives of the patient.

Results with the SDAS have shown that the scale, containing 21 items, has two major factors: a factor or subscale of outward aggression (in total nine items, SDAS-9), and a second factor or subscale of inward aggression (in total six items, SDAS-6) (ERAG, 1992). Furthermore, an item of self-mutilation did not correlate significantly with either SDAS-9 or SDAS-6. For the SDAS-9 (outward aggression) it was found meaningful to score both the generalized aggression and for episodes of aggression. In both cases, the total score seemed a sufficient statistic when tested with latent structure analyses (Bech, 1993). The interobserver reliability of SDAS-9 was found to be adequate.

The SDAS-6 (inward aggression) included anxiety and depression items (among them suicidal thoughts). This scale seemed most meaningful as a generalized scale. No correlation was found between SDAS-9 and SDAS-6; they are orthogonal factors. The self-mutilation item should be measured as a separate dimension (Bech, 1993).

The ERAG study included mainly psychiatric inpatients with schizophrenia, manic–melancholic disorders and personality disorders. Studies are ongoing to evaluate the SDAS in other patient populations, especially with dementia and mental handicaps.

While the OAS and SDAS have been developed as generic aggression scales, i.e. applicable across diagnoses, attempts have been made to develop disease-specific aggression scales for measuring outcome of treatment. An example is the Rating Scale for Aggression in the Elderly (RAGE) developed by Patel and Hope (1992). This scale contains 21 items, using frequency as a quantifier. The scale is specifically tailored for institutionalized (aggressive) geriatric patients who, most typically, are demented. Although the validation studies still are limited, the results are promising.

When analyzing the concurrent validity of a scale, the global impression assessed by the treating physician or another skilled observer is the most frequently used index. There are several types of global impression scales. The most widely used scale in psychopathology is the Global Clinical Impression Scale (Guy, 1976). This scale measures the severity of a syndrome: from 1 = not present, to 7 = among the most extremely ill. However, so far, this scale has not been frequently used in aggression studies. The ERAG (1992) study included the Global Clinical Severity Scale (published by Bech et al., 1986) which previously has been used in the validation of depression and mania rating scales. As a GAS it is an 11-point scoring scale with the following specifications: 0 = not present, 1 = doubtfully present, 2–4 = mild degrees of aggression, 4–7 = moderate degrees of aggression, and 8–10 = severe to extreme degrees of aggression.

These global scales have often a high validity but low reliability as the scores are very much dependent on the skill of the rater. A physician who is in charge of a department or ward that has severely aggressive patients will often tend to give lower global scores than will a physician who has only a little contact with such patients. This is a type of contrast error (Bech, 1993), i.e. the tendency to underrate a dimension which is very familiar to the rater.

From the ERAG study experience and from trials using eltoprazine as an anti-aggressive drug, it seems that the GAS correlates adequately with the SDAS-9 and, therefore, poorly with the SDAS-6. In an ongoing study, the GAS has been further developed to have separate scores for outward aggression and for inward aggression. Table 3 shows the preliminary results, which indicate that the correlation is adequate between SDAS-9 and outward GAS. However, the correlations between SDAS self-mutilation and GAS are inadequate (most so for the outward GAS).

Self-rating scales

Questionnaires on hostile attitudes or aggressive impulses have a much longer history than the observer scales, for example the Hostility Scale (Cook and Medley, 1954), the Buss–Durkee Hostility Inventory (BDHI; Buss and Durkee, 1957), and the Hostility and Direction of Hostility Questionnaire (HDHQ; Caine et al., 1967). These scales have been developed as psychometric instruments for the measurement of "level of aggressiveness" in various populations, often nonpatient populations. The HDHQ is basically quite similar to the BDHI in terms of the format of the items and their dichotomous answers, but it has the advantage of differentiating between outward directed aggression (extrapunitive behavior) and inward aggression (intrapunitive behavior). This scale has been analyzed by Philip (1969). It was concluded that the outward subscale is different from the inward subscale (which included self-criticism and guilt items). This

Table 3 Spearman coefficients of correlation between the Global Aggression Scale (GAS) scores and subscales for outward- and inward-directed aggression

	GAS	GAS outward	GAS inward
SDAS 9-item outward	0.75	0.71	0.26
SDAS self-mutilation	–	0.24	0.53

finding has been supported by Arrindell et al. (1984) and Miller and Haffner (1989). In studies of attempted suicides, Vinoda (1966) showed that they scored high on General Hostility as well as on intropunitive aggression. Studies using the HDHQ in depression, mania, and schizophrenia have shown that during episodes of acute illness, depressed patients, and also some patients with schizophrenia, have increased inward scores, whereas manic patients score high on outward aggression. Post-treatment, the scores for all patients tended to be within normal values after 8 weeks of treatment (Tsiantis et al., 1981; Price and O'Kearney, 1982). This means that the HDHQ is a scale sensitive to change during treatment, and that it can be applied in groups of inpatients who have different degrees of aggression but apparently no severe psychotic symptoms. However, there are problems using questionnaires as the only outcome measure in aggression. First, they give no information at all about the real acting out by the patient. Second, the information given by the patients about urges to act aggressively is often coloured by social desirability. Their limitation is that they can only be applied in cognitively competent patients and in patients without psychotic symptoms. When used in cross-national studies it has been shown for the BDHI and for the Spielberger State/Trait Anxiety Scale that it is often difficult to make translations, and adapted items are required (Selg, 1966; van der Ploeg, 1980).

Table 4 shows the advantages and disadvantages of the various aggression scales when used for psychiatric patients.

CONCLUSIONS

This chapter has focused on aggressive behavior, including both outward and inward aggression. While impulsivity is only partially associated with suicidal behavior, inward aggression is clearly associated with suicidal behavior and specific depression rating scales are recommended here, such as the Hamilton Depression Scale.

We have especially focused on the principles in the selection of rating scales, and only the most frequently used scales have been discussed. Self-rating scales like the Buss–Durkee and Spielberger scales have their main application in the minor forms of aggression and in covering the coaxial syndrome between personality (or trait) aggression and clinical aggression. The scales measuring the peak or acts of physical aggression are scales to be administered by the clinical staff (e.g. the OAS). The scale with the broadest range of items is the SDAS with indicators of both minor and major aggression. At the clinical syndrome level (Axis I of DSM-III-R), aggression often coexists with or is part of specific syndromes such as dementia, mental handicap, schizophrenia, or mania. In these cases, it has been recommended that aggression scales are used in connection with the

Table 4 Examples of specific aggression scales: advantages and disadvantages of use in psychiatric patients

	Advantages	Disadvantages
OBSERVER SCALES		
All	Basis for intervention	Inter-rater reliability? (Training required)
Event scales		
Overt Aggression Scale	"Hard data"	Time-consuming
Staff Observation Aggression Scale		Reliability of completion?
Disease-specific scales	Broad picture of behavior	For limited population
Aberrant Behavior Checklist		Too detailed for global impression
Scale for Aggressive Behavior in the Elderly		Value of total score?
Disease-independent scales		
Social Dysfunction and Aggression Scale	Use across diagnoses Core symptoms of aggression	Not adequate for inward aggression
Global assessments		
Clinical Global Impression (severity)	Single score Major relevance	Contents of judgment?
Global Aggression Scale		Inter-rater reliability?
SELF-RATINGS (questionnaires)		
All	Patient's own information Suitable for outpatients	No data on real acts Influenced by: Social desirability Culture differences Cognitive competence
Examples:		
Hostility and Direction of Hostility Questionnaire	Useful subscales	Precise contents: trait or state?
Buss–Durkee Inventory		Questionable validity in patients
Spielberger State/Trait Anger	Clear trait and state parts	Hardly used in patients

appropriate psychopathological rating scale (e.g. the PANSS, the BPRS, or the Mania Scale). At the personality level, aggression is often associated with extroversion and/or antisocial behavior. In these cases, the Hare scale for psychopathic or antisocial behavior is recommended. Finally, self-mutilating might be considered as an indicator of borderline symptomatology rather than of aggression.

In conclusion, it can be stated that there has been progress in the psychometrics of aggression. However, many problems still remain, as indicated in this chapter.

REFERENCES

American Psychiatric Association (1987). *Diagnostic and Statistical Manual of Mental Disorders, Third Revised Version (DSM-III-R)*. American Psychiatric Press, Washington, DC.

Andersen, J., Larsen, J.K., Schültz, V., et al. (1989). The Brief Psychiatric Rating Scale. Dimension of Schizophrenia. *Psychopathology*, 22, 168–176.

Angst, J., and Clayton, P. (1986). Premorbid personality of depressive, bipolar, and schizophrenic patients with special reference to suicidal issues. *Compr. Psychiatry*, 27, 511–532.

Arrindell, W.A., Hafkenscheid, A.J.P., and Emmelkamp, P.M.G. (1984). The hostility and direction of hostility questionnaire (NDHQ): a psychometric evaluation in psychiatric outpatients. *Pers. Indiv. Diff.*, 5, 221–231.

Ban, T.A., and Guy, W. (eds) (1982). *The Manual for the Assessment and Documentation of Psychopathology (AMDP System)*. Springer, Berlin.

Barratt, E.S. (1990). Impulsiveness and aggression. Paper presented at the McArthur Foundation Program of Research and Mental Behavior, Pittsburgh, Pennsylvania, 27 Sept 1990.

Bech, P. (1981). Rating scales for affective disorders. Their validity and consistency. *Acta Psychiatr. Scand.*, 64 (suppl. 295), 1–101.

Bech, P. (1993). *Rating Scales for Psychopathology, Health Status, and Quality of Life. A Compendium on Documentation in Accordance with the DSM-III-R and WHO Systems*. Springer, Berlin.

Bech, P., Allerup, P., and Rosenberg, R. (1978). The Marke–Nyman Temperament Scale. Evaluation of transferability using the Rasch item analysis. *Acta Psychiatr. Scand.*, 59, 420–430.

Bech, P., Bolwig, T.G., Kramp, P., Rafaelson, O.J. (1979). The Bech-Rafaelsen Mania Scale and the Hamilton Depression Scale. *Acta Psychiatr. Scand.*, 59, 420–430.

Bech, P., Kastrup, M., and Rafaelsen, O.J. (1986). Mini-compendium of rating scales. *Acta Psychiatr. Scand.*, 73 (suppl. 326), 7–37.

Blackburn, R. (1993). Psychopathic disorder, personality disorders and aggression. In: *Violence. Basic and Clinical Science* (eds C. Thompson and P. Cowen), pp. 101–118. Butterworth–Heinemann, London.

Bond, A.J. (1992). Pharmacological manipulation of aggressiveness and impulsiveness in healthy volunteers. *Progr. Neuropsychopharmacol. Biol. Psychiatr.*, 16, 1–7.

Brizer, D.A., Convit, A., Krakowski, M., and Volavka, J. (1987). A Rating Scale for Reporting Violence on Psychiatric Wards. *Hosp. Community Psychiatry*, 38, 769–770.

Buss, A.H., and Durkee, A. (1957). An inventory for assessing different kinds of hostility. *J. Consult. Psychol.*, 21, 343–349.

Buss, A.H., and Perry, M. (1992). Personality processes and individual differences; the aggression questionnaire. *J. Pers. Soc. Psychol.*, 63, 452–459.

Caine, T.M., Foulds, G.A., and Hope, K. (1967). *Manual of the Hostility and Direction of Hostility Questionnaire*. University of London Press, London.

Coccaro, E.F., Harvey, P.D., Kupsan-Lawrence, E., Herbert, J.L., and Bernstein, D.P. (1991). Development of neuropharmacologically based behavioral assessments of impulsive aggressive behavior. *J. Neuropsychiatry*, 3 (suppl.), 44–51.

Cook, W.W., and Medley, D.M. (1954). Proposed hostility and pharisaic-virtue scales for the MMPI. *J. Appl. Psychol.*, 38, 414–418.

Eichelman, B., and Hartwig, A. (1990). The Carolina Nosology of Destructive Behavior (CNBD). *J. Neuropsychiatry*, 2, 288–296.

ERAG (1992). Social dysfunction and aggression scale (SDAS-21) in generalized aggression and in aggressive attacks: A validity and reliability study. *Int. J. Meth. Psychiatr. Res.*, 59, 420–430.

Eysenck, H.J., and Eysenck, S.B.G. (1976). *Psychoticism as a Personality Dimension*. Hodder and Stoughton, London.

Eysenck, S.B.G., and Eysenck, H.J. (1977). The place of impulsiveness in a dimensional system of personality description. *Br. J. Soc. Clin. Psychol.*, 16, 57–68.

Guy, W. (1976). *Early Clinical Drug Evaluation (ECDEU) Assessment Manual for Psychopharmacology*. National Institute of Mental Health, Rockville.

Hare, R.D. (1980). A research scale for the assessment of psychopathology in criminal populations. *Pers. Indiv. Diff.*, 1, 111–119.

Holmes, N., Shah, A., and Wing, L. (1982). The Disability Assessment Schedule: a brief screening device for use with mentally retarded. *Psychol. Med.*, 12, 879–890.

Honigfeld, G., Gillis, R.D., and Klett, C.J. (1966). NOSIE-30: a treatment sensitive ward behavior scale. *Psychol. Rep.*, 19, 180–182.

Jenkins, C.D., Zymanski, S.J., and Rosenbaum, R.H. (1979). *Jenkins Activity Survey*. The Psychological Corporation, New York.

Kaplan, H.I., and Sadock, B.J. (1990). *Handbook of Clinical Psychiatry*. Williams and Wilkins, New York.

Kay, S.R., Fiszbein, A., and Opler, L.A. (1987). *The Positive and Negative Syndrome Scale (PANNS). Rating Manual*. San Rafael Social and Behavioral Documents, New York.

Kay, S.R., Wolkenfeld, F., and Murrell, L.M. (1988). Profiles of aggression among psychiatric patients. *J. Nerv. Dis.*, 176, 539–546.

Kernberg, O.F. (1992). *Aggression in Personality Disorders and Perversions*. Yale University Press, New Haven.

Kiloh, L.G., and Garside, R.F. (1977). Depression: A multivariate study of Sir Aubrey Lewis's data on melancholia. *Aust. N. Z. J. Psychiatr.*, 11, 149–156.

Lorr, M., and Wunderlich, R.A. (1985). A measure of impulsiveness and its relation to extroversion. *Education and Psychological Measurement*, 45, 251–257.

Lund, J. (1989). Measuring behaviour disorder in mental handicap. *Br. J. Psychiatr.*, 155, 379–383.

Miller, R.J., and Hafner, R.J. (1989). HDHQ test properties for normal respondents. *Pers. Indiv. Diff.*, 10, 1311–1318.

Olff, M., and Endresen, I. (1990). The Dutch and Norwegian translations of the Plutchik questionnaire for psychological defense. In: *Qualification of Human Defense Mechanisms* (eds M. Olff, G. Godaert, and H. Ursin). Springer, Berlin.

Overall, J., and Gorham, D.R. (1962). The Brief Psychiatric Rating Scale. *Psychol. Rep.*, 10, 799–812.

Palmstierna, T., and Wistedt, B. (1987). Staff observation aggression scale. SOAS: presentation and evaluation. *Acta Psychiatr. Scand.*, 76, 657–663.

Palmstierna, T., and Wistedt, B. (1989). Risk factors for aggressive behaviour are of limited value in predicting the violent behaviour of acute involuntarily admitted patients. *Acta Psychiatr. Scand.*, 81, 152–155.

Patel, V., and Hope, R. (1992). A rating scale for aggressive behaviour in the elderly. The RAGE. *Psychol. Med.*, 22, 211–221.

Philip, A.E. (1969). The development and use of the hostility and direction of hostility questionnaire. *J. Psychosom. Res.*, 13, 283–287.

Pietzcker, A., Gebhardt, R., Straus, A., Stöckel, M., Langer, C., and Freudenthal, K. (1983). The syndrome scales in the AMDP system. In: *The AMDP System in Pharmacopsychiatry* (eds D. Bobon, U. Baumann, J. Angst, H. Helmchen, and H. Hippius) pp. 88–99. Karger, Basel.

Plutchik, R., and van Praag, H. (1989). The measurement of suicidality, aggressivity, and impulsivity. *Progr. Neuropsychopharmacol. Biol. Psychiatr.*, 13, 23–34.

Plutchik, R., Kellerman, H., and Conte, H.R. (1979). A structural theory of ego defences and emotions. In: *Emotions and Psychopatholgy* (ed. C.E. Izard). Plenum, New York.

Price, J., and O'Kearney, R. (1982). Changes in hostility during the course of hypomanic illness. *Br. J. Clin. Psychol.*, 6, 63–68.

Selg, H., and Lischke, G. (1966). Eine Faktorenanalyse von Aggressionsvariablen. *Z. Exp. Angew. Psychol.*, 13, 502–526.

Silver, J.M., and Yudofsky, S.C. (1988). Documentation of aggression in the assessment of the violent patient. *Psychiatr. Ann.*, 17, 375–383.

Silver, J.M., and Yudofsky, S.C. (1991). The Overt Aggression Scale: overview and guiding principles. *J. Neuropsychiatry*, 3 (suppl.), 22–29.

Sjöbring, H. (1973). Personality structure and development. *Acta Psychiatr. Scand.*, (suppl. 244).

Sorgi, P., Ratey, J., Knoedler, D.W., Markert, R.J., and Reichman, M. (1991). Rating aggressions in the clinical setting. A retrospective adaptation of the overt aggression scale: preliminary results. *J. Neuropsychiatry*, 3 (suppl.), 552–555.

Spielberger, C.D., Westberry, L., Barker, L., Russell, S., Silva de Crane, R., and Ozer, A.K. (1980). *Preliminary Manual for the State–Trait Anger Scale*. Center for Research in Community Psychology, College of Social and Behavioural Science, University of South Florida, Tampa.

Spielberger, C.D., Johnson, E.H., Russell, S.F., Crane, R.J., Jacobs, G.A., and Worden, T.J. (1985). The experience and expression of anger: construction and validation of an anger expression scale. In: *Anger and Hostility in Cardiovascular and Behavioural Disorders* (eds M.A. Chesney and R.H. Rosenman) pp. 5–30. Hemisphere/McGraw-Hill, New York.

Tsiantsis, J., Blackburn, J.M., and Lyketsos, G.C. (1981). Changes in hostility of schizophrenic patients during treatment. *Br. J. Med. Psychol.*, 54, 251–258.

van der Ploeg, H.M., Defaris, P.B., and Spielberger, C.D. (1980). *Handleiding bij de Zelf-Analyse Vragenlijst. Een Vragenlijst voor het Meten van Boosheid en Woede, als Toestand en als Dispositie*, pp. 7–20. Swets and Zeitlinger, Lisse, The Netherlands.

Verdoux, H., and Bourgeois, M. (1993). A comparison of manic patient subgroups. *J. Affective. Dis.*, 27, 267–273.

Vinoda, K.S. (1966). Personality characteristics of attempted suicides. *Br. J. Psychiatr.*, 112, 1143–1148.

Wing, L. (1980). The MRC handicaps, behaviour skills (HBE) schedule. *Acta Psychiatr. Scand.*, 62 (suppl. 285), 241–247.

Wistedt, B., Rassmussen, A., Pedersen, L., et al. (1990). The development of an observer scale for measuring social dysfunction and aggression. *Pharmacopsychiatry*, 23, 249–252.

Yudofsky, S.C., Silver, J.M., Jackson, W., Endicott, J., and Williams, D. (1986). The overt aggression scale for the objective rating of verbal and physical aggression. *Am. J. Psychiatr.*, 143, 35–39.

4 The Epidemiology of Aggression

LEE N ROBINS

Department of Psychiatry, Washington University School of Medicine, St. Louis, MO, USA

INTRODUCTION

The study of impulsive and aggressive behavior has long been of interest to the psychologists and psychiatrists who must treat people with these problems, to the justice system and criminologists who are concerned with the identification, prosecution, incarceration, and rehabilitation of people with these difficulties, to teachers and military personnel who must manage these behaviors in a troublesome few assigned to them as students or recruits, and to sociologists, to whom deviant behavior, as an example of social failure, illuminates the processes through which societies generally achieve consensus and cooperation from the vast majority.

Each of these disciplines has been concerned with impulsive and aggressive behavior as a deviant exception to normal life, a sign of pathology. Yet in recent years, a common perception has arisen that the incidence of impulsivity and aggression is increasing at such a pace that it can no longer be viewed as characterizing a troublesome but isolated minority, and must rather be seen as threatening the tradition of social civility in society as a whole and limiting the freedom of the ordinary citizen. This change in perception of the scope of the problem has moved the study of impulsivity and aggression as a medical problem from the exclusive province of psychiatry or neurology into a primary focus of those concerned with public health (Koop and Lundberg, 1992). Yet a public concern with violent crimes is not new. In 1969 a report was published by the National Commission on the Causes and Prevention of Violence (Mulvihill and Tumin, 1969), and about the same time the sociological literature was rich in articles attempting to verify a rise in delinquency (Chilton and Spielberger, 1971). By the time of publication of the Surgeon General's 1979 report *Healthy People*, in 1979, there was awareness of the contribution of violence to mortality. The *Report of the Secretary's Task Force on Black and Minority Health* (US Department of Health and Human Services, 1985) documented that violence substantially elevated minority groups, mortality and morbidity. Recently, however, the concern with violence has become more central to public policy. The

Impulsivity and Aggression. Edited by E. Hollander and D.J. Stein
© 1995 John Wiley & Sons Ltd

Centers for Disease Control have adopted violence as a major research topic for the Youth Risk Behavior Survey. The *Journal of the American Medical Association* recently devoted two consecutive issues (10 and 17 June, 1992) to violence. In 1993, President Clinton called on the US Congress to take action to reduce the level of aggression in the community, and Congress did finally pass the Brady Bill, a first step toward better control of firearms, in an effort to reduce the costs of violence.

As aggression has been approached by different disciplines, it has been given a variety of meanings, even some relatively positive ones. In this chapter, we will take it to mean what the literature generally terms "violence", i.e. physical assault upon another person, leading to injury or death. This volume also covers the topic of impulsivity. There is no such well-defined synomym to help us operationalize impulsivity. It is a less popular topic for the various disciplines and is not clearly defined even within single disciplines. A look at its use in the psychiatric nomenclature has been of no help. The DSM-III-R denotes as disorders of impulse control a set of disorders that includes kleptomania (stealing things that are not desired for their monetary value or usefulness), fire setting, hair pulling, pathological gambling, psychoactive substance use disorders, paraphilias, and Impulsive Personality Disorder. It also lists impulsivity among the symptoms of antisocial personality disorder, borderline personality disorder, attention deficit disorder, and conduct disorder. Psychiatrists also commonly consider suicide attempts for which no advance planning has taken place as impulsive, and use the term to describe the shopping sprees and sexual behavior typical of mania. This list of behaviors that fit under the rubric of impulsivity is too long, and the correlates of the behaviors are too various to allow a coherent picture of its epidemiology in the current chapter. Yet we will inevitably cover some of its territory in discussing aggression, when, as we shall see, we note that violence is closely related to conduct disorder, antisocial personality, and substance abuse.

This chapter will attempt to estimate how large the problem of violence is, how substantial the evidence is that it is increasing, in what parts of the population it appears most frequently, and what its correlates are, in the hope that they may shed light on the causes of its increase.

HOMICIDE

Homicide is the ultimate aggressive act. Its current frequency in the USA, compared with other parts of the world, and changes in its rate over the years give us a sense of how serious the current situation is and what we can expect in the future.

Homicide data come from Vital Statistics reports, which are compiled from death certificates. Death certificates are well known to contain inaccuracies, and violent deaths may be particularly vulnerable to error, because by definition no physician was in attendance around the time of death. The coroner's report has to be the basis for the classification. The quality of coroners' determinations of homicide can vary over the years, making detection of true trends questionable. They should, in general, become more accurate as the science of pathology improves, but there are also competing pressures, both political and economic. Despite possible errors, however, the information on death certificates is uniquely valuable because all deaths get reported and all sudden deaths must be reviewed as possible homicides. Violence that does not result in death, in contrast, is severely under-recorded in public records.

In the USA, death certificates showed a drop in homicide rates from 1948 to 1960, a steep rise from 1960 to 1978, a slight decline in the early 1980s, and a recent trend upwards again. To a large extent, the trends in homicide rates have followed the trends in the 15- to 24-year-old proportion of the population, the age bracket in which most perpetrators fall (Wilbanks, 1981–82). However, the rate of homicides did not drop as low in the 1948–60 period as the proportion of young people did, nor did it peak in 1978 to the extent that the "baby boom" would suggest it should have. In any case, the overall trend since 1960 has been a rise that has doubled the US national rates.

Death certificate data can be compared across countries, subject to caveats about differences in definitions and autopsy procedures. The US homicide rates are far above those of any other Western country—about nine to 10 times the rate in most of Europe, and three times the rate in Canada and in Finland, the European country with the highest rate (National Center for Health Statistics, 1984). Clearly, death certificates suggest that the US has a major problem with aggression. It is important, therefore, to see which groups account for this problem.

The highest rates of death by homicide are among young males living in poverty areas of big cities (Baker et al., 1984), and rates decline linearly with size of city for all age–sex groups. Overall, male rates are about three times female rates. Blacks have much higher rates than whites, among both males and females. Black male rates are about six times as high as white males', and black female rates are about four times as high as white females'. This racial gap has closed slightly over time, as rates have risen faster in whites than in blacks. Still, homicide remains the leading cause of death of black men and women between 15 and 34 years old, the ages during which the excess over white rates is at its peak—eight times the rate for white men in that age bracket and six times the rate for white women of those ages. The fact that homicide is the leading cause of death for young blacks is partly explained by the low rate of natural deaths in the young and partly by the fact that blacks' poverty and concentration in large central

cities protects them from the leading cause of death for young whites—
motor accidents. Nevertheless, it is a staggering fact that one out of every 20
black youths can be expected to die by homicide. The black–white rates are
so discrepant that, for males under 45, homicide alone accounts for 38% of
the excess mortality of blacks over whites. Homicide rates for Hispanic
males fall between those of black men and white men, while the rates for
Hispanic females do not differ much from those for whites. Native American
rates also fall between those of blacks and whites, and are about double
white rates.

While appallingly high, these figures for homicide victims might seem to
tell us little about who is violent. It is, after all, the perpetrators with whom
we are concerned. It turns out, however, that facts about the victims are
informative because the race of perpetrator and victim is almost always the
same (in over 90% of cases). Furthermore, most male homicides occur as a
result of conflicts with male acquaintances of approximately the same age,
living in the same neighborhood, and with the same behavioral patterns
(Jason et al., 1983). For example, high blood alcohol levels are frequently
found in the victims, and perpetrators often report that they had been
drinking at the time of the act; drugs are also commonly found in both,
though not as frequently as alcohol (MacDonald, 1986; Welte and Abel,
1989). The similarity between perpetrator and victim was poignantly put by
a black mother in St. Louis who was spending much effort seeing that her
son's murderer came to justice, only to have another son charged with a
different murder. As quoted by William McClenahan (*St. Louis Post
Dispatch*, 26 November 1993), she said: "I've got two fears for all the black
babies. One is that they'll be killed. The other is that they'll kill somebody."
Of course, not all victims are like their perpetrators. When male acquaintances were not responsible for the homicide of a young male, the most
likely perpetrator was a wife or lover (Mann, 1986).

One explanation for the current extraordinary level of homicides in the
USA appears to be the increasing availability of firearms. About two-thirds
of all homicides are committed with firearms, with knives running a poor
second. Firearms are particularly the weapons of men; women are more
likely to use knives or other sharp instruments. The greater availability of
firearms in large cities than elsewhere may be an important explanation for
the fact that homicide rates increase with city size. The increase with city
size appears to be limited to firearm homicides; rates of homicide by other
means are reasonably constant across population sizes (Fingerhut et al.,
1992). The easy availability of firearms to young Americans is remarkable.
A survey of public school 11th graders in Seattle found that 34% claimed
easy access to guns, and access was easiest for just those sections of the
population responsible for the highest homicide rates—black males of low
social status (Callahan and Rivara, 1992). But more convincing than correlations between gun access and characteristics associated with violence is the
fact that passage of a law in Washington, DC, banning firearms sales led to

an immediate decline in homicides by firearms, while there was no decline in homicides by other means.

PHYSICAL ASSAULT

The frequency of physical assault has been studied in populations of prisoners and psychiatric inpatients, in whom its frequency is expected to be high because institutionalization of some of them will have been prompted by their use of force or threats that they intended to use force. These cases, however, are not representative of the total population of youths or adults involved in violence. They may not even be representative of the extreme end of the continuum of violence, because public stereotypes about who is dangerous may influence the detection of violence at any stage in the process that results in institutionalization—from a social worker's assessment of a client, to a policeman's decision that someone seen near a crime site might be the perpetrator, to a jury's weighing of trial evidence. When the content of institutional records is used as evidence for violent behavior there are additional possible sources of bias—patients or prisoners may have slanted their responses to questioning in an effort to affect administrative decisions; staff notes may have been distorted to justify administrative actions taken.

Some of these difficulties can be avoided by obtaining data from sample surveys of the general population that ask about the perpetration of violent acts or experiences as the victim of violence. Such surveys have become available only in the last 15 or 20 years. Before then, it was doubted that questions about such socially disapproved behaviors would be answered honestly (Srole et al., 1962). However, it has been shown that answers given to ordinary survey interviewers correspond well with record data when interviewers put the questions in a nonjudgmental fashion after rapport has been established.

Sample surveys, none the less, have other problems. The populations studied vary with respect to age range, living arrangements (i.e. whether the homeless or institutionalized are included), and geographical area. The sample actually interviewed is never exactly the sample targeted. Thus, unlike death certificates, which are available for a total population, survey data can provide only more-or-less fair and precise estimates of parameters of the target population. Unless high-risk portions of the population are oversampled, surveys provide little opportunity to learn much about extreme but rare forms of violence, such as rapes or stabbings. Definitions of aggression vary greatly from study to study, some studies counting a slap or even a threat of violence used to discipline children, while others require physical damage lasting at least a day or two; some including fights between siblings, while others count only fights outside the family. They also vary in the time covered, so that assaults can be reported for the last month, for the respondent's adulthood, or for the whole lifespan. Studies covering the whole lifetime avoid classifying as "nonviolent" those who were last violent years ago, and who therefore should share *early* predictors of aggression with the recently violent. However, recall of these long past episodes of violence are likely to be less accurate than recall of more recent episodes.

These variations in method make it uncertain whether differences in rates reported by two studies carried out in different geographical settings or different eras show that those places or eras truly have different rates of violence. What surveys do best is show what types of violent behavior are linked to what population characteristics, because they collect much more detailed data than are available from public records. They answer questions about the association of violence with social status, childhood aggression, and adult psychiatric disorder. When different surveys find the same correlates with violence *despite* differences in study design and question wording, the argument for a true link is further substantiated.

INFORMATION FROM POLICE AND HOSPITALS AND SOCIAL AGENCIES

Assault

We noted that homicide is the cause of death that most distinguishes between blacks and whites, and that the perpetrators and victims are almost always of the same race and usually of the same gender. It is no surprise, therefore, that assault is the reason for arrest that most distinguishes the races (Federal Bureau of Investigation Uniform Crime Reporting Program, 1984). In 1980, when the overall rate of index crimes for which black males under 18 years old were arrested was 2.4 times the overall rate for whites, blacks were arrested for *violent* index offenses 3.4 times more often than whites. Nor would it surprise us that most of those arrested for assault are male.

A study of a sample of former mental patients found that they reported more violence and more other illegal behaviors than did community controls (Link et al., 1990.) Of special interest is the fact that the higher rate occurred only in those patients with psychotic symptoms; the remainder did not report increased violence. Also of interest is the fact that psychotic symptoms predicted violence in the untreated community sample as well.

Rates of violence in mental patients are found to exceed rates in the general population just prior to admission, and after release (Monahan, 1991). But the meaning of these rates is unclear, since fear of violence is a reason for admission, and belief that there is little risk of violence is a reason for release. What is interesting is that the correlates of violence in mental patients are the same as those in the general population: i.e. the violent ones are predominantly young males who grew up with ineffective parents and who had violent family members (Krakowski et al., 1986).

Child abuse

Although rates of reporting child abuse have grown enormously over the last 15 years, this remains a rare event compared with other types of violence. Unlike homicide and assault, there is no evidence that blacks exceed whites in child abuse. The figures published of cases reported to protective agencies show, if anything, a lower rate for blacks.

A follow up, via criminal records at the age of 20 years, of children known to have been abused or neglected showed that both physical abuse and neglect predicted violent crime (Widom, 1989).

SURVEY DATA IN GENERAL POPULATIONS

Victims

In a yearly victimization survey carried out by the US Department of Justice, victims of violence were more often black and they more often identified the perpetrators as black than would be expected from the proportion of the population that is black. But the excess is more modest than one would expect from death records of homicide or Federal Bureau of Investigation records of arrests for violent crime. The rate of aggravated assaults reported by blacks was about half again as high as the rate reported by whites (1.3% vs 0.8%), and the rate of perpetrators identified as black was about double their rate in the population (27%). The modest excess suggests that blacks' greater representation in death and police records may be explained more by blacks' use of firearms during crimes than by the number of violent crimes committed.

Domestic violence

There are two major US surveys that provide information about domestic violence, a survey devoted exclusively to domestic violence (Straus and Gelles, 1980), and a general psychiatric survey, the Epidemiologic Catchment Area (ECA) project (Robins and Regier, 1991), which included spouse and child hitting as symptoms of antisocial personality. Both attempt to make estimates for the USA as whole. The survey carried out by Straus and Gelles presented the surprising result that women were more likely to attack their husbands than vice versa, upsetting the stereotype of greater aggressivity in men. This result held up even when milder forms of attacks, such as pushing, shoving, slapping, and throwing things, were not counted. The ECA also found about twice as many women as men reporting having been the first to hit their spouse in a fight (Robins et al., 1988). Both studies also found more spouse hitting by blacks than whites. The ECA also suggested that the rate of domestic violence was increasing, because younger men and women, both black and white, reported spouse hitting more than older men and women, even though the younger ones had had fewer years of marriage at risk. The increase in the younger groups was much greater for whites than blacks, reflecting the pattern of whites catching up with blacks that has been noted in deaths by homicide as well.

Self-report of abusing children is much less common than reports of hitting one's spouse. Straus and Gelles found only 0.4% positive, the ECA only 2%. In neither study was there any evidence for a male or a black excess. Indeed, there was somewhat less reporting of child abuse by blacks, agreeing with the published referral data noted above. The correlates of child physical abuse, rather than sex or race, appear to be the parents being very young and in economic difficulty. These results suggest that child abuse is not part of the general pattern of antisocial behavior, but is an independent syndrome. However, the correlates of this behavior have not been extensively studied in general population surveys because of the small numbers who report child abuse.

It has been argued that a primary factor in domestic violence is growing up in a home in which the same behaviors occurred. Results are just beginning to appear from studies that followed abused children long enough to learn how they treat their own children (Widom, 1989). Such studies are needed because people in treatment as a consequence of striking their children or spouses are likely to recall mistreatment in their own childhoods in their search for an explanation for their behavior. Even if such a recapitulation of violent parenting does occur between generations, it is not clear that it was the witnessing or being the recipient of violence that is responsible, since violence in the home is associated with many other adverse circumstances.

Fighting

The ECA provides correlates of fighting for adults, while a survey conducted by the Centers for Disease Control, the Youth Risk Behavior Survey (YRBS), provides correlates for adolescents (Centers for Disease Control, 1991). In both studies, male rates greatly exceed female rates. While fighting might be considered normal behavior for children, it is surprising that so many (about one-quarter) of all men reported physical fights when they were 18 or older. The ECA also found that more young than older people report any adult fighting, despite having had fewer years in which to do it. The one exception was in black men, for whom the frequency was slightly below one-third (31%) in both younger and older age groups.

Differences between black men and white men were modest and disappeared entirely among those under 45 and among those unemployed or with little schooling. For women, on the other hand, blacks were twice as likely as whites to have been in a fight (12 vs 5%), and this difference remained no matter whether age or social level was controlled. The YRBS also found somewhat more fighting in blacks and Hispanics than whites, and that the higher rate for blacks was much more marked in girls than boys. These results suggest two changes over time: women's violence is approaching that of men, and white violence is approaching that of blacks.

One important difference between the sexes and races still exists, and appears to be disappearing more slowly than the difference in fighting: black adults are much more likely to use weapons when they fight than are whites. Half of all blacks in the ECA who had fought had used a weapon; for whites, the rate was less than a quarter. Although the rate of weapon use when fighting is increasing for whites, as shown by a higher proportion in younger than older fighters, the rates are still far below rates for blacks. Weapons use starts very young, particularly among children who have the most severe history of antisocial behavior. Callahan and Rivara (1992) showed that in Seattle high school students, those with the easiest access to guns were males who were gang members, drug sellers, had been arrested, had been suspended from school, who drank and used drugs—and who fought. Thus, weapons are selectively available to the most violent youngsters, who have the poorest prospects of exercising restraint and judgment in their use. Because use of weapons is associated with arrest and fatality, we cannot expect to see rapid equalization of arrests for assault or homicide rates between blacks and whites in the near future, despite the near equality in numbers of black and white men who fight. Unfortunately, what we can expect, given the higher rates of fighting and weapon use in young than older whites, is a further rise in rates of assault and homicides unless vigorous action is taken either to reduce access to firearms or to turn the rising tide of fighting in whites.

The stability of aggression between childhood and adulthood has been demonstrated in a host of studies (Farrington, 1990); thus it is no surprise that fighting in childhood is a good predictor of adult fighting. Indeed, the ECA found that boys and girls who fought as children were more than three times as likely as others to fight as adults. It is surprising, however, that the number of *non*violent childhood conduct problems was an even more powerful predictor of adult fighting. While half the men who fought as children also fought as adults, three-fifths of those with three or more nonviolent conduct problems in childhood did so. Indeed, a history of being a runaway, a rare childhood symptom that occurs almost exclusively late in childhood, was a better predictor of adult fighting than was fighting in childhood. This is strong evidence that violence is not a unique character trait, but is rather one symptom of a general pattern of antisocial behavior of diverse types and long endurance. This observation is supported by a look at other adult antisocial behavior. Two-thirds of the men who had at least three adult antisocial behaviors other than violence were fighters. The criminology literature also notes that efforts to distinguish the violent criminal from the more common property criminal have failed. What one finds is that violent criminals generally have a long history of arrests for property crimes as well (Farrington, 1979). Violent criminals are different only in the severity of their criminal history, not in its kind.

In the ECA, nonviolent, antisocial behaviors were much more strongly correlated with fighting than were economic or marital status. While those who fought were *somewhat* more likely than others to have been unemployed for at least 6 months in the last 5 years and not currently married, these are not necessarily causes, since those who fight may therefore lose their jobs or have their marriages dissolve.

For men and women of both races, heavy drinking and drug use were associated with fighting. The relationship was particularly strong for women's heavy drinking. While women who drank heavily did not fight as often as heavy-drinking men, the male : female ratio of fighting dropped from about 4 : 1 overall to less than 2 : 1 when both were heavy drinkers.

Other psychiatric disorders, schizophrenia, depression, and mania were also somewhat related to violence, whether measured by spouse hitting, child abuse, fighting, or using a weapon (Swanson et al., 1990), but less strongly than substance abuse.

SURVEYS OF PRISONERS

Interviews with prisoners convicted of violent crimes and a control group of people who grew up in the same neighborhoods found significant differences in family backgrounds (Kruttschnitt et al., 1986; Kruttschnitt and Dornfeld, 1991). More of the prisoners had been beaten by their parents, had had scant parental supervision, or had criminal parents. They did not differ in whether one of their parents was abused by the other, or in the level of parental attention or affection they received. They did differ in school performance and, of course, illegal behaviors.

SUMMARY

The epidemiology of violence emphasizes the importance of childhood predisposition, but the striking differences over time and across nations also emphasize that expression of these predispositions in adult life is subject to the impact of historical moments and circumstances. The USA is on an upward trajectory of violence that makes it an outlier among other nations.

The evidence that violence is increasing is overwhelming, even when we consider the contribution of improved reporting and changes in the demographic profile (Smith, 1986). Not only is violence involving increasing segments of the population, but the greater access to firearms makes its expression increasingly serious. Yet its roots are the ones that we have recognized for many years. It is most prevalent in youth, and more frequent in males than females. It is associated with heavy use of a variety of psychoactive substances. It is heralded by childhood behavior problems of all kinds, including but not specific to fighting and other forms of violence. This childhood behavior, in turn, is most likely when parents are antisocial, excessive drinkers, cruel, or inconsistent in their discipline, and when supervision is absent. Severe mental disorders, particularly the presence of psychotic symptoms, make some contribution to the national concern with violence, but their contribution is only modest because they affect such a small part of the population.

This consistency among studies in noting the most violence-prone sections of the population helps us target interventions, but it does not explain the increase in violence. Many explanations for the increase have been proposed. To begin with, there is evidence that most of the well-recognized correlates of violence have increased: there has been a growth in the heavy consumption of drugs and alcohol over the last generation, and more children have behavior problems. As the frequency of aggression rises in the population, more children are exposed to antisocial parents, and children get less supervision as more women work, either because more are single mothers or because it has become the norm for women in two-parent families to work. The frequency of mental disorders appears to be increasing among young people, as indicated by the drop in age of onset noted in epidemiological studies such as the ECA (Robins and Regier, 1991).

Many other explanations have been offered as well, including television and movies that display violence, underemployment or unemployment of young people, low crime clearance rates by police and lenient sentences that reduce deterrence, young adults' growing postponement of or failure ever to undertake family formation, increased availability of firearms, easy access to alcohol, weakening of the church, break up of the "nuclear" family, loss of respect for the government, increasingly racially and economically segregated residential areas, which deprives the poor of middle-class role models and connections to employment opportunities, overcrowded schools, teenage parenting, and others as well. We have no way to estimate the relative contribution of these factors to aggression. Only some of them might be remediable through changes in social policy, but any that are remedied will give an opportunity to see whether a consequent reduction in the prevalence of violence supports their causal role.

REFERENCES

Baker, S.P., O'Neill, B., and Karpf, R.S. (1984). *The Injury Fact Book*. Lexington Books, Lexington, MA.

Callahan, C.M., and Rivara, F.P. (1992). Urban high school youth and handguns: A school-based survey. *JAMA*, 267 (22), 3038–3042.

Centers for Disease Control (1991). Weapon-carrying among high school students—United States, 1990. *MMWR*, 40, 681–684.

Chilton, R., and Spielberger, A. (1971). Is deliquency increasing? Age structure and the crime rate. *Soc. Forces*, 49, 487–493.

Farrington, D.P. (1979). Longitudinal research on crime and deliquency. In: *Crime and Justice*, vol. I. (eds N. Morris and M. Tonry) pp. 303–304. University of Chicago Press, Chicago.

Farrington, D.P. (1990). Childhood aggression and adult violence: Early precursors and later-life outcomes. In: *The Development of Childhood Aggression* (eds D.J. Pepler and K.H. Rubin) pp. 5–29. Erlbaum, Hillsdale, NJ.

Federal Bureau of Investigation Uniform Crime Reporting Program (1984). *Age-Specific Arrest Rates 1965–1983*. US Department of Justice, Washington, D.C.

Fingerhut, L.A., Ingram, D.D. and Feldman, J.J. (1992). Firearm and nonfirearm homicide among persons 15 through 19 years of age: Differences by level of urbanization, United States, 1979 through 1989. *JAMA*, 267 (22), 3048–3053.

Jason, J., Flock, M., and Tyler, C.W. Jr (1983). Epidemiologic characteristics of primary homicides in the United States. *Am. J. Epidemiol.*, 117 (4), 419–428.

Koop, C.E., and Lundberg, G.D. (1992). Violence in America: A public health emergency. Time to bite the bullet back [editorial]. *JAMA*, 267 (22), 3075–3076.

Krakowski, M., Volavka, J., and Brizer, D. (1986). Psychopathology and violence: A review of literature. *Compr. Psychiatr.*, 27 (2), 131–148.

Kruttschnitt, C., and Dornfeld, M. (1991). Childhood victimization, race, and violent crime. *Criminal Justice Behav.*, 18 (4), 448–463.

Kruttschnitt, C., Heath, L., and Ward, D.A. (1986). Family violence, television viewing habits, and other adolescent experiences related to violent criminal behavior. *Criminology*, 24 (2), 235–267.

Link, B., Cullen, F., and Andrews, H. (1990). Violent and illegal behavior of current and former mental patients compared to community controls. Presented at the meeting of the Society for the Study of Social Problems, Aug 1990.

MacDonald, J.M. (1986). *The Murderer and His Victim*, 2nd edn. Charles C. Thomas, Springfield, IL.

Mann, C.R. (1985). The black female criminal homicide offender in the United States. In: US Department of Health and Human Services, Subcommittee on Homicide, Suicide, and Unintentional Injuries, *Report of the Secretary's Task Force on Black and Minority Health*. US Department of Health and Human Services, Washington DC.

Monahan, J. (1991). *Mental Disorder and Violent Behavior: Perceptions and Evidence. Working Paper Series* #3. John D. and Catherine T. MacArthur Foundation, Research Network on Mental Health and the Law, Chicago.

Mulvihill, D.J., and Tumin, M.M. (1969). *Crimes of Violence. Task Force on Individual Acts of Violence, National Commission on the Causes and Prevention of Violence*. U.S. Government Printing Office, Washington, D.C.

National Center for Health Statistics (1984). *Health of the United States, 1984*. DHHS Pub. No. (PH5), 85–1232. Public Health Service US Government Printing Office, Washington D.C.

Robins, L.N., and Regier, D.A. (eds) (1991). *Psychiatric Disorders in America*. The Free Press, New York.

Robins, L.N., Carlson, V., Bucholz, K., and Sussman, L. (1988). *Intentional and Unintentional Injury in Black Americans—Report to Panel on Health Status and Demography of Black Americans, NRC Committee on the Status of Black Americans*. Washington University, St. Louis, MD.

Smith, M.D. (1986). The era of increased violence in the United States: Age, period, or cohort effect? *Sociol. Q.*, 27 (2), 239–251.

Srole, L., Langner, T.S., Michael, S.T., et al. (eds) (1962). *Book Two. Mental Health in the Metropolis. The Midtown Manhattan Study*. Harper & Row, New York.

Straus, M.A., Gelles, R.J., and Steinmetz, S.K. (1980). *Behind Closed Doors: Violence in the American Family*. Anchor/Doubleday, Garden City, NY.

Surgeon General's report on health promotion and disease prevention. (1979). *Healthy People*. DHEW publication No. PHS 79/55071, The US Government Printing Office, Washington D.C.

Swanson, J., Holzer, C., Ganju, V., and Jono, R. (1990). Violence and psychiatric disorder in the community: Evidence from the Epidemiologic Catchment Area Surveys. *Hosp. Community Psychiatr.*, 41, 761–770.

US Department of Health and Human Services, Subcommittee on Homicide, Suicide, and Unintentional Injuries (1985). *Report of the Secretary's Task Force on Black and Minority Health*. US Department of Health and Human Services, Washington D.C.

Welte, J.W., and Abel, E.L. (1989). Homicide: Drinking by the victim. *J. Studies on Alcohol*, 50(3), 197–201.

Widom, C.S. (1989). The cycle of violence. *Science*, 244, 160–166.

Wilbanks, W. (1981–82). Trends in violent death among the elderly. *Int. J. Aging Hum. Dev.*, 14(3), 167–175.

Part II

NEUROBIOLOGY

5 Animal and Evolutionary Models of Impulsive Aggression

BURR EICHELMAN
Department of Psychiatry, Temple University School of Medicine,
Philadelphia, PA, USA

INTRODUCTION

Within human evolution should rest the clues to our most basic and primitive behaviors. Aggressive behavior can be considered one of these basic behaviors. MacLean (1958) wrote about the "primitive brain", the archipallium which, he felt, drives the emotional state of the human organism despite the evolutionary development of a modifying neocortex concerned with intellectual functioning. His neurophysiology lent support to the theories of aggressive behavior. Is there an underlying aggressive drive of a destructive nature (e.g. *Thanatos*; Freud, 1930) which must be redirected constructively as Lorenz hypothesized (Lorenz, 1966)? Such theoretical debate has led to heated philosophical arguments as to whether mankind is "bad" or "good" (innately violent or nonviolent). Such debates soon become overburdened with values that may well obscure what we potentially might gain from examining our evolutionary past and laboratory models of "impulsivity" and "aggression".

This chapter proposes that "constructs of impulsivity" may be conceptually useful in understanding alterations of behavior and their evolutionary advantages and disadvantages as they pertain to aggressive behavior. Specifically, this chapter aims to examine "impulsivity" within the framework of a differential ability to inhibit responses, a deficit or a variation in the ability to passively avoid. It illustrates that such deficits are linked to enhanced aggressive behavior and often to a reduction in serotonin (5-hydroxytryptamine, 5-HT) functioning within the brain.

This chapter addresses the evolutionary development of such behaviors and argues that they have evolved as a continuum of behavior providing a rich substrate for natural selection. Finally, this chapter hypothesizes how such behaviors may become "unmasked" for a given species if external, environmental situations change or internal, neuronal systems are injured.

Impulsivity and Aggression. Edited by E. Hollander and D.J. Stein
© 1995 John Wiley & Sons Ltd

The references utilized in support of this theoretical construct are illustrative. An extensive and excellent review of laboratory paradigms and serotonergic manipulation is provided by Soubrie (1986), followed by elaborate commentaries. By no means is the literature review within this chapter intended to be exhaustive. It is selective, and exceptions to the observations reported exist within the literature.

The linkage of behavior to a single neurotransmitter system, as illustrated within this chapter, is an oversimplification. Modification of one neurotransmitter will perturb other systems. Drug, lesion, or environmental effects must, in general, alter multiple neurotransmitter systems. Even a single neurotransmitter may effect opposite behaviors through differing receptor mechanisms. Nevertheless, oversimplification for heuristic purposes has led to substantial and effective medical interventions of complex functions, as illustrated by the β-adrenergic antagonist control of hypertension or the H_2-antagonist effects on peptic ulcers. It is from this simplified, but potentially practical, position that this chapter is written.

IMPULSIVITY AND THE CONCEPTS OF ACTIVE AND PASSIVE AVOIDANCE

Cannon (1939) wrote about the fight versus flight responses to environmental danger. In reality, however, an animal can fight, flee, or *freeze*. Response to threat is actually tripartite. Species show varying degrees of these three behaviors: rabbits freeze or flee; possums freeze or "fight" (threaten); dogs flee or fight, but rarely freeze.

In laboratory environments these behaviors, fight, flight, or freeze, are often tested separately. Sometimes they may be paired to compete with each other.

The ability to "actively" avoid a danger can be illustrated by paradigms of conditioned avoidance responses. Rats placed in a two-way shuttlebox are warned with a stimulus cue (a sound or light) that a footshock is soon to follow. They learn to *actively* move to the other chamber: to actively avoid the footshock.

Linked to the ability to actively avoid is the ability to actively explore a novel environment. This can be studied through the use of an "open-field test". For example, a rat is placed into a novel box with gridded squares. This situation places the rat in conflict between freezing and exploring. The number of squares traversed during a period of time varies with rat strains and physiological characteristics of the rat.

Experimental manipulations may produce animals skilled in active avoidance and very active in the open field. Conversely, these same animals will often show deficits of "passive avoidance". A deficit in passive avoidance is a deficit in "freezing". These may be classified as impulsive behaviors. A normal cat that receives an mild electric shock at a feeding bowl will not return to that bowl. A cat with a neurophysiologically induced deficit in passive avoidance (e.g. caused by surgical ablation of the septal nuclei) will return repeatedly to receive the aversive shock (McCleary, 1961).

Deficits in the inhibition of responding—a variant of passive avoidance—can also be experimentally displayed with appetitive operant conditioning. An example of such an experimental paradigm is the differential reinforcement low-rate (DRL) schedule of operant behavior. The DRL schedule provides reinforcement to an animal (usually a rat within a Skinner box), which can withhold a response during a critical interval. If the rat presses a lever within the DRL interval, the program is reset and the rat "starts over" to obtain a reward. This, in normal rats, produces a very slow but steady rate of responding to reinforcement. Certain brain lesions or drugs will produce "impulsive" animals that are deficient in DRL performance.

When one cross-correlates genetic selection studies, brain lesion studies, and neurochemical or pharmacological manipulations with deficits in passive avoidance or enhanced active avoidance and aggressive behavior, there is a remarkable concurrence of findings. Those manipulations which make animals more adept at active avoidance or less adept at passive avoidance are frequently the same manipulations which enhance aggressive behavior within the laboratory setting. From a neurochemical perspective, those neurochemical manipulations which impair passive avoidance and enhance "active" behaviors (e.g. 5-HT reduction) also appear to enhance aggressive behavior within certain laboratory models.

One illustrative animal laboratory model of aggressive behavior is the model of shock-induced fighting or pain-induced aggression in rats or mice. In this laboratory model, rats (Ulrich and Azrin, 1962) or mice (Tedeschi et al., 1959) are paired in a Skinner box and subjected to footshock. During the footshock they will attack each other in a species-specific pattern. Other laboratory models, including predatory aggression and ethological observation (within free-roving primate colonies), have also affirmed such an association between aggressive behavior and altered brain 5-HT.

SEPTAL BRAIN LESIONS, IMPULSIVITY AND AGGRESSIVE BEHAVIOR

Brain lesion studies suggest an association between impulsivity and aggressive behavior. Lesions to the septal nuclei, a forebrain portion of the limbic system integrally connected to the hypothalamus and hippocampus, in the cat (McCleary, 1961) and the rat (King, 1958) produce enhanced active avoidance under certain conditions (similar to the rats of the Roman High Avoidance Strain) and concurrent deficits in passive avoidance (McCleary, 1961; Miczek et al.; Grossman, 1972). Rats with septal lesions have impaired performance on a DRL schedule of reinforcement if external cues are withheld (Ellen et al., 1964). Rats with septal lesions demonstrate (under reduced lighting conditions) increased activity in the open-field paradigm (Eichelman, 1971) and in spontaneous crossings within an active avoidance paradigm (Schwartzbaum et al., 1967) comparable to Maudsley Nonreactive strains.

Rats with septal lesions show marked increases in shock-induced aggressive behavior (Eichelman, 1971). Under certain circumstances they will also demonstrate enhanced predatory aggression, attacking mice housed with them (Miczek and Grossman, 1972). Entwined with these observations is the finding that rats with large septal lesions (showing increased shock-induced fighting) show reduced levels of 5-HT within the hippocampus (Kantak et al., 1981a). This increase in aggressive behavior as a consequence of septal lesions can be blocked with high doses of 5-HT's precursor, tryptophan, which will partially raise depleted levels of hippocampal 5-HT (Kantak et al., 1981b).

NEUROCHEMICAL MANIPULATION, IMPULSIVITY, AND AGGRESSIVE BEHAVIOR

Manipulation of central levels evaluated within several laboratory paradigms demonstrates an enhancement of aggressive behaviors. Use of the tryptophan hydroxylase inhibitor *para*-chlorophenylalanine (PCPA) to lower brain 5-HT induces an increase in both affective aggression (shock-induced fighting; Sheard and Davis, 1976) and predatory aggression (mouse-killing; Gibbons et al., 1978). In order to demonstrate the increase in shock-induced fighting, a prolonged intershock interval must be used (15 s). Otherwise, it appears that the rats are so active within the cage following footshock that they do not orient effectively to attack. Rats treated with PCPA have a shortened latency before attacking and killing mice, a model of predatory aggression.

Similar behavioral effects can be achieved through other manipulations of the brain 5-HT system. Lesions of the 5-HT-containing raphe nuclei deplete brain 5-HT and produce increased shock-induced fighting (Jacobs and Cohen, 1976). Treatment of the brain with the serotonergic neurotoxin 5,7-dihydroxytryptamine (5,7-DHT) also produces increases in shock-induced fighting (Kantak et al., 1981a). 5,7-Dihydroxytryptamine injures presynaptic 5-HT neurons, causing a depletion of 5-HT (Bjorkland et al., 1975).

In rats, ablation of the median raphe nucleus which sends projections to the hippocampus has been shown to produce an increase in open-field activity (Jacobs and Cohen, 1976). Interestingly, in the same study, median raphe lesions did not alter pain-induced fighting. Dorsal raphe lesions, which affect serotonergic projections to the striatum and hypothalamus, enhanced pain-induced fighting but did not alter open-field behavior. Thus, 5-HT is involved in both behaviors, but these can be modulated independently through differing anatomical loci.

An inability to inhibit a nonaggressive motor response can also be seen in other studies of 5-HT manipulation. Rats treated with PCPA, lowering brain 5-HT, show a lower jump threshold to an electric footshock than normal controls (Tenen, 1967). This may not be the consequence of an altered pain sensitivity in footshock perception, since the current threshold for a flinch response is not significantly altered. The same reduction in the "jump threshold", but not the "flinch threshold", is seen in rats treated with the neurotoxin 5,7-DHT (Kantak et al., 1981a) and in rats that have sustained septal lesions (Eichelman, 1971).

Manipulation of the central 5-HT system also produces impairment of operant conditioning that relies on delays for successful execution. Treatment of rats with 5-HT$_1$ antagonists impairs DRL operant responding, while treatment with 5-HT$_1$ agonists enhances DRL responding (Marek et al., 1990b). Conversely, blockade of 5-HT$_2$ receptors enhances DRL responding (Marek et al., 1990a).

An inability to inhibit responses when a central 5-HT system is injured seems to go beyond simple or complex motor responses. It appears to affect the organism's ability to process external stimuli (see Davis, 1980, for a review). Conner et al. (1970) have demonstrated that rats with impairment in the central 5-HT system, through the depletion of brain 5-HT with PCPA, have a marked deficit in their ability to habituate to auditory stimuli. These animals are impaired in their ability to disregard insignificant external stimuli. They manifest an exaggerated and prolonged startle response to auditory stimuli compared to control rats. A similar observation using *para*-chloroamphetamine (PCA) was observed by Davis and Sheard (1976). The exaggerated startle response appears to be an inability to dampen a sensory input or its significance, rather than simply the inhibition of a simple or complex motor response.

SELECTIVE BREEDING STUDIES

Genetic studies have been less supportive of a definitive association among impulsivity, aggression, and reduced serotonergic activity. Supportive of an association are the observations found with the Maudsley rat strain. The Maudsley Reactive (MR) and Maudsley Nonreactive (MNR) strains were selectively bred by Broadhurst (1975) for performance in open-field behavior. While these strains have typically been discussed in terms of differing levels of "fear" (Gray, 1987), their behavior also fits a differing ability to inhibit behavior. Those rats which froze and had decreased activity in the open field (i.e. rats that were high in inhibition and low in impulsivity) were bred as the MR variant strain. Rats active (which could be viewed as more impulsive or less inhibited) within the open field were bred as the MNR strain.

Rat strains which were more active (more impulsive) demonstrated increased aggressive behavior within the shock-induced fighting paradigm (Eichelman, 1980). The MNR strain was much more aggressive than the MR strain. There was no overlap for the two groups despite the fact that these two strains were selectively bred for locomotor behavior and not evaluated with respect to aggressive behavior until many generations later. Neurochemically, the MNR strain showed lower limbic brain 5-HT levels than the MR strain (Sudak and Maas, 1964).

In contrast, there are discrepant studies utilizing the Roman Low Avoidance (RLA) and Roman High Avoidance (RHA) rat strains developed by Bignami (1965). The RHA rats are more proficient in active avoidance and one could presume more "impulsive" than the RLA rats. They are also more aggressive in the shock-induced paradigm (Eichelman, 1980). Paradoxically, however, they appear to have higher regional levels of brain 5-HT. They also—with monoamine oxidase inhibitor (MAOI) pretreatment—are reported to show a more rapid disappearance of 5-hydroxyindoleacetic acid (5-HIAA) in the midbrain/medulla region. Nevertheless, using MAOI methodology, the RLA strain has been shown to have greater synthesis of 5-HT than the RHA in the midbrain/medulla and subcortical regions (Driscoll et al., 1980).

The RHA/RLA findings may be entirely consistent with the impulsivity–aggression–low 5-HT thesis of this chapter within certain, critical, brain regions. Alternatively, they might better fit another theoretical construct such as "decreased fear" associated with high serotonergic activity. This, too, could be argued to facilitate active avoidance learning and increase attack behavior. The observations even could be accounted for by another neurotransmitter system unassayed for in these studies.

In summary, these reviewed, selected, laboratory studies generally illustrate a close linkage among enhanced fight, flight and lowered central 5-HT activity; or between reduced ability to inhibit, enhanced aggressive behavior, and reduced sertonergic activity.

A GENETIC PERSPECTIVE ON IMPULSIVITY AND AGGRESSION

The genetic breeding of rodent strains of high and low ability in active avoidance (Bignami, 1965) and of active and inactive performance in the open field (Broadhurst, 1975) demonstrate the genetic basis of these behaviors. Such studies implicate an enhanced aggressive behavior and impulsivity or activity (Eichelman, 1980) that may be linked to differences in regional 5-HT function (Sudak and Maas, 1964; Driscoll et al., 1980). While studies of the RHA and RLA or Maudsley strains have not been of central interest to behavioral geneticists, no evidence exists to suggest a single gene responsible for impulsivity. The most likely interpretation of the genetic and behavioral data is that there is a multigenic contribution that produces a graded differential in impulsivity.

Genetic breeding for aggressive behavior can be accomplished with similar success. Domesticated foxes (Popova et al., 1991), domesticated wild Norwegian rats (Naumenko et al., 1989), and laboratory strains of rats can be selectively bred for reduced aggressive behavior. As with those strains separated on the basis of impulsivity parameters, there is a difference in central serotonergic neurochemistry with the less aggressive animals showing higher regional levels of 5-HT.

TOWARDS AN EVOLUTIONARY HYPOTHESIS

The ability to genetically select for "impulsive" or aggressive animals from within a given population reflects the genetic encoding of these factors within given mammalian populations. There undoubtedly will be behavioral "outliers". Whether these outliers become labelled as having a "disorder" may be more a social issue than a biological issue. Certainly, animal studies suggest that impulsivity and enhanced aggressive behavior can be genetically bred by a shift in the behavioral distribution. It can also be induced with central neuronal (serotonergic) injury. Is one a "natural variation" and the other a "disorder", even though the resultant behavior may be identical? From an evolutionary perspective, however, maintaining both deliberate and impulsive populations within a species would provide greater versatility for that species in the event of a changing environment.

In an environment that is exceedingly dangerous but with a low incidence of dangerous events, quick reactions and high levels of arousal or diminished habituation coupled to a high degree of aggressive behavior might be of a selective advantage. In a safer, more constructive environment, such behaviors would become disruptive and offer an increased risk of injury through precipitous response or unnecessary attack. In an environment that is saturated with stimuli of an aversive nature, the inability to habituate would exaggerate stress and inappropriate responses.

While some anthropologists might disagree, human evolution has appeared to move to more deliberate, methodical, and ritualized behaviors (albeit, every bit as dangerous as earlier behaviors). This would produce a selective disadvantage for the more impulsive members of society. It may well also make them more visible. Industrialized society has also become more sensorially stimulating. Such a change might also carry with it a consequence of enhanced stress and maladaptive responses for those on the impulsive side of the response–inhibition continuum.

How would genetic variability interact with social behaviors? Clues to this interaction may be suggested within the clinical and experimental literature. For example, there is an increase in aggressive behavior in certain individuals developing senile or presenile dementias. Upwards of 35% of this population manifest physically aggressive behavior (Hamel et al., 1990). One of the neurochemical consequences of senile dementia is a reduction in the levels of brain 5-HT (Rosser and Iverson, 1986; Palmer et al., 1987).

We do not know the effects of fetal toxin exposure or of various drugs given to the fetus on adult central neurotransmitter systems. We do not know the effects of stressors early in development on brain neurotransmitter systems in adulthood. Reduction in central 5-HT function under these conditions could interact with a genetic diathesis of impulsivity to further increase impulsive aggressive behavior.

In addition, we know that for impulsive animals in the laboratory, external cues are important. Earlier it was noted that rats with septal lesions performed "impulsively" and poorly on a delayed reinforcement schedule of reinforcement (Ellen et al., 1964). This deficit can be "corrected" in the laboratory if the animals are given external cues to assist in determining the length of the required interval (e.g. a light cue; Ellen and Butter, 1969). This concept of "external cueing" might well have relevance for the human condition. For example, if through the modelling of impulsive behavior (by television or neighborhood behavior) the external cues for signalling "appropriate inhibition" are removed, then those individuals so exposed may become more vulnerable to their internal genetic diathesis of impulsivity. Stated another way, as social controls diminish and as greater impulsivity emerges in the organism's environment, the greater the effect of the biochemical–genetic diathesis for impulsive behavior. A subset of this behavior is impulsive aggression.

IMPLICATIONS FOR SOCIAL INTERVENTION AND CLINICAL TREATMENT

Examination of the animal model literature suggests that impulsive behaviors are part of a normally occurring distribution and may have long-term selective advantages for a species, such as species preservation in times of physical danger, or by providing for the dispersal of males as a consequence of aggressive interactions. In this respect, impulsive behaviors are variants of behavior, not a disorder. However, substantially deviant outliers in a given environment may be at a selective disadvantage.

Laboratory studies suggest that both environmental manipulation (sensory cueing) and neurochemical manipulation (enhancement of serotonergic function) produce modifications in impulsivity, and that attenuation of aggressive behavior can occur. Such findings suggest that through social cueing subsets of the population could attenuate their impulsive and aggressive behavior. On an individual level, some subjects with brain injury could receive biological treatment that would enhance serotonergic functioning and also reduce impulsivity and aggressive behavior as illustrated by the impulsivity of patients with frontotemporal injury. Such patients with frontotemporal brain injury have been shown to have reduced cerebrospinal levels of 5-HIAA, the metabolite of 5-HT, suggestive of reduced serotonergic functioning (van Woerkom et al., 1977).

FUTURE RESEARCH

Lacking in the animal laboratory research is a series of combined experiments linking neurochemical function, impulsive behavior, and aggressive behavior within the same experimental subjects. Studies have examined avoidance behavior, but not neurotransmitters; aggressive behavior, but not habituation or avoidance behavior; genetic variability, but not covariance of neurotransmitter function. Only through such multivariate studies will these relationships be defined and the genetic and neural associations of aggression and impulsivity delineated within laboratory models.

Relevant to the human condition is the need for a greater in-depth study of the developmental modifiers of impulsivity. Do intrauterine drug exposures enhance impulsivity? Does significant stress during gestational development alter neuronal systems to enhance impulsivity? Once induced, what behavioral interventions can reduce impulsive behavior? Do reductions in such behavior occur with a concomitant alteration in 5-HT metabolism or despite such changes?

ACKNOWLEDGMENTS

I thank T. Callaghan and P. Kothapa for assistance in the preparation of this chapter.

REFERENCES

Bignami, G. (1965). Selection for high rates and low rates of avoidance conditioning in the rat. *Anim. Behav.,* 13, 221–227.
Bjorkland, A., Baumgarten, H.G., and Rench, A. (1975). 5,7-Dihydroxytryptamine: Improvement of its selectivity for serotonin neurones in the CNS by pretreatment with desipramine. *J. Neurochem.,* 24, 833–835.

Broadhurst, P.L. (1975). The Maudsley Reactive and Nonreactive strains of rats: a survey. *Behav. Genetics*, 5, 299–319.

Cannon, W.B. (1939). *The Wisdom of the Body*. Norton, New York.

Conner, R.L., Stolk, J.M., Barchas, J.D., and Levine, S. (1970). Parachlorophenyla-lanine and habituation to repetitive auditory startle stimuli. *Physiol. Behav.*, 5, 1215–1219.

Davis, M. (1980). Neurochemical modulation of sensory–motor reactivity: Acoustic and tactile startle reflexes. *Neurosci. Biobehav. Rev.*, 4, 241–263.

Davis, M., and Sheard, M.H. (1976). *p*-Chloroamphetamine: Acute and chronic effects on habituation and sensitization of the acoustic startle response in rats. *Eur. J. Pharmacol.*, 35, 261–273.

Driscoll, P., Dedek, J., Martin, J.R., and Baettig, L. (1980). Regional 5-HT analysis in Roman high- and low-avoidance rats following MAO inhibition. *Eur. J. Pharmacol.*, 68, 373–376.

Eichelman, B. (1971). Effects of subcortical lesions on shock-induced aggression in the rat. *J. Comp. Physiol. Psychol.*, 74, 331–339.

Eichelman, B. (1980). Variability in rat irritable and predatory aggression. *Behav. Neural Biol.*, 29, 498–505.

Ellen, P., and Butter, J. (1969). External cue control of DRL performance in rats with septal lesions. *Physiol. Behav.*, 4, 1–6.

Ellen, P., Wilson, A.S., and Powell, E.W. (1964). Septal inhibition and timing behavior in the rat. *Exp. Neurol.*, 10, 120–132.

Freud, S. (1958, original published in 1930). Civilization and its discontents. In: *The Standard Edition of the Complete Works of Sigmund Freud*, vol. 21 (ed. J. Strachey) pp. 64–145. Hogarth Press, London.

Gibbons, J.L., Barr, G.A., and Bridger, W.H. (1978). Effects of *para*-chlorophenyl-lalanine and 5-hydroxytryptophan on mouse killing behavior in killer rats. *Pharmac. Biochem. Behav.*, 9, 91–98.

Gray, J.A. (1987). *The Psychology of Fear and Stress*, 2nd edn. Cambridge University Press, Cambridge.

Hamel, M., Gold, D.P., Andres, D., et al. (1990). Predictors and consequences of aggressive behavior by community-based dementia patients. *Gerontologist*, 30, 206–211.

Jacobs, B.L., and Cohen, A. (1976). Differential health effects of lesions of the median or dorsal raphe nuclei in rats: open field and pain-elicited aggression. *J. Comp. Physiol. Psychol.*, 90, 102–108.

Kantak, K.M., Hegstrand, L.R., and Eichelman, B. (1981a). Facilitation of shock-induced fighting following intraventricular 5,7-dihydroxytryptamine and 6-hydroxy-dopa. *Psychopharmacology*, 74, 157–160.

Kantak, K.M., Hegstrand, L.R., and Eichelman, B. (1981b). Dietary tryptophan reversal of septal lesions and 5,7-DHT lesion elicited shock-induced fighting. *Pharmac. Biochem. Behav.*, 15, 343–350.

King, F.A. (1958). Effects of septal and amygdaloid lesions on emotional behavior and conditioned avoidance responses in the rat. *J. Nerv. Ment. Dis.*, 126, 57–63.

Lorenz, K. (1966). *On Aggression*. Harcourt, Brace and World, New York.

MacLean, P.D. (1958). Limbic system with respect to self preservation and the preservation of the species. *J. Nerv. Ment. Dis.*, 127, 1–11.

McCleary, R.A. (1961). Response specificity in the behavioral effects of limbic system lesions in the cat. *J. Comp. Physiol. Psychol.*, 54, 605–613.

Marek, G.J., Li, A.A., and Seiden, L.A. (1990a). Selective 5-hydroxytryptamine$_2$ antagonists have antidepressant-like effects on differential reinforcement of low-rate 72-second schedule. *J. Pharm. Exp. Ther.*, 250, 52–59.

Marek, G.J., Li, A.A., and Seiden, L.S. (1990b). Evidence for involvement of

5-hydroxytryptamine$_1$ receptors in antidepressant-like drug effects on differential reinforcement of low-rate 72-second schedule. *J. Pharm. Exp. Ther.*, 250, 60–71.

Miczek, K., and Grossman, S.P. (1972). Effects of septal lesions on inter- and intraspecific aggression in rat. *J. Comp. Physiol. Psychol.*, 79, 37–45.

Miczek, K.A., Kelsey, J.E., and Grossman, S.P. (1972). Time course of effects of septal lesions on avoidance response suppression and reactivity to shock. *J. Comp. Physiol. Psychol.*, 79, 318–327.

Naumenko, E.V., Popova, N.K., Nikulina, E.M., et al. (1989). Behavior, adreno-cortical activity, and brain monoamines in Norway rats selected for reduced aggressiveness towards man. *Pharmacol. Biochem. Behav.*, 33, 85–91.

Palmer, A.m., Wilcock, G.K., Esiri, M.M., Francis, P.T., and Bowen, D.M. (1987). Monoaminergic innervation of the frontal and temporal lobes in Alzheimer's disease. *Brain Res.*, 401, 231–238.

Popova, N.K., Voitenkio, N.N., Kulikov, A.V., and Avgustinovich, D.F. (1991). Evidence for the involvement of central serotonin in mechanisms of domestication of silver foxes. *Pharmacol. Biochem. Behav.*, 40, 751–756.

Rosser, M.N., and Iversen, L.L. (1986). Non-cholinergic neurotransmitter abnormalities in Alzheimer's Disease. *Br. Med. Bull.*, 42, 70–74.

Schwartzbaum, J.S., Green, R.H., Beatty, W.W., and Thompson, J.B. (1967). Acquisition of avoidance behavior following septal lesions in the rat. *J. Comp. Physiol. Psychol.*, 63, 95–104.

Sheard, M.H., and Davis, M. (1976). Shock-elicited fighting in rats; importance of intershock interval upon the effect of *p*-chlorophenylalanine (PCPA). *Brain Res.*, 111, 433–437.

Smith, R.F. (1979). Attenuation of septal lesion-induced shuttlebox facilitation by 5-hydroxytryptophan. *Physiol. Psychol.*, 7, 419–421.

Soubrie, P. (1986). Reconciling the role of central serotonin neurons in human and animal behavior. *Behav. Brain Sci.*, 9, 319–364.

Sudak, H.W., and Maas, J.W. (1964). Behavioral–neurochemical correlation in reactive and nonreactive strains of rats. *Science*, 146, 418–420.

Tedeschi, R.E., Tedeschi, D.H., Mucha, A., Cook, L., Mattis, P.A., and Fellows, E.J. (1959). Effects of various centrally acting drugs on fighting behavior of mice. *J. Pharm. Exp. Ther.*, 125, 28–34.

Tenen, S.S. (1967). The effects of *p*-chlorophenylalanine, a serotonin depletor, on avoidance acquisition, pain sensitivity and related behavior in the rat. *Psychopharmacologia*, 10, 204–219.

Ulrich, R., and Azrin, N.H. (1962). Reflexive fighting in response to aversive stimulation. *J. Exp. Anal. Behav.*, 5, 511–520.

van Woerkom, T.C.A.M., Teelken, A.W., and Minderhoud, J.M. (1977). Difference in neurotransmitter metabolism in fronto-temporal-lobe contusion and diffuse cerebral contusion. *Lancet*, i, 812–813.

6 Biological Studies of Impulsivity, Aggression, and Suicidal Behavior

PHILIP I MARKOWITZ AND EMIL F COCCARO

Clinical Neuroscience Research Unit, Department of Psychiatry, Medical College of Pennsylvania at Eastern Pennsylvania Psychiatric Institute, Philadelphia, PA, USA

INTRODUCTION

A longstanding dilemma facing biological psychiatrists is the need to develop valid and reliable biological markers and probes of neuropsychiatric dysfunction. Unlike other body organs, the human brain is not available to direct biological scrutiny on an antemortem basis. Thus, biological psychiatrists are forced to rely on indirect views of brain function through neuroimaging procedures, electrophysiological studies, and peripheral indices of neurochemical and receptor function. For this reason, biological study of brain-behavior relationships is at best an inferential process. The purpose of this chapter is to review the current status of a promising window on central nervous system (CNS) function, neuroendocrine challenge studies, with particular reference to disorders involving impulsive aggression.

As reviewed in other chapters, a large body of evidence is accumulating linking serotonergic dysfunction with aggressive behavior and, specifically, impulsive aggression. Most robust is the finding of decreased cerebrospinal fluid (CSF) 5-hydroxyindoleacetic acid (5-HIAA) concentration in individuals with a history of a past suicide attempt, and perhaps violent suicidal behavior in particular (Coccaro, 1989). Evidence of decreased serotonin (5-hydroxytryptamine, 5-HT) activity has also been demonstrated in violent offenders (Linnoila et al., 1983) and conduct disordered children (Stoff et al., 1987). Measures suggestive of abnormal platelet 5-HT receptor function in depression, suicide, and autism, conditions in which irritability and behavioral dyscontrol may be present, also support a role for the serotonergic system in modulating this aspect of behavior (Coccaro and Murphy, 1990). While potentially informative, these indices are problematic for at least two reasons: (1) because they represent a static measure of function (CSF 5-HIAA), and (2) because they are peripheral to the CNS and may not truly reflect events in the brain. Neuroendocrine challenges, on the other hand, offer a potentially more direct assessment of CNS events

Impulsivity and Aggression. Edited by E. Hollander and D.J. Stein
© 1995 John Wiley & Sons Ltd

of interest because the outcome measures used are mediated by limbic–hypothalamic–pituitary neurotransmitter systems (Coccaro and Kavoussi, 1994).

Neurohypophyseal function is under the control of a complex interaction between different monoamine neurotransmitters. Precise mechanistic factors remain to be elucidated, but an elementary understanding has emerged, suggesting an important role for the serotonergic system. Hormonal synthesis and release is under the control of a complex feedback loop involving the target hormone itself, a stimulatory pituitary hormone, and stimulatory or inhibitory hypothalamic neuropeptides that function as pituitary releasing factors. Control at the level of the hypothalamus involves an exquisitely delicate and sensitive balance of neurotransmitter activity acting in a reciprocal fashion to modulate hypothalamic–pituitary activity. The hypothalamic–pituitary–adrenal axis, for example, appears to be under the control of serotonergic stimulation and noradrenergic inhibition of corticotropin releasing factor, which in turn enhances adrenal release of corticosteroids via pituitary release of adrenocorticotropic hormone (ACTH). Prolactin release, as another important example, is tonically inhibited by dopamine and stimulated by 5-HT via the hypothalamic release of an unidentified prolactin releasing factor (Ben-Jonathan et al., 1989).

Based on the premise of a major stimulatory influence of 5-HT on prolactin and ACTH/cortisol secretion, investigators have attempted to delineate the functional status of the serotonergic system in various psychiatric disorders. Methodologically, this has involved increasing serotonergic activity through the administration of either 5-HT precursors (i.e. tryptophan and 5-hydroxytryptophan) or drugs that enhance serotonergic activity via the release of 5-HT, blockade of its reuptake, or direct stimulation of postsynaptic receptors. In the latter case, the agents most often employed have been fenfluramine, *meta*-chlorophenylpiperazine (mCPP) and relatively selective 5-HT postsynaptic receptor agonists such a buspirone. The magnitude of the end organ response can be interpreted as reflecting the integrity of serotonergic pathways from the midbrain raphe nuclei to the pituitary via the hypothalamus, and, by implication, the status of pathways elsewhere in the brain. This is the case if these disparate pathways are identical anatomically and physiologically, which at this time is unknown. An additional caveat involves the level of inference involved in interpreting the neurophysiological meaning of the change in hormone levels observed. Since fenfluramine stimulation produces an integrated or "net" observation of 5-HT activity including pre- and postsynaptic mechanisms, one cannot localize the point of hypothetically aberrant function unless comparisons with multiple receptor selective agents are available. As will become apparent in this chapter, theoretically contrary results may be reconciled by invoking alternative physiological explanations. An additional cautionary note is that neuroendocrine probes are subject to a variety of extraneous influences, such as age, sex, body habitus, menstrual status, and activity level, that if not controlled for will obfuscate the picture (Coccaro and Kavoussi, 1994).

REVIEW OF THE LITERATURE

While this chapter will focus on data obtained from psychopharmacologic challenge of the central 5-HT system, we will begin with a brief review of relevant studies concerning data from brain and/or cerebrospinal fluid (CSF) levels of 5-HT and its metabolites (5-hydroxyindoleacetic acid: 5-HIAA).

5-HT NEUROCHEMICAL STUDIES

Inverse relationships between assessments of "aggression" (and/or suicidal behavior) and neurochemical indices of 5-HT system function (CSF 5-HIAA) have been reported in human and nonhuman primate subjects. In general, these findings are consistent with those of more invasive studies involving brain tissue itself in victims of violent suicide which found reduced levels of brain 5-HT in suicide, compared with accident, victims (Coccaro and Astill 1990). The first clinical neurochemistry study published in this area was authored by Asberg and collegues (1976). These authors reported a significantly higher proportion of suicide attempters among depressed patients with low (versus high) basal CSF 5-HIAA concentration. This finding has been replicated many times in many patient groups; the only exception being individuals with bipolar affective disorder (Asberg et al., 1987). Given the inverse relationship between 5-HT and inwardly-directed aggressive (i.e. suicidal) behavior, inverse correlations between outwardly-directed aggressive behavior and basal CSF 5-HIAA concentrations constitutes a logical extension from this finding. Within three years of the Asberg et al. publication, Brown et al. (1979) reported an inverse relationship between a life history of aggressive behavior and basal CSF 5-HIAA ($r = -0.78$) in male individuals with DSM-II personality disorder ($r = -0.78$). The same group replicated this finding in a smaller sample of males with DSM-III borderline personality disorder three years later (Brown et al., 1982). In this second study there was a strong inverse correlation with the Psychopathic Deviance subscale of the MMPI ($r = -0.77$); the correlation with history of aggressive events was smaller in magnitude, falling short of statistical significance. The second major finding in this area was reported by Linnoila et al. (1983) who demonstrated that CSF 5-HIAA was reduced in aggressive individuals only if the aggression was impulsive, rather than premeditated, in nature. Both findings of Brown et al. (1979, 1982) and Linnoila et al. (1983) have been replicated in most, though not all, studies. Where these findings have been replicated the correlation coefficients for the aggression/CSF 5-HIAA have been smaller in magnitude. For example, Limson et al. (1991) recently reported a significant, but much smaller, correlation between CSF 5-HIAA and life history of aggressive events in abstinent alcoholics and healthy volunteers ($r = -0.31$, $p < 0.05$). In addition, Kruesi et al. (1990) reported smaller inverse correlation coefficients between various assessments of aggression and CSF 5-HIAA concentration in children and adolescents with either DSM-III behavioral disruptive disorder or obsessive compulsive disorder. Several of these correlations were statistically significant in the raw data set. However, only two remained significant after correcting for the effect of age on CSF 5-HIAA concentration ("aggression against people": $r = 0.40$, $p < 0.05$; "negative expressed emotion about the mother": $r = -0.39$, $p < 0.05$). Notably, at least one nonhuman primate study reports a moderate sized inverse correlation between CSF 5-HIAA and observed overt aggressive behavior in rhesus monkeys ($r = -0.58$, $p < 0.002$; Higgley et al., 1992). Among the nonreplicating studies are those of Coccaro (1992) and Stanley et al. (personal communication, 1993). Previous and ongoing studies in our laboratory (Coccaro 1992; Coccaro and Kavoussi, in press) have not found a significant inverse correlation between assessments of aggression and CSF 5-HIAA in patients with DSM-III-R personality disorder. In addition, a large ongoing study of recent suicide attempters, by Stanley's laboratory, has also been negative in this regard. However, while these two studies have not found inverse correlations between aggression and CSF 5-HIAA, inverse correlations were found with other variables. In the one study (Coccaro 1992) inverse correlations with aggression and history of suicidal behavior were found with the prolactin (PRL) response to 5-HT stimulation with d,l-fenfluramine in the same subjects. In the other study (Stanley et al.), the CSF 5-HIAA concentrations were reduced in suicide attempters compared with nonattempters. Accordingly, while the hypothesized inverse aggression/CSF 5-HIAA correlation was not found in these samples, a significant correlation between aggressive behavior was found with another index of 5-HT function (Coccaro 1992) or was found with a behavior related to aggression (i.e. suicidal behavior).

5-HT CHALLENGE STUDIES

This section will review the current status of studies examining neuroendocrine responses to pharmacological challenge in depression, suicidal behavior, and aggression (see Table 1). The studies are few in number, disparate in the nature of the challenging agent, and somewhat contradictory in their findings. In spite of this, the data suggest an important role for the serotonergic modulation of these particular behaviors, consistent with studies utilizing CSF and peripheral blood indices of 5-HT function. Depression has been included because of the frequent coexistence of a type of aggressive behavior directed toward the self (i.e. suicidal behavior).

Table 1 Summary of all published human and nonhuman primate studies using pharmacochallenge to study biology of suicidal and/or impulsive aggressive behavior*

Probe	Reference	Sample	Outcome variables		Result
			Biological	Behavioral	
5-HTP (p.o.)	Meltzer et al. (1984)	Patients: depressed and manic Controls: healthy volunteers	CORT (5-HTP)	Suicide attempt	Elevated CORT(5-HTP) in suicide attempters
d,l-Fenfluramine (p.o.)	Fishbein et al. (1989)	Patients: mixed substance abusers Controls: none	PRL(FEN)	BDHI/Barratt rating scales of aggression and impulsivity	Elevated PRL(FEN) responses in "impulsive aggressive" substance abusers; positive correlations with Barratt Impulsivity Scales
d,l-Fenfluramine (p.o.)	Coccaro et al. (1989)	Patients: depressed/ personality disorder Controls: healthy volunteers	PRL(FEN)	Suicide attempt BDHI rating scales	Reduced PRL(FEN) in suicide attempters; strong inverse correlations with BDHI scales of "assault" and "irritability" in personality but not depressive disorder patients
d,l-Fenfluramine (p.o.)	López-Ibor et al. (1990)	Patients: suicidal and nonsuicidal Controls: healthy volunteers	PRL(FEN)	Suicide attempt	Reduced PRL(FEN) in suicide attempters

continued over

Table 1 (continued)

Probe	Reference	Sample	Outcome variables		Result
			Biological	Behavioral	
mCPP (p.o.)	Moss et al. (1990)	Patients: antisocial personality disorder with history of substance abuse Controls: healthy volunteers	PRL(mCPP)	Antisocial personality disorder patients vs healthy volunteers BDHI Scales	PRL(mCPP) responses reduced in antisocial personality disorder patients compared with healthy volunteers; inverse correlation with "assault" in whole sample
d-Fenfluramine (p.o.)	O'Keane and Dinan (1991)	Patients: currently depressed Controls: healthy volunteers	PRL(d-FEN)	Suicide attempt	PRL(d-FEN) was blunted in depressive compared to controls but depressives with history of suicide attempt were not reduced compared to those without suicide attempt
Buspirone (p.o.)	Coccaro et al. (1991)	Patients: personality disorder	PRL(BUSP)	BDHI scales	PRL(BUSP) correlated inversely with BDHI ratings in personality disorder patients
Clonidine (i.v.)	Coccaro et al. (1992)	Patients: personality disorder Controls: healthy volunteers	GH(CLON)	BDHI scales	GH(CLON) correlated directly with "irritability", but not "assault", in whole sample
d-Fenfluramine (p.o.)	O'Keane et al. (1992)	Patients: violent offenders with antisocial personality Controls: healthy volunteers	PRL(d-FEN)	AsPd vs healthy volunteers	PRL(d-FEN) responses of antisocial personality disorder subjects were significantly blunted compared with healthy volunteers

Challenge	Reference	Subjects	Hormone	Behavioral measure	Findings
Apomorphine (i.m.)	Pitchot et al. (1992)	Patients: depressed with suicide attempt Controls: depressed without suicide attempt	GH(APO)	Suicide attempt	GH(APO) of major depression with history of suicide attempt blunted compared with major depression without history of suicide attempt
d,l-Fenfluramine (p.o.)	Stoff et al. (1992)	Patients: disruptive behavior disorder Controls: healthy volunteers	PRL(FEN) CORT(FEN)	Disruptive behavior disorder vs healthy volunteers Child/parent rating scales of aggression/hostility	No differences between disruptive behavior disorder and healthy volunteers (either prepubertal or adolescent); no correlation with any of the rating scales
d,l-Fenfluramine mCPP	Handelsman et al. (1993)	Patients: alcohol abusers cocaine abusers	PRL(FEN) PRL(mCPP)	BDHI scales	Inverse correlations with BDHI scales in alcohol abusers; direct correlations with same scales in cocaine abusers
d,l-Fenfluramine	Botchin et al. (1993)	Subjects: macaques	PRL(FEN)	Ratings of overt aggression and social affiliation	Monkeys with reduced PRL(FEN) had higher ratings of overt aggression and lower ratings of social affiliation

*Abbreviations: APO, apomorphine; BDHI, Buss–Durkee Hostility Inventory; BUSP, buspirone; CLON, clonidine; CORT, cortisol; FEN, fenfluramine; GH, growth hormone; 5-HTP, 5-hydroxytryptamine precursor; mCPP, *meta*-chlorophenylpiperazine; PRL, prolactin.

Challenge strategies have been developed to evaluate both noradrenergic and serotonergic mechanism in depression. A consistently replicated finding has been a blunted growth hormone response to the selective α_2-agonist clonidine (Siever, 1987), a finding that appears to be trait rather than state dependent. Cortisol responses to adrenergic challenge have been generally but not consistently blunted (Siever, 1987). Serotonergic dysfunction is suggested by the findings of an enhanced cortisol response to 5-hydroxytryptophan in drug-free patients with depression and mania (Meltzer et al., 1984). Unfortunately, interpretation of this finding is hampered by the observations that 5-hydroxytryptophan is unreliable in its ability to stimulate the release of both cortisol and prolactin and by the possibility that it may release catecholamines as well (van Praag et al., 1987). However, the latter possibility appears to be dependent on dose and possibly route of administration. It is difficult to know whether the cortisol response observed is occurring at a central or peripheral level, since 5-hydroxytryptophan acts peripherally as well as centrally and the adrenal gland is hyper-responsive to ACTH in depression (Pryor and Nemeroff, 1991) and perhaps to other stimulus agents as well. In other studies, however, there has been either a reduction (Golden et al., 1990), or no difference (Asnis et al., 1988; Coccaro et al., 1991; O'Keane and Dinan, 1991), noted in the cortisol response to serotonergic challenge with either clomipramine or d,l- or d-fenfluramine, respectively.

Studies examining the prolactin (PRL) response to serotonergic challenge have yielded mixed data as well. Henninger et al. (1984) observed a blunted response to tryptophan in depressed patients compared with controls. This finding has been replicated in many other studies, although some studies have yielded negative findings possibly due to an increase in the peripheral disposition of tryptophan in depressives compared with controls (Koyama and Meltzer, 1986) or because recent weight loss among depressives enhances the PRL response to tryptophan (Goodwin and Cowan, 1988). Reduced PRL responses to serotonergic stimulation have been obtained with studies using clomipramine (Golden et al., 1990) and d,l-fenfluramine (Siever et al., 1984; Coccaro et al., 1989) or d-fenfluramine (O'Keane and Dinan, 1991). Asnis et al. (1988), however, did not replicate these findings in a study with d,l-fenfluramine. This may in part be due to patient heterogeneity regarding inpatient versus outpatient status, since this confounds severity of depression and may not adequately account for differences in endogenous versus nonendogenous depressive state. Both indices of peripheral as well as central monoaminergic function suggest that biological depression is not a discrete and unitary entity. Future studies need to account for this heterogeneity. Moreover, it may be useful to dissect study populations further and in a different way, such that subsyndromal variants differing on the variables are related to the presence or absence of aggression and irritability (Coccaro et al., 1989). Finally, one of the most cogent and heuristic observations cutting across the biological literature of aggression and suicide is the realization that suicide is not unique to depressive illness. For example, suicidal behavior commonly occurs in the context of major psychoses and personality disorders as well. The recognition that suicide is a behavior that stands on its own and can be studied in its own right separate from its categorical context is a major advance in the attempt to understand the biological determinants of aggressive behavior.

Psychopharmacological challenge studies of aggression and impulsivity have matured considerably since the technique was first employed 10 years ago. The level of sophistication has evolved from 5-HT precursor (5-HTP) challenges to stimulation employing global release/reuptake blockade to the use of selective receptor agonists in order to differentiate pre- from postsynaptic influences as well as to localize better the specific receptor subtypes involved. The goal has evolved from a relatively gross and simplistic effort to implicate serotonergic systems to the more subtle goal of attempting to tease out the multiple and intricate receptor interactions occurring at the synaptic level and better understand reciprocal and modulatory effects. This is coincident with the theoretical premise of faulty synaptic regulation/ interaction as the substrate for neuropsychiatric illness in contrast to the attractive, but simplistic, attempt to relate dysfunction to gross over- or underactivity in specific neurotransmitter systems.

The study by Meltzer et al. (1984) was the first pharmacological challenge study to implicate serotonergic dysfunction in impulsive aggression. This study involved 40 patients with affective disorders (12 unipolar and 13 bipolar depressed, six schizoaffective depressed, and 16 bipolar manic), all of whom were symptomatic and unmedicated at the time of study. 5-Hydroxytryptamine precursor was administered orally (200 mg) followed by serum cortisol assays at 30, 60, 90, 120, 150, and 180 min after challenge. Three prechallenge baseline measurements were obtained for comparison, and peak δ-cortisol levels were then computed. Depressed and manic patients evidenced greater peak cortisol responses than normal controls. When patients were categorized into those with a history of a suicidal act, suicidal thoughts, or no suicidal ideation at all, individuals who had attempted suicide had the most robust cortisol responses to challenge. This was evident in a paired comparison of the suicide attempters with the other two groups pooled, but failed to differentiate the latter two groups individually. The suicidal thought group did not differ from the nonsuicidal group, suggesting that the behavioral dimension of significance was not the suicidal state itself but rather the poor impulse control that allows the individual to execute the act. Additionally, significant correlations with peak δ-cortisol were found on the Present State Exam for suicidal acts but not thoughts, as well as for suicidality as measured by the Hamilton Depression Rating Scale and the change version of the Schedule for Affective Disorders and Schizophrenia (SADS-C).

Meltzer and colleagues interpreted their findings as consistent with the presence of a hyposerotonergic state both in the patients with depression and in those with a history of a suicide attempt. They hypothesized that the increased cortisol response might be due to supersensitive 5-HT receptors occurring as an adaptive response to the chronic hyposerotonergic state. At the same time, they readily acknowledged the multiple nonserotonergic factors potentially involved. Unfortunately, plasma ACTH assay was not performed, leaving unanswered the question of whether the pathology is at the level of the hypothalamus—pituitary or the adrenal. Future studies will need to address the array of intervening hormonal variables in order to clarify their potential role. 5-Hydroxytryptamine appears to exert a stimulatory effect on corticotrophin (ACTH) releasing factor (CRF) and would thus be expected to increase corticosteroid levels. Levels of CRF have been shown to be elevated in depression (Pryor and Nemeroff, 1991). This may result in downregulation of pituitary corticotroph CRF receptors. Whether this would produce compensatory up or downregulation of 5-HT receptors is difficult to predict, although the former remains the most plausible hypothesis given these data.

To date, most investigations have used paradigms involving the serotonergic stimulation of PRL as a probe of impulsivity and aggression. One approach is stimulation with fenfluramine, an agent that stimulates release and blocks reuptake of 5-HT. It may also exert a direct postsynaptic stimulatory effect through its metabolite norfenfluramine. The net result is a temporary increase in 5-HT in the synaptic cleft. 5-Hydroxytryptamine is a potent stimulator of PRL through the limbic–hypothalamic–pituitary axis (Ben-Jonathan et al., 1989). Its effect is opposed by 5-HT antagonists and lesions of the dorsal raphe (van der Klar and Bethea, 1982). Fenfluramine increases plasma PRL levels in a dose-dependent fashion, an action that can be blocked by 5-HT antagonists (Lewis and Sherman, 1985) and lesions of the raphe nuclei (Kuhn et al., 1981). Through this fashion, challenge with fenfluramine should enable an assessment of the responsivity of the serotonergic system in the limbic–hypothalamic–pituitary axis.

Coccaro et al. (1989) examined the effect of d,l-fenfluramine challenge on PRL response across both categorical and dimensional domains in a study of 45 individuals with DSM-III and Research Diagnostic Criteria (RDC) defined major affective disorder (MAD; $n = 25$) and personality disorder (PD; $n = 20$). Personality disorder diagnoses included schizotypal and paranoid in nine subjects, borderline and histrionic in eight, compulsive in four, avoidant in three, antisocial in one, and mixed in three. Fifteen subjects had current major depression and 10 were in remission. The PRL(fenfluramine) response was compared by both diagnostic category as well as by the presence or absence of a life history of suicide and impulsive aggression. Despite the heterogeneity of the sample, robust differences emerged. The PRL(fenfluramine) responses were reduced in both the MAD and PD groups as compared with 18 healthy volunteers. The PRL(fenfluramine) responses were also decreased in patients with a history of suicide attempt, irrespective of diagnostic category, compared with patients without a history of suicide attempt and with normal controls. In fact, patients without a life history of a suicide attempt did not have reduced PRL(fenfluramine) responses compared with the healthy volunteers, suggesting that history of suicide was a stronger predictor of reduced PRL(fenfluramine) responses than the diagnosis of depression. Further analysis revealed significant inverse correlations (r ranging from -0.54 to -0.68) on behavioral dimensions related to clinician-rated life history of aggression and self-reported assessments of "assaultiveness", "irritability", and "motor impulsiveness" in the PD sample. As might be expected, PD patients with a history of suicidal behavior had higher scores on these dimensions than did PD patients without suicidal histories. Once statistically corrected for these differences in assaultiveness and irritability, however, PD patients with suicidal histories no longer displayed lower PRL(fenfluramine) responses compared with PD patients without this history. Accordingly, it appeared that in PD patients, at least, impulsive aggressive behavior was inextricably associated with suicidal behavior. In other words, a reduction of central serotonergic system function was associated with an increased risk of impulsive aggression against both self and others, probably depending on the circumstances leading up to the act.

These findings were essentially replicated in a study by López-Ibor et al. (1990) of a group of 17 suicidal patients in whom a diagnosis of past or present major depressive disorder was an exclusion. Even without the presence of depression, suicidal patients demonstrated a markedly decreased PRL and cortisol response to d,l-fenfluramine challenge compared with 17 matched controls. In addition, patients with a history of suicidal behavior scored higher than their counterparts in a self-reported assessment of aggressive behavior (although this sample also included individuals who did not undergo fenfluramine challenge).

Animal studies involving nonhuman primates also suggest the existence of an inverse relationship between PRL(fenfluramine) responses and aggression. Botchin et al. (1993) administered d,l-fenfluramine challenges in 75 macaques. The animals had been housed in five-member social groups and observed over 28 months. At month 24, d,l-fenfluramine challenges were administered (4 mg/kg intramuscularly). Animals were then observed for another 4 months. Animals were then dichotomized into low and high PRL(fenfluramine) responders, and evaluated on measures of both aggressive and socially affiliative behavior. Low PRL(fenfluramine) responders were significantly more aggressive than high PRL(fenfluramine) responders. While this finding did not relate to their dominance status it did predict social responsivity, with low PRL(fenfluramine) responders being more passive and socially withdrawn.

While these findings suggest an inverse relationship between PRL (fenfluramine) responses and suicidality and/or aggression, d,l-fenfluramine is a racemic mixture and may not be as specific a stimulant of the 5-HT system as previously thought. This is because d,l-fenfluramine can cause the release of dopamine and norepinephrine (noradrenaline) and the l-isomer may have dopaminergic receptor antagonistic activity as well (Invernizzi et al., 1986). Curiously, a recent study (O'Keane and Dinan, 1991) using the d-fenfluramine isomer (specific for the 5-HT release and uptake inhibition) has replicated the finding that depressed patients demonstrate a blunted PRL(fenfluramine) response compared with healthy volunteers, while not replicating the findings of Coccaro et al. (1989) and of López-Ibor et al. (1990) that suicidal behavior is more specifically associated with reduced PRL(fenfluramine) responses. This lack of replication may be due to differences in patient characteristics. However, given that the report by O'Keane and Dinan gives no data on the breakdown of depressed patients as a function of history of suicidal behavior, it is difficult to speculate further regarding this possibility. On the other hand, another study by the same group demonstrates that violent offenders with antisocial PD have a marked blunting of PRL(fenfluramine) responses in comparison with healthy volunteers (O'Keane et al., 1992). Accordingly, there is evidence that PRL responses to challenge with fenfluramine, regardless of its isomeric formulation, correlate in an inverse manner with behavioral parameters reflecting suicidal behavior and/or aggression in patients with depression and/or PD.

Despite these findings with fenfluramine challenge, a contradictory report has been published using the postsynaptic 5-HT agonist mCPP. Wetzler et al. (1991) reported that mCPP induced changes in PRL (and cortisol) release did not differ as a function of history of aggression or of suicidal behavior in two groups of patients with depression and panic disorder, respectively. Methodological differences may partially explain their failure to replicate the findings of those studies utilizing fenfluramine. For one, mCPP is quite a different 5-HT probe from fenfluramine, the former being a direct agonist while the latter is an indirect agonist. It is possible that PRL responses to fenfluramine may be blunted while PRL responses to mCPP could be normal or enhanced. This would be the case if PRL(fenfluramine) responses reflect primarily presynaptic influences. In this case, decreased 5-HT output [i.e. reflected by a reduced PRL(fenfluramine) response] could be associated with either "normal" (an uncompensated state) or "heightened" (a partially compensated state) postsynaptic receptor function. Empirical data suggest, however, the PRL responses to fenfluramine and mCPP may not be that different. Preliminary data from studies in which both challenges were performed on the same individuals suggest that there is a strong and direct relationship between PRL response to fenfluramine and mCPP (Coccaro et al., 1991). Another possible reason for the lack of replication in the study by Wetzler et al. may lie in important differences in the measures used to assess aggression in the patient samples studied. For example, patients were categorized as being aggressive as a function of a dichotomous split on two SADS items reflecting state (i.e. rather than trait) irritability, anger, or annoyance. On the other hand, there was similarly no inverse relationship found with trait aggression scales from the Buss–

Durkee Hostility Inventory. Moreover, there was also no correlation reported with these scales in the depressed patient sample in the study by Coccaro et al. (1989). Accordingly, it is possible, considering potential differences in the noradrenergic system between depressed (and probably panic disorder patients as well) and PD patients, that a fundamental difference in brain physiology between the groups will obscure the hypothesized relationship between 5-HT and aggression (Coccaro et al., 1991). This point is underscored by the fact that Moss et al. (1990) reported significant blunting of PRL(mCPP) responses in patients with antisocial PD (with a history of substance abuse) compared with healthy volunteers. In addition, there was a significant inverse correlation among all subjects between PRL(mCPP) responses and a self-report measure of assaultiveness [one of the same scales used in the investigation by Coccaro et al. (1989)].

COMORBIDITY WITH SUBSTANCE ABUSE

The presence of substance-abusing PD patients in the study by Moss et al., for example, raises the issue to which comorbidity of aggression, suicide, and PD with substance abuse confounds biological findings. Alcoholism may represent a hyposerotonergic state (Coccaro et al., 1993). Alcohol is a potent releaser of 5-HT, suggesting than some alcoholics may be self-medicating. 5-Hydroxytryptamine uptake inhibitors may be useful in the treatment of binge alcohol intake. In all pharmacological challenge studies to date directly addressing aggressive patient populations, substance abuse has been present as well. Interestingly, O'Keane's and Dinan's study of depression specifically excluded substance abusers and failed to find an association between hormonal response and suicidality. Coccaro et al. (1989) statistically controlled for the effects of alcohol use in their study and found a strong main effect for alcohol although not for abuse of other drugs. In spite of this, polysubstance abuse may still be a confounding factor, since chronic cocaine abuse has been found to decrease plasma PRL and increase plasma growth hormone levels (Gawin and Kleber, 1985). That this must be taken into account is suggested by a recent study comparing PRL and cortisol responses to a 0.35 mg/kg challenge of mCPP and 60 mg challenge of fenfluramine in 13 alcoholics and nine cocaine addicts (Handelsman et al., 1993). Both groups of patients were studied 2–4 weeks following detoxification. The PRL responses to the two challenge agents were correlated in both groups, although to a greater extent in the cocaine abusers (alcohol, $r = 0.64$; cocaine, $r = 0.91$). Alcoholics demonstrated the expected inverse relationship between PRL response and selected scales on the Buss–Durkee Hostility Inventory. Cocaine addicts, on the other hand, demonstrated a direct and positive relationship between the two parameters. Thus, chronic substance abuse may induce changes in neuroendocrine responsivity that are diverse and substance specific (see later discussion of

Fishbein et al., 1989). This has implications for the evaluation of studies involving heterogeneous populations of substance abusers, as well as raising questions about the interactive effect of polysubstance use on the neuro-endocrine responsivity of any particular individual.

O'Keane et al. (1992) partially controlled for this potentially confounding factor by studying nine individuals with antisocial PD, six of whom had a history of alcohol abuse but had been abstinent for a mean of 4.2 years. A blunted PRL response to d-fenfluramine was still obtained, suggesting that although substance abuse and aggressive personality characteristics may biologically covary, an independent role for aggressive behavior may still exist. Unfortunately, the question of persistent trait-dependent biological characteristics pertaining to alcohol abuse remains unanswered.

Two studies have specifically addressed comorbid aggression and sub-stance abuse, with contradictory findings. Fishbein et al. (1989) examined neuroendocrine responses in polysubstance abusers stratified as having high or low levels of aggressiveness. This was operationalized as scoring in the upper or lower quartile on a composite measure of aggression derived from the Early Experience Questionnaire, the Antisocial Hostility Scale, com-posed from items from the Buss–Durkee Hostility Inventory, and the Jenkins Composite Hostility Scale, based on items from the Minnesota Multiphasic Personality Inventory (MMPI). Subjects with both high levels of aggressiveness and impulsivity demonstrated elevated PRL and cortisol responses to fenfluramine challenge. Hormonal response correlated with and was a strong predictor of impulsivity, contributing 47% of the variance. Cognizant of the fact that chronic cocaine use can alter hypothalamic–pituit-ary responsivity and baseline levels of PRL (although findings are contradic-tory as to whether baseline PRL levels are elevated or reduced), various statistical techniques were used to control for the magnitude of cocaine use. When this was done, group differences remained robust and significant. In contrast, Moss et al. (1990) found a blunted PRL response to mCPP in a group of 15 substance-abusing patients with antisocial PD. The discrepancy could be explained by differences in subject sample characteristics as the latter study employed a patient group with diagnosed PD, while the former examined volunteers admitted to a specialized addiction research center and screened for high levels of psychopathology other than hostility. Interest-ingly, in the study by Moss et al., cortisol responses in the antisocial group were significantly elevated, suggesting a differential effect of substance abuse on serotonergic function, as well as the possibility, as previously articulated by Coccaro et al. (1992), that PRL and cortisol responses may be mediated by different serotonergic receptors. Finally, in the study by Fishbein et al., baseline plasma PRL levels were significantly elevated in the high aggressiveness group compared with the low aggressiveness group, suggesting the possibility that the former might be in a state of hypothala-mic–pituitary hyperactivity and be hyper-responsive to any provocative challenge.

CHILDREN AND ADOLESCENTS

Research in the biology of aggression, as in other behavioral questions, will need to address not only the current biological substrate of brain–behavior relationships, but also the longitudinal antecedents, both biological and phenomenological. Does childhood aggression predict similar behavior in the adult? Conversely, how commonly is childhood aggression an antecedent of adult aggression? If there is a biological substrate which predisposes for aggressive behavior, at what age does it emerge and how does it vary over time? There appears to be a strong genetic component to temperament and personality in general and impulsivity, hyper-reactivity, and aggression in particular (Plomin et al., 1990). With this in mind, the obvious question to be answered is whether putative biological markers demonstrable in adults are present in children as well. The few studies performed utilizing peripheral markers such as whole-blood 5-HT (Pliszka et al., 1988) or platelet-[H^3]imipramine binding (Stoff et al., 1987) suggest that this may be the case. Only one pharmacological challenge study has been performed in children. Stoff et al. (1992) looked at 15 prepubertal males and eight male adolescents. Diagnoses in both groups were mixed, including conduct disorder, oppositional defiant disorder, and attention deficit disorder, and in some cases comorbid. Prolactin and cortisol responses to fenfluramine challenge in the preadolescent sample, although not compared with normal controls, failed to correlate with parent-rated measures of aggression, hostility or antisocial behavior. The absence of other adult ratings, such as teachers', may have inadvertently biased the results, as teacher ratings of hyperactivity have proved to be better predictors of response to treatment with stimulant medication than those of parents. The small adolescent sample was not distinguished from controls in their hormonal response. In addition, hormonal response failed to correlate with clinician-rated measures of aggression and hostility. Although the patient sample differed from controls on measures of aggression and therefore was clearly a deviant group, the gross and relatively poor predictability of adult sociopathy from disruptive behavior disorders of childhood may have obscured any significant biological variability.

5-HT RECEPTOR SELECTIVITY

Most pharmacological challenge studies have utilized either 5-HT amino acid precursors or drugs with activity at both the pre- and postsynaptic level. The net status or activity of the serotonergic system can thereby be assessed, but distinctions at the pre/postsynaptic or synaptic subtype level are lost. This can be addressed by the additional use of more selective serotonergic agents. To date this has been done with only two agents, mCPP and buspirone. At the postsynaptic level mCPP is selective, although its receptor activation profile is nonselective in that it stimulates all serotonergic receptors, and also demonstrates activity at α_1- and α_2-adrenergic receptors, β-adrenergic receptors, and to a lesser extent dopaminergic and muscarinic receptors (Kahn and Wetzler, 1991). The issue of receptor nonselectivity is mitigated by the observation that the general 5-HT antagonist metergoline can nearly completely block the hormonal response to mCPP. Buspirone is a selective 5-HT$_{1A}$ agonist, although it has weak antidopaminergic activity as well. While it is likely that the PRL response to buspirone challenge reflects activation of the 5-HT system, it is certainly possible that buspirone's antidopaminergic properties may play a role as well (Coccaro et al., 1990).

In addition to the aforementioned reports using mCPP as a challenge (Moss et al., 1990; Wexler et al., 1991; Handlesman et al., 1993), preliminary studies by Coccaro et al. (1990, 1991) have reported an inverse relationship between the PRL responses to mCPP and buspirone and self-reported measures of aggression in patients with PDs. Both published reports involve 10 subjects each (with some overlap in subjects). With mCPP the correlation between the sum score of Buss–Durkee Assault + Irritability and PRL(mCPP) was $r = -0.66$. The correlation with buspirone as challenge agent was $r = -0.69$. A larger sample of PD patients with mCPP challenge, however, reveals an inverse, but not significant correlation. Curiously, the mathematical product of CSF 5-HIAA concentration and PRL(mCPP) responses reveals a much higher, and significant, inverse correlation with Buss–Durkee Assault Scores ($r = -0.71$ vs -0.41; Coccaro et al., 1993). This suggests the possibility that postsynaptic hormonal responses are less reflective of the behavioral correlation with 5-HT activity than are biological assessments, which integrate pre- and postsynaptic factors (e.g. fenfluramine).

CHALLENGE STUDIES OF THE NOREPINEPHRINE AND DOPAMINE SYSTEMS

There are few studies examining suicidal or impulsive aggressive type behaviors using challenges that target the noradrenergic system or the dopaminergic system. Coccaro et al. (1991) reported a positive correlation between the growth hormone (GH) response (log-transformed) to intravenous clonidine challenge and the Buss–Durkee scale "irritability" ($r = 0.71$) in a pilot sample of 18 individuals who were either healthy volunteers or patients with a DSM-III personality disorder. Since GH(clonidine) responses did not correlate with PRL(fenfluramine) responses in these individuals, the investigators suggested that the α_2-noradrenergic system may exert an influence on irritability (a trait which appears to prime individuals towards aggressive responding), which is independent of that of 5-HT which is inversely related to this behavioral dimension. This interpretation is consistent with animal data, which suggest that increased noradrenergic function is associated with aggression (Stolk, 1974; Eichelman and Barchus, 1975). Finally, Pitchot et al. (1992) have reported that GH responses to challenge with the dopamine agonist apomorphine are blunted in major depressed patients who have a history of a suicide attempt. The control group was age- and sex-matched with current depression but no history of suicidal behavior. One confounding factor, however, is that all subjects were depressed and it is difficult to know if the reduction in GH(apomorphine) responses were not simply reflecting a sample with a greater proportion of endogenous depression and/or of a more retarded nature [both of which could be associated with blunted GH(apomorphine) responses as well; Ansseau et al., 1988]. Interestingly, this finding is consistent with findings from CSF monoamine metabolite studies, which suggest that reduced CSF homovanillic acid concentrations in depressives are associated suicidal behavior (Roy et al., 1986). Clearly, more research is needed in the area of the responsivity of central catecholaminergic systems with respect to suicidal and impulsive aggressive behavior.

CONCLUSIONS

Like much of the data from studies of CSF 5-HIAA concentration in patients at risk for suicidal and/or aggressive behavior, the consensus from data from the various pharmacochallenge studies that have been performed in this area suggest that net 5-HT function in the limbic–hypothalamic–pituitary axis is inversely correlated with history of suicidal behavior and/or dimensional assessments of aggressive and/or impulsive aggressive behavior. Data from studies using indirect 5-HTP stimulation or direct postsynaptic 5-HT agonists (mCPP) are mixed, with the former suggesting the possibility of heightened postsynaptic responsivity in depressed patients with history of suicidal behavior and the latter suggesting either reduced or "normal" postsynaptic responsivity.

In summary these studies generally suggest an important role for aberrant 5-HT (and possibly catecholamine) system function in selected psychiatric patients at risk for suicidal and/or aggressive behavior. Future studies should focus on at least three areas: (1) exploration of the stability of these pharmacological challenge measures, as well as the impact of factors that affect the magnitude and nature of the hormonal response to challenge (e.g. differential response as a function of drugs of abuse); (2) a better understanding of the 5-HT receptor subtypes(s) that underlie the hormonal response to these probes; and (3) correlation between the baseline, and post-treatment, status of the 5-HT system in the limbic–hypothalamic–pituitary axis with the pharmacological response to treatment interventions such as lithium or 5-HT uptake inhibitors.

REFERENCES

Ansseau, M., von Frenckell, R., Certontaine, J.L., et al. (1988). Blunted response of growth hormone to clonidine and apomorphine in endogenous depression. *Br. J. Psychiatry*, 153, 65–71.

Asberg, M., Traksman, L., and Thoren, P. (1976). 5-HIAA in the cerebrospinal fluid: A biochemical suicide predictor? *Arch. Gen. Psychiatry*, 33, 1193–1197.

Asberg, M., Schalling, D., Traksman-Bendz, L., and Wagner, A. (1987). Psychobiology of suicide, impulsivity, and related phenomena. In: *Psychopharmacology: Third Generation of Progress*, (ed. H.Y. Meltzer) pp. 655–688. Raven Press, New York.

Asnis, G.M., Eisenberg, J., van Praag, H.M., Lemus, C.Z., Harkavy Friedman, J.M., and Miller, A.H. (1988). The neuroendocrine response to fenfluramine in depressives and normal controls. *Biol. Psychiatry*, 24, 117–120.

Ben-Jonathan, N., Abbogast L.A., and Hyde, J.F. (1989). Neuroendocrine regulation of prolactin release. *Progr. Neurobiol.*, 33, 399–447.

Brown, G.L., Goodwin, F.K., Ballenger, J.C., Goyer, P.F., and Major, L.F. (1979). Aggression in humans correlates with cerebrospinal fluid amine metabolites. *Psychiatry Res.*, 1, 131–139.

Brown, G.L., Ebert, M.H., Goyer, P.F., et al. (1982). Aggression, suicide, and serotonin: Relationships to CSF amine metabolites. *Am. J. Psychiatry*, 139, 741–746.

Botchin, M.B., Kaplan, J.R., Manuck, S.B., and Mann, J.J. (1993). Low versus high prolactin responders to fenfluramine challenge: Marker of behavioral differences in adult male cynmolgus macaques. *Neuropsychopharmacology*, 9, 93–99.

Coccaro, E.F. (1989). Central serotonin and impulsive aggression. *Br. J. Psychiatry*, 155 (suppl. 8), 52–62.

Coccaro, E.F. (1992). Impulsive aggression and central serotonergic system function in humans: an example of a dimensional brain–behavioral relationship. *Int. J. Clin. Psychopharmacol.*, 7, 3–12.

Coccaro, E.F., and Astill, J. (1990). Central serotonergic function in parasuicide. *Prog. Neuro-Psychopharmacol. Biol. Psychiatry*, 14, 663–674.

Coccaro, E.F., and Kavoussi, R.J. (1994). The neuropsychopharmacologic challenge in biological psychiatry. *Clin. Chemistry*, 40, 319–327.

Coccaro, E.F., and Kavoussi, R.J. In: *The Neurobiology of Clinical Aggression* (eds D.M. Stoff and R.B. Cairns). Lawrence Erlbaum Associates, N.J. (in press).

Coccaro, E.F., and Murphy, D.L. (1990). *Serotonin in Major Psychiatric Disorders*. American Psychiatric Press, Washington, D.C.

Coccaro, E.F., Siever, L.J., Klar, H., et al. (1989). Serotonergic studies in affective and personality disorder patients: Correlates with suicidal and impulsive aggressive behavior. *Arch. Gen. Psychiatry*, 46, 587–599.

Coccaro, E.F., Gabriel, S., and Siever, L.J. (1990). Buspirone challenge: Preliminary evidence for a role for central 5-HT-1a receptor function in impulsive aggressive behavior in humans. *Psychopharmacol. Bull.*, 26, 393–405.

Coccaro, E.F., Lawrence, T., Trestman, R., Gabriel, S., Klar, H.M., and Siever, L.J. (1991). Growth hormone responses to intravenous clonidine challenge correlates with behavioral irritability in psychiatric patients and in healthy volunteers. *Psychiatry Res.*, 39, 129–139.

Coccaro, E.F., Kavoussi, R.J., and Lesser, J. (1992). Self- and other-directed human aggression: The role of the central serotonergic system. *Int. J. Clin. Psychopharmacology*, 6 (suppl. 6), 70–83.

Coccaro, E.F., Kavoussi, R.J., and Stehle, S. (1993). Serotonin and impulsive aggression: Relationship to alcoholism. In: *The Science and Psychiatry of Violence* (eds C. Thompson and P.J. Cowen) pp. 62–75. Butterworth–Heinemann, Oxford.

Coccaro, E.F., Kavoussi, R.J., Trestman, R.L., and Siever, L.J. (1993). 5-HT and aggression: Assessment of pre- and postsynaptic indices of 5-HT. *Biol. Psychiatry*, 33, 87 [abstr.].

Eichelman, B., and Barchus, J. (1975). Facilitated shock-induced aggression following antidepressant medication in the rat. *Pharmacol. Biochem. Behav.*, 3, 601–604.

Fishbein, D.H., Lozovsky, D., and Jaffe, J.H. (1989). Impulsivity, aggression, and neuroendocrine responses to serotonergic stimulation in substance abusers. *Biol. Psychiatry*, 25, 1049–1066.

Gawin, F.H., and Kleber, H.D. (1985) Neuroendocrine findings in chronic cocaine abusers: A preliminary report. *Br. J. Psychiatry*, 147, 569–573.

Golden, R.N., Ruegg, R., Brown, T.M., et al. (1990). Abnormal neuroendocrine responsivity to clomipramine in depression. *Psychopharm. Bull.*, 26, 317–320.

Goodwin, G.M., Fairnairn, C.G., and Cowen, P.J. (1987). The effects of dieting and weight loss on neuroendocrine responses to L-tryptophan, clonidine and apomorphine in volunteers: important implications for neuroendocrine investigation in depression. *Arch. Gen. Psychiatry*, 44, 952–955.

Handelsman, L., Holloway, K., Shiekh, I., Sturiano, C., and Bernstein, D. (1993). Serotonergic challenges in cocaine addicts and alcoholics. New Research Abstracts (NR 433), 146th Meeting of the American Psychiatric Association, San Francisco.

Heninger, G.R., Charney, D.S., and Sternberg, D.E. (1984). Serotonergic function in depressed patients and healthy subjects. *Arch. Gen. Psychiatry*, 41, 398–402.

Higley, J.D., Mehlman, P.T., Taub, D.M., et al. (1992). Cerebrospinal fluid monoamine and adrenal correlates of aggression in free-ranging rhesus monkeys. *Arch. Gen. Psychiatry*, 49, 436–441.

Invernizzi, R., Berettera, C., Garatitini, S., and Samanin, R. (1986). D- and L-isomers of fenfluramine differ markedly in their interaction with brain serotonin and catecholamines in the rat. *Eur. J. Pharmacol.*, 120, 9–15.

Kahn, R.S., and Wetzler, S. (1991). *m*-Chlorophenylpiperazine as a probe of serotonin function. *Biol. Psychiatry*, 30, 1139–1166.

Koyama, T., and Meltzer, H.Y. (1986). A biochemical and neuroendocrine study of the serotonergic system in depression. In: *New Results in Depression Research* (eds H. Hippius, G.L. Klerman, and N. Matussek) pp. 169–188. Springer-Verlag, Berlin.

Kruesi, M.J.P., Rapoport, J.L., Hamberger, S., et al. (1990). Cerebrospinal fluid metabolites, aggression, and impulsivity in disruptive behavior disorders of children and adolescents. *Arch. Gen. Psychiatry*, 47, 419–462.

Kuhn, C.M., Vogel, R.A., Mailman, R.B., Mueller, R.A., Schanberg, S.M., and Bresse, G.R. (1981). Effect of 5,7-dihydroxytryptamine on serotonergic control of prolactin secretion and behavior in rats. *Psychopharmacology*, 73, 188–193.

Lewis, D.A., and Sherman, B.M. (1985). Serotonergic regulation of prolactin and growth hormone secretion in man. *Acta Endocrinol.*, 110, 152–157.

Limson, R., Goldman, D., Roy, A., et al. (1991). Personality and cerebrospinal fluid monoamine metabolites in alcoholics and controls. *Arch. Gen. Psychiatry*, 48, 437–441.

Linnoila, M., Virkkunen, M., Scheinin, M., Nuutila, A., Rimon, R., and Goodwin, F.K. (1983). Low cerebrospinal fluid 5-hydroxyindolacetic acid concentration differentiates impulsive from nonimpulsive violent behavior. *Life Sci.*, 33, 2609–2614.

López-Ibor, J.J., Lana, F., and Saiz Ruiz, J. (1990). Conductas autoliticas impulsivas y serotonina. *Actas Luso-Esp. Neurol. Psiquiatr.*, 18, 316–325.

Meltzer, H.Y., Perline, R., Tricou, B.J., Lowry, M.T., and Robertson, A. (1984). Effect of 5-hydroxytryptophan on serum cortisol levels in major affective disorders.

II. Relation to suicide, psychosis, and depressive symptoms. *Arch. Gen. Psychiatry*, 41, 379–387.

Moss, H.B., Yao, Y.K., and Panzak, G.L. (1990). Serotonergic responsivity and behavioral dimensions in antisocial personality disorder with substance abuse. *Biol. Psychiatry*, 28, 325–338.

O'Keane, V., and Dinan, T.G. (1991). Prolactin and cortisol responses to *d*-fenfluramine in major depression: Evidence for diminished responsivity of central serotonergic function. *Am. J. Psychiatry*, 148, 1009–1015.

O'Keane, V., Moloney, E., O'Neill, H., O'Connor, A., Smith, C., and Dinan, T.G. (1992). Blunted prolactin responses to *d*-fenfluramine in sociopathy: Evidence for subsensitivity of central serotonergic function. *Br. J. Psychiatry*, 160, 643–646.

Pitchot, W., Hansennes, M., Gonzalez-Moreno, A., and Asseau, M. (1992). Suicidal behavior and growth hormone response to apomorphine test. *Biol. Psychiatry*, 31, 1213–1219.

Pliszka, S.R., Rogeness, G.A., Renner, P., Sherman, J., and Broussard, T. (1988). Plasma neurochemistry in juvenile offenders. *Am. Acad. Child. Adolesc. Psychiatry*, 27, 558–594.

Plomin, R., Nitz, K., and Rowe, D.C. (1990). Behavioral genetics and aggressive behavior in childhood. In: *Handbook of Developmental Psychopathology* (eds M. Lewis and S.M. Miller) pp. 119–133. New York, Plenum Press.

Pryor, J.C., and Nemeroff, C.B. (1991). Stress-associated psychiatric disorders. Focus on the role of neuropeptides. In: *Stress Neurobiology and Neuroendocrinology* (eds M.R. Brown, G.F. Koof, and C. Rivier) p. 381. Marcel Dekker, New York.

Roy, A., Agren, A., Picklar, et al. (1986). Reduced CSF concentrations of homovanillic acid and homovanillic acid to 5-hydroxyindoleacetic acid ratios in depressed patients: Relationship to suicidal behavior and dexamethasone nonsuppression. *Am. J. Psychiatry*, 143, 1539–1545.

Siever, L.J. (1987). Role of noradrenergic mechanisms in the etiology of the affective disorders. In: *Psychopharmacology: Third Generation of Progress* (ed. H.Y. Meltzer) pp. 493–504. Raven Press, New York.

Siever, L.J., Murphy, D.L., Slater, S., and de la Vega Lipper, S. (1984). Plasma prolactin changes following fenfluramine in depressed patients compared to controls: An evaluation of central serotonergic responsivity in depression. *Life Sci.*, 34, 1029–1039.

Stoff, D.M., Pollock, L., Vitiello, B., Behar, D., and Bridger, W.H. (1987). Reduction of ^{3}H-imipramine binding sites on platelets of conduct disordered children. *Neuropsychopharmacology*, 1, 55–62.

Stoff, D.M., Pastiempo, A.P., Yeung, J.H., Cooper, T.B., Bridger, W.H., and Rabinovich, H. (1992). Neuroendocrine responses to challenge with *d,l*-fenfluramine and aggression in disruptive behavior disorders of children and adolescents. *Psychiatry Res.*, 43, 263–276.

Stolk, J.M., Connor, R.L., Levine, S., and Barchus, J.D. (1974). Brain norepinephrine metabolism and shock induced fighting behavior in rats: Differential effects of shock and fighting on the neurochemical response to a common footshock stimulus. *J. Pharmacol. Exp. Ther.*, 190, 193–209.

Wetzler, S., Kahn, R.S., Asnis, G.M., Korn, M., and van Praag, H.M. (1991). Serotonin receptor sensitivity and aggression. *Psychiatry Res.*, 37, 271–279.

van der Klar, L.D., and Bethea, C.L. (1982). Pharmacological evidence that serotonergic stimulation of prolactin release is mediated via the dorsal raphe nucleus. *Neuroendocrinology*, 35, 225–230.

van Praag, H.M., Lemus, C., and Kahn, R. (1987). Hormonal probes of central serotonergic activity: Do they really exist? *Biol. Psychiatry*, 22, 86–98.

7 The Neuropsychiatry of Impulsive Aggression

DAN J STEIN*, JAMES TOWEY‡, AND ERIC HOLLANDER†
*Department of Psychiatry, University of Stellenbosch, Tygerberg, South Africa
‡Department of Biopsychology, New York State Psychiatric Institute, New York, NY, USA
†Department of Psychiatry, Mount Sinai School of Medicine, NY, USA

INTRODUCTION

Clinicians have long known that patients with neurological lesions may present with symptoms of aggression. Early case studies provided some of the first hypotheses about the nature of the brain structures involved in impulsive aggressive behavior. More recently, researchers have attempted to demonstrate subtle neurological impairment in patients who present with symptoms of aggression. This work has proved valuable in clarifying the neurobiological factors that contribute to the etiology of aggression and impulsive aggression. In this chapter, we will review the contribution that neuropsychiatric studies have made towards understanding these phenomena.

NEUROLOGICAL STRUCTURES MEDIATING AGGRESSION

Clinical reports of aggressive patients with specific neurological lesions may help delineate the structures that mediate these symptoms. Animal studies provide further support for the involvement of specific brain regions in aggression (Hess, 1957). Drawing closely on the work of previous authors (Weiger and Bear, 1988), we will focus on the role of the hypothalamus, amygdala, and prefrontal cortex.

HYPOTHALAMUS

The hypothalamus can be conceptualized as the principal ganglion of the autonomic nervous system (ANS). The hypothalamus receives input from a variety of chemoreceptors and osmoreceptors, and sends efferents to

Impulsivity and Aggression. Edited by E. Hollander and D.J. Stein
© 1995 John Wiley & Sons Ltd

neurons in the pituitary and to motor centers in the brainstem. The hypothalamus is therefore able to monitor various internal states, for example hunger, and to regulate them.

It might be postulated that aggression is also under hypothalamic regulation (Siegel and Edinger, 1981). Indeed, early work with decorticate cats provided evidence in support of this. Bard (1928) demonstrated that in cats in which there were lesions of structures rostral to the hypothalamus, there was marked sympathetic arousal and apparent anger. In contrast, sectioning of the brain caudal to the hypothalamus did not result in this behavior. Later animal studies confirmed the role of the hypothalamus in offensive (and defensive) aggression (Wasman and Flynn, 1962; Eichelman, 1971).

Clinical data provides further support of a role for the hypothalamus in aggression. Thus, structural lesions of the hypothalamus may be associated with unplanned and undirected aggressive symptoms that often appear unprovoked but may be in response to physical discomfort (Reeves and Plum, 1969; Killefer and Stern, 1970; Haugh and Markesbery, 1983; Ovsiew and Yudofksy, 1993).

AMYGDALA

Limbic structures in the temporal lobe consist of the amygdala and the hippocampus. The amygdala receives inputs from multiple cortical areas, and has efferents to the extrapyramidal system and the hypothalamus. Thus, the amygdala may have a role in associating sensory experience with (hypothalamically directed) affects and behaviors, including anger (Bear, 1991).

Bilateral temporal lobectomy in monkeys leads to the Klüver–Bucy syndrome, characterized by hyperorality, hypersexuality, and loss of aggressive responses (Klüver and Bucy, 1939). It is as though there is a dissociation between sensory information (about the environment) and regulatory affects and behaviors (involving food, sex, and aggression). Similarly, removal of the amygdala from monkeys results in decreased aggression (Downer, 1961). However, amygdalectomy in submissive monkeys may result in increased aggression (Dicks et al., 1969), suggesting that the amygdala may function as a rheostat—not simply acting to increase regulatory affects and behaviors, but rather mediating their control. Similarly, in cats, aggressive behavior following stimulation of the amygdala varies according to pre-existing temperament (Adamec, 1990).

Bilateral temporal lobe damage in humans may also lead to the Klüver–Bucy syndrome, with a decrease in regulatory affects and behaviors (Terzian and Ore, 1955; Marlowe et al., 1975; Isern, 1987). Amgydalectomy has been suggested as a treatment for aggressive behavior (Narabayashi et al., 1963; Kiloh et al., 1974). On the other hand, in disorders with temporal lobe excitation, there may be an increase in aggression. Thus patients with temporal lobe epilepsy (TLE) may demonstrate hyperemotionality and increased aggression (Weiger and Bear, 1988; Elliott, 1992).

While TLE is occasionally characterized by ictal or postictal aggression, more commonly patients have interictal aggression. Conversely, Elliott (1982) found that 30% of 286 patients with intermittent violent outbursts had TLE. Similarly, Lewis et al. (1982) found psychomotor epilepsy in 18 of 97 incarcerated delinquent boys with a history of violence. Several studies indicate that the majority of TLE patients with increased aggression have a left temporal lobe focus (Serafetinides, 1965; Nachson, 1988), suggesting left-hemisphere dysfunction. Whereas ictal and postictal aggression are unplanned and undirected, interictal aggression often involves intense affect in response to an environmental stimulus.

PREFRONTAL CORTEX

The prefrontal cortex receives input from a variety of cortical associative areas. In addition, it receives afferents from the hypothalamus via the dorsal medial nucleus of the thalamus, and afferents from the temporolimbic system via the uncinate fasciculus. It has efferents to the pyramidal motor system and the striatum. Thus, this structure has access to environmental stimuli, internal states, and past experience (Weiger and Bear, 1988). It integrates this information in order to plan future goals and ensure goal execution (Luria, 1980).

Prefrontal lesions are classically associated with impairment in these "executive" functions. An early case of prefrontal lesioning was that of Phineas Gage (Elliott, 1978; Macmillan, 1986), who demonstrated marked changes in personality after injury to his frontal lobes. Subsequent cases of head injury and of frontal lobe surgery have led to reports of many further patients with similar symptoms (Kandel and Freed, 1987; Lishman, 1968, 1987). Dorsal lesions of the prefrontal cortex are associated with impairment in long-term planning and increased apathy (pseudodepression). Orbital lesions of the prefrontal cortex are associated with increase in reflexive emotional responses to environmental stimuli (pseudopsychopathy; Luria, 1980). Weiger and Bear (1988) suggest that whereas TLE patients may express deep remorse over an aggressive act, patients with prefrontal lesions often indicate indifference.

DISCUSSION

A number of authors have suggested that a typology of aggressive symptoms can be based on the specific brain structures that mediate different kinds of aggression. Reis (1971), for example, has divided aggression into affective and predatory aggression. Affective aggression is characterized by sympathetic arousal, and usually occurs between animals of the same species. It can be subdivided into offensive and defensive forms (Blanchard et al., 1977). Predatory aggression, on the other hand, does not lead to sympathetic arousal, and generally occurs between animals of different species.

In the rat, lesions of the septal nuclei lead to an increase in defensive affective aggression, whereas lesions of the ventromedial nucleus of the hypothalamus lead to an increase in offensive affective aggression. Tricyclic antidepressants increase affective aggressive behavior, but decrease predatory aggressive behavior (Eichelman, 1992).

Weiger and Bear (1988) have suggested that aggressive symptoms can be divided into three kinds. Aggressive symptoms that are motivated by internal or visceroreceptive states (e.g. hunger and fatigue) are mediated by hypothalamus and related brainstem structures. Such symptoms may be stereotyped in nature, showing little relationship to environmental stimuli, and with little response to learning. On the other hand, aggressive acts that are a result of broadened emotional associations to external stimuli or events are mediated by temporolimbic structures. Finally, aggressive acts that are impulsive unreflective responses to environmental frustration point to impairment of prefrontal cortex and associated structures (e.g. the striatum).

Different pharmacological effects may be associated with each of these neuroanatomical regions. Thus, for example, cholinergic stimulation of hypothalamic receptors may be associated with increased aggression (Bear et al., 1986). On the other hand, anticonvulsants such as carbamazepine may decrease aggression by altering temporolimbic events. Finally, serotonergic agents may exert serenic effects via their action on prefrontal cortical function. While this scheme comprises a useful clinical and research heuristic, and is compatible with an hierarchical approach to brain structure and function (MacLean, 1990), further work is necessary to determine whether these outlines for a typology of aggression are valid.

SOFT SIGNS IN IMPULSIVITY AND AGGRESSION

Neurological soft signs are nonlocalizing neurological phenomena that occur in the absence of evidence of gross neurological disease. They include involuntary movements, a variety of apraxias, difficulties in performing rapid alternating movements, difficulties in discerning double simultaneous stimulation, and dysgraphesthesia (Shaffer et al., 1985). Neurological soft examination appears reliable (Stokman et al., 1986) and stable (Shafer et al., 1986).

Work on patients with personality disorders characterized by impulsivity supports an association between these disorders and increased soft signs. Quitkin et al. (1976) found that 22 patients with "emotionally unstable character disorder", characterized by impulsive and antisocial behaviors, had increased neurological soft signs compared with 108 patients with other personality disorders. Many of the patients with emotionally unstable character disorder would presumably meet DSM-III-R criteria for borderline personality disorder (BPD). In an uncontrolled study of 24 latency-age children with symptoms consistent with BPD, Bemporad et al. (1982) found that 16 of 24 subjects demonstrated neurological soft signs. More recently, Gardner et al. (1987) found that, on an unblinded soft sign examination, patients with DSM-III BPD had significantly more soft sign neurological abnormalities than normal controls. Vitiello et al. (1990) found that increased soft signs were associated with impulsive responding on cognitive tests, but not with global cognitive functioning or with clinical ratings of impulsivity.

Stein et al. (1993a) found that patients with DSM-III-R BPD had increased left-sided neurological soft signs, whereas patients with a history of aggression had increased right-sided neurological soft signs. These findings are consistent with a specific association between impulsive aggression and left-hemisphere dysfunction. This hypothesis is consistent with a number of neuropsychological studies, reviewed in the next section of this chapter. In view of their nonspecificity and unclear etiology, neurological soft signs provide only a limited window on the neuropsychiatry of aggression. However, neurological soft signs may be an efficient tool for delineating subgroups of patients, and they may have specific correlations with findings on brain imaging (Stein et al., 1993b) and with response to treatment (Hollander et al., 1991).

NEUROPSYCHOLOGICAL STUDIES OF IMPULSIVITY AND AGGRESSION

Several authors have attempted to use neuropsychological studies to demonstrate that patients with aggressive symptoms manifest subtle neuropsychiatric impairment. Much of this research has been conducted on criminals and juvenile delinquents, a proportion of whom meet diagnostic criteria for antisocial personality disorder (ASPD) or conduct disorder. There has also been increasing work on BPD, a core feature of which is impulsivity.

ANTISOCIAL PERSONALITY DISORDER

A variety of literature supports Weschler's (1958) hypothesis that psychopathy is characterized by a higher performance IQ relative to verbal IQ (Miller, 1987; Nachson, 1988). On the other hand, some have argued that this pattern may reflect learning disability associated with psychopathy rather than psychopathy *per se* (Prentice and Kelly, 1963). In his comprehensive review, Miller (1987) concluded that more impulsive and violently aggressive psychopaths tend to be less intelligent, but that there is no clear causal relationship between low IQ and psychopathy.

In line with a relative decrease in verbal IQ, an early hypothesis was that left-hemisphere dysfunction was associated with psychopathic behavior (Flor-Henry, 1973). Using the Halstead–Reitan battery, Yeudall and colleagues (Yeudall and Fromm-Auch, 1979) studied laterality of cerebral dysfunction in various subject groups. They found predominantly left-hemisphere dysfunction in psychopaths, violent criminals, alcoholics with personality disorders, and adolescents with conduct disorders, but predominantly right-hemisphere dysfunction in nonviolent criminals, alcoholics with affective disorders, and affective personality disorders. However, using a similar battery of tests, Fedora and Fedora (1983) found left-hemisphere dysfunction in both psychopathic and nonpsychopathic criminals, and suggested that these results reflected impulsivity in both groups.

Hare (1979) criticized this research, arguing that impairment on these neuropsychological batteries did not necessarily indicate specific hemisphere dysfunction. Furthermore, he found no differences between psychopaths and nonpsychopaths in handedness or lateral preference. Similarly, various studies of lateral preference in delinquents have reached disparate conclusions (Nachson, 1988).

Spellacy (1978) compared violent and nonviolent male penitentiary inmates on cognitive, language, perceptual, and psychomotor abilities. In each of these categories, violent subjects performed worse than nonviolent subjects. Spellacy concluded that organic factors played a role in mediating impulse dyscontrol in violent subjects. Subsequent studies have similarly found increased neuropsychological impairment in more violent subjects compared with less violent subjects. Bryant et al. (1984), for example, found impaired performance on tests requiring complex information processing, goal-directed executive functions, and sustained attention.

Impairment on tests of executive function have been interpreted as consistent with frontal lobe dysfunction. Indeed, a number of early authors posited a role for frontal lobe dysfunction in psychopathic behavior (Pontius, 1972). Gorenstein (1982) therefore chose to study male psychopaths, nonpsychopathic psychiatric patients, and normal controls on tests of frontal lobe function such as the Wisconsin Card Sort Test (WCST). Subjects in the psychopathic group demonstrated poorer performance on several measures of frontal lobe function (e.g. WCST perseveratory errors), but not on scores unrelated to frontal lobe function (e.g. WCST nonperserveratory errors).

The foregoing studies have, however, been criticized for their lack of adequate diagnostic assessment, and for the failure to control for such factors as education and substance abuse (Hare, 1984; Kandel and Freed, 1989). Hare (1984), employing structured diagnostic assessments and relevant controls, compared psychopaths and normal controls. No significant differences were found between groups on tests of frontal lobe function, such as the WCST. Other studies have also not found a relationship between psychopathy and frontal lobe dysfunction (Hoffman et al., 1987; Hart et al., 1990).

It is possible that the different conclusions reached by these studies are due to heterogeneity of subjects in terms of diagnostic subtype (Devonshire et al., 1988) or intelligence (Sutker and Allain, 1987). Nevertheless, the causal role of neuropsychological impairment in ASPD symptoms remains controversial (Miller, 1987). Hart et al. (1990) suggest that rather than focusing on cerebral impairment, it may be more useful to emphasize alterations in cognitive processing in psychopaths. For example, there appear to be distinct differences in verbal processing between psychopaths and controls (Hare et al., 1988).

BORDERLINE PERSONALITY DISORDER

There have been fewer neuropsychological studies of BPD than of ASPD. However, BPD patients have commonly been thought to have cognitive impairment on the basis of clinical observation of "ego-deficits" (Kernberg, 1975). A traditional distinction is that patients with BPD have intact performance on structured psychological tests, such as the Weschler Adult Intelligence Scale (WAIS), but disturbed performance on unstructured projective tests, such as the Rorschach test (Singer, 1977), although there is only limited empirical support for this (Gartner et al., 1989). Such a distinction suggests that cognitive capacities in BPD are vulnerable to affective disruption and that patients lack stable self-organizing strategies.

Work on the neuropsychology of BPD supports the notion that this disorder is associated with impairment in complex information processing. Burgess (1992) found that, compared with normal controls, BPD patients had deficits on tests that required planning multiple operations and the maintenance of a prolonged response over time. O'Leary et al. (1991) found that BPD patients were similar to normal controls on simple auditory and visual memory tasks (visual reproduction and associate learning on the Wechsler Memory Scale), but were significantly impaired on more complex auditory and visual memory tasks (Rey–Osterrieth test, and story recall on the Wechsler Memory Scale). Patients also had significant impairment on tests of visual filtering and discrimination.

CONDUCT DISORDER

Moffitt and Henry (1991) have provided an extensive review of neuro-psychological studies of conduct disorder. Most of the research has been conducted on juvenile delinquents. Across studies, the consistent findings are impairment in language-based verbal skills and "executive" self-control functions. The latter include sustaining attention and concentration, abstract reasoning and concept formation, formulating goals and planning, initiating purposive sequences of behavior, interrupting or inhibiting inappropriate or impulsive behaviors, and self-monitoring.

IMPULSIVITY AS A PERSONALITY DIMENSION

Impulsivity can be approached not only in terms of its manifestations as an Axis I or II disorder but also as a basic personality dimension (Stein et al., 1993c). There has also been interest in investigating the neuropsychiatry of this construct. Barratt and Patton (1983), for example, have noted that time appears to be passing more slowly (experientially) for highly impulsive subjects and that impulsivity is inversely related to mean reaction time. These researchers have also correlated task performance measures with psychophysiological ones, arguing that such external criterion measures are essential for a definitive approach to the definition and study of impulsivity.

DISCUSSION

A number of neuropsychological studies indicate that violent subjects have poorer performance than nonviolent subjects on a variety of neuropsychological measures. Furthermore, some studies are consistent with hypotheses that specific anatomical structures mediate impulsivity and aggression. However, several limitations to this kind of attempt to localize neurological deficits using neuropsychological tests should be noted. First, neuropsychological impairment on any particular test cannot readily be related to a single brain area. For example, impairment on tests of frontal lobe function may also be seen in basal ganglia disease. Second, the absence of neuropsychological impairment does not imply the absence of neurological deficits. Neurological deficits may be too subtle to lead to neuropsychological impairment. Third, neuropsychological dysfunction does not allow assessment of a particular process as primary or secondary. Neuropsychological impairment may, for example, represent a compensation strategy.

Neuropsychological studies are nevertheless able to contribute to an understanding of the cognitive processes that are impaired in impulsive and aggressive behaviors. An information-processing perspective of both impulsivity as a personality dimension, and of impulsive and aggressive symptoms, requires further elaboration. Combining research on cognitive processes with other psychiatric methodologies may foster an integrated psychobiological approach to etiology. In addition, increased understanding of how cognitive processes are impaired in impulsivity and aggression may have direct clinical implications. O'Leary et al. (1991), for example, suggest that in BPD cueing techniques may allow deficits in cognitive processing to be overcome.

ELECTROPHYSIOLOGY IN IMPULSIVE AGGRESSION

An association between aggression and electroencephalogram (EEG) abnormalities has long been posited (Hill and Sargent, 1943; Monroe, 1970). Early work focused on criminal offenders and patients with ASPD. Results of this research were inconclusive, with some studies reporting an increase of nonspecific EEG abnormalities compared with normal controls, while other studies failed to find such differences (Syndulko, 1978; Volavka, 1990). An early study of BPD found that a small percentage of these patients have nonspecific EEG abnormalities (Andrulonis, 1981). Snyder and Pitts (1984) and Cowdry et al. (1985) found that patients with BPD have significantly more EEG dysrhythmias than depressed controls, but others (Cornelius et al. 1986, 1989; Archer et al., 1988) have found no significant differences between BPD patients and controls.

The use of event-related potentials (ERPs) can extend information learned from baseline EEGs (Raine and Venables, 1987, 1988; Forth and Hare, 1989). Increased impulsivity in normal volunteers has been associated with augmentation of early ERP components (Carrillo-de-la-Pena and Barratt, 1993). However, several studies have found that criminal offenders (Drake et al., 1988) and patients with BPD (Blackwood et al., 1986; Kutcher et al., 1987; Drake et al., 1991) have increased latency and smaller amplitude of P300, a late ERP component (Blackwood et al., 1986; Kutcher et al., 1987; Drake et al., 1991).

Electrophysiological findings have also supported the hypothesis of a link between left-hemisphere dysfunction and increased impulsive aggression. Yeudall and Wardell (1978) found that during the processing of verbal stimuli, violent criminals failed to show a normal activation pattern, particularly over the left hemisphere. Hare and his colleagues have demonstrated abnormal verbal processing in psychopaths, particularly of affective material (Hare and McPherson, 1984; Williamson et al., 1991).

We examined ERP correlates of selective attention (i.e. Processing Negativity; Naatanen and Picton, 1987) during an auditory "oddball" task which used ear channel as a condition (Attend Left versus Attend Right). There was significantly *less* negativity in the N1 region for unmedicated BPD patients ($n = 11$) than normal controls ($n = 15$) across these conditions for both stimuli (i.e. target and nontarget tones). This reduced negativity in BPD patients was more pronounced over left than right hemispheres, and persisted throughout most of the 0.5 seconds after stimulus onset. During the second half of the recording epoch (i.e. Slow Wave region), ERPs of BPD patients were *more* negative than normal controls, especially over right hemisphere sites. Processing Negativity is thought to reflect a frontal lobe mechanism responsible for regulating directed attention and inhibiting external interfering stimuli (e.g., Baxter et al., 1987). Hence, this brain region may be dysfunctional in BPD.

Volavka (1990) has noted that several technical and theoretical problems are often present in electrophysiological studies of aggression. Future studies must ensure reliability of EEG readings, control for within-subject variables, acknowledge sampling bias, and improve characterization of subjects' aggressive symptoms. Longitudinal studies are required to distinguish the antecedents of violence from its consequences. Finally, electrophysiological variables need to be combined with other predictors of violence in order to ensure an integrated approach.

BRAIN IMAGING

Patients who have impulsive and aggressive symptoms on the basis of neurological disorders may of course be found on brain imaging to have lesions. For example, Tonkonogy (1991) found that some patients with organic mental syndromes characterized by violent symptoms had lesions in the anterior–inferior temporal lobe on computerized tomography or magnetic resonance imaging. He concluded that unilateral destruction of the amygdala or adjacent structures may lead to aggression.

Brain imaging is now also being applied to the study of impulsive and aggressive symptoms in patients without gross neurological disorders. Preliminary findings using positron emission tomography include the demonstration of a relationship between decreased prefrontal or global cerebral glucose metabolism and increased aggression (Goyer et al., 1991; Amen and Paldi, 1993). This area of investigation appears to have particular promise for understanding the neuropsychiatry of impulsivity and aggression.

CONCLUSIONS

It is clear that both impulsivity and aggression must be understood within their sociological and cultural context. Nevertheless, neuropsychiatric factors should not be ignored. In some cases of pathological aggression, neurological disorder is the most important factor in the pathogenesis of symptoms, and adequate diagnosis may lead to appropriate treatment. In patients with impulsivity and aggression that is not secondary to a gross neurological disorder, an understanding of the underlying neuropsychiatry of impulsive and aggressive behaviors may inform the diagnosis and treatment.

A neurological perspective on impulsivity and aggression provides the outlines of a logical approach to the classification of these symptoms. Important advances have been made since the work of such early authors as Lombroso (1874), who investigated the physical stigmata of criminals. Nevertheless, further work is required in order to provide a rational and empirical diagnostic approach to cases of impulsivity and aggression in which there are no gross underlying neurological lesions. The relationship between impulsivity and aggression in the presence and absence of such lesions needs to be better understood.

Neurological soft signs and neuropsychological batteries provide an initial approach to understanding the neuropsychiatry of impulsivity and aggression. Nevertheless, methodological problems hamper their ultimate contributions. For example, these techniques often demonstrate a relative lack of neuroanatomical specificity. Furthermore, impairment on a neuropsychological battery may be indicative of either a primary dysfunction or of a secondary compensatory mechanism. A cognitive science or information processing approach to impulsivity and aggression requires further elaboration.

More recent methodologies, such as measurement of event-related potentials and brain imaging techniques, provide more promise of ultimately understanding the neuropsychiatry of impulsivity and aggression. Combining these techniques, together with a focus on the neurochemical and biological challenge studies discussed elsewhere in this book, may lead to more comprehensive neurobiological models. Ultimately, integration of these neurobiological models with cognitive and social models of impulsivity and aggression is also required.

REFERENCES

Adamec, R. (1990). Does the kindling model reveal anything clinically significant? *Biol. Psychiatry*, 27, 249–279.

Amen, D.G., and Paldi, J.H. (1993). Brain SPECT findings in aggressive behavior. *Biol. Psychiatry*, 33, 106 [abstr.].

Andrulonis, P.A., Glueck, B.C., Stroebel, C.F., et al. (1981). Organic brain dysfunction and the borderline syndrome. *Psychiatr. Clin. North Am.*, 4, 47–66.

Archer, R.P., Struve, F.A., Ball, J.D., and Gordon, R.A. (1988). EEG in borderline personality disorder. *Biol. Psychiatry*, 24, 731–732.

Bard, P. (1928). A diencephalic mechanism for the expression of rage with special reference to the sympathetic nervous system. *Am. J. Psychol.*, 84, 490–515.

Barratt, E.S., and Patton, J.H. (1983). Impulsivity: cognitive, behavioral, and psychophysiological correlates. In: *Biological Bases of Sensation Seeking, Impulsivity, and Anxiety* (ed. M. Zuckerman). Lawrence Erlbaum, Hillsdale.

Baxter, L.R. Jr., Phelps, M.E., Mazziotta, J.C., et al. (1987). Local cerebral glucose metabolic rates in obsessive-compulsive disorder: a comparison with rates in unipolar depression and in normal controls. *Arch. Gen. Psychiatr.*, 55, 211–218.

Bear, D.M. (1991). Neurological perspectives on aggression. *J. Neuropsychiatry Clin. Neurosci.*, 3 (suppl. 1), 3–8.

Bear, D.M., Rosenbaum, J.F., and Norman, R. (1986). Aggression in cat and man precipitated by a cholinesterase inhibitor. *Psychosomatics*, 26, 535–536.

Bemporad, J.R., Smith, H.F., Hanson, G., and Ciccetti, D. (1982). Borderline syndromes in childhood: Criteria for diagnosis. *Am. J. Psychiatr.*, 5, 596–602.

Blackwood, D.H.R., St. Clair, D.M., and Kutchen, S.P. (1986). P300 event-related potentials in BPD. *Biol. Psychiatry*, 21, 557–560.

Blanchard, R.J., Blanchard, D.C., Takahashi, T., and Kelley, M. (1977). Attack and defensive behaviour in the albino rat. *Anim. Behav.*, 25, 622–634.

Bryant, E.T., Scott, M.L., Golden, C.J., and Tori, C.D. (1984). Neuropsychological deficits, learning disability and violent behavior. *J. Consult. Clin. Psychol.*, 52, 323–324.

Burgess, J.W. (1992). Neurocognitive impairment in dramatic personalities: Histrionic, narcissistic, borderline and antisocial disorders. *Psychiatry Res.*, 42, 283–290.

Carrillo-de-la-Pena, M.T., and Barratt, E.S. (1993). Impulsivity and ERP augmenting/reducing. *Pers. Indiv. Diff.*, 15, 25–32.

Cornelius, J.R., Brenner, R.P., Soloff, P.H., et al. (1986). EEG abnormalities in borderline personality disorder. Specific or nonspecific. *Biol. Psychiatry*, 21, 974–977.

Cornelius, J.R., Soloff, P.H., George, A.W.A., et al. (1989). An evaluation of the significance of selected neuropsychiatric abnormalities in the etiology of borderline personality disorder. *J. Pers. Disord.*, 3, 19–25.

Cowdry, R.W., Pickar, D., and Davies, R. (1985). Symptoms and EEG findings in the borderline syndrome. *Int. J. Psychiatr. Med.*, 15, 201–210.

Devonshire, P.A., Howard, R.C., and Sellars, C. (1988). Frontal lobe functions and personality in mentally abnormal offenders. *Pers. Indiv. Diff.*, 9, 339–344.

Dicks, P., Myers, R.E., and Kling, A. (1969). Uncus and amygdala lesions: Effects on social behavior in the free-ranging monkey. *Science*, 165, 69–71.

Downer, J.L. (1961). Changes in visual gnostic functions and emotional behavior following unilateral temporal pole damage in the "split-brain" monkey. *Nature*, 191, 50–51.

Drake, M.E., Phillips, B.B., and Pakalnis, A. (1991). Auditory evoked potentials in borderline personality disorder. *Clin. Electroencephalogr.*, 22, 188–192.

Eichelman, B. (1971). Effect of subcortical lesions on shock-induced aggression in the rat. *J. Comp. Physiol. Psychol.*, 74, 331–339.

Eichelman, B. (1992). Aggressive behavior: From laboratory to clinic. Quo vadit? *Arch. Gen. Psychiatry*, 49, 488–492.

Elliott, F.A. (1978). Neurological aspects of antisocial behavior. In: *The Psychopath: A Comprehensive Study of Antisocial Disorders and Behaviors* (ed. W.H. Reid) pp. 146–189. Brunner/Mazel, New York.

Elliott, F.A. (1982). Neurological findings in adult minimal brain dysfunction and the dyscontrol syndrome. *J. Nerv. Ment. Dis.*, 170, 680–687.

Elliott, F.A. (1992). Violence: The neurological contribution: An overview. *Arch. Gen. Neurol.*, 49, 595–603.

Fedora, O., and Fedora, S. (1983). Some neuropsychological and psychophysiological aspects of psychopathic and nonpsychopathic criminals. In: *Laterality and Psychopathology* (eds P. Flor-Henry and J. Gruzelier). Elsevier, Amsterdam.

Flor-Henry, P. (1973). Psychiatric syndromes considered as manifestations of lateralized temporal-limbic dysfunction. In: *Surgical Approaches in Psychiatry* (eds L.V. Latiner and K.E. Livingston). Medical and Technical Publishing, Lancaster.

Forth, A.E., and Hare, R.D. (1989). The contingent negative variation in psychopaths. *Psychophysiology*, 26, 676–682.

Gardner, D., Lucas, P.B., and Cowdry, R.W. (1987). Soft sign neurological abnormalities in borderline personality disorder and normal control subjects. *J. Nerv. Ment. Dis.*, 3, 177–180.

Gartner, J., Hurt, S.W., and Gartner, A. (1989). Psychological test signs of borderline personality disorder: A review of the empirical literature. *J. Pers.*

Assess., 53, 423–441.

Goldman, R.G., Bruder, G.E., Stewart, J.W., et al. (1992). Personality and perceptual asymmetry in depression. Presented at the Annual Meeting of the American Psychiatric Association.

Gorenstein, E.E. (1982). Frontal lobe functions in psychopaths. *J. Abn. Psychol.*, 91, 368–379.

Goyer, P.F., Andreasen, P.J., Semple, W.E., et al. (1991). PET and personality disorders. Presented at the Annual Meeting of the American College of Neuropharmacology.

Hare, R.D. (1979). Psychopathy and laterality of cerebral dysfunction. *J. Abnormal Psychol.*, 88, 605–610.

Hare, R.D. (1984). Performance of psychopaths on cognitive tasks related to frontal lobe function. *J. Abnorm. Psychol.*, 93, 133–140.

Hare, R.D., and McPherson, L.M. (1984). Psychopathy and perceptual asymmetry during verbal dichotic listening. *J. Abnorm. Psychol.*, 93, 141–149.

Hare, R.D., Williamson, S.E., and Harpur, T.J. (1988). Psychopathy and language. In: *Biological Contributions to Crime Causation* (eds T.E. Moffitt and S.A. Mednick) pp. 69–92. Martinus Nijhoff, Dordrecht.

Hart, S.D., Forth, A.E., and Hare, R.D. (1990). Performance of criminal psychopaths on selected neuropsychological tests. *J. Abnorm. Behav.*, 99, 374–379.

Haugh, R.M., and Markesbery, W.R. (1983). Hypothalamic astrocytoma: syndrome of hyperphagia, obesity, and disturbances of behavior and endocrine and autonomic function. *Arch. Neurol.*, 40, 560–563.

Hess, W.R. (1957). *The Functional Organization of the Diencephalon*, p. 180. Grune & Stratton, New York.

Hill, D., and Sargent, W. (1943). A case of matricide. *Lancet*, 244, 526–527.

Hoffman, J.J., Hall, R.W., and Bartsch, T.W. (1987). On the relative importance of "psychopathic" personality and alcholism on neuropsychological measures of frontal lobe dysfunction. *J. Abnorm. Psychol.*, 96, 158–160.

Hollander, E., DeCaria, C., Sauoud, J., Klein, D.F., and Liebowitz, M.R. (1991). Neurological soft signs in obsessive–compulsive disorder, *Arch. Gen. Psychiatry*, 48, 278–279.

Isern, R. (1987). Family violence and the Kluver–Bucy syndrome. *South. Med. J.*, 80, 373–377.

Kandel, E., and Freed, D. (1989). Frontal-lobe dysfunction and antisocial behavior: A review. *J. Clin. Psychol.*, 45, 404–413.

Kernberg, O. (1975). *Borderline Conditions and Pathological Narcissism*. Jason Aronson, Dunmore, PA.

Killeffer, F.A., and Stern, W.E. (1970). Chronic effects of hypothalamic injury. *Arch. Neurol.*, 22, 419–429.

Kiloh, R.S., Gye, R.S., Rusworth, R.G., et al. (1974). Stereotaxic amygdalotomy for aggressive behavior. *J. Neurol. Neurosurg. Psychiatry*, 37, 437–444.

Klüver, H., and Bucy, P.C. (1939). Preliminary analysis of functions of the temporal lobes in monkeys. *Arch. Neurol. Psychiatry*, 42, 979–1000.

Kutcher, S.P., Blackwood, D.H.R., St. Clair, D., et al. (1987). Auditory P300 in borderline personality disorder and schizophrenia. *Arch. Gen. Psychiatry*, 44, 645–650.

Lewis, D.O., Pincus, J.H., Shanok, S.S., et al. (1982). Psychomotor epilepsy and violence in a group of incarcerated adolescent boys. *Am. J. Psychiatry*, 139, 882–887.

Lishman, W.A. (1968). Brain damage in relation to psychiatric disability after head injury. *Br. J. Psychiatry*, 114, 373–410.

Lishman, W.A. (1987). *Organic Psychiatry*, 2nd edn. Blackwell Scientific, Oxford.

Lombroso, C. (1874). *L'Uomo Delinquente*. Bocca, Torino.

Luria, A.R. (1980). *Higher Cortical Functions in Man*. Basic Books, New York.

MacLean, P.D. (1990). *The Triune Brain In Evolution: Role In Paleocerebral Functions*. Plenum, New York.

Macmillan, M.B. (1986). A wonderful journey through skull and brains: The travels of Mr. Gage's tamping iron. *Brain Cogn.*, 5, 67–107.

Marlowe, W.B., Mancall, E.L., and Thomas, J.J. (1975). Complete Klüver–Bucy syndrome in man. *Cortex*, 11, 53–59.

Miller, L. (1987). Neuropsychology of the aggressive psychopath: An integrative review. *Aggressive Behav.*, 13, 119–140.

Moffitt, T.E., and Henry, B. (1991). Neuropsychological studies of juvenile delinquency and violence: A review. In: *The Neuropsychology of Aggression* (ed. J.S. Milner). Kluwer Academic, Norwell.

Monroe, R.R. (1970). *Episodic Behavioral Disorders*. Harvard University Press, Cambridge, MA.

Naatanen, R., and Picton, T. (1987). The N1 wave of the human electric and magnetic response to sound: A review and an analysis of the component structure. *Psychophysiology*, 24, 375–425.

Nachson, I. (1988). Hemisphere function in violent offenders. In: *Biological Contributions to Crime Causation* (eds T.E. Moffitt and S.A. Mednick) pp. 55–67. Martinus Nijhoff, Dordrecht.

Narabayashi, H., Nagao, T., Saito, Y., et al. (1963). Stereotaxic amgydalotomy for behavior disorders. *Arch. Neurol.*, 9, 1–16.

O'Leary, K.M., Brouwers, P., Gardner, D.L., et al. (1991). Neuropsychological testing of patients with borderline personality disorder. *Am. J. Psychiatry*, 148, 106–111.

Ovsiew, F., and Yudofsky, S. (1993). Aggression: A neuropsychiatric perspective. In: *Rage, Power, and Aggression: The Role of Affect in Motivation, Development, and Adaptation* (eds R.A. Glick and S.P. Roose) pp. 213–230. Yale University Press, New Haven.

Pontius, A.A. (1972). Neurological aspects in some types of delinquency, especially among juveniles. *Adolescence*, 7, 289–308.

Prentice, N.M., and Kelly, F.J. (1963). Intelligence and delinquency: A reconsideration. *J. Soc. Psychol.*, 60, 327–337.

Quitkin, F.M., Rifkin, A., and Klein, D.F. (1976). Neurological soft signs in schizophrenia and character disorders: Organicity in schizophrenia with premorbid asociality and emotionally unstable character disorders. *Arch. Gen. Psychiatry*, 33, 845–853.

Raine, A., and Venables, P.H. (1987). Contingent negative variation, P3 evoked potentials and antisocial behavior. *Psychophysiology*, 24, 191–199.

Raine, A., and Venables, P.H. (1988). Enhanced P3 evoked potentials and longer P3 recovery times in psychopaths. *Psychophysiology*, 25, 30–38.

Reeves, A.G., and Plum, F. (1969). Hyperphagia, rage and dementia accompanying a ventromedial hypothalamus neoplasm. *Arch. Neurol.*, 20, 616–624.

Reis, D. (1974). Central neurotransmitters in aggression. *Res. Pul. Assoc. Res. Nerv. Ment. Dis.*, 52, 119–148.

Serafetinides, E.A. (1965). Aggressiveness in temporal lobe epileptics and its relation to cerebral dysfunction and environmental factors. *Epilepsia*, 6, 33–42.

Shafer, S.Q., Stokman, C.J., Shaffer, D., Ng, S.C., O'Connor, P.A., and Schonfeld, I.S. (1986). Ten-year consistency in neurological test performance of children without focal neurological deficit. *Dev. Med. Child Neurol.*, 28, 417–427.

Shaffer, D., Schonfeld, I.S., O'Connor, P.A., et al. (1985). Neurological soft signs and their relationship to psychiatric disorder and intelligence in childhood and adolescence. *Arch. Gen. Psychiatry*, 42, 342–351.

Siegel, A., and Edinger, H. (1981). Neural control of aggression and rage behavior. In: *Behavioral Studies of the Hypothalamus* (eds P.J. Morgan and J. Panskepp) pp. 303–340. Marcel Dekker, New York.

Singer, M.T. (1977). The borderline diagnosis and psychological tests: Review and research. In: *Borderline Personality Disorder* (ed. P. Hartocollis) pp. 193–212. International Universities Press, New York.

Snyder, S., and Pitts, W.M. (1984). Electroencephalography of DSM-III borderline personality disorders. *Acta Psychiatr. Scand.*, 69, 129–134.

Spellacy, F. (1978). Neuropsychological discrimination between violent and non-violent men. *J. Clin. Psychol.*, 34, 49–52.

Stein, D.J., Hollander, E., Cohen, L., et al. (1993a). Neuropsychiatric impairment in impulsive personality disorders. *Psychiatry Res.*, 48, 257–266.

Stein, D.J., Hollander, E., Chan, S., et al. (1993b). Computerized tomography and soft signs in obsessive–compulsive disorder. *Psychiatry Res.*, 50, 143–150.

Stein, D.J., Hollander, E., and Liebowitz, M.R. (1993c). Neurobiology of impulsivity and impulse control disorders. *J. Neuropsychiatry Clin. Neurosci*, 5, 9–17.

Stokman, C.J., Shafer, S.Q., Shaffer, D., Ng, S.C., O'Connor, P.A., and Wolff, R.M. (1986). Assessment of neurological soft signs in adolescents: Reliability studies. *Dev. Med. Child. Neurol.*, 28, 428–439.

Sutker, P.B., and Allain, A.N. (1987). Cognitive abstraction, shifting, and control: Clinical sample comparisons of psychopaths and nonpsychopaths. *J. Abnorm. Psychology*, 96, 73–75.

Syndulko, K. (1978). Electrocortical investigations of sociopathy. In: *Psychopathic Behavior: Approaches to Research* (eds R.D. Hare and D. Schalling). Wiley, New York.

Terzian, H., and Ore, J.D. (1955). Syndrome of Klüver and Bucy reproduced in man by bilateral removal of the temporal lobes. *Neurology*, 5, 373–380.

Tonkonogy, J.M. (1991). Violence and temporal lobe lesion: Head CT and MRI data. *J. Neuropsychiatry Clin. Neurosci.*, 3, 189–196.

Vitiello, B., Stoff, D., Atkins, M., and Mahoney, A. (1990). Soft neurological signs and impulsivity in children. *J. Devel. Behav. Pediatr.*, 11, 112–115.

Volavka, J. (1990). Aggression, electroencephalography, and evoked potentials. *Neuropsychiatr. Neuropsychol. Behav. Neurol.*, 3, 249–259.

Wasman, M., and Flynn, J.P. (1962). Directed attack elicited from the hypothalamus. *Arch. Neurol.*, 6, 220–227.

Weiger, W.E., and Bear, D.M. (1988). An approach to the neurology of aggression. *J. Psychiat. Res.*, 22, 85–98.

Wechler, D. (1958). *The Measurement and Appraisal of Adult Intelligence*. Williams & Wilkins, Maryland.

Williamson, S., Harpur, T.J., and Hare, R.D. (1991). Abnormal processing of affective words by psychopaths. *Psychophysiology*, 28, 260–273.

Yeudall, L.T., and Fromm-Auch, D. (1979). Neuropsychological impairments in various psychopathological populations. In: *Hemisphere Asymmetries of Function in Psychopathology* (eds J. Gruzelier and P. Flor-Henry). Elsevier, Amsterdam.

Yeudall, L.T., and Wardell, D.M. (1978). Neuropsychological correlates of criminal psychopathy: Part 2. Discrimination and prediction of dangerous and recidivist offenders. In: *Human Aggression and its Dangerousness* (eds L. Beliveau, G. Canepa, and D. Szabo). Pinel Institute, Montreal.

Part III

DISORDERS OF IMPULSE CONTROL

8 Disorders of Impulse Control

SUSAN L McELROY*, HARRISON G POPE Jr‡, PAUL E KECK
Jr*, AND JAMES I HUDSON‡
*Biological Psychiatry Program, University of Cincinnati College of
Medicine, Cincinnati, OH, USA
‡ Biological Psychiatry Laboratory, Laboratories for Psychiatric Research,
McLean Hospital, Belmont, MA, and Harvard Medical School, Boston, MA,
USA

> *The kleptomaniacs in the old sense cannot even resist the impulse of*
> *appropriating things, and here again it is done regardless of whether they*
> *can make use of the things or not, they hoard them, give them away,*
> *destroy them, and under conditions they even return them to the rightful*
> *owners. The morality of such people may in other respects be quite good.*
>
> Bleuler (1988) p. 539

INTRODUCTION

Despite being recognized since at least the early 19th century, the impulse
control disorders (ICDs) remain a poorly understood group of conditions
that have received little systematic study. Indeed, even their diagnostic
validity, individually and as a category, remains in question. Authors
doubting the legitimacy of the ICDs have generally argued that afflicted
individuals do not really experience impulses that are irresistible, but,
rather, have voluntary control over their impulsive behaviors, or that their
impulsive behaviors are nonspecific symptoms due to other primary psychiatric or medical disorders (Everts, 1887; Antheaume, 1925; Peele, 1989).
Nevertheless, many have argued that the irresistible impulse is a valid
psychopathological symptom and that the ICDs are legitimate mental disorders that are more common than is realized, cause significant morbidity,
and are treatable. The purpose of this chapter is to provide an overview of
the available research on the ICDs, with special focus on their epidemiology, phenomenology, comorbidity, family history, biology, response to
somatic and psychosocial treatments, and relationship to other psychiatric
disorders in general.

Impulsivity and Aggression. Edited by E. Hollander and D.J. Stein
© 1995 John Wiley & Sons Ltd

HISTORY, DEFINITION, AND CLINICAL DESCRIPTION

Although broadly defined as mental disorders characterized by irresistible impulses to perform harmful acts, ICDs have been variously labelled and described by different authors. In 1816 Matthey used "klopemanie" to describe the impulsive stealing of worthless objects, and in 1820 Meckel mentioned "impulsive incendiarism" to describe impulsive fire setting (Lacey and Evans, 1986). In 1838, Esquirol introduced the term "monomanias" to describe conditions in which individuals performed acts which they deplored and did not want to do in response to irresistible impulses; arson, alcoholism, impulsive homicide, and, included later, kleptomania are examples (McElroy et al., 1991a). In the introduction to his chapter on monomanias in *Des Maladies Mentales,* Esquirol (1838, p. 332, translated by H.G. Pope Jr) stresses their irresistible, uncontrollable, and involuntary features:

> . . . voluntary control is profoundly compromised: the patient is constrained to perform acts which are dictated neither by his reason nor by his emotions—acts which his conscience disapproves of, but over which he no longer has willful control; the actions are involuntary, instinctive, irresistible, it is *monomania without delirium* or *instinctive monomania.*

Later in this chapter (1838, p. 337) he writes:

> . . . the irresistible impulses show all of the features of passion elevated to the point of delirium; the patients, furious or otherwise, are drawn *irresistibly* to acts which they repudiate. They can reason and judge about these acts perfectly sanely, just as well as anybody else; they deplore these acts and make efforts to conquer their impulses: are they not therefore a lucid period? Soon afterward the "paroxysm" follows the period of remission. Again prey to their delirium, these monomaniacs are carried away; they yield to their impulse, and reason no longer can control them. Obeying the impulse which presses upon them, they forget the motives that controlled them an instant earlier; they see nothing but the object of their fixation, much like a man who is prey to a powerful moral affectation and sees nothing but the object of his passion.

At the turn of the century Kraepelin (1915) and Bleuler (1988) used the terms pathological impulses and reactive impulses, respectively, to describe these conditions, and included pyromania, kleptomania, buying mania (oniomania), morbid collecting, impulses "to give every one a present", anonymous letter writing, and impulsive poison mixing as examples. Kraepelin (1915) concluded that the motive of one woman's shopping impulses was an attraction to danger, unrest, and excitement, and likened her impulsive shopping to the behavior of the gambler. Both authors stressed the impulsive features of these conditions, including how they may be enacted in an altered state of awareness. In describing buying mania, for example, Bleuler (1988, p. 540) writes:

> The particular element is impulsiveness; they "cannot help it", which sometimes even expresses itself in the fact that not withstanding a good school intelligence, the patients are absolutely incapable to think differently, and to

conceive the senseless consequences of their act, and the possibilities of not doing it. They do not even feel the impulse, but they act out of their nature like the caterpillar which devours the leaves.

Both authors also noted that these disorders had compulsive features, stressing the uncontrollable and senseless nature of the impulses; their association with anxiety, tension, and other negative or unpleasant feelings; and how they can be resisted as well as enacted impulsively. In describing pyromania, for example, Bleuler (1988, p. 539) states:

> The perpetrators of the act cannot find, as a rule, any adequate reason, unless the prosecutor examines it into them; the act is so little their own that even if they are otherwise of a normal nature they cannot even display the proper regret . . . The act is sometimes preceded by distinct moodiness with anxiety, "homesickness", digestive, and similar disturbances. During the accomplishment of the act some seem to be in a kind of twilight state, while others reflect and go through a conscious struggle between their impulse and their morality. In some the impulse comes suddenly and is at once put in operation, leaving no time for an actual reflection.

Touching upon the relationship between the irresistible impulse and impulsivity in general, Frosch and Wortis (1954) divided the "impulse disorders" into two major groups based on whether the abnormal impulsivity was a discrete symptom or a pervasive characterological feature. The first group, characterized by "one or many, more or less isolated impulsive acts usually of a recurring quality", included three subgroups: the impulse neuroses (kleptomania, pyromania, and addictions), the perversions or impulsive sexual deviations (e.g. the paraphilias), and catathymic crisis (an isolated, nonrepetitive act of violence). The second group, also called the character impulse disorders and characterized by "a diffuseness of the impulse disturbance which permeates the personality without specifically attaching itself to any one kind of impulse", included three subgroups: organic syndrome, psychopathic personality, and neurotic character disorder. Describing these conditions further, Frosch and Wortis (1954) defined an impulse as "the sudden unpremeditated welling-up of a drive toward some action, which usually has the quality of hastiness and a lack of deliberation", and "morbid" impulses as characterized by "minimal distortion of the original impulse" and an "irresistible and impelling quality in a setting of extreme tension". Differentiating them from obsessive compulsive symptoms, Frosch and Wortis stated that impulse disorders were further characterized by ego-syntonicity ("the impulse is wholly or partly in harmony with the momentary aims of the psyche") and a pleasurable component at the moment of expression.

Despite this extensive historical literature, the ICDs were not included in the *Diagnostic and Statistical Manual of Mental Disorders* (DSM) until publication of the third edition (DSM-III; American Psychiatric Association, 1980). In DSM-IV (American Psychiatric Association, 1994), the essential feature of an ICD is the failure to resist an impulse, drive, or temptation to perform some act that is harmful to the person or others. DSM-IV further stipulates that for most ICDs, the individual feels an increasing sense of tension or arousal before committing the act, and then experiences pleasure, gratification, or relief at the time the act is committed. After the act is performed, there may or may not be genuine regret, self-reproach, or guilt. Thus, ICD symptoms may be at times ego-syntonic—particularly when relief or even pleasure is experienced at the moment when they are enacted. But, they may also be experienced as ego-dystonic, with the impulses associated with tension or anxiety and the behaviors generating self-reproach, shame, or guilt.

Although the DSM-III, DSM-III-R, and DSM-IV define ICDs similarly and include them under residual categories (neither has a formal category for ICDs), there are minor differences. In the DSM-III, pathological gambling, kleptomania, pyromania, intermittent explosive disorder (IED), isolated explosive disorder, and atypical impulse control disorder are listed under the heading "disorders of impulse control not elsewhere classified". In the DSM-III-R and DSM-IV, these same disorders are listed in the category "impulse control disorders not elsewhere classified", except for the addition of trichotillomania and the deletion of isolated explosive disorder. Also, atypical impulse control disorder was changed to impulse control disorder not otherwise specified. Although specific examples are not provided, potential members of this latter residual category include compulsive buying or shopping (also called buying mania, oniomania, and dressing disorder), compulsive sexual behavior (also called sexual compulsions or nonparaphilic sexual addictions), compulsive facial or skin picking, severe onychophagia (nail biting), some forms of self-injurious behavior [also called repetitive self-mutilation (RSM), autoaggressive behavior, and deliberate self-harm], and binge eating (Frankenburg and Yurgelun-Todd, 1984; Popkin, 1989; Leonard et al., 1991; Winchell and Stanley, 1991; Favazza, 1992; McElroy et al., 1992 and 1994; Favazza and Rosenthal, 1993; Anthony and Hollander, 1993; Christianson et al., 1994). Alcohol and psychoactive substance use disorders, the paraphilias and antisocial personality disorder, although not described as ICDs in the DSM-IV, are given as examples of such in the residual category where ICDs are defined. Personality disorders with impulsive features are categorized as personality disorders, and binge eating is classified as an eating disorder. It is worthy of note that, although there will be minor modifications of the diagnostic criteria for IED, pathological gambling, and trichotillomania, substantive changes in the definition or classification of the ICDs have not been proposed for the DSM-IV. Thus, IED was not deleted, despite concerns that it presents only as an associated feature of another Axis I or Axis II disorder (American Psychiatric Association, 1991). And recommendations to include RSM as a formal ICD were rejected because of concerns that self-mutilation is usually a symptom of borderline personality disorder (Favazza, 1992; see Chapter 12).

It is not entirely clear why some, but not all, of these individual conditions are grouped together. For example, although the DSM-III-R characterizes ICDs by the inability to resist an impulse, drive, or temptation to perform a harmful act, it does not explicitly require this criterion for pathological gambling, pyromania, or the alcohol and psychoactive substance use disorders—presumably because some individuals with these disorders do not experience irresistible impulses. Because of recent research showing that some patients with apparent trichotillomania do *not* experience irresistible impulses to pull hair, mounting tension preceding hair pulling, and/or relief following hair pulling, it has been argued that the DSM-III-R criteria for trichotillomania and, by extension, the DSM-III-R definition of an ICD, are too narrow (Christenson et al., 1991a). Indeed, as alluded to above, some have argued that the ICDs should include all disorders characterized by irresistible impulses and/or problematic impulsive behavior [including binge eating, the paraphilias, alcohol and drug abuse, RSM, the impulsive personality disorders, and even obsessive compulsive disorder (OCD)] (Frosch and Wortis, 1954; Popkin, 1989; López-Ibor, 1990; Kavoussi and Caccaro, 1993). In this chapter, we will focus on those disorders approximating the original and modern conceptualizations of an ICD (the performance of harmful acts in response to irresistible impulses), realizing that there may be subsyndromal or atypical variants of ICDs and that the relationship of the irresistible impulse to impulsivity and compulsivity has not been well studied (McElroy et al., 1991a, 1993; Stein and Hollander, 1993).

PREVALENCE, PATIENT CHARACTERISTICS, COURSE, AND ASSOCIATED FEATURES

Most ICDs are presumed to be rare. Three recent self-report surveys of hair pulling among college students found that only 0.6, 1.0, and 0.005%, respectively, of the populations assessed met the DSM-III-R criteria for trichotillomania (Christenson et al., 1991d; Rothbaum et al., 1993). The prevalence of persons engaging in self-injurious behavior has been estimated to range from 0.04 to 0.07% of the population per year (Whitehead et al., 1972, 1973; Pattison and Kahan, 1983; Favazza and Conterio, 1988). Although behaviors such as impulsive aggressive acts (often called uncontrollable rage, temper outbursts, or episodic dyscontrol), fire setting, shoplifting, gambling, hair pulling, alcohol and drug abuse, and sexual abuse are common in the general population, studies generally have not systematically assessed the proportion of these behaviors performed in response to irresistible impulses. Those studies that have suggest that only a small portion of individuals perform these behaviors in response to irresistible impulses and thus represent cases of true ICDs (Lewis and Yarnell, 1951; Gibbens and

Prince, 1962; Robbins and Robbins, 1967; Moran, 1970; Bach-y-Rita et al., 1971; Bradford, 1982; Bradford and Balmaceda, 1983; Prins et al., 1985; Christenson et al., 1991; McElroy et al., 1992; Rothbaum et al., 1993). Furthermore, in studies of impulsive aggression, many of the individuals do not appear to have IED according to the DSM-III-R criteria, because the aggression is attributed to a primary neurological or organic mental disorder (Elliott, 1976).

However, for most of the established and potential ICDs, systematic studies using operational diagnostic criteria to determine prevalence rates in the general population have not been done. Thus, there are no systematic data regarding the general population prevalence rates of DSM-III-R defined IED, kleptomania, pyromania, or paraphilias; of potential ICDs such as compulsive buying, compulsive picking, compulsive sexual behavior, and binge eating; and thus, of ICDs in general. Also, studies indicate that pathological gambling (the only ICD for which systematic prevalence data are available) is common and that its prevalence is increasing (Lesieur and Rosenthal, 1991; see Chapter 9). Indeed, a recent large-scale epidemiological survey of psychiatric morbidity in a Chinese community using the Diagnostic Interview Schedule found a lifetime prevalence of DSM-III pathological gambling of 3.0% among men and 0.16% among women (Chen et al., 1993). Also, among men, pathological gambling was the third most common psychiatric disorder. Although similar studies have not yet been carried out for compulsive buying, an expanding consumer behavior literature suggests that it may also be frequent, afflicting 1.1–5.9% of the general population, depending on how narrowly or broadly it is defined (Aber and O'Guinn, 1991). Also, lifetime prevalence rates of bulimia nervosa in girls and women range from 1.7 to 4.2% (Kendler et al., 1991), the frequency of current binge eating in women has been estimated to be 35% (Fairburn and Beglin, 1990), and estimates of binge eating in overweight adults seeking treatment for weight loss range from 23 to 82% (O'Neil and Jarrell, 1992). Furthermore, impulsive aggression, impulsive fire setting, and self-injurious behavior are common among prison populations (Winchel and Stanley, 1991).

 In short, the apparent rarity of the ICDs may not be real for a number of reasons. First, prevalence rates of most ICDs in the general population have not yet been systematically determined; those ICDs that have been studied appear to be common. Second, ICDs may not always be associated with impulses, tension, or relief, and thus current diagnostic criteria may be too narrow (McElroy et al., 1991a). Third, the ICDs are "secret disorders" and, thus, their apparent rarity may be due in large part to afflicted individuals concealing their symptoms. It is therefore noteworthy that many ICDs, including IED, kleptomania, trichotillomania, the paraphilias, RSM, and binge eating, have been hypothesized to be more common than realized (Maletzky, 1973; Kilmann et al., 1982; Favazza and Conterio, 1988;

McCann and Agras, 1990; McElroy, et al. 1991a; Swedo and Rapoport, 1991; Swedo, 1993).

Although few systematic data are available, ICDs appear to have different sex ratios. Thus, IED, pathological gambling, pyromania, compulsive sexual behavior, and the paraphilias appear to be more common in men, whereas kleptomania, trichotillomania, compulsive shopping, RSM, and binge eating appear to be more common in women (McElroy et al., 1992a). In contrast, the ICDs do appear to share similar ages of onset and courses. Many cases begin in adolescence or early adulthood (although a substantial number may also begin in childhood or late adulthood), and follow an episodic or chronic course. It has been suggested that episodic dyscontrol and RSM may decrease in severity or frequency with increasing age (Maletzky, 1973; Favazza and Rosenthal, 1993). However, there are few systematic studies of the natural course of most of the ICDs, and little is known about their evolution with advanced age.

Furthermore, few systematic data are available on the associated features of the ICDs. Nevertheless, episodic dyscontrol has been associated with various neurological abnormalities (Maletzky, 1973; Elliot, 1976), and RSM has been associated with childhood sexual and/or physical abuse (Favazza and Conterio, 1989). Also, increased access to shopping and gambling has been associated with increased rates of shoplifting and problematic gambling, respectively (Dubuisson, 1901; Rosenthal, 1993).

ASSOCIATED PSYCHOPATHOLOGY AND COMORBIDITY

There are no controlled studies examining the associated psychopathology and/or comorbidity of any of the ICDs. Nevertheless, operational diagnostic criteria have been used to systematically assess associated psychopathology in four studies of impulsive aggression ($n = 24$), three of which used the same cohort of patients and were extensions of the first (Linnoila et al., 1983; Virkkunen et al., 1989); in one study of kleptomania ($n = 20$) (McElroy et al., 1991b); in three cohorts of patients with pathological gambling ($n = 99$) (McCormick et al., 1984; Linden et al., 1986; Roy et al., 1988); in two studies of trichotillomania ($n = 64$) (Swedo et al., 1989; Christenson et al., 1991a); and in three studies of compulsive buying ($n = 80$) (Christenson et al., 1994; McElroy et al., 1994; Schlosser et al., 1994). All but two of these studies showed high lifetime rates of comorbid mood disorder. Thus, 83 (84%) of 99 pathological gamblers, all (100%) of 20 kleptomanic patients, 46 (62%) of 64 trichotillomanic persons, and 45 (56%) of 80 compulsive buyers displayed mood disorder. In one of the negative studies, only one of 124 patients with impulsive aggression (18 of whom had IED as defined by the DSM-III criteria) had concomitant major depression

(Virkkunen et al., 1989). In the other, Christenson et al. (in press) found that 24 compulsive buyers recruited by newspaper advertisement were no more likely to have a mood disorder, compared with 24 normal spenders. However, the compulsive buyers displayed a higher rate of generalized anxiety disorder (GAD) (which is viewed by some to be a prodrome or variant of major mood disorder) (Dubovsky, 1990) and higher ratings on scales measuring depression, anxiety, and compulsiveness.

We have not been able to find comparable studies of DSM-III-R pyromania. However, in a study of 22 impulsive arsonists [some of whom presumably met the DSM-III-R criteria for pyromania and 15 (68%) of whom also met the DSM-III criteria for IED], 21 (95%) met the DSM-III criteria for dysthymia or major depression (Virkkunen et al., 1989). Furthermore, in a recent study of 72 female "psychopaths" meeting the DSM-III criteria for borderline personality disorder, 69 (96%) of whom reported "compulsions to carry out at least one form of deviant or criminal activity", 51 (71%) met lifetime DSM-III criteria for major depression, 18 (25%) for mania/atypical bipolar disorder, and 19 (26%) for dysthymia (Coid, 1993). Of note was that the deviant behaviors included self-mutilation (93% of patients), property damage (82%), anorectic episodes (78%), fire setting (76%), assaultiveness (76%), drug overdoses (76%), thefts (61%), binge eating (58%), alcohol abuse (50%), homicidal urges/fantasies (44%), promiscuity (38%), and drug abuse (36%). Further supporting a relationship between ICDs and mood disorder are case reports and small case series describing comorbid mood disorders in patients with apparent IED (Fava et al., 1990), apparent pyromania (Warner, 1932), kleptomania (McElroy et al., 1991a), compulsive buying (McElroy et al., 1991c), various paraphilias and sexual compulsions (Kafka 1991; Stein et al., 1992), and RSM (Favazza and Rosenthal 1993); high rates of mood disorders in individuals with bulimia nervosa (Keck et al., 1990) and in obese people who binge eat without purging (McCann and Agras et al., 1990); and high rates of suicide attempts in patients with episodic dyscontrol (Maletzky, 1973), pathological gambling (Moran, 1969), and RSM (Favazza, 1992).

Several studies have compared the age at onset of the ICD with that of the comorbid mood disorder. In 20 patients with concomitant kleptomania and mood disorder, the onset of mood disorder preceded the onset of kleptomania by at least 1 year in 12 (60%), occurred within the same year in three (15%), and occurred after the onset of kleptomania in five (25%) (McElroy et al., 1991b). Of 19 patients with comorbid compulsive buying and mood disorder, 14 reported the onset of depression before, and eight after, the onset of compulsive buying. And in a study of 25 pathological gamblers, 18 (72%) experienced major depressive episodes around the time they first stopped gambling, and 13 (52%) patients experienced additional major affective episodes (major depression in 11 and mania in two) either before or after they stopped gambling (Linden et al., 1986).

Although the mood disorder most often comorbid with ICDs is major depression, particularly high rates of bipolar disorders (Type I, Type II, and cyclothymia) have been reported in patients with kleptomania (McElroy et al., 1991b), pathological gambling (McCormick et al., 1984; Linden et al., 1986), and compulsive buying (McElroy et al., 1994). Moreover, some patients described relationships between their ICD and affective symptoms, stating that their irresistible impulses would change in intensity or frequency when they were depressed or manic, or that their impulsive behaviors would affect their affective symptoms. Some patients reported that stealing, gambling, or shopping produced a pleasurable "rush" that alleviated their depressive symptoms, and likened this rush to their spontaneously occurring hypomanias (McElroy et al., 1991b). We have recently observed several bipolar patients with kleptomania whose stealing impulses and behavior increased when they experienced antidepressant-induced rapid cycling and/ or dysphoric hypomania. Interestingly, in Coid's (1993) study of 72 female psychopaths meeting the DSM-III criteria for borderline personality disorder, 96% of whom reported compulsions to perform at least one form of deviant behavior, 18 (25%) met the DSM-III criteria for a lifetime history of mania or atypical bipolar disorder—despite current symptoms of mania or major depression at the time of interview being an exclusion criterion (Coid, 1993). Coid further noted that 55 (76%) of the patients described "a marked bipolar quality" to their affective instability, that the sense of compulsion associated with their deviant activities increased with increased intensity of their affective symptoms, and that enactment of the deviant behaviors, especially self-mutilation, often relieved these symptoms.

Studies have also shown high rates of concomitant anxiety, alcohol and psychoactive substance abuse, and eating disorders in patients with ICDs. Of 24 impulsive offenders, 18 of whom met the DSM-III criteria for IED, all met the DSM-III criteria for alcohol abuse (Virkkunen et al., 1989). Of 20 patients with kleptomania, 16 (80%) met lifetime DSM-III-R criteria for at least one anxiety disorder (panic disorder, agoraphobia, social phobia, simple phobia, and/or OCD); 12 (60%) met criteria for an eating disorder; and 10 (50%) met criteria for a psychoactive substance use disorder (most commonly alcohol, amphetamine, or cocaine) (McElroy et al., 1991b). Of 49 pathological gamblers from two studies, 11 (22%) had at least one anxiety disorder, including OCD, panic disorder, GAD, and simple phobia (Linden et al., 1986; Roy et al., 1988). Of 100 pathological gamblers from three studies, 42 (42%) had histories of alcohol or substance abuse (Ramirez et al., 1983; Linden et al., 1986; Roy et al., 1988); and in a study of female pathological gamblers, 20% called themselves compulsive overeaters (Lesieur, 1988). In two studies, 39 out of 74 patients (53%) with trichotillomania had histories of anxiety disorders, and 17 (23%) had histories of alcohol or drug abuse (Swedo et al., 1989; Christenson et al., 1991a). In one study of 20 compulsive buyers, 16 (80%) had a lifetime diagnosis of an anxiety disorder (panic disorder, social phobia, simple phobia, and/or OCD), eight (40%) had a history of alcohol or substance abuse, and seven (35%) had a history of an eating disorder (McElroy et al., 1994). In another study, 24 compulsive buyers had significantly higher lifetime rates of GAD, alcohol abuse or dependence, and the proposed DSM-IV diagnosis of binge eating disorder than 24 normal spenders (Christenson et al., 1994). And in a study of 22 impulsive arsonists, 21 (95%) met criteria for alcohol abuse (Virkkunen et al., 1989).

These findings are supported by numerous case reports and case series of individuals with apparent ICDs who also have concurrent OCD, panic disorder, eating disorders, or alcohol or substance abuse (McElroy et al., 1992). Studies have also shown relatively high rates of impulsive stealing or kleptomania in patients with eating disorders (Hudson et al., 1983; McElroy et al., 1991a), high rates of pathological or problem gambling in alcoholics (Lesieur et al., 1986), and, for episodic dyscontrol and pathological gambling, a relationship with attention deficit disorder (Bach-Y-Rita et al., 1971; Maletzky, 1973; Carlton et al., 1987; Mattes, 1990). Finally, individuals with one ICD may have high rates of other ICDs (Lacey and Evans, 1986). Eight (40%) of 20 patients with kleptomania in one study (McElroy et al., 1991b) and 13 (29%) of 20 patients with compulsive buying in two other studies (Christenson et al., in press; McElroy et al., in press) had a lifetime history of at least one other ICD. Also, women who are pathological gamblers have been reported to have high rates of compulsive shopping and sexual addictions (Lesieur, 1988; Lesieur and Rosenthal, 1991); and self-injurious behaviors have been noted to occur in pathological gamblers (McCormick et al., 1984), women with eating disorders (Favazza et al., 1989), men with episodic dyscontrol (Bach-Y-Rita et al., 1971), and female arsonists (Tennent et al., 1971).

Although personality disorders with impulsive features (especially borderline and antisocial personality disorders) have been hypothesized to be primarily disorders of impulse control, the relationship between personality disorders and ICDs has not been well studied (see Chapter 10). There are few studies using structured diagnostic instruments to assess personality disorders in individuals with ICDs or, conversely, to assess ICDs in individuals with personality disorders. Nevertheless, preliminary studies suggest that some ICDs, including IED, pyromania, pathological gambling, and RSM, may be associated with impulsive personality disorders and/or antisocial behaviors. Of 54 violent offenders and impulsive fire setters, 29 of whom had DSM-III IED, 37 (69%) had borderline and nine (17%) had antisocial personality disorders, whereas six (11%) had paranoid and five (9%) had passive–aggressive personality disorders (by the DSM-III criteria) (Linnoila et al., 1989). Of 51 adult chronic hair pullers evaluated with the Structured Clinical Interview for DSM-III-R Personality Disorders (SCID-II) (Spitzer and Williams, 1986), 21 (41%) met the DSM-III-R criteria for at least one personality disorder, with histrionic personality disorder being the most common (13.7%) (Christenson and Chernoff, 1991). Furthermore, pathological gamblers have been shown to have elevated scores on the psychopathic deviation (pd) scale of the Minnesota Multiphasic Personality Inventory (MMPI), to engage in a wide variety of illegal behaviors, and to have possibly increased rates of antisocial and narcissistic personality disorders (Moran, 1970; Blaszczynski et al., 1989; Lesieur and Rosenthal, 1991). However, in the study by Christenson and Chernoff (1991), avoidant, dependent, and obsessive compulsive personality disorders were the most common personality disorders after histrionic in their group of trichotillomanic patients. In our study of 20 individuals with kleptomania, although some engaged in isolated antisocial behaviors other than stealing, none met the DSM-III-R criteria for antisocial personality disorder (McElroy et al., 1991b). And despite binge eating being listed as a symptom of borderline personality disorder, Herzog et al. (1992) found that of 210 women seeking treatment for anorexia nervosa, bulimia nervosa, or both, assessed with the SCID-II (27% of whom had at least one personality disorder), only 18 (9%) met criteria for borderline personality disorder.

Nevertheless, high rates of RSM, episodic dyscontrol, and other impulsive harmful behaviors have been reported in patients with borderline, antisocial, and histrionic personality disorders (Virkkunen, 1976; Pattison and Kahan, 1983). However, many of the specific behaviors of ICDs overlap with those listed as diagnostic criteria for these personality disorders. For example, two of the DSM-III-R criteria for borderline personality disorder are: (1) "impulsiveness in at least two areas that are potentially self-damaging, e.g., spending, sex, substance use, shopping, reckless driving, binge eating"; and (2) "recurrent suicidal threats, gestures, or behavior, or self-mutilating behavior". Since few studies have evaluated whether personality disorder patients perform these behaviors in response to irresistible impulses, it is unknown whether there are in fact high rates of bona fide ICDs among individuals with impulsive personality disorders, or whether the impulsive acts of ICDs and personality disorders are distinct phenomena. Interestingly, in his study of 72 female psychopaths detained in three British maximum-security hospitals and meeting the DSM-III criteria for borderline personality disorder, 69 (96%) of whom reported compulsions to carry out deviant or criminal behaviors, Coid (1993) reported that these behaviors were sometimes described as "impossible to resist" and frequently followed by symptom relief. Coid also noted, however, that the population of patients chosen for study was highly unusual, and thus possibly not representative of individuals with personality disorders or ICDs in general. In short, because available data are insufficient, it is unknown whether ICDs and impulsive personality disorders represent separate but related conditions that are highly comorbid, identical entities (with impulsive personality disorders possibly representing the most severe cases or persons with multiple ICDs), or independent entities that may co-occur by chance, but which are easily misdiagnosed as one or the other.

FAMILY STUDIES

At present, there are no controlled family history studies of individuals with ICDs. However, open studies have found relatively high rates of mood and substance use disorders in first-degree relatives of individuals with IED or episodic dyscontrol (Bach-Y-Rita et al., 1971; Maletzky, 1973; Linnoila et al., 1983; Virkkunen et al., 1989; Mattes and Fink, 1987; Linnoila et al., 1989), kleptomania (McElroy et al., 1991b), pathological gambling (McCormick et al., 1984; Linden et al., 1986; Roy et al., 1988), and compulsive buying (McElroy et al., in press). Of 54 violent offenders and impulsive fire setters (29 of whom had DSM-III IED and 52 of whom had DSM-III alcohol abuse), Linnoila et al. (1989) found that 44 (81%) had first- or second-degree relatives with alcoholism and 35 (65%) had alcoholic fathers. Also, subjects with alcoholic fathers were more often impulsive and had a lower mean cerebrospinal fluid (CSF) 5-hydroxyindoleacetic acid (5-HIAA) concentration than subjects without alcoholic fathers. Our group reported that of 103 first-degree relatives of 20 individuals with kleptomania (McElroy et al., 1991b), 22 (21%) had a major mood disorder and 21 (20%) had an alcohol or substance abuse disorder. Similarly, Ramirez et al. (1983) reported that 50% of 51 pathological gamblers each had an alcoholic parent, and Roy et al. (1988) reported that 33% and 25% of 24 pathological gamblers had a first-degree relative with mood disorder and alcohol abuse, respectively. Other studies, however, have found lower rates. For example, of 132 first-degree relatives of 33 patients with temper outbursts (22 of whom had DSM-III IED), Mattes and Fink (1987) reported that 11% had depression and 8% had alcohol or drug abuse. And Linden et al. (1986) found that among 175 first-degree relatives of 25 pathological gamblers, 18 (10%) displayed a major mood disorder and 19 (11%) displayed alcohol abuse or dependence.

Other findings include relatively high rates of anxiety disorders in the families of individuals with kleptomania (McElroy et al., 1991b) and trichotillomania (Swedo and Rapoport, 1991); high rates of violent behavior and attention deficit hyperactivity disorder (ADHD; Mattes and Fink, 1987) in the families of individuals with episodic dyscontrol (Bach-Y-Rita et al., 1971; Maletzky, 1973; Mattes and Fink, 1987); and possibly higher than normal rates of the same ICD in the families of patients with IED (6.9%; Mattes and Fink, 1987), kleptomania (2%; McElroy et al., 1991b), pathological gambling (23%; Ramirez et al., 1983), and trichotillomania (5%; Swedo and Rapoport, 1991). Finally, Winokur et al. (1969) have reported a high prevalence of pathological gambling in the families of individuals with bipolar disorder.

STUDIES OF BIOLOGICAL TESTS

Biological studies of the ICDs have primarily examined serotonin (5-hydroxytryptamine, 5-HT), norepinephrine (NE—noradrenaline), and/or dopamine (DA) neurotransmission, and, to a lesser extent, hypothalmic–pituitary–adrenal axis function, glucose metabolism, opiate system function, neurological findings, and positron emission tomography. They have focused on individuals with impulsive aggression, impulsive fire setting, self-injurious behavior, pathological gambling, and trichotillomania (Winchel and Stanley, 1991; McElroy et al., 1992; Ninan et al., 1992). Some of this research will be briefly discussed below; for a thorough review of these findings, see Chapter 6.

The most consistent findings in individuals with ICDs have been abnormalities in serotonergic neurotransmission (Stein et al., 1993). For instance, in a study of 58 violent offenders and impulsive fire setters, 33 (57%) of whom had DSM-III IED, Virkkunen et al. (1989) found lower CSF concentrations of 5-HIAA and 3-methoxy-4-hydroxyphenylglycol (MHPG) in the impulsive offenders and fire setters than in the non-impulsive offenders and normal control subjects. Moreover, low CSF 5-HIAA and MHPG concentrations were associated with a lifetime history of suicide attempts. Brown et al. (1989) found that mean platelet [^{3}H]5-HT uptake was significantly lower in 15 male outpatients with episodic aggression than in 15 nonaggressive comparison subjects. In a study of 21 patients with major depression, the five patients who exhibited self-aggressive behaviors had significantly lower CSF 5-HIAA concentrations than the other 16 patients (López-Ibor et al., 1985). In a controlled study of subjects with RSM and borderline personality disorder, Simeon et al. (1992) similarly found that lower serotonergic activity (as measured by platelet imipramine binding sites and affinity) was related to greater severity of self-mutilation. And, although CSF concentrations of 5-HIAA, homovanillic acid (HVA), MHPG, and cortisol in eight women with trichotillomania (diagnostic criteria not specified) were not different from those of controls and did not correlate with baseline scores of severity of trichotillomania symptomatology, the degree of response to treatment with 5-HT reuptake inhibitors (SRIs) was significantly negatively correlated with baseline CSF 5-HIAA concentrations (Ninan et al., 1992).

In contrast, Roy et al. (1988) reported that individuals who were pathological gamblers by the DSM-III-R criteria had significantly lower plasma MHPG concentrations, greater centrally produced fractions of CSF MHPG, and greater urinary output of NE than comparison subjects, but similar CSF 5-HIAA concentrations. In a subsequent study of 17 pathological gamblers, Roy et al. (1989) found highly significant positive correlations between measures of extraversion and indices of noradrenergic function, including concentrations of CSF MHPG, plasma MHPG, urinary vanillylmandelic acid, and the sum of urinary NE and its major metabolites. Because noradrenergic systems play a role in arousal, and because arousal (or excitement) may be important in the genesis of pathological gambling, Roy et al. concluded that state or trait disturbances in central noradrenergic function might underlie pathological gambling (see Chapter 9). However, pharmacological challenge tests with clomipramine in pathological gamblers have revealed a blunted prolactin response, suggesting serotonergic dysfunction (Moreno et al., 1991). Although available data do not permit firm conclusions, perhaps interactions between the serotonergic and noradrenergic neurotransmitter systems are important in the genesis of ICDs, with serotonergic abnormalities underlying some of their compulsive features (e.g. irresistibility) and noradrenergic abnormalities underlying some of their impulsive features (i.e. pleasure with enactment). Indeed, women with bulimia nervosa have been shown to have alterations in central 5-HT and NE activity. Because serotonergic systems appear to inhibit eating whereas noradrenergic systems appear to facilitate it, it has been similarly hypothesized that binge eating may reflect underactivity of hypothalamic serotonergic systems, hyperactivity of hypothalamic nonadrenergic systems, or a combination of both defects (Kaye and Weltzin, 1991).

RESPONSE TO TREATMENT

Few studies have systematically examined the treatment of patients with ICDs. Regarding psychological treatments, there have been three controlled studies and numerous case reports and case series suggesting that various forms of behavior therapy may be effective in pathological gambling, trichotillomania, kleptomania, the paraphilias, and sexual compulsions (Azrin et al., 1980; Kilmann et al., 1982; McConaghy et al., 1983; Allcock, 1986; Swedo and Rapoport, 1991; McElroy et al., 1991a and 1992). In one of the controlled trials, a three-arm crossover comparisons in 12 men with exhibitionism, electrical aversion was more effective than self-regulation techniques, with relaxation being of no efficacy (Rooth and Marks, 1974). In another, habit reversal was twice as effective as negative practice training in suppressing hair pulling in 34 patients with trichotillomania (Azrin et al., 1980). And in the third controlled study, imaginal desensitization was more effective than aversive therapy in reducing the urge to gamble, gambling, and anxiety in 20 compulsive gamblers—at both 1 month and 1 year after treatment (McConaghy et al., 1983). Also, controlled studies suggest that cognitive behavior therapy and interpersonal psychotherapy may reduce binge eating over the long term in patients with bulimia nervosa (Fairburn et al., 1993). Although there are no controlled studies of psychoanalytically oriented psychotherapy in ICDs, open studies of psychoanalytical psychotherapy and inpatient treatment have shown varying degrees of success in pathological gamblers (Bergler, 1957; Allcock, 1986; Taber et al., 1987), and there are isolated case reports and case series of successful treatment of kleptomania, pathological gambling, trichotillomania, and various paraphilias with insight-oriented psychotherapy (Kilmann et al., 1982; McElroy et al., 1992). However, many authors have commented on the difficulties involved in psychological treatment of individuals with ICDs, citing patient's refusal to take responsibility for their behavior, lack of insight, denial, and concomitant legal difficulties, antisocial behaviors, and alcohol and drug abuse (Greenson, 1947; Kilmann et al., 1982; Allcock, 1986; Swedo and Rapoport, 1991; Favazza and Rosenthal, 1993).

Regarding somatic therapies, few controlled trials of pharmacological agents in the treatment of individuals with ICDs (including potential forms with the exception of binge eating) have been conducted. Those that have been done have primarily examined antidepressant or anticonvulsant agents in individuals with impulsive aggression and trichotillomania. Thus, in a controlled comparison of carbamazepine and propranolol in 80 patients with rage outbursts due to a variety of diagnoses, including IED ($n = 51$) and attention deficit disorder, residual type ($n = 38$), the two drugs were equally beneficial in reducing rage outbursts (Mattes, 1990). Also, the diagnosis of IED was associated with better response to carbamazepine, whereas the diagnosis of attention deficit disorder was associated with preferential response to propranolol. Similarly, in a placebo-controlled crossover study of two doses of phenytoin (100 and 300 mg/day) administered for 4 weeks to 13 male inmates in a maximum-security prison with impulsive aggression defined as "spontaneous hair trigger acts", phenytoin at 300 mg/day—but not placebo or phenytoin at 100 mg/day—significantly reduced the frequency of aggressive acts as well as ratings of tension–anxiety and depression–dejection. Anger–hostility scores, however, were not reduced (Barratt et al., 1991). In a 10-week double-blind crossover trial of clomipramine and desipramine in 13 women with severe trichotillomania by the DSM-III-R criteria, clomipramine was significantly more effective than desipramine in reducing trichotillomania symptoms (Swedo et al., 1989). Specifically, patients reported a reduction in the frequency and intensity of hair pulling urges and an increased ability to resist the urges during treatment with clomipramine, but not during treatment with desipramine. By contrast, in an 18-week placebo-controlled double-blind crossover study of fluoxetine up to 80 mg/day in 21 adult chronic hair-pullers (in which 6-week trials of fluoxetine and placebo were separated by a 5-week wash-out period), fluoxetine was not superior to placebo in suppressing hair pulling symptoms. Other controlled studies include a 10-week crossover trial showing that clomipramine was superior to desipramine in decreasing nail biting in 14 patients with severe onychophagia (Leonard et al., 1991), a crossover comparison showing that cyproterone acetate and ethyl oestradiol were equally effective and better than no treatment in lowering sexual interest and sexual activity in 12 inpatients with various paraphilias (Bancroft et al., 1974), and a

6-week placebo-controlled double-blind crossover study demonstrating that benperidol—but not chlorpromazine or placebo—decreased ratings of sexual interest in 12 men with pedophilia (Tennent et al., 1974). Finally, over 15 double-blind placebo-controlled studies have shown that a variety of antidepressants from many different classes suppress binge eating in women with bulimia nervosa (Walsh, 1991) and in obese persons who binge eat but do not purge (McCann and Agras, 1990).

Despite the paucity of controlled trials, there are numerous case reports and case series of a wide range of agents with antidepressant or mood-stabilizing properties having efficacy in a variety of ICDs. These include desipramine, clomipramine, lithium, carbamazepine, and valproate for apparent IED (Cutler and Heiser, 1978; Mattes, 1986; Fava et al., 1990; Szymanski and Olympia, 1991); amitriptyline, imipramine, nortriptyline, trazodone, fluoxetine, lithium, and valproate for kleptomania (Fishbain, 1987; McElroy et al., 1989, 1991a–c); clomipramine and lithium for pathological gambling (Moskowitz, 1980; Hollander et al., 1992); imipramine, desipramine, clomipramine, isocarboxazid, fluoxetine, trazodone, and lithium for trichotillomania (Christenson et al., 1991a, b; Swedo and Rapoport, 1991; Ninan et al., 1992; Winchel et al., 1992); bupropion, nortriptyline, and fluoxetine for compulsive shopping (McElroy et al., 1992, in press); fluoxetine for compulsive facial picking and skin picking in Prader–Willi syndrome (Stout, 1990; Warnock, 1993); and fluoxetine and lithium for sexual compulsions and various paraphilias (Kafka, 1991; Anthony and Hollander, 1993). Also, individuals with kleptomania and transvestism have been reported to respond to ECT (Eyers, 1960; Fishbain, 1987). In most cases, patients reported reductions in the frequency and intensity of their irresistible impulses and/or behaviors, usually after several weeks of treatment with doses typically effective for mood disorder. In some instances, the ICD symptoms recurred after discontinuation of medication and remitted again when medication was reinstituted (Fishbain, 1987; McElroy et al., 1989).

Many of the above cited thymoleptic agents affect serotonergic neurotransmission to some degree. It is therefore of interest that other agents with potent serotonergic properties have been reported to reduce aggressive, self-destructive, and other harmful impulsive behaviors. For instance, fenfluramine (a 5-HT releasing agent) has been reported to decrease binge eating in women with bulimia nervosa (Blouin et al., 1988); and buspirone (a 5-HT_{1A} agonist) has been reported to decrease cross-dressing behavior in transvestic fetishism (Fedoroff, 1988). Finally, there are reports of IED responding to β-blockers (Mattes, 1985); paraphilias responding to anti-androgen agents (Gottesman and Schubert, 1993); impulsive aggression due to various causes (i.e. personality disorder, organic mental disorder, dementia, ADHD, and schizophrenia) responding to a variety of antiepileptics (including carbamazepine, phenytoin, and ethosuximide), lithium, psychostimulants, antidepressants, β-blockers, and various hormonal manipulations (in particular, antiandrogen treatments) (Monroe, 1970; Maletzky, 1973; Mattes, 1986; Cowdry and Gardner, 1988); and self-injurious behavior responding to opiate antagonists (Richardson and Zaleski, 1983; see Chapters 12, 13, and 15).

CONCLUSIONS

Although some continue to doubt the diagnostic legitimacy of the ICDs, there are numerous descriptions, from different countries and different historical periods, of individuals who perform harmful behaviors in response to irresistible impulses. Moreover, the modern literature contains increasing numbers of reports of different types of irresistible impulses responding to treatment with medications with antidepressant, mood-stabilizing, serotonergic, and/or anticonvulsant properties. The consistency of the "structure" of the irresistible impulse (a core disturbance of impulsivity and compulsivity), and reports of it responding to psychopharmacological agents—regardless of the "content" or the specific behavior performed—strongly suggest that it is as a valid psychopathological symptom and further suggest that the ICDs are in fact related and should be grouped together.

Indeed, as mentioned, some have argued that ICDs should include a broader range of impulsive symptoms and behaviors, or, even more broadly, all conditions characterized by abnormal impulsivity. Thus, this family of conditions might also include other Axis I disorders with impulsive symptoms (e.g. ADHD, some forms of alcohol and substance abuse, bulimia nervosa, and the proposed DSM-IV diagnosis binge eating disorder), Axis II disorders with impulsive features (e.g. borderline and antisocial personality disorders), and possibly even some medical and neurological disorders characterized by impulsivity (e.g. organic personality disorder, especially the explosive type, tic disorders, and Prader–Willi syndrome) (Frosch and Wortis, 1954; Lacey and Evans, 1986; McElroy et al., 1992; Stein and Hollander, 1993). This conceptualization is supported by many of these latter conditions sharing with the "classic" ICDs similar comorbidity with other psychiatric disorders as well as with each other, abnormalities in serotonergic neurotransmission, and/or favorable response to serotonergic agents (Stein and Hollander, 1993; Stein et al., 1993). Some proponents of this hypothesis have suggested that impulsivity, especially impulsive aggression, represents a psychopathological dimension which is possibly due to abnormal serotonergic neurotransmission and which crosses a variety of psychiatric disorders (Caccaro et al., 1989; Kavoussi and Caccaro, 1993; Stein and Hollander, 1993). In contrast, others have hypothesized that impulsivity reflects maladaptive attempts to relieve a variety of uncomfortable symptoms stemming from psychological trauma or psychiatric illness in general (Favazza and Rosenthal, 1993). However, studies suggesting that the ICDs may be related to other psychiatric conditions, including addictive disorders, mood disorders, and OCD, have lead some authors to posit that they should be viewed as variants of these latter disorders.

Supporting the view that the ICDs (especially pathological gambling, compulsive shopping, and sexual compulsions) would be better conceptualized as addictive disorders are the observations that the irresistible impulse resembles the craving to drink or use drugs and the "high" sometimes experienced with enactment of the impulsive behavior is similar to that induced by alcohol or drugs (Anderson et al., 1984; Gudjonsson, 1987; McElroy et al., 1991a; Rosenthal, 1993). Indeed, some ICD patients claim to be addicted to their behaviors (Favazza and Rosenthal, 1993). Thus, the self-medication of benzodiazepine withdrawal symptoms through the thrill of kleptomanic stealing has been reported (Fishbain, 1987); gambling has been described as inducing "a stimulating, tranquilizing, or pain relieving response" (Custer, 1984), as well as being an "anesthetic" with hypnotizing properties (Lesieur and Rosenthal, 1991); and individuals with RSM frequently state that they do not feel pain upon self-mutilation (Favazza, 1992). One compulsive buyer told us that in the act of buying, she felt "a high like taking cocaine", which was quickly followed by a "crash" characterized by anxiety, depression, and guilt (McElroy et al., 1991c). In addition, pathological gamblers have been reported to develop tolerance (increasing the size of their bets in order to achieve the same degree of desired "high"; Anderson and Brown, 1984), as well as physiological withdrawal symptoms—including tremulousness, abdominal pain, diarrhea, nightmares, cold sweats, and headaches—after abrupt discontinuation of gambling (Wray and Dickerson, 1981). There are also high rates of alcohol and substance abuse in individuals with episodic dyscontrol, kleptomania, pathological gambling, impulsive fire setting, compulsive buying, and RSM; high rates of pathological or problem gambling among individuals with alcohol or substance abuse (Lesieur et al., 1986); and MMPI profiles in problem gamblers similar to those of alcohol and drug abusers (Lesieur and Rosenthal, 1991). Finally, self-help groups modeled on Alcoholics Anonymous (e.g. Gamblers Anonymous) may be helpful in the treatment of some individuals with pathological gambling, and are emerging for patients with kleptomania, paraphilias, compulsive buying, and RSM (Brown, 1985).

Other authors have argued that the ICDs are related to mood disorders. Supporting this view are high rates of mood disorders in individuals with ICDs and in their families, reports of irresistible impulses and their consequent acts altering in frequency and/or intensity in relation to affective symptoms, reports of impulsive behaviors having antidepressant effects and/or inducing hypomanic symptoms, and reports of many different types of ICDs responding to a wide range of medications with antidepressant, mood-stabilizing, and/or serotonergic properties (McElroy et al., 1992). Our group has hypothesized that the ICDs (especially highly impulsive or pleasurable types such as IED, pathological gambling, and kleptomania) may be related to bipolar disorder, because of their phenomenological similarities (e.g. the "rush" associated with an impulsive act resembles hypomania), relatively high comorbidity with one another in some studies, and their shared response to agents with mood-stabilizing effects (McElroy et al., 1991b, 1993).

Noting the phenomenological similarities between the irresistible impulses and acts of ICDs and the obsessions and compulsions of OCD, many have postulated that the ICDs are either variants of OCD or members of a larger family of obsessive compulsive spectrum disorders (Tynes et al., 1991; Jenike, 1989; McElroy et al., 1992, 1993; Hollander, 1993; Stein and Hollander, 1993). Both impulses and obsessions are often experienced as senseless or repugnant, intrusive, irresistible, and associated with anxiety or tension; impulsive acts and compulsions are often experienced as uncontrollable and anxiety or tension relieving. Indeed, both the DSM-III-R and ICD-10 use the term "impulse" to define OCD obsessions. Moreover, although obsessive compulsive and impulse control disorder symptoms have usually been distinguished with respect to how harmful they are, how senseless they seem, the degree to which they are performed impulsively or resisted, the nature of the relief associated with their performance, and the degree to which they are ego-syntonic or ego-dystonic (with ICD symptoms generally being more harmful, less senseless, more spontaneous, more likely associated with pleasure, and more ego-syntonic), in actuality both sets of symptoms vary considerably with respect to these variables (McElroy et al., 1993). Thus, "compulsive" forms of ICDs (Dupouy, 1905; Warner, 1932), individuals with OCD and high degrees of impulsivity (Hoehn-Saric and Barksdale, 1983; Stein et al., 1991), and impulsive individuals with obsessive compulsive behaviors (Kernberg, 1985; Coid, 1993) have all been described.

Further supporting a relationship between the ICDs and OCD are high rates of OCD in various ICDs (the prevalence of ICDs in patients with OCD has not yet been studied); their similar comorbidity with other Axis I disorders; relatively high rates of OCD in families of individuals with kleptomania and trichotillomania; abnormalities in serotonergic neurotransmission (e.g. decreased CSF 5-HIAA concentrations) in patients with impulsive aggression, impulsive fire setting, and RSM, similar to those in some, but not all, patients with OCD; the finding that clomipramine may be more effective than desipramine in the treatment of trichotillomania and onychophagia; and (although controlled comparison trials have not yet been done) the possibility that they both respond better to behavioral than to psychoanalytical or insight-oriented psychotherapy (Swedo et al., 1989; Leonard et al., 1991; McElroy et al., 1993). This conceptualization, however, does not account for some apparent differences between the ICDs and

OCD, including the possibility that at least some ICDs may respond to a broader range of thymoleptic agents (including non-SRI antidepressants and mood stabilizers) rather than preferentially to SRIs. Of note, attempts to explain these apparent similarities and differences have included unidimensional models with variation or oscillation along a single dimension of impulsivity versus compulsivity (with pure impulsivity at one extreme, pure compulsivity at the other extreme, and mixed compulsive–impulsive conditions situated in between), as well as orthogonal models in which impulsivity and compulsivity represent separate but potentially co-occurring psychopathological states (Lacey and Evans, 1986; Rasmussen and Eisen, 1992; Hollander, 1993; McElroy et al., 1993).

Our group has argued that viewing the ICDs as their own separate group of conditions or as variants of addictive disorders, mood disorders, or OCD does not fully account for their overlap with other Axis I disorders, including anxiety disorders other than OCD and eating disorders. To explain this large overlap, we have hypothesized that the ICDs, and, more broadly, all disorders characterized by irresistible impulses to perform senseless or harmful behaviors, may be forms of "affective spectrum disorder" (ASD) (McElroy et al., 1991a, 1992). Affective spectrum disorder is a hypothesized family of disorders (including OCD, bulimia nervosa, panic disorder, and ADHD) sharing response to antidepressants from several different classes, high comorbidity with mood disorder, and high familial rates of mood disorder, and thus possibly sharing a common pathophysiological abnormality with mood disorder (Hudson and Pope, 1990). Support for the hypothesis that ICDs are forms of ASD comes from the phenomenological similarities of the ICDs not only with OCD but also with bulimia nervosa, panic disorder, and bipolar disorder; high rates of mood, anxiety, and eating disorders in individuals with a variety of ICDs; findings of abnormalities in serotonergic and/or noradrenergic neurotransmission in individuals with episodic dyscontrol, impulsive fire setting, pathological gambling, and RSM similar to that occurring in mood disorders; and the response of a wide range of ICDs to a variety of compounds with antidepressant or mood-stabilizing effects (McElroy et al., 1991a, 1992). Although speculative, this conceptualization might also account for a number of other observations, including the relationship of pathological gambling and episodic dyscontrol with ADHD and, because of the high rates of mood disorder found among alcoholics (Weissman et al., 1980), the overlap of ICDs with alcohol and substance abuse.

The hypothesis that ICDs are forms of ASD is, of course, affected by several methodological limitations. Most important is the lack of systematic, controlled studies of individuals with ICDs diagnosed by operational criteria. Second is the argument that the irresistible impulses and impulsive acts are not disorders in and of themselves, but are merely nonspecific behaviors exhibited with greater than normal frequency by individuals with mood disorders. Also, this theory does not explain the phenomenological similarity of some ICDs, especially IED, with that of complex partial seizures; the experience of withdrawal symptoms upon abrupt discontinuation of the impulsive behavior; the possible overlap of some ICDs with personality disorder; and the response of episodic dyscontrol to nonthymoleptic agents (e.g. β-blockers) (McElroy et al., 1992, 1993).

In summary, despite a descriptive literature dating back over 150 years and their inclusion in the formal American psychiatric nomenclature since 1980, the ICDs have received relatively little systematic study and remain poorly understood. However, even though debate over their diagnostic validity lingers, available research indicates that the ICDs are legitimate mental disorders that are more common than realized, cause significant morbidity, have significant comorbidity with other psychiatric disorders (particularly mood disorder), may be associated with abnormalities in serotonergic and possibly noradrenergic neurotransmission, and may respond to agents with thymoleptic, serotonergic, and/or anticonvulsant properties and to behaviorally oriented psychological treatments. Although further research is clearly needed, it should be realized that the ICDs as a group represent a significant public health problem, are under-recognized, and may respond to available treatments.

ACKNOWLEDGMENT

The authors gratefully acknowledge Ms Rose M. Brumfield for preparation of the manuscript.

REFERENCES

Aber, R.J., and O'Guinn, T.C. (1991). Beyond phenomenology: Emerging theoretical notions on compulsive buying. Paper presented at the American Psychological Association Conference, San Francisco, CA.

Allcock, C.C. (1986). Pathological gambling. *Aust. N.Z. J. Psychiatry*, 20, 259–265.

American Psychiatric Association (1980). *Diagnostic and Statistical Manual of Mental Disorders*, 3rd edn. American Psychiatric Press, Washington, D.C.

American Psychiatric Association (1987). *Diagnostic and Statistical Manual of Mental Disorders*, 3rd edn—revised. American Psychiatric Press, Washington, D.C.

American Psychiatric Association (1994). *Diagnostic and Statistical Manual of Mental Disorders*. 4th edn. American Psychiatric Press, Washington, D.C.

American Psychiatric Association (1991). *DSM-IV Options Book*. American Psychiatric Press, Washington, D.C.

Anderson, G., and Brown, R.I. (1984). Real and laboratory gambling, sensation-seeking and arousal. *Br. J. Psychol.*, 75, 401–410.

Anderson, G., and Brown, R.I. (1987). Some applications of reversal theory to the explanation of gambling and gambling addictions. *J. Gambling Behav.*, 3, 179–189.

Antheaume, A. (1925). La legende de la kleptomanie, affection mentale fictive. *L'Encephale*, 20, 368–388.

Anthony, D.T. and Hollander, E. (1993). Sexual compulsions. In: *Obsessive-Compulsive Related Disorders*, pp. 139–150. (ed. E. Hollander) American Psychiatric Press, Inc., Washington, D.C.

Azrin, N.A., Nunn, R.G., and Frantz, S.E. (1980). Treatment of hair-pulling (trichotillomania): A comparative study of habit reversal and negative practice training. *J. Behav. Ther. Exp. Psychiatry*, 11, 13–20.

Bach-y-Rita, G., Lion, J.R., Climent, C.E., and Ervin, F.R. (1971). Episodic dyscontrol: a study of 130 violent patients. *Am. J. Psychiatry*, 127, 1473–1478.

Bancroft, J., Tennent, G., Loucas, K., and Cass, J. (1974). The control of deviant sexual behavior by drugs: 1. Behavioral changes following estrogens and anti-androgens. *Br. J. Psychiatry*, 125, 310–315.

Barratt, E.S., Kent, T.A., Bryant, S.G., and Felthous, A.R. (1991). A controlled trial of phenytoin in impulsive aggression [letter]. *J. Clin. Psychopharmacol.*, 11, 388–389.

Bergler, E. (1957). *The Psychology of Gambling*. Hill & Wang, New York.

Blaszczynski, A., McConaghy, N., and Frankova, A. (1989). Crime, antisocial personality and pathological gambling. *J. Gambling Behav.*, 5, 137–152.

Bleuler, E. (1988). *Textbook of Psychiatry*. The Classics of Psychiatry & Behavioral Sciences Library, Gryphon Editions, Birmingham, AL.

Blouin, A.G., Blouin, J.H., Perez, E.L., Bushnik, T., Zuro, C., and Mulder, E. (1988). Treatment of bulimia with fenfluramine and desipramine. *J. Clin. Psychopharmacol.*, 8, 261–269.

Bradford, J.M.W. (1982). Arson: a clinical study. *Can. J. Psychiatry*, 27, 188–193.

Bradford, J., and Balmaceda, R. (1983). Shoplifting: is there a specific psychiatry syndrome? *Can. J. Psychiatry*, 28, 248–254.

Brown, I.R. (1985). The effectiveness of gamblers anonymous. In: *Gambling and the Gambling Papers, Proceeding of the Sixth National Conference on Gambling and Risk Taking* (ed. W. Eadington). University of Nevada, Reno.

Brown, G.L., Goodwin, F.K., Ballenger, J.C., Goyer, P., and Major, L. (1979). Aggression in humans correlates with cerebrospinal fluid amine metabolites. *Psychiatry Res.*, 1, 131–139.

Brown, C.S., Kent, T.A., Bryant, S.G., et al. (1989). Blood platelet uptake of serotonin in episodic aggression. *Psychiatry Res.*, 27, 5–12.

Carlton, P.L., Manowitz, P., McBride, H., Nora, R., Swartzburg, M., and Goldstein, L. (1987). Attention deficit disorder and pathological gambling. *J. Clin. Psychiatry*, 48, 487–488.

Chen, C-N., Wong, J., Lee, N., Chan-Ho, M-W., Tak-Fai, J., and Fung, M. (1993). The Shatin community mental health survey in Hong Kong II. Major findings. *Arch. Gen. Psychiatry*, 50, 125–133.

Christenson, G.A., and Chernoff, E. (1991). Personality disorders in trichotillomania. New Research Program and Abstracts (NR 191), American Psychiatric Association Annual Meeting, New Orleans, Louisiana, 11–16 May 1991, NR 191 [abstr.].

Christenson, G.A., Faber, R.J., de Zwaan, M., et al. (1994). Compulsive buying: descriptive characteristics and psychiatric comorbity. *J. Clin. Psychiatry*, 55, 5–11.

Christenson, G.A., Mackenzie, T.B., and Mitchell, J.E. (1991a). Characteristics of 60 adult chronic hair pullers. *Am. J. Psychiatry*, 148, 365–370.

Christenson, G.A., Mackenzie, T.B., Mitchell, J.E., and Callies, A.L. (1991b). A placebo-controlled, double-blind crossover study of fluoxetine in trichotillomania. *Am. J. Psychiatry*, 148, 1566–1571.

Christenson, G.A., Popkin, M.A., Mackenzie, T.B., and Realmuto, G.M. (1991c).

Lithium treatment of chronic hair pulling. *J. Clin. Psychiatry*, 52, 116–120.

Christenson, G.A., Pyle, R.L., Mitchell, J.E. (1991d). Estimated lifetime prevalence of trichotillomania in college students. *J. Clin. Psychiatry*, 52, 415–417.

Coccaro, E.F., Siever, L.J., Klar, H.M., et al. (1989). Serotonergic studies in patients with affective and personality disorders: correlations with suicidal and impulsive aggressive behavior. *Arch. Gen. Psych.*, 46, 587–599.

Coid, J.W. (1993). An affective syndrome in psychopaths with borderline personality disorder? *Br. J. Psychiatry*, 162, 641–650.

Cowdry, R.W., and Gardner, D.L. (1988). Pharmacotherapy of borderline personality disorder. *Arch. Gen. Psychiatry*, 45, 111–119.

Custer, R.L. (1984). Profile of the pathological gambler. *J. Clin. Psychiatry*, 45, 35–38.

Cutler, N., Heiser, J.F. (1978). Retrospective diagnosis of hypomania following successful treatment of episodic violence with lithium: a case report. *Am. J. Psychiatry*, 135, 753–754.

Dubovsky, S.L. (1990). Generalized anxiety disorder: New concepts and psychopharmacologic therapies. *J. Clin. Psychiatry*, 51 (suppl.), 3–10.

Dupouy, R. (1905). De la kleptomania. *J. Psychol. Norm. Pathol.*, 2, 404–426.

Dubuisson, P. (1901). Les voleuses des grand magasins. *Arch Anthropol. Criminelle Criminol. Psychol. Norm. Pathol.*, 16, 23–370.

Elliott, F.A. (1976). The neurology of explosive rage. The dyscontrol syndrome. *Practitioner*, 217, 51–60.

Esquirol, E. (1838). *Des Maladies Mentales.*, J.B. Ballière, Paris.

Everts, O. (1887). Are dipsomania, kleptomania, pyromania, etc, valid forms of mental disease? *Am. J. Insanity*, 44, 52–59.

Eyers, A.E. (1960). Transvestism: Employment of somatic therapy with subsequent improvement. *Dis. Nerv. Syst.*, 21, 52–53.

Fairburn, C.G., Beglin, S.J. (1990). Studies of the epidemiology of bulimia nervosa. *Am. J. Psychiatry*, 147, 401–408.

Fairburn, C.G., Jones, R., Peveler, R.C., Hope, R.A., and O'Connor, M. (1993). Psychotherapy and bulimia nervosa: longer-term effects of interpersonal psychotherapy, behavior therapy, and cognitive behavior therapy. *Arch. Gen. Psychiatry*, 50, 419–428.

Fava, M., Anderson, K., and Rosenbaum, J.F. (1990). Anger attacks: Possible variants of panic and major depressive disorders. *Am. J. Psychiatry*, 147, 867–870.

Favazza, A.R. (1992). Repetitive self-mutilation. *Psychiatr. Ann.*, 22, 60–63.

Favazza, A.R., and Conterio, K. (1988). The plight of chronic self-mutilators. *Community Ment. Health J.*, 24, 22–30.

Favazza, A.R., and Rosenthal, R.J. (1993). Diagnostic issues in self mutilation. *Hosp. Community Psychiatry*, 44, 134–140.

Favazza, A.R., DeRosear, L., and Conterio, K. (1989). Self-mutilation and eating disorders. *Suicide Life Threat. Behav.*, 19, 352–361.

Fishbain, D.A. (1987). Kleptomania as risk taking behavior in response to depression. *Am. J. Psychotherapy*, 41, 598–603.

Fedoroff, J.P. (1988). Buspirone hydrochloride in the treatment of transvestic fetishism. *J. Clin. Psychiatry*, 49, 408–409.

Frankenburg, F.R., and Yurgelun-Todd, D. (1984). Dressing disorder [letter]. *Am. J. Psychiatry*, 141, 147.

Frosch, J. (1977). The relation between acting out and disorders of impulse control. *Psychiatry*, 40, 295–314.

Frosch, J., and Wortis, S.B. (1954). A contribution to the nosology of the impulse disorders. *Am. J. Psychiatry*, 111, 132–138.

Geller, J.L., Erlen, J., and Pinkus, R.L. (1986). A historical appraisal of America's experience with "pyromania"—a diagnosis in search of a disorder. *Int. J. Law Psychiatry*, 9, 201–229.

Gibbens, T.C.N., and Prince, J. (1962). *Shoplifting*. Institute for the Study and Treatment of Delinquency, London.

Goldstein, L., Manowitz, P., Nora, R., Swartzburg, M., and Carlton, P. (1985). Differential EEG activation and pathological gambling. *Biol. Psychiatry*, 20, 1232–1234.

Gottesman, H.G., and Schubert, D.S.P. (1993). Low-dose oral medroxyprogesterone acetate in the management of the paraphilias. *J. Clin. Psychiatry*, 54, 182–188.

Greenson, R.R. (1947). On gambling. *Am. Imago*, 4, 61–77.

Gudjonsson, G.H. (1987). The significance of depression in the mechanism of compulsive shoplifting. *Med. Sci. Law*, 27, 171–176.

Herzog, D.B., Keller, M.B., Lavori, P.W., Kenny, G.M., and Sacks, N.R. (1992). The prevalence of personality disorders in 210 women with eating disorders. *J. Clin. Psychiatry*, 53, 147–152.

Hoehn-Saric, R., and Barksdale, V.C. (1983). Impulsiveness in obsessive–compulsive patients. *Br. J. Psychiatry*, 143, 177–182.

Hollander, E. (ed.) (1993). *Obsessive–Compulsive Related Disorders*. American Psychiatric Press, Washington, D.C.

Hollander, E., Frenkel, M., DeCaria, C., Trungold, S., and Stein, D.J. (1992). Treatment of pathological gambling with clomipramine [letter]. *Am. J. Psychiatry*, 149, 710–711.

Hudson, J.I., and Pope, H.G. Jr (1990). Affective spectrum disorder: Does antidepressant response identify a family of disorders with a common pathophysiology? *Am. J. Psychiatry*, 147, 552–564.

Hudson, J.I., Pope, H.G. Jr, Jonas, J.M., and Yurgelun-Todd, D. (1983). Phenomenologic relationship of eating disorders to major affective disorder. *Psychiatry Res.*, 9, 345–354.

Jenike, M.A. (1989). Obsessive–compulsive and related disorders: A hidden epidemic. *N. Engl. J. Med.*, 321, 39–541.

Kafka, M.P. (1991). Successful antidepressant treatment of non-paraphilic sexual addictions and paraphilias in men. *J. Clin. Psychiatry*, 52, 60–65.

Kavoussi, R.J., and Caccaro, E.F. (1993). Impulsive personality disorders and disorders of impulse control. In: *Obsessive–Compulsive Related Disorders* (ed. E. Hollander) pp. 179–202. American Psychiatric Press, Washington, D.C.

Kaye, W.H., and Weltzin, T.E. (1991). Neurochemistry of bulimia nervosa. *J. Clin. Psychiatry*, 52, 21–28.

Keck, P.E. Jr, Pope, H.G. Jr, Hudson, J.I., McElroy, S.L., Yurgelun-Todd, D., and Hundert, E.M. (1990). A controlled study of phenomenology and family history in outpatients with bulimia nervosa. *Comp. Psychiatry*, 31, 275–283.

Kendler, K.S., MacLean, C., Neale, M., Kessler, R., Heath, A., Eaves, L. (1991). The genetic epidemiology of bulimia nervosa. *Am. J. Psychiatry*, 148, 1627–1637.

Kernberg, O. (1985). *Borderline Conditions and Pathological Narcissism*. Jason Arnonson, New Jersey.

Kilmann, P.R., Sabalis, R.R., Gearing, II, M.L., Bukstel, L.H., and Scovern, A.W. (1982). The treatment of sexual paraphilias: A review of the outcome research. *J. Sex Res.*, 18, 193–252.

Kraepelin, E. (1915). *Psychiatrie*, 8th edn, pp. 408–409. Verlag Von Johann Ambrosius Barth, Leipzig.

Lacey, J.H., and Evans, C.D.H. (1986). The impulsivist: A multi-impulsive personality disorder. *Br. J. Addict.*, 81, 641–649.

Leonard, H.L., Lenane, M.D., Swedo, S.E., Rettew, D.C., and Rapoport, J.L. (1991). A double-blind comparison of clomipramine and desipramine treatment of severe onychophagia (nail biting). *Arch. Gen. Psychiatry*, 48, 821–827.

Lesieur, H.R. (1988). The female pathological gambler. In: *Gambling Studies, Proceedings of the 7th International Conference in Gambling and Risk Taking* (ed. W.R. Eadington). University of Nevada, Reno.

Lesieur, H.R., Blume, S.B., Zoppa, R.M. (1986). Alcoholism, drug abuse, and gambling. *Alcoholism (NY)*, 10, 33–38.

Lesieur, H.R., and Rosenthal, R.J. (1991). Pathological gambling: A review of the literature. *J. Gambling Stud.*, 7, 5–39.

Lewis, N.D.C., and Yarnell, H. (1951). *Pathological Firesetting (Pyromania): Nervous and Mental Disease Monograph 82*. Coolidge Foundation, New York.

Linden, R.D., Pope, H.G. Jr, and Jonas, J.M. (1986). Pathological gambling and major affective disorder: Preliminary findings. *J. Clin. Psychiatry*, 47, 201–203.

Linnoila, M., Virkkunen, M., Scheinin, M., Nuutila, A., Rimon, R., and Goodwin, F.K. (1983). Low cerebrospinal fluid 5-hydocyindoleacetic acid concentration differentiates impulsive from nonimpulsive violent behavior. *Life Sci.*, 33, 2609–2614.

Linnoila, M., DeJong, J., and Virkkunen, M. (1989). Family history of alcoholism in violent offenders and impulsive firesetters. *Arch. Gen. Psychiatry*, 46, 613–616.

López-Ibor, J.J. Jr, (1990). Impulse control in obsessive–compulsive disorder: A biopsychopathological approach. *Neuropsychopharmacol. Biol. Psychiatry*, 14, 709–718.

López-Ibor, J.J. Jr, Saiz-Ruiz, J., Perez de los Cobos, J.C. (1985). Biological correlations of suicide and aggressivity in major depressions (with melancholia): 5-Hydroxyindoleacetic acid and cortisol in cerebrospinal fluid, dexamethasone suppression test and therapeutic response to 5-hydroxytryptophan. *Neuropsychobiology*, 14, 67–74.

McCann, U.D., and Agras, W.S. (1990). Successful treatment of nonpurging bulimia nervosa with desipramine: A double-blind, placebo-controlled study. *Am. J. Psychiatry*, 147, 1509–1513.

McConaghy, N., Armstrong, M., Blaszczynski, A., and Allcock, C. (1983). Controlled comparison of aversive therapy and imaginal desensitization in compulsive gambling. *Br. J. Psychiatry*, 142, 366–372.

McCormick, R., Russo, A.M., Ramirez, L.F., and Taber, J.I. (1984). Affective disorders among pathological gamblers seeking treatment. *Am. J. Psychiatry*, 1, 215–218.

McElroy, S.L., Hudson, J.I., Pope, H.G. Jr, and Keck, P.E. Jr (1991a). Kleptomania: Clinical characteristics and associated psychopathology. *Psychol. Med.*, 21, 93–108.

McElroy, S.L., Keck, P.E., Jr, Pope, H.G., Jr, Hudson, J.I. (1989). Pharmacological treatment of kleptomania and bulimia nervosa. *J. Clin. Psychopharmacol.*, 9, 358–360.

McElroy, S.L., Pope, H.G. Jr, Hudson, J.I., Keck, P.E. Jr, and White, K.L. (1991b). Kleptomania: A report of 20 cases. *Am. J. Psychiatry*, 148, 652–657.

McElroy, S.L., Satlin, A., Pope, H.G. Jr, Hudson, J.I., and Keck, P.E. Jr, (1991c). Treatment of compulsive shopping with antidepressants. A report of three cases. *Ann. Clin. Psychiatry*, 3, 199–204.

McElroy, S.L., Hudson, J.I., Keck, P.E. Jr, Pope, H.G. Jr, and Aizley, H. (1992) The DSM-III-R impulse control disorders not elsewhere classified: Clinical characteristics and relationship to other psychiatric disorders. *Am. J. Psychiatry*, 149, 318–327.

McElroy, S.L., Hudson, J.I., Phillips, K.A., Keck, P.E., and Pope, H.G. Jr, (1993). Clinical and theoretical implications of a possible link between obsessive–compulsive and impulse control disorders. *Depression*, 1, 121–132.

McElroy, S.L., Keck, P.E. Jr, Pope, H.G. Jr, Smith, J.M.R., and Strakowski, S.M. (1994). Compulsive buying: A report of 20 cases. *J. Clin. Psychiatry*, 55, 242–248.

Maletzky, B.M. (1973). The episodic dyscontrol syndrome. *Dis. Nerv. Syst.*, 36, 178–185.

Markovitz, P.J., Calabrese, J.R., Schultz, S.C., and Meltzer, H.Y. (1991). Fluoxetine in the treatment of borderline and schizotypical disorders. *Am. J. Psychiatry*, 148, 1064–1067.

Mattes, J.A. (1985). Metoprolol for intermittent explosive disorder. *Am. J. Psychiatry*, 142, 1108–1109.

Mattes, J.A. (1986). Psychopharmacology of temper outbursts: A review. *J. Nerv. Ment. Dis.*, 174, 464–478.

Mattes, J.A. (1990). Comparative effectiveness of carbamazepine and propranolol for rage outbursts. *J. Neuropsychiatry Clin. Neurosci.*, 2, 159–164.

Mattes, J.A., and Fink, M. (1987). A family study of patients with temper outbursts. *J. Psychiatry Res.*, 21, 249–255.

Monroe, R.R. (1970). *Episodic Behavioral Disorders*. Harvard Univ. Press, Cambridge, MA.

Moran, E. (1970). Varieties of pathologic gambling. *Br. J. Psychiatry*, 116, 593–597.

Moreno, I., Saiz-Ruiz, J., and López-Ibor, J.J. (1991). Serotonin and gambling dependence. *Hum. Psychopharmacol.*, 6 (suppl.), 9–12.

Moskowitz, J.A. (1980). Lithium and lady luck: Use of lithium carbonate in compulsive gambling. *N. Y. J. Med.*, 80, 785–788.

Ninan, P.T., Rothbaum, B.O., Stipetic, M., Lewine, R.J., and Risch, S.C. (1992). CSF 5-HIAA as a predictor of treatment response in trichotillomania. *Psychopharmacol. Bull.*, 28, 451–455.

O'Neil, P.M., and Jarrell, M.P. (1992). Psychological aspects of obesity and dieting. In: *Treatment of the Seriously Obese Patient* (eds T.A. Wadden and T.B. Van Itallie) pp. 252–270. The Guilford Press, New York.

Pattison, E.M., Kahan, J. (1983). The deliberate self harm syndrome. *Am. J. Psychiatry*, 140, 867–872.

Peele, S. (1989). *Diseasing of America: Addiction Treatment Out of Control*. D.C. Heath, Lexington, MA.

Prins, H., Tennent, G., and Trick, K. (1985). Motives for arson (fire setting). *Med. Sci. Law.*, 25, 275–278.

Popkin, M.K. (1989). Impulse control disorders not elsewhere classified. In: *Comprehensive Textbook of Psychiatry*, vol. II (eds H.I. Kaplan and B.J. Saddock) pp. 1145–1154. Williams & Wilkins, Baltimore.

Pyle, R.L., Mitchell, J.E., and Eckert, E.D. (1981). Bulimia: a report of 34 cases. *J. Clin. Psychiatry*, 42, 60–64.

Ramirez, L.F., McCormick, R.A., Russo, A.M., Taber, T.I. (1983). Patterns of substance abuse in pathological gamblers undergoing treatment. *Addict. Behav.*, 8, 425–428.

Rasmussen, S.A., and Eisen, J.L. (1992). The epidemiology and differential diagnosis of obsessive compulsive disorder. *J. Clin. Psychiatry*, 53 (suppl.), 4–10.

Reeve, E.A., Bernstein, G.A., and Christenson, G.A. (in press). Clinical characteristics and psychiatric comorbidity in children with trichotillomania. *J. Am. Acad. Child Adolesc. Psychiatry*.

Richardson, J.S., and Zaleski, W.A. (1983). Naloxone and self-mutilation. *Biol. Psychiatry*, 18, 99–101.

Robbins, E., and Robbins, L. (1967). Arson with special reference to pyromania. *N. Y. State J. Med.*, 67, 795–798.

Rooth, F.G., and Marks, I.M. (1974). Persistent exhibitionism: Short term response to aversion, self-regulation, and relaxation treatments. *Arch. Sexual Behav.*, 3, 227–248.

Rosenthal, R.J. (1993). Pathological gambling. *Psychiatr. Ann.*, 22, 72–78.

Rothbaum, B.O., Shaw, L., Morris, R., and Ninan, P.T. (1993). Prevalence of trichotillomania in a college freshmen population [letter]. *J. Clin. Psychiatry*, 54, 72.

Roy, A., Adinoff, B., Roehrick, L., et al. (1988). Pathological gambling: A psychobiological study. *Arch. Gen. Psychiatry*, 45, 369–373.

Roy, A., DeJong, J., and Linnoila, M. (1989). Extraversion in pathological gamblers. *Arch. Gen. Psychiatry*, 46, 679–681.

Schlosser, S., Black, D.W., Repertinger, S., Freet, D. (1994). Compulsive buying: demography, phenomenology, and comorbidity in 46 subjects. *Gen. Hosp. Psychiatry*, 16, 205–212.

Simeon, D., Stanley, B., Frances, A., et al. (1992). Self-mutilation in personality disorders: Psychological and biological correlates. *Am. J. Psychiatry*, 149, 221–226.

Spitzer, R.L., and Williams, J.B.W. (1986). *Structured Clinical Interview for DSM-III-R Personality Disorders (SCID-II)*. Biometrics Research Department, New York State Psychiatric Institute, New York.

Stein, D.J., and Hollander, E. (1993). The spectrum of obsessive–compulsive-related disorders. In: *Obsessive–Compulsive Related Disorders* (ed. E. Hollander) pp. 241–271. American Psychiatric Press, Washington, D.C.

Stein, D.J., Hollander, E., DeCaria, C.M., and Trungold, S. (1991). OCD: A disorder with anxiety, aggression, impulsivity, and depressed mood. *Psychiatry Res.*, 36, 237–239.

Stein, D.J., Hollander, E., Anthony, D.T., et al. (1992). Serotonergic medications for sexual obsessions, sexual addictions, and paraphilias. *J. Clin. Psychiatry*, 53, 267–271.

Stein, D.J., Hollander, E., and Liebowitz, M.R. (1993). Neurobiology of impulsivity and the impulse control disorders. *J. Neuropsychiatry Clin. Neurosci.*, 5, 9–17.

Stout, R.J. (1990). Fluoxetine for the treatment of compulsive facial picking [letter]. *Am. J. Psychiatry*, 147, 370.

Sunkureddi, K., and Markovitz, P. (1993). Trazodone treatment of obsessive–compulsive disorder and trichotillomania [letter]. *Am. J. Psychiatry*, 150, 523–524.

Swedo, S.E. (1993). Trichotillomania. In: *Obsessive–Compulsive Related Disorders* (ed. E. Hollander) pp. 93–111. American Psychiatric Press, Washington, D.C.

Swedo, S.E., and Rapoport, J.L. (1991). Annotation: Trichotillomania. *J. Child Psychol. Psychiatry*, 32, 401–409.

Swedo, S.E., Leonard, H.L., Rapoport, J.L., Lenane, M.L., Goldberg, E.L., and Cheston, D.L. (1989). A double-blind comparison of clomipramine and desipramine in the treatment of trichotillomania (hairpulling). *N. Engl. J. Med.*, 321, 495–501.

Szymanski, H.V., and Olympia, J. (1991). Divalproex in post traumatic stress disorder [letter]. *Am. J. Psychiatry*, 148, 1086–1087.

Taber, J.I., McCormick, R.A., Russo, A.M., Adkins, B.J., and Ramirez, L.F. (1987). Follow-up of pathological gamblers after treatment. *Am. J. Psychiatry*, 144, 757–761.

Tennent, T.G., Bancroft, J., and Cass, J. (1974). The control of deviant sexual behavior by drugs: A double-blind controlled study of benperidol, chlorpromazine, and placebo. *Arch. Sexual Behav.*, 3, 261–271.

Tennent, T.G., McQuaid, A., Loughnane, T., and Hands, A.J. (1971). Female arsonists. *Br. J. Psychiatry*, 119, 497–502.

Tynes, L.L., White, K., and Steketee, G.S. (1991). Toward a new nosology of obsessive compulsive disorder. *Comp. Psychiatry*, 31, 465–480.

Virkkunen, M. (1976). Self-mutilation in antisocial personality (disorder). *Acta. Psychiatrica Scand.*, 54, 347–352.

Virkkunen, M., DeJong, J., Bartko, J., and Linnoila, M. (1989). Psychobiological concomitants of history of suicide attempts among violent offenders and impulsive fire setters. *Arch. Gen. Psychiatry*, 46, 604–606.

Volberg, R.A., and Steadman, H.J. (1988). Refining prevalence estimates of pathological gambling. *Am. J. Psychiatry*, 145, 502–505.

Volberg, R.A., and Steadman, J.J. (1989). Prevalence estimates of pathological gambling in New Jersey and Maryland. *Am. J. Psychiatry*, 146, 1618–1619.

Walsh, B.T. (1991). Psychopharmacologic treatment of bulimia nervosa. *J. Clin. Psychiatry*, 52 (suppl.), 34–38.

Warner, G.L. (1932). A few representative cases of pyromania. *Psychiatr. Q.*, 6, 675–690.

Warnock, J.K. (1993). Selective serotonin reuptake inhibitors in treatment of skin picking in Prader–Willi Syndrome. New Research Program and Abstracts, American Psychiatric Association Annual Meeting, American Psychiatric Association, San Francisco, CA, p. 248.

Weissman, M.M., Meyers, J.K., Harding, P.S. (1980). Prevalence and psychiatric heterogeneity of alcoholism in a United States urban community. *J. Study Alchol*, 41, 672–681.

Whitehead, P.C., Ferreno, R., and Johnson, F.G. (1972). Physicians' reports of self-injury cases among their patients not seen in hospital. *Suicide Life Threat. Behav.*, 2, 137–146.

Whitehead, P.C., Johnson, F.G., and Ferreno, R. (1973). Measuring the incidence of self injury. *Am. J. Orthopsychiatry*, 43, 142–148.

Winchel, R.M., and Stanley, M. (1991). Self-injurious behavior: A review of the behavior and biology of self mutilation. *Am. J. Psychiatry*, 148, 306–317.

Winchel, R.M., Jones, J.S., Stanley, B., Molcho, A., and Stanley, M. (1992). Clinical characteristics of trichotillomania and its response to fluoxetine. *J. Clin. Psychiatry*, 53, 304–308.

Winokur, G., Clayton, P.J., and Reich, T. (1969). *Manic Depressive Illness*. C.V. Mosby, St. Louis.

Wray, I., Dickenson, M.G. (1981) Cessation of high frequency gambling and "withdrawal symptoms". *Br. J. Addict.*, 76, 401–405.

9 Pathological Gambling

JUAN JOSÉ LÓPEZ-IBOR AND JOSÉ LUIS CARRASCO
Department of Psychiatry, San Carlos Hospital, Complutense University,
Madrid, Spain

*Is gambling such a terrible vice. Like all waters that flow down to the sea,
all vices meet at the gambler.*

Mateo Alemán, Spanish writer, 17th century

INTRODUCTION

Gambling is an ancient and common activity in the general population.
Egyptian pharaohs and Roman-emperors are known to have enjoyed betting
on dice. The famous Spanish poet, Gongora, was evicted from his house as a
consequence of his persistent gambling, as was Dostoyevsky.

Gambling exists in many forms, such as betting on horse races or sporting
events, playing card games or coin-operated machines, or just betting on
coin tosses. These activities provide forms of entertainment for many people
without negatively interfering in their lives.

For a small group of gamblers, however, this behavior takes on an
excessive importance in their lives, to the extent that it interferes with other
demands on their money and time. This maladaptive use of gambling is the
main feature of pathological gambling.

CLINICAL PICTURE

The inclusion of pathological gambling among the disorders of impulse
control, as it appears both in DSM-III-R (American Psychiatric Association,
1987) and in the ICD-10 (World Health Organization, 1992), is relatively
recent. Over the last decade, the concept of gambling has undergone
significant changes. Before the publication of the DSM-III in 1980, the
clinical syndrome of morbid gambling was labelled as compulsive gambling
(in the 9th edition of the ICD).

The difference between a compulsion and an impulse was defined some
time ago as the presence or absence of ego-dystonic perception by the
subject. Unlike compulsions, the impulsive act is pleasurable at the time of

Impulsivity and Aggression. Edited by E. Hollander and D.J. Stein

performance and is consonant with the conscious wish of the subject, though some remorse and guilt may occur afterwards.

Unlike other impulse disorders, in gambling the DSM-III-R does not require the criterion of "inability to resist the impulse to . . .", probably reflecting the existence of socially sanctioned gambling. The essential feature of pathological gambling is the maladaptive use and the harmful sequelae of the behavior. The clinical features are summarized in the list of diagnostic criteria from the DSM-III-R (Table 1).

EPIDEMIOLOGY

PREVALENCE AND COURSE

Pathological gambling is more frequent among the general population than are other impulse control disorders. The prevalence is estimated at 0.2–3.3% (Volberg and Steadman, 1988) and it seems to be much higher than it was a decade ago (Allcock, 1986). Gambling behavior is common in the general population, but only a small number of such individuals represent cases of true impulse control disorders (Dickerson et al., 1990). The disorder is more frequent in males than in females, and most cases begin in adolescence and early adulthood. Typically, the course is chronic or episodic and often occurs in "bouts" of uncontrolled gambling.

The following phases are usually present in the development of pathological gambling. A first phase, or winning phase, is characterized by a big win that accelerates gambling behavior. Winnings are followed by a losing phase, in which losses mount, leading the gambler to gamble to recover the lost money. At this point, the gambler adopts a chasing attitude, by which

Table 1 The DSM-III-R diagnostic criteria for pathological gambling

1. Frequent preoccupation with gambling or with obtaining money to gamble
2. Frequent gambling of larger amounts of money or over a longer period of time than intended
3. A need to increase the size or frequency of bets to achieve the desired excitement
4. Restlessness or irritability if unable to gamble
5. Repeated loss of money by gambling and returning another day to win back losses ("chasing")
6. Repeated efforts to reduce or stop gambling
7. Frequent gambling when expected to meet social or occupational obligations
8. Sacrifice of some important social, occupational, or recreational activity in order to gamble
9. Continuation of gambling despite inability to pay and mounting debts, or despite other significant social, occupational, or legal problems that the person knows to be exacerbated by gambling

he or she continues to gamble in order to get even. As losses keep mounting, negative social, family, and occupational consequences arise, giving way to a "desperation phase".

FAMILY STUDIES

Pathological gambling is more prevalent among the first-degree relatives of pathological gamblers, affecting about 20% (Saiz et al., 1992). Family studies of pathological gamblers have also shown an increased association with substance abuse disorders and mood disorders. It has been reported that 25–50% of all pathological gamblers have a first-degree relative with alcohol abuse (Ramírez et al., 1983), and 11% of first-degree relatives display alcohol abuse or dependence (Linden et al., 1986).

Mood disorders are present in about 10% of first-degree relatives of pathological gamblers (Roy et al., 1988a).

There is currently no information from twin studies on genetic inheritance.

COMORBIDITY

Other psychiatric disorders are frequently associated with pathological gambling. Cross-sectional studies indicate that comorbid major depression may be present in up to 70% of pathological gamblers. The incidence is higher at the time the gambling is stopped, but additional depressive episodes have been identified in 50% of gamblers before or after stopping gambling (McCormick et al., 1984). High rates of bipolar I and II disorders and cyclothymia have also been reported in pathological gamblers (Linden et al., 1986). The only follow-up study available to date showed a rate of clinical depression of 18% among pathological gamblers who were abstinent for 6 months, despite improvement in work and family life (Taber et al., 1987).

Pathological gambling is also associated with a high prevalence (30–40%) of substance abuse disorders (Ramírez et al., 1983; Sáiz et al., 1992).

PATHOGENESIS OF PATHOLOGICAL GAMBLING

Attempts to explain the nature and pathogenesis of pathological gambling have been influenced by various theoretical approaches. Initial behavioral and psychodynamic theories have been complemented in recent decades by psychophysiological and cognitive research and, more recently, a neurobiological perspective. At present, no one separate theory can satisfactorily explain the disorder and a comprehensive model combines different contributions.

PSYCHOANALYTICAL THEORIES

Psychoanalysts propose that gambling represents a displacement of sexual satisfaction. By enjoyment and subsequent punishment (financial losses), gambling behavior activates unconscious forbidden drives related to Oedipal wishes (Bergler, 1936). However, other psychoanalytical authors have emphasized the pre-Oedipal nature of gambling manifested by the regressed and demanding attitude of these patients. Heavy gambling involves feelings of omnipotence and expectations of magical intervention that can modify the outcome of luck (Greenson, 1947).

LEARNING THEORIES

Under the rubric of learning theory, gambling develops as an operant conditioned behavior. Financial rewards are the positive reinforcement in gambling. More than 70% of gamblers entering treatment report that winning money is the main reason for gambling (Dickerson et al., 1990). What differentiates gambling from other operant behaviors, however, is the variable nature of reinforcement, without a fixed-interval schedule.

This variable form of reinforcement is one of the most powerful behavior maintainers known (Custer, 1982). Although the gambler knows that the odds are against him in the long run, partial reinforcements are likely to produce gambling behavior highly resistant to cessation. The importance of financial reinforcement contingencies in the development of pathological gambling is supported by the fact that those types of gambling with rapidly provided reinforcement (e.g. casinos and poker machines) lead more frequently to pathological gambling than do slowly reinforced games, such as weekly lotteries (Dickerson, 1990).

COGNITIVE DISTORTIONS

The persistence of gambling, despite the acknowledgment of a predictable negative outcome in the long term, cannot be understood without the existence of special types of cognition in the gambler. Gamblers tend to feel a greater degree of control over the outcome of the game than they actually have, as well as an unrealistic optimism. Some studies show that 80% of gamblers think that they will be successful on their next bet and many of them think that they can influence the outcome of the game (Gadboury and Ladouceur, 1989). Another typically biased cognition in pathological gamblers is the idea that chasing is a positive strategy. A run of bad luck must always come to an end and be followed by a run of wins. The gambler has the perception of being owed money and a feeling of deserving reparation (Legg England and Götestam, 1991), which is in consonance with the omnipotence and magical thinking described by psychoanalytical researchers.

ADDICTIVE THEORIES

The similarities of pathological gambling to other addictive behaviors have been widely suggested as indicating the addictive nature of this behavior. Several clinical features of addiction have been reported in pathological gambling, including tolerance (the gambler needs to make larger bets every time) and withdrawal symptoms. Irritability, depression, restlessness, decreased concentration, and obsessional thoughts have been described upon cessation of gambling (Wray and Dickerson, 1981). Like other addictions, gambling displaces other major aspects of life, relegating them to secondary importance, and there is also a craving for gambling that often results in "bouts" of the behavior. For some authors, gambling behavior resembles the pharmacological model of benzodiazepines (Custer, 1982). As with these drugs, in gamblers, there is a facilitation of punished responses. Thus, gambling does not seem to be affected by negative consequences and negative responses in the environment. Gambling may also activate the opiate system, since gambling withdrawal is often associated with diarrhea, tremor, headaches, abdominal pain, and other symptoms reminiscent of opiate withdrawal (Custer, 1982).

GAMBLING AS AN AFFECTIVE DISORDER

The idea that gambling is a behavioral attempt to modify the individual's internal state has recently drawn much attention. Gambling represents an important emotional and physiological event. Gambling is generally accompanied by increases in peripheral sympathetic activity, as manifested by changes in heart rate, and is associated with a subjective feeling of activation (Dickerson et al., 1987). Activation is reported as a sense of euphoria or excitement with an increase in mood and a decrease in tiredness that resembles the effects of amphetamines or opiates (Hickey et al., 1986). Most gamblers report that they initiated gambling to forget troubles and to ward off emotional states such as loneliness, depression, or anxiety (Blaszczynsky and McConaghy, 1989). Moreover, the duration of gambling sessions and persistence of gambling while losing is longer when associated with a depressed mood.

Interestingly, depression is usually associated with negative expectations, feelings of worthlessness, and a loss of self-esteem, implying that a depressed gambler should feel less likely to win. However, it could be argued that the illusion of control and omnipotent expectations associated with gambling could be an attractive feature for the depressed individual (Legg England and Götestam, 1991). To this extent, animal research shows that being in a position of control over events acts as a reinforcer and is associated with a reduction in stress and possibly with opioid secretion (Miller, 1979).

As noted before, several authors have found that gambling is associated with high rates of comorbid depression. The conclusion from these studies is that gambling represents an antidepressant behavioral mechanism, which explains the fact that gambling is often the only activity that really interests pathological gamblers. However, these data must be interpreted cautiously regarding the etiopathogenic role of depression. In this light, it has also been reported that most gamblers perceive that their negative life events and subsequent distress is mostly dependent on gambling itself, suggesting that a significant proportion of their dysphoric symptoms stems from the primary gambling disorder (Roy et al., 1988a).

GAMBLING AS A SENSATION-SEEKING BEHAVIOR

Other lines of research have investigated the relationship between gambling and the individual's internal arousal. Underaroused states are usually associated with impaired attention and dysphoric mood. Zuckerman (1980) hypothesized that high-sensation seeking subjects have a propensity to gamble as an attempt to elevate their persistently low levels of arousal. In *The Gambler*, Dostoyevsky wrote: "... I really was overcome by a terrible craving for risk. Perhaps the soul passing through such a wide range of sensations is not satisfied but only exacerbated by them ...". Studies of sensation seeking among gamblers, however, have produced inconsistent results, ranging from positive to negative and nonsignificant relationships between sensation seeking and gambling (Anderson and Brown, 1984; Blaszczynsky et al., 1986). This lack of uniformity may result from methodological differences and the time at which assessment was made. For instance, the degree of sensation seeking can be affected by depression or anxiety, which are commonly present in gamblers at the time of seeking treatment (Blaszczynsky et al., 1986).

GAMBLING AS A DISORDER OF IMPULSE CONTROL

Finally, it has been stated that the core feature of pathological gambling is the low ability to control the impulse to gamble. As in many other pleasurable activities, many people feel attracted to gamble without developing any maladaptive behavior. Only those subjects with a reduced impulse control fail to stop gambling when it becomes a pernicious behavior. This idea has predominated in the nosological discussion of the DSM-III-R and ICD-10, leading to the inclusion of pathological gambling among other impulse control disorders.

Some authors have suggested that pathological gambling could lie in a spectrum of compulsive impulsive disorders (Hollander, 1993). This spectrum is characterized by the emergence of morbid impulses and ideas, with the presence or absence of cognitive resistance as the differentiating factor in various disorders, including obsessive compulsive disorder, trichotillomania, kleptomania, pathological gambling, and some forms of borderline personality disorder (Jenike, 1989). Of note is that high rates of obsessive compulsive disorder have been reported among pathological gamblers (Linden et al., 1986), and some recent neurobiological and pharmacological findings indicating a dysfunction of central serotonergic activity (Moreno et al., 1991; Hollander et al., 1992; Carrasco et al., 1993) seem to support this hypothesis (see later).

Close to the impulsivity hypothesis, some findings show that recovered gamblers might have EEG patterns similar to those of children with attention deficit disorder (ADD) (Goldstein et al., 1985). This relationship was confirmed by the demonstration of a correlation between adult gambling and childhood behaviors related to attention deficit disorders in the same patients (Carlton et al., 1987).

NEUROBIOLOGY OF PATHOLOGICAL GAMBLING

The nosological delimitation of pathological gambling by the DSM-III only in 1980 encouraged researchers to study the physiological mechanisms of the disorder but explains why investigation of the neurobiology of gambling is still in its infancy.

DEXAMETHASONE RESPONSE

Despite the previously demonstrated association between pathological gambling and depression, the only study that has investigated the dexamethasone response in pathological gamblers found that all subjects in the sample were supressors, i.e. had a normal response (Ramírez et al., 1988). However, the authors found significantly higher diurnal fluctuations of basal cortisol levels in a subgroup of gamblers with depressive characteristics as measured by the Minnesota Multiphasic Personality Inventory (MMPI), indicating that some hypothalamic–pituitary axis dysfunction might be present.

NORADRENERGIC FUNCTION

Noradrenergic function in pathological gambling has been the focus of some studies. Central noradrenergic activity is thought to regulate internal arousal and brain activation, and a number of studies have found alterations in plasma and cerebrospinal fluid (CSF) metabolites of norepinephrine (noradrenaline) in high-sensation seeking individuals (Ballenger et al., 1983).

In consonance with these findings, Roy et al. (1988b) found that pathological gamblers had a significantly higher centrally produced fraction of CSF 3-methoxy-4-hydroxyphenylglycol (MHPG), as well as significantly greater urinary output of norepinephrine than normal controls. Moreover, concentrations of MHPG (Roy et al., 1989) were positively correlated with the degree of extraversion as measured on the Eysenck Personality Inventory (EPI). This study contained a subgroup of gamblers who met the DSM-III criteria for major depressive disorder, which might itself explain a dysregulation of the noradrenergic system. However, no differences were found between the depressed and nondepressed gamblers on any of the indexes of noradrenergic function measured. A primary noradrenergic dysfunction, probably reflecting specific differences in internal arousal, might therefore be present in association with pathological gambling.

SEROTONERGIC FUNCTION

The phenomenological similarities between pathological gambling and other impulsive disorders have stimulated the search for abnormalities in serotonergic function. There is a well-established association between high degree of impulsivity and low CSF 5-hydroxyindoleacetic acid (5-HIIA). However, in one study pathological gamblers had similar CSF 5-HIIA levels to controls (Roy et al., 1988b). None the less, individuals with antisocial personality were excluded from this study, as was stated by DSM-III guidelines. Since antisocial subjects tend to have the lowest CSF 5-HIIA levels (Linnoila et al., 1983), the biased sample might have excluded the very gamblers with decreased 5-HIIA concentrations.

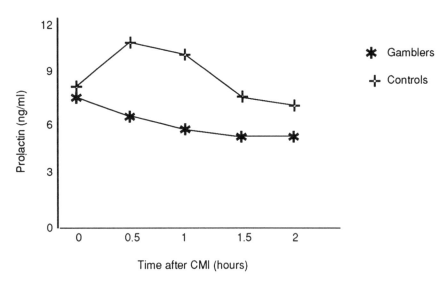

Figure 1 Prolactin response to intravenous clomipramine (CMI) in gamblers and controls (figure provided by I. Moreno).

A more sensible strategy to investigate central serotonergic function is the use of serotonergic challenges. Several reports have shown that hormonal responses to serotonergic agonists are reduced in impulsive patients, such as suicidal depressives (López-Ibor et al., 1990) and individuals with impulsive personality disorders (Coccaro et al., 1990; Hollander et al., in press), supporting the idea of reduced serotonergic activity. To date, there has been only one study that has applied this procedure to pathological gamblers (Moreno et al., 1991a). By using a challenge of 12.5 mg of intravenous clomipramine, it was demonstrated that a sample of eight pathological gamblers had significantly blunted prolactin response compared with a group of controls matched for sex and age (Figure 1). The cortisol response was also blunted in this study, but the differences did not reach statistical significance. These findings support the existence of reduced serotonergic postsynaptic activity in pathological gambling. It is of note that gamblers with associated major depression were excluded from the study, which suggests that serotonin (5-hydroxytraptamine) abnormalities were related specifically to the gambling behavior.

PLATELET MONOAMINE OXIDASE ACTIVITY

As has been demonstrated previously (Schalling et al., 1987; Ward et al., 1987), low platelet monoamine oxidase (MAO) activity is associated with high levels of sensation seeking. Low levels of platelet MAO have also been reported in pathological gambling in one study (Carrasco et al., 1993). Gamblers showed a significantly lower platelet MAO activity than controls. Monoamine oxidase changes were not correlated with scores on sensation-seeking scales in this study but were correlated with measures of impulsivity, which supports the impulsive nature of gambling. Of note is that all

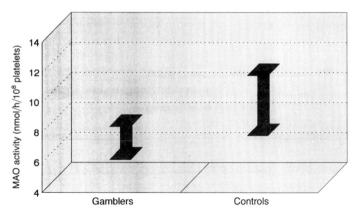

Figure 2 Platelet monoamine oxidase (MAO) activity in pathological gamblers and controls [data from Carrasco et al. (1994)].

gamblers in the sample had low platelet MAO, indicating that MAO reduction could reflect a discrete pathological factor. Since platelet MAO activity is a marker of serotonergic activity, it can be hypothesized that low platelet MAO in gamblers reflects a dysfunction of serotonergic activity.

TREATMENT

The treatment of pathological gambling involves a multifactorial approach, including psychological, social, and probably pharmacological measures. A wide range of therapeutic interventions in gamblers has been described, but the lack of controlled methodologies precludes making generalized conclusions. In the literature, only one controlled treatment study can be found (McConaghy et al., 1983) that shows that imaginal desensitization is more effective than aversive therapy in reducing the urge to gamble and gambling behavior. Isolated case reports and case series have shown insight-oriented therapies, various types of behavior therapy, cognitive restructuring, and cognitive behavior therapy to be effective for pathological gambling. However, a number of authors have noted that treating pathological gamblers, like other patients with impulse control disorders, is difficult given the patient's lack of insight, refusal to take responsibility for their own behavior, denial, concomitant legal difficulties, and associated alcohol abuse (McElroy et al., 1992).

Psychosocial interventions in the treatment of pathological gambling should be oriented to the modification of several factors:

1. Reducing conditioning stimili for gambling: gambling sites or gambling images (such as advertisements) should be avoided. Contact with money must be reduced by removing credit cards and controlling bank accounts.
2. Maintenance of abstinence: there is no general agreement on the need for complete abstinence to achieve a good outcome. Generally, total abstinence from gambling is required to prevent gambling "bouts". However, some selected patients may benefit from learning new styles of gambling without impulsive and uncontrolled decisions.
3. Cognitive restructuring of unrealistic expectations of winning and of beliefs that chasing is a sensible strategy to regain losses is needed. Also, some depressive attributional styles that induce the subject to gamble in response to negative events should be restructured.
4. Financial needs should be reduced by counselling about job opportunities and improving budgeting skills.
5. Negative internal states must be modified. Also, the pathological dependence of the patient's self-esteem on winning at gambling must be confronted. Marital or social problems are usually associated with

pathological gambling, producing dysphoric states that can precipitate further gambling.

6. The role of self-help groups, such as Gamblers Anonymous, in the treatment seems to be highly beneficial if long-term attendance is achieved, but most gamblers drop out after a few visits (Stewart and Brown, 1988).

As in other impulsive disorders, it is expected that the pharmacological treatment of pathological gambling may have beneficial effects, though only a few isolated reports are available as yet. A promising report by Hollander et al. (1992) of preliminary findings from an ongoing controlled study shows significant improvement of pathological gambling during clomipramine treatment. In addition, case reports suggest that lithium treatment is effective (Moskovitz, 1980; Moreno and Saiz, 1991b).

REFERENCES

Allcock, C.C. (1986). Pathological gambling. *Aust. N. Z. J. Psychiatry*, 4, 369–373.
American Psychiatric Association (1987). *Diagnostic and Statistical Manual of Mental Disorders*, 3rd edn—revised. American Psychiatric Press, Washington, D.C.
Anderson, G., and Brown, R.I.F. (1984). Real and laboratory gambling, sensation seeking and arousal. *Br. J. Psychol.*, 75, 401–410.
Ballenger, J.C., Post, R.M., Jimerson, D.C., et al. (1983). Biochemical correlates of personality in normals. *Pers. Indiv. Diff.*, 4, 615–625.
Bergler, E. (1936). The psychology of the gambler. *Imago*, 22, 409.
Blaszczynsky, A., and McConaghy, N. (1989). Anxiety and or depression in the pathogenesis of addictive gambling. *Int. J. Addict.*, 24, 337–350.
Blaszczynsky, A.P., Wilson, A.C., and McConaghy, N. (1986). Sensation seeking and pathological gambling. *Br. J. Addict.*, 81, 111–117.
Carlton, P.L., Manowitz, P., McBride, H., Nora, R., Swartzburg, M., and Goldstein, L. (1987). Attention deficit disorder and pathological gambling. *J. Clin. Psychiatry*, 48, 487–488.
Carrasco, J.L., Saiz, J., Moreno, I., and López-Ibor, J.J. (1994). Low platelet MAO activity in pathological gambling. Acta Psych Scand. (in press).
Coccaro, E.F., Siever, L.J., Klar, H.M., et al. (1990). Serotonergic studies in patients with affective and personality disorders: Correlates with suicidal and impulsive aggressive behavior. *Arch. Gen. Psychiatry*, 46, 587–599.
Custer, R.L. (1982). An overview of compulsive gambling. In: *Addictive Disorders Update: Alcoholism, Drug Abuse, Gambling* (eds P.A. Carone, S.F. Yolles, and S.N. Kieffer). Human Sciences Press, New York.
Dickerson, M., Hinchy, J., and Fabre, J. (1987). Chasing, arousal and sensation seeking in off-course gamblers. *Br. J. Addict.*, 82, 673–680.
Dickerson, M.G. (1990). Internal and external determinants of persistent gambling; implications for treatment. In: *Self Control and the Addictive Behaviors* (eds N. Heather, W.R. Willer, and J. Greely). Pergamon Press.
Dickerson, M.G., Walker, G., Legg England, S., and Hinchy, J. (1990). Demographic, personality, cognitive and behavioral correlates of off-course betting involvement. *J. Gambling Behav.*, 6, 165–182.

Gadboury, A., and Ladouceur, R. (1989). Erroneous perceptions and gambling. *J. Soc. Behav. Pers.*, 4, 411–420.

Goldstein, L., Manowitz, P., and Nora, R. (1985). Differential EEG activation and pathological gambling. *Biol. Psychiatry*, 20, 1232–1234.

Greenson, R.R. (1947). On gambling. *Am Imago*, 4, 61–77.

Hickey, J.E., Haertzen, C.A., and Henningfield, J.E. (1986). Simulation of the gambling responses on the Addiction Research Center Inventory. *Addict. Behav.*, 11, 345–349.

Hollander, E. (ed.) (1993a). *Obsessive–Compulsive Related Disorders*. American Psychiatric Press, Washington, D.C.

Hollander, E., Frenkel, M., DeCaria, C., Trungold, S., and Stein, D.J. (1992). Treatment of pathological gambling with clomipramine [letter]. *Am. J. Psychiatry*, 149(5), 710–711.

Hollander, E., Stein, D.J., DeCaria, C.M., et al. (in press). Serotonergic sensitivity in borderline personality disorder: Preliminary findings. *Am. J. Psychiatry*.

Jenike, M.A. (1989). Obsessive–compulsive and related disorders: A hidden epidemic. *N. Engl. J. Med.*, 321, 539–541.

Legg England, S., and Götestam, K.G. (1991). The nature and treatment of excessive gambling. *Acta Psychiatr. Scand.*, 84, 113–120.

Linden, R.D., Pope, H.G. Jr, and Jonas, J.M. (1986). Pathological gambling and major affective disorder: Preliminary findings. *J. Clin. Psychiatry*, 47, 201–203.

Linnoila, M., Virkunnen, M., Scheinin, M., Nuutila, A., Rimon, R., Goodwin, F. K. (1983). Low cerebrospinal fluid 5-hydroxyindoleacetic acid concentration differentiates impulsive from nonimpulsive violent behavior. *Life Sci.*, 33, 2609–2614.

López-Ibor, J.J., Lana, F., and Saiz, J. (1990). Conductas autolíticas impulsivas y serotonina. *Actas Luso Esp. Neurol. Psiquiatr. Cienc. Afines*, 18(5), 316–325.

McConaghy, N., Armstrong, M., Blaszczynsky, A., and Allcock, C. (1983). Controlled comparison of aversive therapy and imaginal desensitization in compulsive gambling. *Br. J. Psychiatry*, 142, 366–372.

McCormick, R.A., Russo, A.M., Ramírez, L.F., and Taber, J.L. (1984). Affective disorders among pathological gamblers seeking treatment. *Am. J. Psychiatry*, 141, 215–218.

McElroy, S.L., Hudson, J.I., Harrison, G.P., Keck, P.E., and Aizley, H.G. (1992). The DSM-III-R impulse control disorders not elsewhere classified: Clinical characteristics and relationships to other psychiatric disorders. *Am. J. Psychiatry*, 149, 318–327.

Miller, S.M. (1979). Controllability and human stress: Method, evidence and theory. *Behav. Res. Ther.*, 17, 287–304.

Moreno, I., and Saiz, J. (1991). Tratamiento de un caso de ludopatía (juego patológico) con sales de litio. *An. Psiquiatr.*, 2, 249–254.

Moreno, I., Saiz-Ruiz, J., and López-Ibor, J.J. (1991). Serotonin and gambling dependence. *Hum. Psychopharmacol.*, 6 (suppl.), 9–12.

Moskowitz, J.A. (1980). Lithium and lady luck. *N. Y. State J. Med.*, 80, 785–788.

Ramírez, L.F., McCormick, R.A., Russo, A.M., and Taber, J.L. (1983). Patterns of substance abuse in pathological gamblers undergoing treatment. *Addict. Behav.*, 8, 425–428.

Ramírez, L.F., McCormick, R.A., and Lowy, M.T. (1988). Plasma cortisol and depression in pathological gamblers. *Br. J. Psychiatry*, 153, 684–686.

Roy, A., Custer, R., Lorenz, V., and Linnoila, M. (1988a). Depressed pathological gamblers. *Acta Psychiatr. Scand.*, 77, 163–165.

Roy, A., Adinoff, B., Roehrich, L., et al. (1988b). Pathological gambling: A psychobiological study. *Arch. Gen. Psychiatry*, 45, 369–373.

Roy, A., De Jong, J., and Linnoila, M. (1989). Extraversion in pathological gamblers. *Arch. Gen. Psychiatry*, 46, 679–681.

Saiz, J., Moreno, I., and López-Ibor, J.J. (1992). Ludopatía: Estudio clínico y terapéutico-evolutivo de un grupo de jugadores patológicos. *Actas. Luso Esp. Neurol. Psiquiatr.*, 20(4), 189–197.

Schalling, D., Asberg, M., Edman, G., and Levander, S. (1987). Markers for vulnerability to psychopathology: Temperaments traits associated with platelet MAO activity. *Acta Psychiatr. Scand.*, 76, 172–182.

Stewart, R.M., and Brown, R.I.F. (1988). An outcome study of Gamblers Anonymous. *Br. J. Psychiatry*, 152, 284–288.

Taber, J.L., McCormick, R.A., Russo, A.M., Adkins, B.J., and Ramírez, L.F. (1987). Follow-up of pathological gamblers after treatment. *Am. J. Psychiatry*, 144, 757–761.

Volberg, R.A., and Steadman, H.J. (1988). Refining prevalence estimates of pathological gambling. *Am. J. Psychiatry*, 145, 502–505.

Ward, P.B., Catts, S.V., Norman, T.R., Burrows, G.D., and McConaghy, N. (1987). Low platelet monoamine oxidase and sensation seeking in males: An establish relationship? *Acta Psychiatr. Scand.*, 75, 86–90.

World Health Organization (1992). *International Classification of Mental Disorders and Behaviors*. World Health Organization, Geneva.

Wray, I., and Dickerson, M.G. (1981). Cessation of high frequency gambling and "withdrawal" symptoms. *Br. J. Addict.*, 76, 401–405.

Zuckerman, M., Buchsbaum, M.S., and Murphy, D.L. (1980). Sensation seeking and its biological correlates. *Psychol. Bull.*, 88, 187–214.

Part IV

IMPULSIVE AGGRESSIVE PERSONALITY DISORDERS

10 Borderline Personality Disorder

ANTONIA S NEW*, ROBERT L TRESTMAN‡, AND LARRY J
SIEVER‡
*Formerly: Department of Psychiatry, Mount Sinai Medical Center,
Bronx, NY, USA. Currently: University of Pittsburgh School of Medicine,
Pittsburgh, PA, USA.
‡Bronx Veterans Affairs Medical Center and The Mount Sinai Medical
Center, Bronx, NY, USA

INTRODUCTION

The term "borderline" was first used to describe a pathological condition in 1938, when it was applied to patients who had both psychotic and neurotic features and was thus "bordering" these two domains (Zanarini, 1993). In the 1950s, terms like "borderline schizophrenia", "pseudoneurotic schizophrenia", and "latent schizophrenia" were used to describe a similar group of patients thought to have an allied condition "on the border" of schizophrenia (Stone et al., 1992).

The borderline diagnosis has subsequently evolved through a number of conceptualizations. Kernberg used the term "borderline personality organization" to describe a level of personality organization lying between neurosis and psychosis: a severe impairment in ego-integration in patients with intact reality testing (Kernberg, 1977). To establish this diagnosis, the clinician employs a psychoanalytically oriented interview focusing on the patient's interpersonal relationships and internal image of self and others (Kernberg, 1977). With the advent of the DSM-III, the borderline diagnosis was made by criteria including a cluster of behaviors and definable cognitions. This approach allowed the diagnosis to be made through operationalized criteria and had the advantage of allowing more reliable comparisons of patients meeting the diagnosis. Subsequently, borderline personality disorder (BPD) was viewed as an illness in the affective disorder spectrum (Akiskal et al., 1981); more recently, the diagnosis has also been thought of as a disorder of impulse control, in the spectrum of antisocial personality disorder, substance abuse disorders and perhaps eating disorders (Zanarini, 1992).

Impulsivity and Aggression. Edited by E. Hollander and D.J. Stein
© 1995 John Wiley & Sons Ltd

THE BORDERLINE DIAGNOSIS

A test of diagnostic validity may reasonably consist of (Robins and Guze, 1970):

1. Phenomenological distinctness. Are there a core set of symptoms characteristic of BPD? Do these symptoms differentiate it from other diagnoses? Can the diagnosis be made reliably by different examiners?
2. Family history. Do first-degree relatives of patients with the diagnosis have an increased morbid risk for the illness?
3. Treatment. Is there a reproducible response to biological treatments?
4. Long-term outcome. Does the diagnosis remain phenomenologically distinct from other diagnoses over time?

Clinical studies assessing whether BPD can be differentiated from other major psychiatric diagnoses and whether a core set of symptoms defining the diagnosis can be identified have yielded mixed results. These studies have employed a number of semi-structured interviews to delineate a group of definable behaviors and cognitions that comprise the diagnosis. The principal instruments used are the Diagnostic Interview for Borderline Patients (DIB; Gunderson et al., 1981), the Schedule for Interviewing Borderlines (SIB; Baron and Gruen, 1980), the Structured Clinical Interview for DSM-III-R Personality Disorders (SCID-II; Spitzer et al., 1987), the Personality Disorders Examination (PDE; Loranger, 1988), and the Structured Interview for DSM-III Personality Disorders (SIDP; Pfohl et al., 1982). In the studies which did not exclude patients with major psychotic disorders, BPD was reliably differentiated from schizophrenia, though one study found a 10–20% comorbidity (McGlashan, 1983; Pope et al., 1983). Many studies have also reported a high degree of comorbidity of BPD with major mood disorders (bipolar disorder and major depression), ranging from 35 to 51.5% (McGlashan, 1983; Pope et al., 1983; Frances et al., 1984). Comorbidity of BPD with a major mood disorder does not inherently bring into question the validity of the BPD diagnosis, in view of the clear criteria established for major affective disorders. Although affective lability is a part of the BPD diagnosis, the clinical phenomenology of affective lability is clearly distinct from unipolar major depression and classical bipolar disorder. There are potential areas of diagnostic overlap, however, between severe affectively unstable BPD and rapid cycling or mixed bipolar disorder.

There is more of a concern, however, with BPD criteria that overlap those of other less clearly delineated diagnoses. Specifically, BPDs distinctness from other personality disorders has been questioned. Under the DSM-III criteria, the rate of concomitant histrionic personality disorder (HPD) has been reported to be as high as 55–73% (Pope et al., 1983; Grueneich, 1992). The overlap with HPD may be diminished under the DSM-III-R criteria, as self-injurious behavior was dropped from criteria for HPD (Grueneich, 1992). The rate of concomitant antisocial diagnosis in borderline patients has varied in the literature from 9 to 67%; the rate of a comorbid schizotypal personality disorder diagnosis in borderline patients has varied from 0 to 43% (Pope et al., 1983; Grueneich, 1992). It is apparent that not only is there significant overlap between BPD and histrionic, antisocial, and schizotypal personality disorders, but also there is great variability in the reported rates of overlap. Some of this variability may result from methodological differences in the studies, including the use of retrospective data from charts and the use of non-blind raters for the diagnostic interviews. However, the studies also vary in the diagnostic instrument used and hence the clinical criteria applied to make the diagnosis. While inter-rater reliability has been reported to be high with all of the instruments cited (median $\kappa = 0.78$, range 0.72–0.96) (Frances et al., 1984; Grueneich, 1992), the agreement among three scales (DIB, SIB, and SCID-II) in a study rating the same patients was only 52% (Kavoussi et al., 1990). Other assessments of interscale reliability between the SCID-II and the PDE showed a diagnostic agreement of 0.53–0.62. Ratings using self-report questionnaires and clinical interviews as comparison assessments yielded even lower diagnostic agreement (Perry, 1992).

Efforts to identify a core set of symptoms within the borderline diagnosis show some, but not complete, agreement. Most studies have attempted to define which of the DSM-III or DSM-III-R criteria for BPD are the most discriminating. In borderline patients diagnosed by DIB criteria, three of the eight DSM-III criteria for BPD were found to be the most discriminating: unstable interpersonal relationships, impulsivity, and self-damaging acts. Inappropriate anger and intolerance of aloneness were the least discriminating (McGlashan, 1987). In a prospective study of borderline patients using DSM-III-R criteria and non-blinded raters, a hierarchy of discriminating symptoms was delineated in descending order: disturbed interpersonal relationships, impulsivity, feelings of emptiness, self-destructive behaviors, intense anger, and abandonment avoidance (Nurnberg et al., 1991). There is reasonably good agreement between these studies in that three criteria from one study fall within the other study's top four. Data accumulated from a number of studies showed the most effective inclusion criteria for BPD to be unstable interpersonal relationships and self-damaging acts. Impulsivity was prevalent in borderline patients but was also present in patients with other personality disorder diagnoses. One review also cited "intolerance of being alone" as the least discriminating criteria (Grueneich, 1992). It should be noted that this criterion was changed in the DSM-III-R to "frantic efforts to avoid real or imagined abandonment". By the revised DIB (DIB-R) criteria, seven symptoms were found to discriminate BPD from other diagnoses: quasipsychotic thought, self-mutilation, manipulative suicide efforts, abandonment/engulfment/annihilation concerns, demandingness/entitlement, treatment regressions, and countertransference difficulties (Zanarini et al., 1990). Again, these features overlap with the DSM-III-R criteria but they include features like psychotic episodes not used in the DSM-III-R system.

Although BPD appears to be distinguishable from schizophrenia and from major affective disorders (with some comorbidity), a categorical approach to the diagnosis has led to difficulties in distinguishing BPD from other personality disorders and to a lack of agreement among diagnostic instruments. One solution to these difficulties is to shift the focus of research from the diagnostic category to dimensions of the diagnosis; this chapter focuses on impulsivity as a trait of BPD. Impulsivity is a particularly important aspect of the diagnosis, because it is prevalent and accounts for a substantial portion of the morbidity (self-injurious behavior, substance abuse, and destruction of property) and mortality associated with BPD. Viewing BPD as a disorder of impulse control, as are antisocial personality disorder and substance abuse disorders, provides a theoretical way of explaining the overlap of certain criteria among diagnoses. It may be that the trait of impulsivity itself characterizes a cluster of diagnoses. Impulsivity might be viewed as a heritable trait, and the factors determining the other characteristics of a patient's illness might be a combination of other heritable traits and environmental factors (Siever and Davis, 1991). Family studies might therefore address the question of whether the BPD diagnosis *per se* is inherited, or whether there is a stronger pattern of inheritance of traits such as impulsivity.

FAMILY STUDIES

A number of studies have investigated the possibility of familial transmission of BPD. In a retrospective study reviewing charts of patients diagnosed with BPD by the DSM-III criteria, schizophrenia, and bipolar disorder, first-degree relatives of borderline probands had an 11.6% morbid risk for borderline personality disorder, compared with a 1.4% risk for BPD in schizophrenic probands and a 0.7% risk for BPD in bipolar probands (Loranger et al., 1982). Prospective studies have shown a range of 15.3–24.9% morbid risk of BPD in first-degree relatives of borderline probands (Baron et al., 1985; Links et al., 1988b; Zanarini et al., 1988). This risk was significantly greater than the risk for BPD in first-degree relatives of probands with schizotypal personality disorder (STPD; 3.0–6.9%), dysthymia (9.6%), antisocial personality disorder (ASPD; 4.1%), and normal controls (4.1%). One chart review contradicts these findings, reporting 0.8% morbid risk of BPD in relatives of borderline probands (Pope et al., 1983). These studies suffer from methodological difficulties in that family history of the disorder was gleaned at least in large part from the proband, not from direct interviews with family members. Furthermore, there remains the problem of a lack of agreement between diagnostic instruments used for BPD. Nevertheless, these studies tend to support the presence of some degree of familial transmission of BPD.

Studies have not shown an increased morbid risk of schizophrenia in relatives of borderline probands (Loranger et al., 1982; Links et al., 1988b; Zanarini et al., 1988; Schulz et al., 1989). An increased risk of schizophrenia, however, has been reported in relatives of probands with both borderline and schizotypal features (Schulz et al., 1989). A number of studies have reported an increased risk of unipolar depression in relatives of borderline patients (Loranger et al., 1982; Links et al., 1988b). This has been used as an argument for including BPD in the spectrum of affective disorders. However, it appears that the increase in depression in relatives of borderlines is largely accounted for by comorbid depression in the borderline proband himself (Zanarini et al., 1988): no increased rate of BPD over other personality disorders was found in first-degree relatives of probands with unipolar depression (Maier et al., 1992). Taken together, these data suggest the possibility of a familial transmission of BPD; however, to assess whether this derives from environmental factors or whether there is genetic transmission, one would need to look at adoption or twin studies. The one study that attempted to do this did not show a greater concordance in monozygotic twins ($n = 3$) compared with dizygotic twins ($n = 7$) for BPD (Torgersen, 1984). The results of this preliminary study supported neither a genetic component to BPD nor a genetic relationship between BPD and schizophrenia, though the number of patients used was small. A subsequent pilot study suggests that while the borderline syndrome may not be genetically influenced, certain features of the syndrome may be. A genetic influence was found specifically in the following features in descending order: instability of relationships, impulsivity, anger, and affective instability (Torgersen, 1992). This finding highlights the usefulness of looking at the borderline syndrome in dimensional terms: investigating traits associated with the disorder, rather than investigating the disorder itself in purely categorical terms.

If the trait of impulsivity is itself heritable, one would expect to find an increase in impulsivity in the first-degree relatives of borderline patients. Impulsivity has been reported as one of the features of BPD found most frequently in the relatives of borderline patients (Links et al., 1988b). Impulsive personality disorder traits have also been reported to be increased in the relatives of borderline patients compared with relatives of probands with schizophrenia or with other personality disorders (a mix of histrionic, schizotypal, compulsive, antisocial, paranoid, narcissistic, avoidant, and dependent). Impulsive personality traits in that study were specifically defined as including three of the following criteria: (1) physical fighting not associated with alcohol use, (2) stealing, (3) alcohol or drug abuse, (4) binge eating, (5) problem with gambling, (6) promiscuity, (7) self-damaging acts, (8) irrational angry outbursts, and (9) over-reaction to minor events (Silverman et al., 1991). A high incidence of ASPD, itself a diagnosis with impulsivity as a prominent feature, has been found in the relatives of patients with ASPD or BPD compared with relatives of patients with dysthymia (Zanarini et al., 1993). The suggestion that antisocial and borderline personality disorders are found together within families might support the notion of a cluster of impulse control disorders in which impulsivity itself is a heritable trait.

Biological measures associated with impulsivity have also been used to distinguish those personality disordered patients who might have a heritable trait for impulsivity. It has been reported that a decreased prolactin response to the serotonergic agonist, fenfluramine, correlates with impulsive aggression in personality disordered patients (Coccaro et al., 1989a); this discussed in more detail later in this chapter. The morbid risk of impulsive personality traits in relatives of personality disordered probands with a decreased prolactin response to fenfluramine was 25.8%, compared with 7.0% in relatives of personality disordered probands with a normal prolactin response to fenfluramine. Though the reduced prolactin response to fenfluramine was correlated with measures of aggression in the probands, correlation of clinical scores of impulsivity and aggression with increased family risk for impulsivity was not significant. This suggests the possibility that biological markers may be more sensitive markers for the heritable trait of impulsivity than clinical assessments of impulsivity itself (Coccaro et al., in press).

DEVELOPMENTAL ISSUES

Little has been published about the stability over time of the syndrome of BPD. One follow-up study into adulthood (ages 16–30 years) of a group of children (ages 6–10 years) diagnosed as borderline by Bemporad's criteria developed no major affective disorders or schizophrenia; Bemporad's criteria include a fluctuation in functioning, susceptibility to extreme anxiety, bizarre thinking, disturbed interpersonal relationships, and inability to control anger and to delay gratification (Bemporad et al., 1982). In adulthood, 16 out of 19 had personality disorder diagnoses, but only three out of 16 continued to a BPD diagnosis (Lofgren et al., 1991). This does not necessarily argue against stability of the diagnosis over time, as the criteria used for childhood diagnosis in this study are not the same as the DSM-III-R criteria. Furthermore, the diagnosis may appear differently in children than in adults. More research in longitudinal follow up of BPD into adulthood needs to be done.

If BPD is viewed as having multiple causes, certain features, such as impulsivity, may be inherited. Environmental factors, however, may also have a role in the etiology of the disorder. Certain childhood disorders are associated with an increased risk of BPD in adulthood. In one study, 25.5% of BPD adults were reported to have a childhood history of attention deficit disorder with hyperactivity (ADHD) or learning disabilities, whereas 18.2% of schizophrenic patients had this history (Andrulonis et al., 1982); the statistical significance of this difference was not assessed. Male patients with BPD, in particular, had a high incidence of childhood disorders: 39.6% had a history of learning disabilities, developmental delays or ADHD, as opposed to 13.8% in female BPD patients. Other reports, however, comparing borderline, schizophrenic, and depressed patients, found no increased incidence of delayed "milestones", learning difficulties, or hyperactivity in borderlines (Soloff and Millward, 1983). A higher incidence of reading difficulties and school failure was found in BPD patients than in depressed patients, but less than in schizophrenic patients. An early onset of head banging, temper tantrums, and drug abuse in BPD compared with both control groups was also reported (Soloff and Millward, 1983). Although BPD patients appear to have a high incidence of childhood ADHD, developmental delays, and learning disabilities, there appears to be little evidence that this is a specific finding when compared to other psychiatric diagnoses.

Another developmental factor that has been associated with BPD is a history of head trauma. In 91 borderline patients diagnosed by DSM-III criteria, an 11% incidence of head trauma, encephalitis, or epilepsy was reported (Andrulonis et al., 1980). In a comparison of BPD patients and schizophrenic patients, 14.2% of BPD and 7.3% of schizophrenic patients reported a history of head trauma, encephalitis, or epilepsy (Andrulonis et al., 1982). In a contradictory report, no difference was found between BPD, depressed, and schizophrenic patients (excluding patients with known CNS deficits, organic brain syndromes, current alcohol or drug abuse, or medical illnesses) in history of head trauma, CNS infections, general anesthesia, severe illnesses, or fever with delirium (Soloff and Millward, 1983). BPD patients did have a higher incidence of complications from pregnancy (17.8%) associated with their gestation, compared with schizophrenic (4.8%) and depressed patients (0%) (Soloff and Millward, 1983). As with a history of certain childhood disorders, a history of head trauma and other insults to the brain does not appear to be specific to BPD. Furthermore, even if such an increase were documented, the causal connection would not be established. If borderline patients have early evidence of impulsive traits, such as head banging and drug abuse, they might place themselves at increased risk for head injury as a secondary phenomenon.

A history of child abuse or neglect has been associated with BPD. History of child abuse has been a particularly difficult area to assess, in that the reliability of reporting has come into question. Both under- and over-reporting has been postulated, and external corroboration is unavailable in most cases. The rate of childhood physical abuse reported in patients with BPD ranges from 46 to 71% (Herman et al., 1989; Zanarini et al., 1989; Ludolph et al., 1990); the rate of sexual abuse reported in BPD ranges from 26 to 71% (Herman et al., 1989; Zanarini et al., 1989; Ludolph et al., 1990; Ogata et al., 1990). These rates of abuse were significantly higher than in comparison groups examined, such as patients with other personality disorders, dysthymia, and bipolar disease. Witnessing violence (Herman et al., 1989) and verbal abuse (Zanarini et al., 1989) appeared also to be more prevalent in the childhood history of patients with BPD than in comparison groups. Children with BPD, compared with other children coming to a clinic for outpatient psychiatric evaluation, had significantly more reported sexual or physical abuse (38.6% in BPD, 9% in other disorders). These rates are somewhat lower than most of the reports in adults; this may be related to the fact that patients were considered abused only when there was external corroboration of the abuse by parents or by the authorities (Goldman et al., 1992). Furthermore, this population of borderline patients was comprised of a greater proportion of males than is seen in the adult population, and abuse may be somewhat less common in males. Among military subjects coming for psychiatric evaluation, 32% had experienced sexual or physical abuse as children; of the abused group 69% were diagnosed with BPD, whereas in the nonabused group 35% were diagnosed with BPD (Raczek, 1992). In a group of patients coming to a general emergency room for evaluation, 70% reported a history of sexual abuse when asked specifically; of the abused group, 37% were diagnosed with BPD and 7% of the nonabused group were diagnosed with BPD (Briere and Zaidi, 1989).

Some studies have tried to correlate particular features of BPD with a history of abuse. Impulsive traits have been reported to be increased in BPD patients with a history of sexual abuse, such as suicidality, substance abuse, and promiscuity (Briere and Zaidi, 1989; Ogata et al., 1990; Raczek et al., 1992). Alcohol abuse and illicit drug use have been associated with a history of physical abuse in borderline patients, and combined sexual and physical abuse has been associated with a family history of alcohol abuse in the male relatives of borderline patients (Brown and Anderson, 1991). One hypothesis about the relationship between abuse in childhood and the development of BPD is that the abuse causes the emergence of the disorder. Another equally plausible hypothesis is that the proclivity towards impulsive acts is an inherited facet of the disorder. In that case, family members may also be impulsive and therefore be at higher risk for abusing their children. Borderline personality disorder patients would then be seen as coming from impulsive families and inheriting the tendency toward impulsivity. The degree to which they manifest impulsive behavior may be influenced by childhood experiences of abuse, for which they are at risk because of the impulsivity of their family members.

NEUROPSYCHOLOGICAL CHANGES

Neuropsychological disturbances, particularly disturbances of memory, have been posited as a contributing factor to some of the symptoms of BPD; defects of memory have been hypothesized to contribute to the unstable involvement in interpersonal relationships that BPD patients frequently demonstrate. Empirical studies have suggested that memory defects, including the recall of learned material, are present in some BPD patients. However, cueing seems to bring performance back to normal (O'Leary et al., 1991). Poor performance on neurocognitive tasks, particularly involving multistep, multielement associative operations (e.g. delayed memory, similarity comparisons, and proverb interpretations) have also been reported (Burgess, 1992). Other studies have found no evidence of defects in neuropsychological testing in BPD patients compared with historical values (Cornelius et al., 1989). No clearly reproducible neuropsychological deficit has been found in BPD. One might expect individuals with impulsive behaviors to manifest defects in attention, motivation and psychomotor performance, but these have not been seen in the neuropsychological testing of BPD (Cornelius et al., 1989; O'Leary et al., 1991). However, self-injurious behavior *per se* has been observed to correlate with a variety of deficits in memory in BPD patients (Burgess, 1991).

ELECTROPHYSIOLOGICAL STUDIES

Abnormalities on electroencephalogram (EEG) have been reported to be more prevalent in BPD than in control groups of patients with other psychiatric disorders, including depression and dysthymia (Andrulonis et al., 1980; Snyder and Pitts, 1984; Cowdry et al., 1985). The site of the reported abnormalities varies: posterior sharp wave activity has been reported (Cowdry et al., 1985); slow, fast and mixed wave activity have been reported diffusely, in the frontal, frontotemporal, and occipital regions (Snyder and Pitts, 1984). Other authors have not found EEG abnormalities in BPD patients compared with depressed patients (Archer et al., 1988; Cornelius et al., 1989). Attempts to correlate EEG abnormalities with specific symptoms of BPD have not, in general, been productive; however, pooled parasagittal mean frequency values from spectral analysis did correlate with anxiety levels in borderline patients after pharmacological amphetamine challenge (Cornelius et al., 1988). Increased risk for head injury might exist in patients with BPD because of their impulsivity. This explanation might account for the different locations in the brain of the findings of EEG abnormalities as well as the differing configurations of the findings.

Abnormal sleep patterns have been reported in BPD patients compared with normal controls. In particular, decreased sleep continuity, decreased

Stage 3 and 4 sleep, and decreased rapid eye movement (REM) latency have been reported (McNamara et al., 1984). However, these abnormalities were the same as those seen in a depressed group, and in fact all of the borderline patients in that study had as many depressive symptoms as the depressed group. Others found decreased REM latency and density only in those borderline patients who also had depressive symptoms (Lahmeyer et al., 1988). Sleep abnormalities may correlate with depression *per se*, cutting across other diagnostic categories.

Auditory event-related EEG potentials (ERPs) have been used as markers for psychiatric diagnostic groups. Borderline personality disorder patients have manifested longer P300 (a late ERP component of auditory stimulation) latency and smaller amplitude in a number of studies (Blackwood et al., 1986; Kutcher et al., 1987; Drake et al., 1991). This pattern is similar to that reported in schizophrenic patients, and different from depressed patients and from normal controls (Kutcher et al., 1987). Longer latency and lower amplitudes were also seen in the early ERP components in one study of BPD patients (Drake et al., 1991).

Various electrophysiological approaches have suggested that there is some abnormality associated with BPD; however, no finding has reached a level of reliability that would make it clinically useful. Further research needs to be done to define subgroups within the BPD population which might show a more reliable association.

NEUROBIOLOGY

NEUROIMAGING

Structural brain abnormalities as seen on computerized tomography (CT) scan have been reported in schizophrenia and other populations of psychiatric patients. The abnormalities reported in EEG and ERP studies of BPD patients suggest that structural brain abnormalities might exist in BPD as well. However, neither gross inspection nor quantitative measures have revealed CT abnormalities in BPD patients more frequently than in normal controls (Snyder et al., 1983; Lucas et al., 1989). Magnetic resonance imaging (MRI) studies have not been reported in this population. Results of a preliminary positron emission tomography (PET) study in BPD did show an inverse correlation of global cerebral glucose metabolic rate with measures of aggression. This finding was specific to the BPD group ($n = 6$), compared with other personality disorders. Regional metabolic glucose rates in the frontal and parietal lobes were also depressed in BPD (Goyer et al., 1991). These PET results are provocative but come from a small number of patients and require further investigation.

SEROTONERGIC ABNORMALITIES

Abnormalities in serotonergic function have been studied in relationship to BPD, and particularly in relation to impulsive and aggressive behaviors. A central hyposerotonergic state has been hypothesized to be associated with impulsive behavior, especially in personality disordered populations. The evidence for this hypothesis comes from a number of different areas including animal studies, and clinical studies of peripheral and central serotonergic measures. Animal studies have consistently shown a correlation between disturbed serotonergic function and aggressive behavior (reviewed by Modai et al., 1989). Clinical studies have examined peripheral measures of serotonin (5-hydroxytryptamine; 5-HT) function using the platelet as a model for central 5-HT activity. A decrease in platelet 5-HT uptake has been associated with impulsivity in males with episodic aggression (Brown et al., 1989). However, no correlation between violence or aggressive behavior and 5-HT uptake by platelets was found in one study of BPD patients (Modai et al., 1989). Platelet 5-HT content has been reported to be decreased in depression but increased in BPD; platelet 5-HT content has been found to be specifically correlated with current hostility and with a lifetime history of aggression in borderline patients (Mann et al., 1992).

Decreased platelet monoamine oxidase (MOA) levels have been associated with sensation seeking, impulsivity, suicidality, and substance abuse (reviewed by Yehuda et al., 1989). In a study of PBD, platelet MAO was significantly decreased compared with controls, and especially decreased in the presence of comorbid antisocial personality disorder (Yehuda et al., 1989). In contrast, another study found no relationship between BPD symptoms and platelet MAO, but did find a decrease in platelet MAO in patients with self-reported hostility and antisocial, manipulative behavior in the week prior to study (Soloff et al., 1991). These apparently contradictory findings may reflect the complexity of the neuronal systems involved in producing any behavior such as impulsivity. It may be that more than one neurotransmitter system is involved; MAO is involved in the breakdown of a number of monoamines, and so is relatively nonspecific. Furthermore, the activity of MAO in platelets may not reflect MAO activity in the central nervous system.

Studies of cerebrospinal fluid (CSF) have demonstrated a decrease in 5-hydroxyindoleacetic acid (5-HIAA), a 5-HT metabolite, associated with suicidal, and particularly violently suicidal, behavior across personality disorder diagnoses (Linnoila and Virkkunen, 1992). While this association of lowered 5-HIAA in CSF with aggressive/impulsive behavior has been supported by a number of reports (Linnoila and Virkkunen, 1992), one negative finding was in a study of BPD patients *per se*. This study was unable to demonstrate any decrease in CSF 5-HIAA associated with violence or self-mutilation in women with BPD (Gardner et al., 1990). This negative finding may reflect a genuine difference between BPD and violent offenders, but it may also be the result of patient selection bias, inadequate power ($n = 17$), or, perhaps, the exclusive use of women in the study.

Neuroendocrine challenge studies may reflect the functional status of the central 5-HT system more directly than peripheral markers. Fenfluramine, which acts as a 5-HT reuptake inhibitor, a presynaptic 5-HT releaser, and a postsynaptic agonist, has been used in personality disordered patients as a serotonergic challenge. The prolactin response to fenfluramine challenge has been taken to reflect net central 5-HT activity (Coccaro et al., 1989a). A blunted prolactin response to fenfluramine was reported in male patients with major affective disorder and in personality disordered patients, compared with controls. The blunted response correlated with a history of suicide attempt in all patients, but was correlated with impulsive aggressive behavior in personality disordered patients only (Coccaro et al., 1989a). Buspirone (a selective 5-HT$_{1A}$ receptor agonist) and *meta*-chlorophenyl-piperazine (mCPP; a selective 5-HT$_{1C,2}$ receptor agonist) also produce a plasma prolactin response. In personality disordered patients, the prolactin response to these agents was inversely correlated with self-reported irritability and aggression, respectively, potentially reflecting decreased receptor sensitivity (Coccaro et al., 1989b, 1990a). The blunted prolactin response to selective and nonselective serotonergic agents may therefore reflect multiple abnormalities at different functional levels of the serotonergic system.

The primary serotonergic defect remains unclear: low 5-HIAA in CSF suggests the possibility of a decrease in endogenous agonist to stimulate the receptor, while reduced responses to challenge suggest receptor or postsynaptic disturbances. If the former were the case, one might expect to see an upregulation of postsynaptic receptor sensitivity, rather than a blunted response to pharmacological stimulation. A hypothesis that remains consistent with the evidence is that in personality disordered populations (and violent offenders, many of whom may have personality disorders), diminished net central serotonergic function is associated with impulsive behaviors.

NORADRENERGIC ABNORMALITIES

A peripheral study of the noradrenergic system showed a decrease in α_2-receptor number on platelets by [^{3}H]rauwolscine binding in nonmedicated BPD patients compared with controls (Southwick et al., 1990). Impulsivity in this group of patients was not assessed. Cerebrospinal 3-methoxy-4-hydroxyphenylglycol (MHPG), a metabolite of norepinephrine (noradrenaline), has been correlated directly with impulsive aggressive behavior (Brown et al., 1979) and with extroverted behavior (Roy et al., 1989); however, an inverse correlation of CSF MHPG with impulsivity was found in violent offenders (Linnoila et al., 1983). In one study of female BPD patients, however, no difference in CSF MHPG was found between BPD patients and normals; within the borderline group, MHPG levels were neither correlated with a history of self-injury nor with violence directed against others, two indicators of impulsivity (Gardner et al., 1990).

Challenge studies with amphetamine, a dopaminergic/noradrenergic sympathomimetic drug, in BPD have demonstrated clinical responses of psychosis, especially in those patients with concomitant schizotypal personality disorder (Schulz et al., 1985). Whether the response of psychosis is the result of stimulation of the dopaminergic, noradrenergic, or both systems is not clear. Patients with BPD without comorbid schizotypal personality disorder have variably been reported to have an improved sense of wellbeing or dysphoria (Schulz et al., 1988). The influence of amphetamine on impulsivity itself has not been studied.

Clonidine, a central α_2-agonist, functions at the level of the hypothalamus, ultimately resulting in the release of plasma growth hormone in normals. Neuroendocrine challenge with clonidine in personality disordered patients and normal controls has demonstrated a significant correlation between plasma growth hormone response and the Buss–Durkee Hostility Inventory's irritability subscale, which has been shown in turn to correlate with impulsivity (Coccaro et al., 1991).

In summary, these studies of noradrenergic function and impulsivity and aggression suggest that a hyperadrenergic state may be associated with impulsive behaviors in some populations. However, given the inconsistency of the results overall and the limited work done with BPD patients in particular, it is likely premature to hypothesize a specific pathophysiology relating norepinephrine and impulsive behavior in this population at this time.

TREATMENT STUDIES OF IMPULSIVITY AND AGGRESSION IN BPD

Treatment studies of BPD have largely been directed at alleviating specific features of the disorder, as no drug has been identified which effectively treats all facets of the syndrome. Lithium has been shown to produce global improvement in BPD (Links et al., 1990), and has been shown to reduce impulsive aggressive behavior in prison inmates (Tupin et al., 1973). Lithium has been reported to enhance presynaptic transmission of 5-HT, which supports the notion that impulsivity in some populations may be associated with a decrease in serotonergic activity (Coccaro et al., 1991). Fluoxetine, a selective 5-HT reuptake inhibitor, has been reported to reduce global psychopathology and to reduce impulsive aggressive behaviors in BPD (Norden, 1989; Coccaro et al., 1990; Cornelius et al., 1990). Although the fluoxetine treatment studies have been open trials, and so the implications of the findings are limited, the results suggest that pharmacological enhancement of serotonergic neurotransmission improves impulsivity in BPD patients, and again supports the hypothesis that a decrease in serotonergic transmission may underlie impulsive behaviors in these patients.

Treatment studies with drugs that enhance noradrenergic function, such as tricyclic antidepressants and MOA inhibitors, have been shown to increase agitation and irritability in some BPD patients (Soloff et al., 1986a; Cowdry and Gardner, 1988). These treatment studies support the notion that increases in noradrenergic function may be associated with the tendency to act aggressively in some populations.

Other medications have been shown to be useful in treating the impulsive behaviors of BPD patients, including antipsychotic agents and anticonvulsants. Haloperidol has been reported to be superior to amitriptyline in reducing a number of symptoms of BPD, including impulsive behaviors (Soloff et al., 1986b). In view of the evidence for worsening of aggressive behavior with noradrenergic enhancing agents, the comparison with a tricyclic antidepressant may falsely suggest a beneficial effect of haloperidol. Uncontrolled studies have also suggested that a diminution of hostility occurs in BPD patients on antipsychotic medication (Brinkley et al., 1979; Leone, 1982). The anticonvulsant, carbamazepine, has been shown to decrease the severity and the frequency of episodes of behavioral dyscontrol in BPD (Cowdry and Gardner, 1988). The reason for the effectiveness of these agents has not been established. If impulsivity were viewed as a seizure disorder, as might be suggested from the improvement on anticonvulsants and the suggestion of electrophysiological abnormalities noted earlier, one would expect a worsening on antipsychotic drugs that lower the seizure threshold. At this time there is little evidence for such a view. More research is needed to select a subpopulation of BPD patients who may respond to specific pharmacological interventions.

CONCLUSIONS

In the light of the difficulties in finding specific criteria that differentiate the BPD diagnosis from other diagnostic categories, particularly from other personality disorders, it is useful to look at the syndrome in terms of salient features. The dimensional approach has not only yielded greater clarity in the search for biological markers of the disease, but has also been the principle that has guided pharmacological treatment of BPD.

Several lines of research support the hypothesis that there is a biological basis for the impulsivity seen in BPD. Family studies show a high rate of BPD and/or impulsivity in relatives of BPD patients; preliminary twin studies have provided evidence for a genetic basis for certain traits associated with the diagnosis, including impulsivity. Neuropsychological studies have shown a variety of disturbances in BPD, including deficits in recall of learned material and completion of complex cognitive tasks. However, it is of note that no defects in continuous performance or concentration, which might be expected to be associated with impulsivity, have been seen.

Electrophysiological studies have demonstrated a variety of EEG abnormalities in some BPD patients; whether this is the result of risk-taking behavior or child abuse, or alternatively, the proximate cause of some impulsive behaviors is not clear. Event-related EEG potential studies have more consistently revealed abnormalities in BPD patients and may in the future lead to more specific hypotheses. Computerized tomography studies of the brain have not yielded any specific finding associated with BPD, or with impulsive behavior. Functional brain imaging technology, such as PET or single proton emission computerized tomography (SPECT), is still in its early stages in this group of patients, but may provide specific information in the future.

The search for a biological basis for impulsive behavior in BPD has progressed the furthest in the area of neurotransmitter studies. Reduced CSF 5-HIAA and a blunted prolactin response to fenfluramine, both markers for abnormalities in serotonergic function, have been associated with suicidal behaviors in a number of diagnostic groups, including personality disordered and mood disordered patients. A blunted prolactin response to fenfluramine, however, has been associated with other-directed aggression in personality disordered patients only. This finding raises the possibility that there is an interaction with other neurotransmitter systems, which may act to modify the expression of the serotonergic abnormalities. Reduced noradrenergic function has been associated with depression in human beings; increased noradrenergic activity has been associated with impulsive behaviors, particularly in other-directed aggression. One possible explanation of these findings is that norepinephrine modulates the expression of serotonergic abnormalities. In populations with reduced 5-HT activity, the behavioral expression of that defect might then depend on the activity level of norepinephrine. In depression, for example, a decrease in both serotonergic and noradrenergic activity might lead to self-directed aggression: suicidal behavior. In impulsive patients with personality disorders (most common in BPD), reduced 5-HT in the setting of increased noradrenergic activity might allow for both self- and other-directed expression of the impulsive characteristic. If the 5-HT system is intact, the driving force for impulsive behavior may not be present. In this case, deficits in noradrenergic behavior might be associated with depression without suicidal behavior. There is preliminary evidence from animal studies of a modulatory interaction between the two systems (Hodge and Butcher, 1975; Janowsky et al., 1982; Chamberlain et al., 1987). The hypothesis about the modulating relationship between noradrenergic and serotonergic activity and its implications for behavior has yet to be studied in human beings and is a promising area for future research.

A number of lines of research, including family studies, electrophysiological studies, neuroimaging, and measures of central and peripheral serotonergic and noradrenergic function are suggestive of biological disturbances associated, in particular, with the impulsive aspect of BPD. While a pathophysiology explaining the etiology of impulsivity in BPD remains to be clarified, some of the biological findings may suggest treatment strategies for BPD. For example, identification of memory defects in BPD might suggest trials of specific cognitive treatments. Preliminary evidence of a hyposerotonergic state provides a theoretical foundation for the use of 5-HT enhancing agents for the clinical treatment of impulsivity in BPD; placebo-controlled trials of the effect of 5-HT reuptake inhibitors on impulsivity in adequate numbers of well-characterized patients are currently in progress.

ACKNOWLEDGMENTS

This research was supported in part by grants from the National Institutes of Health, National Center for Research Resources, RR00071, for the Mt. Sinai Medical Center General Medical Clinical Research Center, the National Institutes of Mental Health, RO1-MH41131, and the Department of Veterans Affairs Merit Award 7609004.

REFERENCES

Akiskal, H.S. (1981). Subaffective disorders: dysthymic, cyclothymic and bipolar II disorders in the "borderline" realm. *Psychiatr. Clin. North Am.*, 4, 25–46.

Andrulonis, P.A., Glueck, B.C., Stroebel, C.F., Vogel, N.G., Shapiro, A.L., and Aldridge, D.M. (1980). Organic brain dysfunction and the borderline syndrome. *Psychiatr. Clin. North Am.*, 4, 47–66.

Andrulonis, P.A., Glueck, B.C., Stroebel, C.F., and Vogel, N.G. (1982). Borderline personality subcategories. *J. Nerv. Ment. Dis.*, 170, 670–679.

Archer, R.P., Struve, F.A., Ball, J.D., and Gordon, R.A. (1988). EEG in borderline personality disorder (letter). *Biol. Psychiatry*, 24, 731–732.

Baron, M., and Gruen, R. (1985). *The Schedule for Interviewing Borderlines*. New York State Psychiatric Institute, New York.

Baron, M., Gruen, R., Asnis, L., and Lord, S. (1985). Familial transmission of schizotypal and borderline personality disorders. *Am. J. Psychiatry*, 142, 927–934.

Bemporad, J.R., Smith, H.F., Hanson, G., and Cicchetti, D. (1982). Borderline syndromes in childhood: Criteria for diagnosis. *Am. J. Psychiatry*, 139, 596–602.

Blackwood, D.H.R., St. Clair, D.M., and Kutchen, S.P. (1986). P300 event-related potential abnormalities in BPD. *Biol. Psychiatry*, 21, 557–560.

Briere, J., and Zaidi, L.Y. (1989). Sexual abuse histories and sequelae in female psychiatric emergency room patients. *Am. J. Psychiatry*, 146, 1602–1606.

Brinkley, J.R., Beitman, B.D., and Freidel, R.O. (1979). Low dose neuroleptic regimes in the treatment of borderline patients. *Arch. Gen. Psychiatry*, 36, 319–326.

Brown, G.L., Goodwin, F.K., Ballenger, J.C., Goyer, P.F., and Major, L.F. (1979). Aggression in humans correlates with cerebrospinal fluid amine metabolites. *Psychiatry Res.*, 1, 131–139.

Brown, G.R., and Anderson, B. (1991). Psychiatric morbidity in adult inpatients with childhood histories of sexual and physical abuse. *Am. J. Psychiatry*, 148, 55–61.

Burgess, J.W. (1991). Relationship of depression and cognitive impairment to self-injury in borderline personality disorder, major depression, and schizophrenia. *Psychiatry Res.*, 38, 77–87.

Chamberlain, G., Ervin, F.R., Pihl, R.O., and Young, S.N. (1987). The effect of raising or lowering tryptophan levels on aggression in vervet monkeys. *Pharmacol. Biochem. Behav.*, 28, 503–510.

Coccaro, E.F., Siever, L.J., Klar, H.M., et al. (1989a). Serotonergic studies in patients with affective and personality disorders. *Arch. Gen. Psychiatry*, 46, 587–599.

Coccaro, E.F., Siever, L.J., Kavoussi, R., Rinaldi, P., Morrison, V., and Howard, L. (1989b). Postsynaptic function in aggression. In: *New Research Abstracts of the American Psychiatric Association*. Presented APA meeting, May 1989, San Francisco. American Psychiatric Press, Washington DC.

Coccaro, E.F., Gabriel, S., and Siever, L.J. (1990a). Buspirone challenge: preliminary evidence for a role for central 5-HT_{1a} receptor function in impulsive aggressive behavior in humans. *Psychopharmacol. Bull.*, 26, 393–405.

Coccaro, E.F., Astill, J.L., Herbert, J.L., and Schut, A.G. (1990b). Fluoxetine treatment of impulsive aggression in DSM IIIR personality disorder patients. *J. Clin. Psychopharmacol.*, 10, 373–375.

Coccaro, E.F., Lawrence, T., Trestman, R., Gabriel, S., Klar, H.M., and Siever, L.J. (1991). Growth hormone response to intravenous clonidine challenge correlate with behavioral irritability in psychiatric patients and healthy volunteers. *Psychiatry Res.*, 39, 129–139.

Coccaro, E.F., Silverman, J.M., Klar, H.M., Horvath, T.B., and Siever, L.J. (*Arch. Gen. Psychiatry*, in press). Familial correlates of reduced central serotonergic system function in personality disorder patients.

Cornelius, J.R., Schulz, S.C., Brenner, R.P., Soloff, P.H., and Ulrich, R.F. (1988). Changes in EEG mean frequency associated with anxiety and with amphetamine challenge in BPD. *Biol. Psychiatry*, 24, 587–594.

Cornelius, J.R., Soloff, P.H., George, A.W.A., et al. (1989). An evaluation of the significance of selected neuropsychiatric abnormalities in the etiology of borderline personality disorder. *J. Pers. Disord.*, 3, 19–25.

Cornelius, J.R., Soloff, P.H., Perel, J.M., and Ulrich, R.F. (1990). Fluoxetine trial in borderline personality disorder. *Psychopharmacol. Bull.*, 26, 151–154.

Cowdry, R.W., and Gardner, D.L. (1988). Pharmacotherapy of borderline personality disorder: alprazolam, carbamazepine, trifluoperazine, and tranylcypromine. *Arch. Gen. Psychiatry*, 45, 111–119.

Cowdry, R.W., Pickar, D., and Davies, R. (1985). Symptoms and EEG findings in the borderline syndrome. *Int. J. Psychiatr. Med.*, 15, 201–211.

Drake, M.E., Phillips, B.B., and Pakalnis, A. (1991). Auditory evoked potentials in borderline personality disorder. *Clin. Electroencephalogr.*, 22, 188–192.

Frances, A., Clarkin, J.F., Gilmore, M., Hurt, S.W., and Brown, R. (1984). Reliability of criteria for borderline personality disorder: A comparison of DSM-

III and the diagnostic interview for borderline patients. *Am. J. Psychiatry*, 141, 1080–1084.

Gardner, D.L., Lucas, P.B., and Cowdry, R.W. (1990). CSF metabolites in borderline personality disorder compared with normal controls. *Biol. Psychiatry*, 28, 247–254.

Goldman, S.J., D'Angelo, E.J., DeMaso, D.R., and Mezzacappa, E. (1992). Physical and sexual abuse histories among children with borderline personality disorder. *Am. J. Psychiatry*, 149, 1723–1726.

Goyer, P.F., Andreason, P.J., Semple, W.E., Clayton, A.H., King, A.C., and Schulz, C. (1991). Pet and personality disorders. Abstracts, American College of Neuropsychopharmacology Annual Meeting, December 1991, p. 121 San Juan, Puerto Rico.

Grueneich, R. (1992). The borderline personality diagnosis: reliability, diagnostic efficiency, and covariation with other personality disorder diagnoses. *J. Pers. Disord.*, 149, 1645–1653.

Gunderson, J.G., Kolb, J.E., and Austin, V. (1981). The diagnostic interview for borderline patients. *Am. J. Psychiatry*, 138, 896–903.

Herman, J.L., Perry, J.C., and van der Kolk, B.A. (1989). Childhood trauma in borderline personality disorder. *Am. J. Psychiatry*, 146, 490–495.

Hodge, G.K., and Butcher, L.L. (1975). Catecholamine correlates of isolation-induced aggression in mice. *Eur. J. Pharmacol.*, 31, 81–93.

Janowsky, A., Okada, F., Manier, D.H., Applegate, C.D., Sulser, F., and Steranka, L.R. (1982). Role of serotonergic input in the regulation of the B-adrenergic receptor coupled adenylate cyclase system. *Science*, 218, 900–901.

Kavoussi, R.J., Coccaro, E.F., Klar, H.M., Bernstein, D., and Siever, L.J. (1990). Structured interviews for borderline personality disorder. *Am. J. Psychiatry*, 147, 1522–1525.

Kernberg, O.F. (1977). The structural diagnosis of borderline personality organization. In: *Borderline Personality Disorders* (ed. P. Hartcollis) pp. 87–121. International University Press, New York.

Kutcher, S.P., Blackwood, D.H.R., St. Clair, D., Gaskell, D.F., and Muir, W.J. (1987). Auditory P300 in borderline personality disorder and schizophrenia. *Arch. Gen. Psychiatry*, 44, 645–650.

Lahmeyer, H.W., Val, E., Gaviria, M., et al. (1988). EEG sleep, lithium transport, dexamethasone suppression, and monoamine oxidase activity in borderline personality disorder. *Psychiatry Res.*, 25, 19–30.

Leone, N.F. (1982). Response of borderline patients to loxapine and chlorpromazine. *J. Clin. Psychiatry*, 43, 148–150.

Links, P.S., Steiner, M., Offord, D.R., and Eppel, A. (1988a). Characteristics of borderline personality disorder: a Canadian study. *Can. J. Psychiatry*, 33, 336–340.

Links, P.S., Steiner, M., and Huxley, G. (1988b). The occurrence of borderline personality disorder in the families of borderline patients. *J. Pers. Disord.*, 2, 14–20.

Links, P.S., Steiner, M., Boiago, I., and Irwin, D. (1990). Lithium therapy for borderline patients: preliminary findings. *J. Clin. Psychopharmacol.*, 4, 173–181.

Linnoila, V.M.I., and Virkkunen, M. (1992). Aggression, suicidality and serotonin. *J. Clin. Psychiatry*, 53 (suppl.), 46–51.

Linnoila, V.M.I., Virkkunen, M., Scheinin, M., Nuutila, A., Rimon, R., and Goodwin, F.K. (1983). Low cerebrospinal fluid 5-hydroxyindolacetic acid concentration differentiates impulsive from nonimpulsive violent behavior. *Life Sci.*, 33, 2609–2614.

Lofgren, D.P., Bemporad, J., King, J., Lindem, K., and O'Driscoll, G. (1991). A prospective follow-up study of so-called borderline children. *Am. J. Psychiatry*, 148, 1541–1547.

Loranger, A.W. (1988). *Personality Disorders Examination (PDE)*. DV Communications, Yonkers, NY.

Loranger, A.W., Oldham, J.M., and Tulis, E.H. (1982). Familial transmission of borderline personality disorder. *Arch. Gen. Psychiatry*, 39, 795–799.

Lucas, P.B., Gardner, D.L., Cowdry, R.W., and Pickar, D. (1989). Cerebral structure in borderline personality disorder. *Psychiatry Res.*, 27, 111–115.

Ludolph, P.S., Westen, D., Misle, B., Jackson, A., Wixom, J., and Wiss, F.C. (1990). The borderline diagnosis in adolescents: Symptoms and developmental histories. *Am. J. Psychiatry*, 147, 470–476.

McGlashan, T.H. (1983). The borderline syndrome: II: Is it a variant of schizophrenia or affective disorder? *Arch. Gen. Psychiatry*, 40, 1319–1323.

McGlashan, T.H. (1987). Testing DSM-III symptom criteria for schizotypal and borderline personality disorders. *Arch. Gen. Psychiatry*, 44, 143–148.

McNamara, E., Reynolds, C.F., Soloff, P.H., et al. (1984). EEG sleep evaluation of depression in borderline patients. *Am. J. Psychiatry*, 141, 182–186.

Maier, W., Lichtermann, D., Minges, J., and Heun, R. (1992). The familial relation of personality disorders (DSM-III-R) to unipolar depression. *J. Affect. Disord.*, 26, 151–156.

Mann, J.J., McBride, P.A., Anderson, G.M., and Mieczkowski, T.A. (1992). Platelet and whole blood serotonin content in depressed inpatients: correlations with acute and life-time psychopathology. *Biol. Psychiatry*, 32, 243–257.

Modai, I., Apter, A., Meltzer, M., Tyano, S., Walevski, A., and Jerushalmy, Z. (1989). Serotonin uptake by platelets of suicidal and aggressive adolescent psychiatric inpatients. *Neuropsychobiology*, 21, 9–13.

Norden, M.J. (1989). Fluoxetine in borderline personality disorder. *Prog. Neuropsychopharmacol. Biol. Psychiatry*, 13, 885–893.

Nurnberg, H.G., Raskin, M., Levine, P.E., Pollack, S., Siegel, O., and Prince, R. (1991). Hierarchy of DSM-III-R criteria efficiency for the diagnosis of borderline personality disorder. *J. Pers. Disord.*, 5, 211–224.

Ogata, S.N., Silk, K.R., Goodrich, S., Lohr, N.E., Westen, D., and Hill, E.M. (1990). Childhood sexual and physical abuse in adult patients with borderline personality disorder. *Am. J. Psychiatry*, 147, 1008–1013.

O'Leary, K.M., Brouwers, P., Gardner, D.L., and Cowdry, R.W. (1991). Neuropsychological testing of patients with borderline personality disorder. *Am. J. Psychiatry*, 148, 106–111.

Perry, J.C. (1992). Problems and considerations in the valid assessment of personality disorders. *Am. J. Psychiatry*, 149, 1645–1653.

Pfohl, B., Stangl, D.A., Zimmerman, M., Bowers, W., and Corenthal, C. (1982). *Structured Interview for DSM-III Personality Disorders (SIDP)*. University of Iowa, Iowa City.

Pope, H.G., Jonas, J.M., Hudson, J.I., Cohen, B.M., and Gunderson, J.G. (1983). The validity of DSM-III borderline personality disorder: A phenomenologic, family history, treatment response, and long-term follow-up study. *Arch. Gen. Psychiatry*, 40, 23–30.

Raczek, S.W. (1992). Childhood abuse and personality disorders. *J. Pers. Disord.*, 6, 109–116.

Robins, E., and Guze, S.B. (1970). Establishment of diagnostic validity in psychiatric illness: Its application to schizophrenia. *Am. J. Psychiatry*, 126, 983–987.

Roy, A., DeJong, J., and Linnoila, M. (1989). Extraversion in pathological gamblers: Correlates with indexes of noradrenergic function. *Arch. Gen. Psychiatry*, 46, 679–681.

Schulz, P.M., Soloff, P.H., Kelly, T., Morgenstern, M., Di Franco, R., and Schulz, S.C. (1989). A family history study of borderline subtypes. *J. Pers. Disord.*, 3, 217–229.

Schulz, S.C., Schulz, P.M., Dommisse, C., et al. (1985). Amphetamine response in borderline patients. *Psychiatry Res.*, 15, 97–108.

Schulz, S.C., Cornelius, J., Schulz, P.M., and Soloff, P.H. (1988). The amphetamine challenge test in patients with borderline disorder. *Am. J. Psychiatry*, 145, 809–814.

Siever, L.J., and Davis, K.L. (1991). A psychobiological perspective on the personality disorders. *Am. J. Psychiatry*, 148, 1647–1658.

Silverman, J.M., Pinkham, L., Horvath, T.B., et al. (1991) Affective and impulsive personality disorder traits in the relatives of patients with borderline personality disorder. *Am. J. Psychiatry*, 148, 1378–1385.

Snyder, S., and Pitts, W.M. (1984). Electroencephalography of DSM-III borderline personality disorder. *Acta Psychiatr. Scand.*, 69, 129–134.

Snyder, S., Pitts, W.M., and Gustin, Q. (1983). CT scans of patients with borderline personality disorder [letter]. *Am. J. Psychiatry*, 140, 272.

Soloff, P.H., and Millward, J.W. (1983). Developmental histories of borderline patients. *Compr. Psychiatry*, 24, 574–588.

Soloff, P.H., George, A., Nathan, R.S., Schulz, P.M., and Perel, J.M. (1986a). Paradoxical effect of amitriptyline on borderline patients. *Am. J. Psychiatry*, 143, 1603–1605.

Soloff, P.H., George, A., Nathan, R.S., Schulz, P.M., Ulrich, R.F., and Perel, J.M. (1986b). Progress in pharmacology of borderline disorders. *Arch. Gen. Psychiatry*, 43, 691–697.

Soloff, P.H., Cornelius, J., Foglia, J. George, A., and Perel, J.M. (1991). Platelet MAO in borderline personality disorder. *Biol. Psychiatry*, 29, 499–502.

Southwick, S.M., Yehuda, R., Giller, E.L., and Perry, B.D. (1990). Altered platelet alpha$_2$-adrenergic receptor binding sites in borderline personality disorder. *Am. J. Psychiatry*, 147, 1014–1017.

Spitzer, R.L., Williams, J.B.W., and Gibbon, M. (1987). *Structured Interview for DSMIII-R Personality Disorders (SCID-II)*. New York State Psychiatric Institute, Biometrics Research, New York.

Stone, M.H. (1992). Borderline personality disorder. In: *Psychiatry*, vol. 1, revised edn, (eds R. Michels, A.M. Cooper, S.B. Guze et al.). J.B. Lippincott, New York.

Torgersen, S. (1984). Genetic and nosological aspects of schizotypal and borderline personality disorders. *Arch. Gen. Psychiatry*, 41, 546–554.

Torgersen, S. (1992). The genetic transmission of borderline personality features displays multidimensionality. Abstract from American College of Neuropsychopharmacology Annual Meeting, December 1992, p. 23, San Juan, Puerto Rico.

Tupin, J.P., Smith, D.B., Clanon, T.L., Kim, L.I., Nugent, A., and Groupe, A. (1973). The long-term use of lithium in aggressive prisoners. *Compr. Psychiatry*, 14, 311–317.

Yehuda, R., Southwick, S.M., Edell, W.S., and Giller, E.L. (1989). Low platelet monoamine oxidase activity in borderline personality disorder. *Psychiatry Res.*, 30, 265–273.

Zanarini, M.C. (1993). Borderline personality disorder as an impulse spectrum disorder. In: *Borderline Personality Disorder: Etiology and Treatment* (ed. J. Paris) pp. 67–85. American Psychiatric Press, Washington, D.C.

Zanarini, M.C., Gunderson, J.G., Marino, M.F., Schwartz, E.O., and Frankenburg, F.R. (1988). DSM-III disorders in the families of borderline outpatients. *J. Pers. Disord.*, 2, 292–302.

Zanarini, M.C., Gunderson, J.G., Marino, M.F., Schwartz, E.O., and Frankenburg, F.R. (1989). Childhood experiences of borderline patients. *Compr. Psychiatry*, 30, 18–25.
Zanarini, M.C., Gunderson, J.G., Frankenburg, F.R., and Chauncey, D.L. (1990). Discriminating borderline personality disorder from other axis II disorders. *Am. J. Psychiatry*, 147, 161–167.

11 Impulsivity and Aggression in Antisocial Personality

WILLIAM H REID

Texas Mental Health and Mental Retardation System, University of Texas System, and Texas A&M College of Medicine, Austin, TX, USA

INTRODUCTION

This chapter will address a rather narrow section of the overall spectrum of persons with impulsive and/or aggressive disorders: those with antisocial personality disorder (APD). Because of space limitations, it will not discuss in detail the general concept of antisocial personality, nor the broad realm of childhood and adolescent conduct disorders and aggressive behaviors that are sometimes seen as precursors to—and often confused with—a diagnosis of antisocial personality. There is widespread misunderstanding about the prevalence of APD in aggressive people and the appropriateness of diagnosing APD in adolescents. Both of these are discussed below.

For the purposes of this chapter, APD is defined by the DSM-III-R criteria (American Psychiatric Association Task Force on Nomenclature and Statistics, 1987). The DSM-IV draft criteria were available when this chapter was prepared, but are not yet published, and do not differ sufficiently from the earlier definition to merit particular atttention herein (American Psychiatric Association Task Force on DSM-IV, 1993). When the term "psychopathy" is used in the text, it should be assumed to be identical to APD.

DIAGNOSIS OF APD IN IMPULSIVE AND AGGRESSIVE PEOPLE

Impulsivity and aggression appear in many of the DSM-III-R diagnostic criteria for APD and are even more prominent in DSM-IV. Nevertheless, they are neither diagnostic for APD nor always found with it. When one encounters violent and antisocial behavior, it should not be assumed to be associated with APD, or even with a psychiatric disorder. Indeed, the material covered by this book is an excellent example of the many sources of impulsivity and aggression, and the variety of clinical and social possibilities associated with the presentation, diagnosis, etiology, and treatment or management of impulsivity and aggression.

Impulsivity and Aggression. Edited by E. Hollander and D.J. Stein
© 1995 John Wiley & Sons Ltd

As is the case for other DSM-III-R and DSM-IV disorders, it is important to consider the diagnostic criteria, and weigh the patient's history and presentation in the light of clinical training and experience. This usually means having access to both the patient and corroborative information. Diagnosis from either history or examination alone—as might be asked of clinicians in some legal, law enforcement, or emergency settings, for example—is generally unreliable. One should resist the temptation to base diagnosis on antisocial, violent, impulsive and/or manipulative behavior *per se*.

One should remember the three important principles of diagnosis. First, are the inclusion criteria fully met? If not, the diagnosis should not be made (although it may be made "provisionally" if clinical suspicion is high and data are incomplete). Second, are the exclusion criteria met? Antisocial symptoms in the presence of an exclusionary diagnosis (such as a manic episode or schizophrenia) are not indicative of APD (and may rule it out). Finally, have the behaviors/symptoms caused the patient significant distress or loss of function? This is a "threshold" concept in DSM-III-R and DSM-IV, without which no psychiatric disorder should be diagnosed.

PREDATORY AGGRESSION

For some, psychopathy is the *sine qua non* of predatory killers or sex offenders, devoid of compassion, driven by irresistible and primitive impulses to seek out their victims. I would recommend caution when considering APD as a diagnosis for such people. Antisocial personality disorder is often described as a "primitive" personality disorder. Cleckley considered the psychopath's handicap virtually neurological in pathology (cf. "semantic aphasia"; Cleckley, 1986). Nevertheless, most people who meet the DSM-III-R or DSM-IV criteria are not so inherently primitive. A simple diagnosis of APD is not usually sufficient to describe those who commit such heinous crimes.

NEUROBIOLOGY, IMPULSIVITY, AGGRESSION, AND APD

Many studies of aggression and violence focus on sociocultural factors. Poverty, family violence, oppression, and other untenable social situations are routinely blamed for much of the brutality in the world. One of the premier neurologists in the field of impulsive and explosive violence, Dr Frank Elliott, warns clinicians to pay attention to both biological and sociological factors and to be alert for biological elements in our culture (Elliott, 1992).

Lewis (1991) considered possible relationships among early serotonin (5-hydroxytryptamine, 5-HT) metabolism, learning deficits, inappropriate emotions, and chronic antisocial behavior. The work of Moss et al. (1990) suggests that altered 5-HT function is associated with aggression, although not with impulsivity, in patients with APD. Many other authors have studied 5-HT and glucose metabolism abnormalities in primitive or impulsive violence (not always in personality disordered patients) (Roy et al., 1986; Virkkunen and Narvanen, 1987).

Fishbein et al. (1989) are among many authors who have studied electroencephalographic tracings and evoked potentials in an effort to find brain abnormalities that might explain or predict antisocial behavior. They found that subjects who met criteria for APD were not significantly different from controls with respect to either EEG or brainstem auditory evoked potentials. Some such studies have been weakly positive, but none has proved clinically useful to date.

Brain damage is often associated with personality change and impulse disinhibition. Some clinicians refer to antisocial behavior caused by such damage as "secondary psychopathy". It rarely has all the characteristics of APD, however, and in my opinion APD should not be diagnosed when the symptoms are due to trauma or a general medical condition. Kandel (1992) studied Danish birth cohorts to assess the role of perinatal insult in later violent criminal behavior and APD. The results indicated an interesting separation of the two concepts. That is, perinatal factors associated with later impulsivity and violence did not appear to be associated with APD itself, suggesting that organically-based violent behavior and APD do not share certain etiological factors.

Although sometimes carried out in subjects with APD, most neurological and other biological studies of violence or impulsivity do not separate antisocial personality disorder from the target symptoms being addressed. Aggressive behavior is modulated in various ways in many parts of the brain, including the cortex, basal ganglia, hypothalamus, and others (Weiger and Bear, 1988), and is affected by a great many endogenous and exogenous substances. Some antisocial syndromes are characteristic of a particular locus or chemical; others are not. The results of the studies cited thus should not be construed to represent characteristics of psychopaths alone. Indeed, the opposite—that the syndromes are usually unrelated to such a heterogenous measure as a personality diagnosis—is probably more often the case.

The neurochemistry and neurophysiology of impulsive and aggressive behavior are discussed in more detail elsewhere in this volume.

ASSOCIATIONS WITH SUBSTANCE ABUSE AND CRIMINALITY

Many authors and clinicians associate substance abuse with APD, perhaps because of the assumption that psychopaths seek the artificial stimulation offered by drugs or alcohol (even though many of the substances are central nervous system depressants and the abusing lifestyle may be more passive than stimulating). Hesselbrock and Hesselbrock (1992) describe certain alcohol-seeking behaviors as "risk-taking," and suggest a relationship with APD and other personality traits. Several studies have attempted to show causative associations between APD and the violence that sometimes accompanies substance abuse, usually with little success. Jaffe et al. (1988) found that when childhood aggression was considered separately from an adult diagnosis of APD in alcoholics, the contribution of APD to adult violence was "negligible" compared with that of alcohol consumption and childhood antecedents.

Psychopathy is over-represented among substance abusers, but the relationship is far from diagnostic or etiological. Among intravenous drug abusers, well under half meet both the early-onset and adult DSM-III-R criteria for APD (Brooner et al., 1992); some studies find the prevalence of psychopathy in such populations reaches only about 20%, even in highly criminal groups such as crack abusers (Kleinman et al., 1990). Conversely, there is no reason to believe that substance-abusing psychopaths are representative of all people with antisocial personality. Nevertheless, APD research populations are often chosen from patients in drug programs (e.g. Haertzen et al., 1990).

The same can be said of incarcerated populations, which are a frequent source of research subjects with APD and other antisocial syndromes. It seems reasonable to assume that impulsive and aggressive psychopaths are likely to become incarcerated at some point in their careers. One should remember, however, that not all prisoners are psychopaths, not all psychopaths are criminals, and incarcerated offenders do not necessarily represent all people with APD.

TREATMENT/MANAGEMENT OF IMPULSIVITY AND AGGRESSION IN APD

There are several review papers on the treatment of personality disorders, but few report controlled research and even fewer focus on APD (Kellner, 1986). Accurate diagnosis is very important, since discovering the source of impulsive or aggressive behavior to be other than a personality disorder may lead the clinician down more optimistic therapeutic avenues. Treatment of APD itself is difficult and often unsuccessful; nevertheless, there are approaches that can be explored.

The search for biological therapies has not proved fruitful. Carbamazepine, lithium carbonate, or propranolol may be considered for patients exhibiting impulsive or explosive violence (Wickham and Reed, 1987; Tyrer and Sievewright, 1988; Mattes, 1990); however, their actions are generic for the behavior or the disinhibiting syndrome involved, not for APD. A few clinicians still suggest antipsychotic medications for antisocial personality, but I recommend against prescribing them because of their lack of effectiveness for either impulse control or the personality disorder, and their obvious potential for side effects and adverse effects. Experience with the "nontraditional" neuroleptics, such as clozapine, is lacking to date. Benzodiazepines are not indicated, due to their abuse potential and their ineffectiveness for these symptoms and behaviors.

The role of central serotonergic function in the regulation of aggressive impulses suggests that 5-HT-enhancing agents may be helpful. This hypothesis has not been well tested, but Coccaro et al. (1990) reported clinical success with fluoxetine in three patients with characterologically based impulsive aggression, one of whom met DSM-III-R criteria for APD. Central serotonergic agonists and precursors may be a promising area for future research, although, again, one should not expect them to affect the personality disorder.

Stereotactic neurosurgery for intractable violence has not been used in the USA for several years. Modern techniques suggest its usefulness for certain patients, particularly those with an ictal locus or other organic lesion (Sano and Mayanagi, 1988). It should not be recommended for patients whose impulsive aggression stems primarily from a personality disorder such as APD.

The only therapies that are arguably effective for a greater range of APD symptoms, including impulsivity and aggression, are those that attempt to restructure the personality itself (or at least the patient's responses that try to fill the needs created by the personality disorder). Individual psychotherapy for this purpose, although sometimes effective, has largely been abandoned. Part of the reason for abandoning long-term, reconstructive psychotherapy or psychoanalysis is the requirement for a highly specialized therapist, an unusually motivated patient, and several years of concerted effort. One must also recognize the almost complete lack of resources and low priority given to this form of treatment, even if efficacy can be shown.

A few studies of short-term or superficial psychotherapy report some acquisition of social skills, improved self-esteem, and modest changes in aggressive traits, particularly using cognitive and/or behavioral approaches (Valliant and Antonowicz, 1991); however, such approaches have not been shown effective in the long run for antisocial, impulsive, or aggressive behavior. Individual or group psychotherapy of low intensity or short duration is simply ineffective, in my opinion, no matter what the type.

Highly controlled, usually highly structured milieu treatment settings have been tried, with varying amounts of success. I have described several forms elsewhere, for incarcerated populations as well as outpatients (Reid, 1985). A more recent, prospective, study by Ravndal and Vaglum (1991) describes long-term treatment of aggressive, antisocial drug abusers in a hierarchical therapeutic community. Wilderness treatment programs have perhaps the most cost-effective results, provided they are planned and staffed by people with experience and expertise in both wilderness programs and psychotherapy (Reid, 1981, 1989).

Treatment and management are not the same thing. Both are important. Psychiatrists and other mental health professionals may be called upon to treat or to assist in the management of behaviors—in clinical settings or in such places as jails and prisons—when "treatment" is not the primary concern. One should be cautious about accepting a "management" role, and about confusing it with clinical "treatment".

Clinicians are not usually trained or expert in social issues (although we may have interests in them, and opinions about them). We are not able to predict the detailed social behavior of any person, not even a psychopath, although we may comment with some validity on the resilience of the diagnosis and intractability of the symptoms. In addition, although we are sometimes asked to provide advice about people in special social settings (e.g. jails, prisons, or the military), our backgrounds do not usually make us knowledgeable about, for example, inmate management.

RESPONSIBILITY AND CULPABILITY

Other chapters in this book refer to legal issues and concepts related to impulsivity and aggression. It is important, however, to point out a few considerations that apply to APD.

First, no diagnosis or disorder, in and of itself, should be assumed to limit a person's responsibility for his or her actions. Even schizophrenia does not imply incompetence or inability to form intent unless (1) there is impairment of function sufficient to impair competence, *and* (2) that impairment is relevant to the behavior being considered. In the case of personality disorders in general, and APD in particular, it is very difficult for a person's symptoms to reach the threshold necessary to prevent society from holding him responsible for his acts.

I do not object to excusing the behaviors of some people, in some situations. However, it is a truism that if society *expects* a person to adhere to laws and social mores, he or she is far more likely to do so than if that same society is ambivalent about legal and social responsibility. Most states have statutes which, in one way or another, prevent a person with a mental disorder from being exonerated when antisocial behavior is the sole (or even the primary) symptom of the disorder. Thus a person with APD cannot escape culpability simply because the disorder is listed in DSM-III-R or DSM-IV. Barring other, nonpsychiatric, considerations, his acts are considered intentional and voluntary. This concept applies to several other diagnoses as well (e.g. pedophilia and pyromania), and is addressed in the introductory pages of both DSM-III-R and DSM-IV.

Are there any situations in which illegal or aggressive acts arising from APD should not be viewed as voluntary and intentional? One should rarely say "always" or "never"; however, the *psychiatric* aspects of psychopathy do not support the idea that it removes a person's responsibility for his actions, in spite of the poor judgment and lack of consideration of consequences that are often associated with the syndrome. I see these deficits as related more to conscious choice than to any *inability* to see alternatives to impulsive or aggressive behavior, or to choose them. The role of ego defenses and the unconscious in determining perception and behavior is significant; but, for a number of psychological, social, and practical reasons, we should not give them sway over the day-to-day decisions for which we are all responsible.

REFERENCES

American Psychiatric Association Task Force on DSM-IV (1993). *DSM-IV Draft Criteria*. American Psychiatric Press, Washington, D.C.

American Psychiatric Association Task Force on Nomenclature and Statistics (1987). *Diagnostic and Statistical Manual of Mental Disorders*, 3rd edn—revised. American Psychiatric Press, Washington, D.C.

Brooner, R.K., Schmidt, C.W., Felch, L.J., and Bigelow, G.E. (1992). Antisocial behavior of intravenous drug abusers: Implications for diagnosis of antisocial personality disorder. *Am. J. Psychiatry*, 149(4), 482–487.

Cleckley, H. (1988). *The Mask of Sanity*. C.V. Mosby, St. Louis.

Coccaro, E.F., Astill, J.L., Herbert, J.L., and Schut, A.G. (1990). Fluoxetine treatment of impulsive aggression in DSM-III-R personality disorder patients [letter]. *J. Clin. Psychopharmacol.*, 10(5), 373–375.

Elliott, F.A. (1992). Violence. The neurologic contribution: An overview. *Arch. Neurol.*, 46(6), 595–603.

Fishbein, D.H., Herning, R.I., Pickworth, W.B., Haertzen, C.A., Hickey, J.E., and Jaffe, J.H. (1989). EEG and brainstem auditory evoked response potentials in adult male drug abusers with self-reported histories of aggressive behavior. *Biol. Psychiatry*, 26(6), 595–611.

Haertzen, C.A., Hickey, J.E., Rose, M.R., and Jaffe, J.H. (1990). The relationship between a diagnosis of antisocial personality and hostility: Development of an antisocial hostility scale. *J. Clin. Psychol.*, 46(5), 679–686.

Hesselbrock, M.N., and Hesselbrock, V.M. (1992). Relationship of family history, antisocial personality disorder and personality traits in young men at risk for alcoholism. *J. Stud. Alcohol*, 53(6), 619–625.

Jaffe, J.H., Babor, T.F., and Fishbein, D.H. (1988). Alcoholics, aggression and antisocial personality. *J. Stud. Alcohol*, 49(3), 211–218.

Kandel, E. (1992). Biology, violence and antisocial personality. *J. Forensic Sci.*, 37(3), 912–918.

Kellner, R. (1986). Personality disorders. *Psychother. Psychosom.*, 46(1–2), 58–66.

Kleinman, P.H., Miller, A.B., Millman, R.B., et al. (1990). Psychopathology among cocaine abusers entering treatment. *J. Nerv. Ment. Dis.*, 178(7), 442–447.

Lewis, C.E. (1991). Neurochemical mechanisms of chronic antisocial behavior (psychopathy). A literature review. *J. Nerv. Ment. Dis.*, 179(12), 720–727.

Mattes, J.A. (1990). Comparative effectiveness of carbamazapine and propranolol for rage outbursts. *J. Neuropsychiatry Clin. Neurosci.,* 2(2), 159–164.

Moss, H.B., Yao, J.K., and Panzak, G.L. (1990). Serotonergic responsivity and behavioral dimensions in antisocial personality disorder with substance abuse. *Biol. Psychiatry,* 28(4), 325–338.

Ravndal, E., and Vaglum, P. (1991). Changes in antisocial aggressiveness during treatment in a hierarchical therapeutic community: A prospective study of personality changes. *Acta Psychiatr. Scand.,* 84(6), 524–530.

Reid, W.H. (ed.) (1981). *The Treatment of Antisocial Syndromes.* Van Nostrand Reinhold, New York.

Reid, W.H. (1985). The antisocial personality: A review. *Hosp. Community Psychiatry,* 36(8), 831–837.

Reid, W.H. (1989). *The Treatment of Psychiatric Disorders.* Brunner/Mazel, New York.

Roy, A., Virkkunen, M., Guthrie, S., and Linnoila, M. (1986). Indices of serotonin and glucose metabolism in violent offenders, arsonists and alcoholics. *Ann. N. Y. Acad. Sci.,* 487, 202–220.

Sano, K., and Mayanagi, Y. (1988). Posteromedial hypothalamotomy in the treatment of violent, aggressive behavior. *Acta Neurochir.,* 44 (suppl.), 145–151.

Tyrer, P., and Seivewright, N. (1988). Pharmacological treatment of personality disorders. *Clin. Neuropharmacol.,* 11(6), 493–499.

Valliant, P.M., and Antonowicz, D.H. (1991). Cognitive behavior therapy and social skills training improves personality and cognition in incarcerated offenders. *Psychol. Rep.,* 68(1), 27–33.

Virkkunen, M., and Narvanen, S. (1987). Plasma insulin, tryptophan and serotonin levels during the glucose tolerance test among habitually violent and impulsive offenders. *Neuropsychobiology,* 17(1–2), 19–23.

Weiger, W.A., and Bear, D.M. (1988). An approach to the neurology of aggression. *J. Psychiatr. Res.,* 22(2), 85–89.

Wickham, E.A., and Reed, J.V. (1987). Lithium for the control of aggressive and self-mutilating behavior. *Int. Clin. Psychopharmacol.,* 2, 181–190.

Part V

RELATED DISORDERS

12 Self-Mutilation

ARMANDO R FAVAZZA* AND DAPHNE SIMEON‡
*Department of Psychiatry, University of Missouri–Columbia, Columbia, MO, USA
‡Department of Psychiatry, Mount Sinai School of Medicine, New York, NY, USA

INTRODUCTION

Self-mutilation (SM) is a vexing behavior that has been present since the earliest days of humankind. The earliest example is graphically depicted by 20 000-year-old hand imprints found on the walls of a cave at Gargas in southern France (Janssens, 1957). Of 92 recognizable imprints, the most common mutilation seen is the absence of the tip of the four fingers, with the thumb being spared. The finger tip amputations probably resulted from healing rituals or religious rituals associated with mourning.

The oldest pathological "case", found in Book 6 of Herodotus (about 450 BC), is that of Cleomenes. He was a Spartan leader who left the city after a series of political intrigues, and eventually was restored to a high position. However:

> He always was a little queer in the head, but no sooner had he returned to Sparta than he lost his wits completely, and began poking his staff into the face of everyone he met. As a result of this lunatic behavior his relative put him in the stocks. As he was lying there, fast bound, he noticed that all his guards had left him except one. He asked this man to lend him his knife. At first the fellow refused, but Cleomenes, by threats of what he would do to him when he recovered his liberty, so frightened him that he at last consented. As soon as the knife was in his hands, Cleomenes began to mutilate himself, beginning on his skin. He sliced his flesh into strips, working upwards to his thighs, hips, and sides until he reached his belly, which he chopped into mincemeat.

The earliest reference to a repetitive self-mutilator is found in the New Testament Gospel of St. Mark, Chapter 5. Jesus entered the land of the Gadarenes and was called upon to help with a man who lived among the tombs and who "night and day, cried and cut himself with stones."

The 19th and early 20th century medical literature contained many, often spectacular, case reports of SM. One patient, for example, periodically slashed herself while in an asylum; at final count 94 pieces of glass, 34 splinters, four shoe nails, one pin, and one needle had been removed from her arms (Channing, 1877–78). Karl Menninger, in 1938, was the first to

Impulsivity and Aggression. Edited by E. Hollander and D.J. Stein

review the literature and to classify SM into types: neurotic, psychotic, organic, and religious. The topic was relatively neglected for many decades until, in the 1960s, wrist cutting became the focus of psychiatric attention. In 1979 Ross and McKay published the first book devoted to SM; it dealt with epidemic skin carving in a Canadian correctional institution for adolescent girls. An article by Pattison and Kahan (1983) on the deliberate self-harm syndrome was the major early impetus for renewed psychiatric interest in SM. The widely reviewed book, *Bodies Under Siege: Self-Mutilation in Culture and Psychiatry* (Favazza, 1987), served to stimulate both researchers and clinicians who generally had dismissed most acts of SM simply as epiphenomena of borderline personality disorder. Numerous scientific reports have appeared in the ensuing years, and SM is now regarded as a legitimate topic of concern.

In this chapter we will (1) provide a classification of self-mutilative behaviors, (2) discuss SM in the context of aggression, and (3) present evidence about the role of impulsivity in SM.

SELF-MUTILATIVE BEHAVIORS

Self-mutilation, the deliberate, direct alteration or destruction of body tissue without conscious suicidal intent, can be divided into two categories. Culturally sanctioned SM includes practices (earlobe-piercing, tattoos, etc.) as well as rituals (subincision of the penis in rites of passage, scarification, etc.) that reflect society's traditional beliefs and symbols. The eye and the anus are the only organs that have not been subjected to culturally sanctioned mutilation probably because the former is the most intellectually valuable and magically endowed organ, while the later responds angrily to wounding and its refusal to heal may result in chronic inanition (Favazza, 1987).

The categorization of deviant SM is problematic. Winchel and Stanley (1991) categorized SM by the clinical contexts in which it mainly occurs: these include mental retardation, psychosis, penal institutionalization, and character disorder, primarily borderline personality disorder. However, since SM is found in a variety of mental and neuropsychiatric disorders, a broader phenomenological classification based on degree of tissue destruction and rate and pattern of behavior is more useful (Favazza and Rosenthal, 1990, 1993).

Table 1 lists the types of SM.

MAJOR SELF-MUTILATION

Major SM results in significant, even potentially lethal, damage. Examples include eye enucleation and amputation of various body parts. The behavior usually occurs suddenly but may be carefully planned, for example in some

Table 1   Categories of self-mutilation

Culturally sanctioned	Practices Rituals

Deviant	Major
	Stereotypical
	Superficial/moderate:
	  Compulsive
	  Episodic
	  Repetitive

cases of transsexual self-castration. Major SM is a relatively rare phenomenon and, while not an essential symptom of any mental disorder, may be an associated feature primarily of psychosis (Clark, 1981; DeMuth et al., 1983), intoxications (Rosen, 1972; Moskovitz and Byrd, 1983), and transsexualism (Krieger et al., 1982). It also has been reported in cases of encephalitis (Goodhart and Savitsky, 1933), congenital sensory neuropathy (Dubovsky, 1978), schizoid personality disorder (Beresford, 1980), mental retardation (Bishop, 1960), and the residual phase of schizophrenia (Talbott and Linn, 1978).

Some patients are indifferent to their behavior: a 16-year-old girl with chronic encephalitis enucleated her right eye during the night, did not complain of pain, and told the nurse that the eye had spontaneously fallen out of her head while she was sleeping (Goodhart and Savitsky, 1933). Some offer idiosyncratic explanations: a 22-year-old schizophrenic who thought he was Leonardo da Vinci removed his testicles because the voice of God told him to do so for no apparent reason (Goldfield and Glick, 1973). Comprehensible, albeit delusional reasons given by patients usually have religious and/or sexual themes: an 18-year-old youth who was forced into a homosexual episode while under the influence of LSD decided that he should obey the Bible and pluck out his eye because he had offended God (Rosen, 1972); a middle-aged depressed man cut off his testicles because he felt guilty over his sexual interest in prepubertal girls (Thompson and Abraham, 1983).

STEREOTYPICAL SELF-MUTILATION

Stereotypical SM involves acts such as head banging, eyeball pressing, and finger biting, that have a repetitive and fairly fixed mode of expression, seem to be devoid of symbolism, thought content or associated affect, and are often rhythmic. The prevalence of this behavior in institutionalized mentally retarded persons is in the range of 10–15% (Griffin et al., 1986). It is also encountered as a symptom or associated feature of autistic disorder, acute psychosis, Lesch–Nyhan syndrome (Christie et al., 1982), Tourette's syndrome (Robertson et al., 1989), and Prader–Willi syndrome (Dan J

Stein, personal communication). The behavior may appear briefly during the course of an episodic mental disorder or may be chronic. One study reported a mentally retarded, autistic child who engaged in head banging at the rate of 5400 times an hour (Romanzyk and Goren, 1975).

SUPERFICIAL/MODERATE SELF-MUTILATION

Superficial/moderate SM comprises acts that result in relatively little tissue damage. Its prevalence has been estimated to be 400–1400 per 100 000 per year (Whitehead et al., 1973; Pattison and Kahan, 1983; Favazza and Conterio, 1988). It may be divided into three types, namely compulsive, episodic, and repetitive.

Compulsive self-mutilation

This includes repetitive, ritualistic behaviors that typically occur many times daily, such as trichotillomania (hair pulling), onychophagia (nail biting), skin picking, and skin scratching.

Of these, only trichotillomania is diagnostically classified as a discrete disorder, specifically an impulse control disorder, i.e. a behavior occurring in response to an irresistible urge and resulting in gratification or relief of the urge. Clinical studies show that most trichotillomanics do report mounting tension or gratification associated with the behavior, suggesting both compulsive and impulsive features (Christenson et al., 1991). Patients commonly describe these behaviors occurring automatically or without conscious intent, and often without extensive or elaborate thought content or affective experience. In this respect, they are phenomenologically similar to those patients with obsessive compulsive disorder (OCD) who have compulsions with little or no obsessions. A relief of mounting anxiety is thus experienced, which differs from the more mechanistic nature of stereotypical self-mutilation. The phenomenological similarity between compulsive self-mutilation and OCD is supported by high comorbidity rates for the two disorders. In one series of trichotillomanic patients, 15% had a history of lifetime OCD and another 18% had a history of obsessive compulsive symptoms (Christenson et al., 1991). When the two disorders co-occur, the OCD obsessions and compulsions are usually unrelated in time or theme to the compulsive self-injury. However, this is not always the case. For example, Stinnet and Hollender (1970) reported a case of a young man with OCD who compulsively pressed his eyeballs and experienced relief of anxiety in response to dystonic obsessive images of his naked mother. Compulsive self-mutilating behaviors other than hair pulling have been very poorly characterized and studied. For example, skin picking appears to be a rather common and potentially impairing problem, especially in women with histories of mild acne (D Simeon and E Hollander, personal communication). Similarly, neurotic excoriations are commonly encountered by dermatologists but have received little attention from psychiatrists (Doran et al., 1985; Gupta et al., 1986). In summary, it can be said that compulsive self-mutilation contains a mix of compulsive and impulsive elements.

Episodic self-mutilation

The episodic type includes behaviors such as cutting, carving, and burning of the skin, interference with wound healing, needle sticking, bone breaking, and self-punching. Among the disorders in which it may appear either as a symptom or associated feature are borderline (Schaffer et al., 1982), histrionic (Pfohl, 1991), and antisocial personality disorders (Virkkunen, 1976), post-traumatic stress disorder (Greenspan and Samuel, 1989; Pitman, 1990) dissociative disorders (Miller and Bashkin, 1974; Bliss, 1988, Coons and Milstein, 1990), benign intracranial hypertension (Ballard, 1990), and eating disorders (Favazza et al., 1989; Parkin and Eagles, 1993). These behaviors are understood generally to be a morbid form of self-help that provides brief and often rapid relief from a broad variety of distressing feelings. Among the effects of the behavior are tension release, termination of depersonalization, euphoria, decreased troublesome or enhanced positive sexual feelings, release of anger, satisfaction from self-punishment, a sense of security, control and uniqueness, manipulation of others, and relief from feelings of depression, loneliness, loss, and alienation (Favazza, 1989). Episodic SM may be endemic in repressive total-care institutions (Toch, 1975) and may spread by contagion (Rada and James, 1965; Walsh and Rosen, 1985).

Repetitive self-mutilation

For some people the behaviors described in the episodic type become an overwhelming preoccupation. These persons may describe themselves as being addicted to the behaviors and may adopt an identity as a "cutter" or "burner". Typically they first deliberately harm themselves during early adolescence and then continue to harm themselves. The self-harm then may become a habitual response to distressing internal and external stimuli and may persist for decades, interspersed with periods of quiescence, eating disorders and episodic alcohol and substance abuse, or kleptomania (Favazza, 1992). This pattern of behavior is known as the repetitive SM syndrome.

The diagnostic criteria for this syndrome are:

1. Preoccupation with harming oneself physically.
2. Recurrent failure to resist impulses to harm oneself physically, resulting in the destruction or alteration of body tissue.

3. An increasing sense of tension immediately before the act of self-harm.
4. Gratification or a sense of relief when committing the act of self-harm.
5. The act of self-harm is not associated with conscious suicidal intent and is not in response to a delusion, hallucination, transsexual fixed ideas, or serious mental retardation.

Favazza and Conterio (1989) reported that 57% of people with the syndrome had attempted suicide by an overdose, usually as a result of demoralization over an inability to control their SM. Interestingly, a long term follow-up study of patients who had made a serious suicide threat or attempt revealed that a majority of the patients who did not commit suicide had a history of impulsivity, manipulative suicide attempts, or SM (Dingman and McGlashan, 1988). On the basis of phenomenological and biochemical evidence, Stanley et al. (1992) have conceptualized self-harm behaviors along a spectrum: "the more serious end of the spectrum would be occupied by suicide attempters and the less serious endpoint by trichotillomania with self-mutilation falling between these two behaviors".

Siomopoulos (1974) was the first to refer to repeated self-cutting as an "impulse neurosis". Pattison and Kahan (1983) described a deliberate self-harm syndrome, the precursor of the repetitive SM syndrome, as an impulse disorder. Favazza and Rosenthal (1993) clearly place the syndrome among the "impulse disorders not elsewhere classified" in the DSM-III-R (i.e. intermittent explosive disorder, pathological gambling, kleptomania, pyromania, and trichotillomania). In a recent major review, Tantam and Whittaker (1992) argue for a "distinct diagnostic category of repeated, deliberate self-harm, *sui generis*, which could also include the impulsive and self-destructive behaviors . . ."

The differentiation between compulsive and repetitive SM is not always sharp and clear. For example, repetitive SM can at times become so habitual as to occur daily and without clearly identifiable emotional precipitants or affective states. On the other hand, compulsive SM sometimes occurs in individuals with histories of childhood trauma, severe character pathology, and identifiable acute precipitants, such as feelings of anger, rejection, and self-punishment. In addition, some individuals display multiple types of self-mutilation of both the compulsive and repetitive type. More attention may need to be paid to the unique combination of obsessive compulsive and impulsive traits that characterize individuals and possibly shape the type, frequency, and other characteristics of their self-injurious behavior.

AGGRESSION AND SELF-MUTILATION

The word aggression often is used loosely by both laymen and scientists and has many cognates and references, for example violence, suicidality, criminality, hostility, pugnacity, obsessiveness, destructiveness, explosiveness, and anger. We consider aggression to be any behavior directed toward the goal of harming or injuring a living human being. Most aggression is directed outward against others. In suicidality it is directed deeply inward against the self with the goal of total destruction of one's body (although the behavior may be accompanied by beliefs or fantasies about the immortality of one's soul, reincarnation, reunion with a deceased loved one, etc.). In SM it is directed superficially inward against the covering and appendages of the self. Unlike suicidality, its goal is not the complete destruction of the body but rather the alleviation of painful psychological symptoms. In SM, aggression acts in service of the ego to facilitate the restoration of feelings of normality.

Ethologists such as Lorenz (1966), Morris (1967), and Eibl-Eibelsfeldt (1972) consider aggression to be an instinctive behavior. In this view, "man's aggressive behavior as manifested in war, crime, personal quarrels, and all kinds of destructive and sadistic behavior is due to a phylogenetically programmed, innate instinct which seeks for discharge and waits for the proper occasion to be expressed" (Fromm, 1973, p. 23). Self-mutilation also belongs on this list of aggressive behaviors. Among animals aggression is a positive, species-preserving instinct that affects sexual selection, the development of a ranking order, and territoriality. According to ethologists, however, the spontaneity of the instinct makes it dangerous, especially in humans. While aggression may be a reaction to external stimuli, it also may explode without demonstrable stimuli. When aggression is dammed up or when the central nervous system lowers its (hypothetical) aggression threshold, then an organism will search for a "missing stimulus" against which aggression can be unleashed. Thus, monkeys might bite, and humans cut their own arms.

Storr (1968), a psychiatrist, notes that the sexual and aggressive instincts share certain components, and that the physiological condition of the body in both sexual and aggressive arousal is quite similar. Just as we accept the idea that sex creates an internal tension which may be reduced either with the help of a partner or through masturbation, so too aggressive tension may be reduced through activities such as war, hunting, and athletic competition (Storr, 1968). Self-mutilation may be analogous to masturbation as a tension-relieving device. In fact, the relief of unbearable tension is commonly cited by self-mutilators as a reason for this behavior (Favazza, 1989).

A classic psychoanalytical formulation by Menninger (1938) is that (1) the prototype of all SM is self-castration and the substituted organ is an unconscious representative of the genital; (2) the aggression in SM may be directed toward an introjected object or towards real and present objects; (3) SM atones for past aggressive wishes and acts, and also permits future aggressive indulgences by the advance payment of a penalty; and (4) SM is a compromise formation to avoid suicide. Anna Freud (1946, p. 56), however, regarded turning against the self to be an early defense mechanism that was "as old as the instincts themselves, or at least as old as the conflict between instinctual impulses and any hindrance which they may encounter on their way to gratification".

Instinct has a somewhat static, first-cause connotation. Aggression may also be regarded as a plastic drive that is aroused when a person is frustrated (Dollard et al., 1939). As an example, early childhood self-attack has generally been explained as a result of aggression forced inward because its outward expression is blocked, for example by motor disabilities, external motor restrictions, physical distance from an intended object of aggression, or fears of loss of love, of punishment, and of destroying the love object (Cain, 1961). In a regressive slide from object to self, an object of hate may be incorporated or introjected so that the internalized representation becomes the target of aggression (Beres, 1952).

Another process described by psychoanalysts is the temporary disassociation of the body from the boundaries of the self so that body is perceived as an external object and receives the brunt of aggression aimed at the self (Freud, 1946; Beres, 1958). The stimulation of self-attack caused by the turning inward of aggression may serve the purpose of "establishing or reinforcing body boundaries—anywhere from the external boundaries or rind of the body ego to the more internal arousal of greater ego feeling" (Cain, 1961). It is well known that SM is an effective method of terminating episodes of dissociation and depersonalization (Rosenthal et al., 1972; Miller and Bashkin, 1974; Favazza, 1989). Kernberg (1987) believes that under conditions of intense frustration, dysphoria, or rage, the act of SM often is the "relieving enactment of revenge" in the effort to control an important person. Stone (1987) notes that "there are strong sociocultural pressures operating in Western society (shaped partly by underlying biological differences between the sexes) that conduce women to inhibit the direct expression of violent feelings against the offending parties, whereas men who feel violent tend more readily to become aggressive."

Aggression also has been described as a learned behavior (Baron, 1985). Thus, persons may self-mutilate because they have learned the behavior from others—an example is the reported spread of SM in institutions (Walsh and Rosen, 1985)—or because they either receive or anticipate rewards for the behavior, for example a caring response from a loved one or relief from undesirable duties.

Studies of self-mutilators show that 18–45% of individuals report anger towards themselves and 10–32% report anger towards others leading up to the acts of self-injury (Gardner and Gardner, 1975; Roy, 1978; Bennum, 1983). Bennum (1983) found that self-mutilators had greater outwardly directed hosility than nonmutilating depressives, while not differing in inwardly directed hostility. Simeon et al. (1992) reported that, compared with nonmutilating personality-disordered controls, self-mutilators had lifetime histories of greater aggression. Furthermore, the frequency of self-mutilation correlated with chronic anger.

A characteristic that distinguishes episodic and repetitive from compulsive self-mutilation is the aggression involved in the behavior. Compulsive self-injurers usually do not demonstrate or experience overt angry affect, and lifetime histories of aggressive or sociopathic traits have not been reported. Indeed, such patients are often quite surprised to come across terms such as self-injury or self-mutilation regarding their behaviors, since they do not view them as such. Instead, some researchers have proposed a neuro-ethological model to explain compulsive self-injury, such as hair pulling, as well as OCD compulsions, such as washing (Swedo and Rapoport, 1991). The model postulates that the compulsions comprise dysregulated, excessive, and repetitive versions of normal and adaptive grooming behaviors, secondary to an underlying neurochemical brain dysfunction. Comparison, then, of repetitive versus compulsive self-mutilation could offer a way of teasing apart the neurochemistry of impulsive aggression and that of non-aggressive impulsiveness.

IMPULSIVITY AND SELF-MUTILATION

Descriptive and systematic data reveal that repetitive self-mutilation is a typical impulsive act. Bennum (1983) reported that 70% of self-mutilators feel that they have no control over the act. Favazza and Conterio (1989) reported that 78% of individuals in their sample decided to self-mutilate on the spur of the moment, and another 15% made the decision within an hour of the act. The act was then always (30%) or almost always (51%) carried out. In another sample, less than 15% of self-mutilators reported any inner struggle to resist the behavior (Gardner and Gardner, 1975). Simeon et al. (1992) found a significant correlation between the frequency of self-mutilation and a measure of impulsivity.

Biological research in psychiatry over the last two decades, starting with the work of Asberg et al. (1976) in Sweden, has highlighted the role of the serotonergic system in impulsive aggression. Initially focusing on serotonergic dysregulation in attempted or completed suicide, research later demonstrated similar neurochemical derangement in outwardly directed acts of impulsive aggression (Brown et al., 1982; Linnoila et al., 1983; Coccaro et al., 1989), as well as in inwardly directed aggression without suicidal intent (SM).

López-Ibor et al. (1985) found that inpatient depressives with histories of self-injury without suicidal intent had lower cerebrospinal fluid (CSF) 5-hydroxyindoleacetic acid (5-HIAA) than those without SM histories; 5-HIAA is similarly low in those who have attempted suicide. Coccaro et al. (1987; 1989) reported a significant correlation between self-damaging acts and a blunted prolactin response to the serotonin (5-hydroxytryptamine, 5-HT) agonist fenfluramine in patients with personality disorders. Simeon et al. (1992) reported a significant negative correlation between the frequency of SM and platelet imipramine binding, a peripheral serotonergic index. In contrast to these studies, Gardner et al. (1990) compared CSF 5-HIAA levels in borderline personality disorder patients with and without SM, and found no difference. However, it cannot be ruled out that the different incidence of suicide attempt histories in the two groups may have concealed an association between CSF 5-HIAA and SM. In this regard, Simeon et al. (1992) found a 44% reduction in CSF 5-HIAA in a small subsample of self-mutilators who had never made suicide attempts, compared with non-mutilators without suicide attempt histories.

Indirect evidence for underlying serotonergic dysfunction in SM comes from open-treatment studies utilizing serotonin (5-HT) reuptake inhibitors (SRIs). Coccaro et al. (1990) reported that fluoxetine resulted, as least initially, in a marked decrease in self-directed assault in three personality disordered patients, independent of affective changes. Markovitz et al. (1991) openly treated borderline and schizotypal patients with fluoxetine for 12 weeks and reported a 97% decrease in self-mutilating episodes. Further pharmacological trials, conducted in a double-blind fashion, and assessing larger numbers of patients, are needed to determine conclusively whether SRIs are efficacious in treating self-injury and whether the response is selective in comparison to other pharmacological agents, as well as to clarify the time course and maintenance of the therapeutic response.

In the biology of compulsive self-mutilation, as with repetitive self-mutilation, serotonergic dysfunction has been implicated. Ninan et al. (1991) preliminarily reported that a small group of trichotillomanics did not differ from normal controls in CSF 5-HIAA, yet treatment response to SRIs correlated with the magnitude of CSF 5-HIAA decrease. Hollander et al. (1988) reported a patient with multiple self-mutilating compulsions who underwent double-blind challenge with the partial serotonin agonist *meta*-chlorophenylpiperazine (mCPP): following the administration of mCCP, there was an exacerbation and emergence of new self-mutilating compulsions. Unfortunately, systematic neurochemical studies of series of patients with compulsive self-injury have not been reported yet. More extensive, while indirect, evidence for serotonergic involvement in compulsive self-injury comes from the multiple reports of response to pharmacological treatment with SRIs in hair pulling (Swedo et al., 1989), nail biting (Leonard et al., 1991), skin picking (Jan Stout, 1990; Stein et al., 1993), and neurotic excoriations (Gupta et al., 1986).

Other neurotransmitter systems may be involved in the neurobiology of self-mutilation, but have been even less studied. Siever et al. (1992) have suggested that, in addition to serotonergic dysfunction, noradrenergic dys-regulation may be implicated in the expression of impulsive aggression. Specifically, noradrenergic hyper-reactivity may mediate increased arousal and irritability and may trigger acts of impulsive aggression, in conjunction with behavioral disinhibition mediated by serotonergic dysfunction. We are not aware of studies of the noradrenergic system specifically in self-injurers.

Dopaminergic dysfunction has been implicated in the execution of repetitive stereotypical behaviors. Although hardly explored in SM, there is one report of a depressed patient who acutely developed skin picking as part of an amphetamine toxic syndrome induced by bupropion (Van Putten and Shaffer, 1990). Two personality disordered patients with self-mutilating behavior are reported to have responded to the stimulant methylphenidate (Lycaki et al., 1979).

Another system implicated in self-mutilation is the opiatergic system. Indeed, habitual self-mutilators commonly report the relief of depersonalization and other dissociative states as the motivation to injure themselves, and relative analgesia to the self-inflicted injury is often present in the emotional state surrounding such acts. In one study of the opiatergic system, Coid et al. (1983) found that habitual self-mutilators had higher plasma met-enkephalin than control subjects.

THE PSYCHOLOGICAL–BIOLOGICAL INTERFACE

If serotonergic or other neurotransmitter abnormalities in part underlie self-mutilation, the question arises as to whether these neurochemical dysfunctions comprise state or trait characteristics. Furthermore, it is unknown if such neurochemical traits are familial and heritable, or arise at some stage in early brain development consequent to environmental life experiences. Childhood trauma has in recent years come increasingly into focus in this respect. Green (1978) reported a significantly greater incidence of self-mutilation in latency-age children who had suffered physical abuse, compared with neglected and normal children. He postulated that the abused child's sense of badness, coupled with ego deficits and poor impulse control, hamper healthy ego and super-ego development and self-esteem regulation at a critical developmental age and so precipitate self-destructive acts. Similarly, van der Kolk and Saporta (1991) found that histories of childhood physical and sexual abuse were highly significant predictors of adult self-cutting, while severe histories of separation and neglect further contributed to the continuation of self-destructive behaviors in the face of treatment. The authors suggested that not only psychological, but also biological, maturity affect how abuse and deprivation is managed at a young age, so that profound disruptions in early care-giving acting on an immature central nervous system may have long-lasting effects on biological self-regulation. Along these lines, it is interesting that even adult trauma, if extreme enough, may result in long-term neurochemical dysfunction, as has been implicated in noradrenergic dysfunction mediating hyperarousal and intrusive symptoms and opiatergic dysfunction mediating numbness and withdrawal symptoms in patients with post-traumatic stress disorder (van der Kolk and Saporta, 1991). The psychological and biological role of trauma in the genesis of self-injurious behaviors is an important area in the future investigation of both compulsive and repetitive self-mutilation.

CONCLUSIONS

Psychological and biological studies demonstrate that pathological SM is characterized by impulsivity and, depending on the type, by aggression or compulsivity. Compulsive SM (hair pulling, nail biting, skin picking, and scratching) contains a mix of compulsive and impulsive elements, but lacks aggression. Episodic/repetitive SM (skin cutting, burning, etc.) is especially associated with measures of aggression and impulsivity. Serotonergic dysregulation has been implicated in both compulsive and repetitive self-mutilation. Although not proven, the noradrenergic and opiatergic systems may also play a role. Negative childhood experiences may influence the development of psychological and biochemical vulnerabilities that result in adult SM. Unlike episodic SM, which can be encountered as a symptom of other disorders, both compulsive and repetitive SM are best conceptualized as Axis I disorders of impulse control. Anecdotal reports and several open studies point to the therapeutic usefulness of SRIs.

REFERENCES

Asberg, M., Traskman, L., and Thoren, P. (1976). 5-HIAA in the cerebrospinal fluid: A biological suicide predictor? *Arch. Gen. Psychiatry*, 33, 1193–1197.

Ballard, C.G. (1990). Benign intracranial hypertension and repeated self-mutilation. *Br. J. Psychiatry*, 155, 570–571.

Baron, R.A. (1985). Aggression. In: *Comprehensive Textbook of Psychiatry*, 4th edn (eds H.I. Kaplan and B.J. Sadock). Williams and Wilkins, Baltimore.

Bennum, I. (1983). Depression and hostility in self-mutilation. *Suicide Life Threat. Behav.*, 13, 71–84.

Beres, D. (1952). Clinical note on aggression in children. In: *The Psychoanalytic Study of the Child*, vol. VII (eds R.S. Eissler, A. Freud, H. Hartman and E. Kris). International Universities Press, New York.

Beres, D. (1958). Vicissitudes of superego function and superego precursors in childhood. In: *The Psychoanalytic Study of the Child*, vol. VIII (eds R.S. Eissler, A. Freud, H. Hartman and E. Kris). International Universities Press, New York.

Beresford, T.Y. (1980). The dynamics of aggression in an amputee. *Gen. Hosp. Psychiatry*, 3, 219–225.

Bishop, W.J. (1960). Some historical cases of auto-surgery. *Scott. Soc. Hist. Med.*, 23, 23–32.

Bliss, E.L. (1980). Multiple personalities. *Arch. Gen. Psychiatry*, 37, 1388–1397.

Brown, G.L., Ebert, M.H., Goyer, P.F., et al. (1982). Aggression, suicide, and serotonin: Relationships to CSF amine metabolites. *Am. J. Psychiatry*, 139, 741–746.

Cain, A.C. (1961). The presuperego turning-inward of aggression. *Psychoanal. Q.*, 30, 171–208.

Channing, W. (1877–88). Case of Helen Miller. *Am. J. Insanity*, 34, 368–378.

Christenson, G.A., Mackenzie, T.B., and Mitchell, J.E. (1991). Characteristics of 60 adult chronic hair pullers. *Am. J. Psychiatry*, 148, 365–370.

Christie, R., Bay, C., and Kaufman, I.A. (1982). Lesch–Nyhan disease. *Dev. Med. Child. Neurol.*, 24, 293–306.

Clark, R.A. (1981). Self-mutilation accompanying religious delusions. *J. Clin. Psychiatry*, 42, 243–245.

Coccaro, E.F., Siever, L.J., Klar, H.M., Friedman, R.A., Moskowitz, A., and David, K.L. (1987). 5-HT function in borderline personality disorders. Presented at New Research, American Psychiatric Association 140th Annual Meeting, Chicago, IL.

Coccaro, E.F., Siever, L.J., Klar, H.M., et al. (1989). Serotonergic studies in patients with affective and personality disorders: Correlates with suicidal and impulsive aggressive behavior. *Arch. Gen. Psychiatry*, 46, 587–599.

Coccaro, E.F., Astill, J.L., Herbert, J.L., and Schut, A.G. (1990). Fluoxetine treatment of impulsive aggression in DSM-III-R personality disorder patients [letter]. *J. Clin. Psychopharmacol.*, 10, 373–375.

Coid, J., Allolio, B., and Rees, L.H. (1983). Raised plasma metenkephalin in patients who habitually mutilate themselves. *Lancet*, ii, 545–546.

Coons, P.M., and Milstein, V. (1990). Self-mutilation associated with dissociative disorder. *Dissociation*, 3, 81–87.

DeMuth, G.W., Strain, J., and Lombardo-Mahar, A. (1983). Self-amputation and restitution. *Gen. Hosp. Psychiatry*, 5, 25–30.

Dingman, C.W., and McGlashan, T.H. (1988). Characteristics of patients with serious suicidal intentions who ultimately commit suicide. *Hosp. Community Psychiatry*, 39, 295–299.

Dollard, J., Doob, L., Miller, N., Mowrer, O.H., and Sears, R.R. (1939). *Frustration and Aggression*. Yale University Press, New Haven.

Doran, A.R., Roy, A., and Wolkowitz, O.M. (1985). Self-destructive dermatoses. *Psychiatr. Clin. North. Am.*, 8, 291–298.

Dubovsky, S.L. (1978). "Experimental" self-mutilation. *Am. J. Psychiatry*, 135, 1240–1241.

Eibl-Eibelsfeldt, I. (1972). *On Love and Hate*. Holt, Rinehart, and Winston, New York.

Favazza, A. (1987). *Bodies Under Siege*. Johns Hopkins University Press, Baltimore.

Favazza, A. (1989). Why patients mutilate themselves. *Hosp. Community Psychiatry*, 40, 137–145.

Favazza, A. (1992). Repetitive self-mutilation. *Psychiatr. Ann.*, 22, 60–63.

Favazza, A., and Conterio, K. (1988). The plight of chronic self-mutilators. *Community Ment. Health J.*, 24, 22–30.

Favazza, A., and Conterio, K. (1989). Female habitual self-mutilators. *Acta Psychiatr. Scand.*, 79, 283–289.

Favazza, A., and Rosenthal, R.J. (1990). Varieties of pathological self-mutilation. *Behav. Neurol.*, 3, 77–85.

Favazza, A., and Rosenthal, R.J. (1993). Diagnostic issues in self-mutilation. *Hosp. Community Psychiatry*, 44, 134–140.

Favazza, A., DeRosear, L., and Conterio, K. (1989). Self-mutilation and eating disorders. *Suicide Life Threat. Behav.*, 19, 352–361.

Freud, A. (1946). *The Ego and and the Mechanisms of Defense*. International Universities Press, New York.

Fromm, E. (1973). *The Anatomy of Human Destructiveness*. Holt, Rinehart, and Winston, New York.

Gardner, A.R., and Gardner, A.J. (1975). Self-mutilation, obsessionality and narcissism. *Br. J. Psychiatry*, 127, 127–132.

Gardner, D.L., Lucas, P.B., and Cowdry, R.W. (1990). CSF metabolites in borderline personality disorder compared to normal controls. *Biol. Psychiatry*, 28, 247–254.

Goldfield, M.D., and Glick, I.A. (1973). Self-mutilation of the genitalia. *Med. Asp. Hum. Sexuality*, 7, 219–232.

Goodhart, S., and Savitsky, N. (1933). Self-mutilation in chronic encephalitis. *Am. J. Med. Sci.*, 185, 674–684.

Green, A.H. (1978). Self-destructive behavior in battered children. *Am. J. Psychiatry*, 135, 579–582.

Greenspan, G.S., and Samuel, S.E. (1989). Self-cutting after rape. *Am. J. Psychiatry*, 146, 789–790.

Griffin, J.C., Williams, D.E., and Stark, M.T. (1986). Self-injurious behavior: A statewide prevalence survey. *Appl. Res. Ment. Retard.*, 7, 105–116.

Gupta, M.A., Gupta, A.K., and Haberman, H.R. (1986). Neurotic excoriations: A review and some new perspectives. *Compr. Psychiatry*, 27, 381–386.

Hollander, E., Papp, L., Campeas, R., DeCaria, C., and Liebowitz, M.R. (1988). More on self-mutilation and obsessive–compulsive disorder [letter]. *Can. J. Psychiatry*, 33, 675.

Jan Stout, R. (1990). Fluoxetine for facial picking [letter]. *Am. J. Psychiatry*, 147, 370.

Janssens, P.A. (1957). Medical news on prehistoric representations of human hands. *Med. Hist.*, 1, 318–322.

Kernberg, O. (1987). The borderline self-mutilator. *J. Pers. Disord.*, 1, 344–346.

Krieger, M.J., McAninch, J.W., and Weimer, S.R. (1982). Self-performed bilateral orchiectomy in transsexuals. *J. Clin. Psychiatry*, 43, 292–293.

Leonard, H.L., Lenane, M.C., Swedo, S.E., Rettew, D.C., and Rapoport, J.L. (1991). A double-blind comparison of clomipramine and desipramine treatment of severe onychophagia. *Arch. Gen. Psychiatry*, 48, 821–827.

Linnoila, M., Virkkunen, M., Scheinin, M., Nuutila, A., Rimon, R., and Goodwin, F.K. (1983). Low cerebrospinal fluid 5-hydroxyindoleacetic acid concentration differentiates impulsive from nonimpulsive violent behavior. *Life Sci.*, 33, 2609–2614.

López-Ibor, J.J., Saiz-Ruiz, J., and de los Cobos, J.C.P. (1985). Biological correlations of suicide and aggressivity in major depressions (with melancholia): 5-Hydroxylindoleacetic acid and cortisol in cerebral spinal fluid, dexamethasone suppression test and therapeutic response to 5-hydroxytryptophan. *Neuropsychiobiology*, 14, 67–74.

Lorenz, K. (1966). *On Aggression*. Harcourt Brace World, New York.

Lycacki, H., Josef, N.C., and Munetz, M. (1979). Stimulation and arousal in self-mutilators. *Am. J. Psychiatry*, 136, 1223–1224.

Markovitz, P.J., Calabrese, J.R., Schulz, S.C., and Meltzer, H.Y. (1991). Fluoxetine in the treatment of borderline and schizotypal personality disorders. *Am. J. Psychiatry*, 148, 1064–1067.

Menninger, K. (1938). *Man Against Himself*. Harcourt Brace World, New York.

Miller, F., and Bashkin, E. (1974). Depersonalization and self-mutilation. *Psychoanal. Q.*, 43, 638–649.

Morris, D. (1967). *The Naked Ape*. McGraw-Hill, New York.

Moskovitz, R.A., and Byrd, T. (1983). Rescuing the angel within: PCP-related self-enucleation. *Psychosomatics*, 24, 402–406.

Ninan, P.T., Eccard, M., Jewart, R.D., Stipetic, M., Lewine, R.J., and Risch, C.S. (1991). Trichotillomania: CSF values and treatment response. Presented at New Research, APA 144th Annual Meeting, New Orleans, LA.

Parkin, J.R., and Eagles, J.M. (1993). Blood letting in bulimia nervosa. *Br. J. Psychiatry*, 162, 246–248.

Pattison, E.M., and Kahan, J. (1983). The deliberate self-harm syndrome. *Am. J. Psychiatry*, 140, 867–872.

Pfohl, B. (1991). Histrionic personality disorder: a review of available data and recommendations for DSM-IV. *J. Pers. Disord.*, 5, 150–156.

Pitman, R.K. (1990). Self-mutilation in combat related PTSD. *Am. J. Psychiatry*, 147, 123–124.

Rada, R.T., and James, W. (1982). Urethral insertion of foreign bodies: a report of contagious self-mutilation in a maximum security hospital. *Arch. Gen. Psychiatry*, 39, 423–429.

Robertson, M.M., Trimble, M.R., and Lees, A.J. (1989). Self-injurious behavior and the Gilles de la Tourette syndrome. *Psychol. Med.*, 19, 611–625.

Romanzyk, R.G., and Goren, E.R. (1975). Severe self-injurious behavior. *J. Consult. Clin. Psychol.*, 43, 730–739.

Rosen, D.H. (1972). Focal suicide. *Am. J. Psychiatry*, 128, 1009–1011.

Rosenthal, R.J., Rinzler, C., Walsh, R., and Klausner, E. (1972). Wrist-cutting syndrome: the meaning of a gesture. *Am. J. Psychiatry*, 128, 1363–1368.

Ross, R.R., and McKay, H.B. (1979). *Self-Mutilation*. Lexington Books, Lexington, MA.

Roy, A. (1978). Self-mutilation. *Br. J. Med. Psychol.*, 51, 201–203.

Schaffer, C.B., Carroll, J., and Alsimowitz, S.I. (1982). Self-mutilation and the borderline personality. *J. Nerv. Ment. Dis.*, 170, 468–473.

Siever, L.J., Trestman, R.L., and Silverman, J.M. (1992). Validation of personality disorder assessment by biologic and family studies. *J. Pers. Disord.*, 6, 301–312.

Simeon, D., Stanley, B., Frances, A., Mann, J.J., Winchel, R., and Stanley, M. (1992). Self-mutilation in personality disorders: psychological and biological correlates. *Am. J. Psychiatry*, 149, 221–226.

Siomopoulos, V. (1974). Repeated self-cutting: an impulse neurosis. *Am. J. Psychother.*, 28, 85–94.

Stanley, B., Winchel, R.M., Molcho, A., Simeon, D., and Stanley, M. (1992). Suicide and the self-harm continuum: Phenomenological and biochemical evidence. *Int. Rev. Psychiatry*, 4, 149–155.

Stein, D.J., Hutt, C., Spitz, J., and Hollander, E. (1993). Compulsive picking and obsessive–compulsive disorder. *Psychosomatics*, 34, 177–181.

Stinnett, J.L., and Hollender, M.H. (1970). Compulsive self-mutilation. *J. Nerv. Ment. Dis.*, 150, 371–375.

Stone, M.H., (1987). The borderline self-mutilator. *J. Pers. Dis.*, 1, 347–349.

Storr, A. (1968). *Human Aggression*. Atheneum, New York.

Swedo, S.E., and Rapoport, J.L. (1991). Annotation: Trichotillomania. *J. Child. Psychol. Psychiatry*, 32, 401–409.

Swedo, S.E., Leonard, H.L., Rapoport, J.L., Lenane, M.C., Goldberger, E.L., and Cheslow, D.L. (1989). A double-blind comparison of clomipramine and desipramine in the treatment of trichotillomania. *N. Engl. J. Med.*, 321, 497–501.

Talbott, J.A., and Linn, L. (1978). Reactions of schizophrenics to life-threatening disease. *Psychiatr. Q.*, 50, 218–227.

Tantam, D., and Whittaker, J. (1992). Personality disorder and self-wounding. *Br. J. Psychiatry*, 61, 451–464.

Thompson, J.N., and Abraham, T.K. (1983). Male genital mutilation after paternal death. *Br. Med. J.*, 287, 727–728.

Toch, H. (1975). *Men in Crisis*. Aldine, Chicago.

van der Kolk, B.A., and Saporta, J. (1991). The biological response to psychic trauma: mechanism and treatment of intrusion and numbing. *Anxiety Res.*, 4, 199–212.

Van Putten, T., and Shaffer, I. (1990). Delirium associated with buproprion. *J. Clin. Psychopharmacol.*, 10, 234.

Virkkunen, M. (1976). Self-mutilation in anti-social personality disorder. *Acta. Psychiatr. Scand.*, 54, 347–352.

Walsh, B.W., and Rosen, P. (1985). Self-mutilation and contagion. *Am. J. Psychiatry*, 125, 119–120.

Winchel, R.M., and Stanley, M. (1991). Self-injurious behavior. *Am. J. Psychiatry*, 148, 306–317.

Whitehead, P.C., Johnson, F.G., and Ferrence, R. (1973). Measuring the incidence of self-injury. *Am. J. Orthopsychiatry*, 43, 142–148.

13 Sexual Impulsivity

MARTIN P KAFKA
Department of Psychiatry, McLean Hospital, Belmont, MA, USA

INTRODUCTION

Before any meaningful discussion can proceed to review the concept "sexual impulsivity", it is necessary to clearly define those syndromes subsumed by this nosological construct. To this end, I will review the defining characteristics of paraphilic disorders and broaden the boundaries for sexual impulsivity by including a group of sexual behaviors designated as "paraphilia-related disorders" (Kafka and Prentky, 1992a; Kafka, 1994a). In addition, I will attempt to highlight any relevant distinctions between sexually aggressive paraphiliacs, nonviolent paraphiliacs, and men with paraphilia-related disorders. Sexually aggressive paraphiliacs include rapists, pedophiles, severe sexual sadists, and paraphilic sexual murderers.

Athough the DSM-III (American Psychiatric Association, 1980) and DSM-III-R (American Psychiatric Association, 1987) categorize paraphilias as disorders of impulse control, other investigators have suggested that this group of behaviors can be more accurately conceptualized as behavioral addictions (Carnes, 1983) or obsessive compulsive spectrum disorders (Coleman, 1987). The purview of this article is not to resolve this dispute, but rather to suggest that empirical research is lacking regarding the form, prevalence, and etiology of these disorders.

PARAPHILIAS

Our current diagnostic nomenclature, both the DSM-III-R (American Psychiatric Association, 1987) and DSM-IV (American Psychiatric Association, 1994) characterize paraphilias as sexual disorders with three component dimensions:

1. Repetitive, intense, socially deviant (i.e. unconventional) sexual arousal.
2. Loss of sexual impulse control, or marked distress from paraphilic arousal or urges.
3. A minimum duration of 6 months.

Impulsivity and Aggression. Edited by E. Hollander and D.J. Stein
© 1995 John Wiley & Sons Ltd

In addition, in DSM IV, impairment of reciprocal sexual and affectionate behaviors can accompany paraphilic sexuality is a necessary criterion for diagnosis.

The common paraphilias are outlined in Table 1.

CHARACTERISTICS COMMON TO PARAPHILIC SEXUAL IMPULSIVITY

Published research as well as clinical data characterizing men with paraphilias is predominantly limited to describing sexually aggressive men, primarily rapists and pedophiles. The following descriptive characteristics of paraphilic sexuality, however, may describe nonviolent paraphiliacs and men with paraphilia-related disorders as well.

For the majority of paraphilic men, the onset of unconventional sexual arousal is during adolescence (Abel et al., 1985). The incidence of sexually aggressive paraphilic behavior, as with many other antisocial impulsive behaviors, peaks between the ages of 15 and 25 years and then gradually

Table 1   The DSM-III-R paraphilic disorders

Paraphilia	Objective for sexual arousal
Exhibitionism	Exposure of one's genitals to an unsuspecting stranger (usually women or children)
Fetishism	Use of nonliving objects (e.g. leather, hair, boots)
Frotteurism	Touching, rubbing against a nonconsenting person
Pedophilia	To a prepubescent child (e.g. 13 years or less)
Masochism	The act of being beaten, bound, humiliated or otherwise made to suffer
Sadism	Acts in which the physical or psychological suffering (including humiliation) of the victim is required
Transvestic fetishism	Crossdressing as a member of the opposite sex
Voyeurism	Observing an unsuspecting person who is naked, undressing, or engaging in sexual activity
Telephone scatologia	Obscene/erotic telephone calls to nonconsenting individuals
Necrophilia	Corpses
Partialism	Exclusive focus on part of the body
Zoophilia	Animals
Coprophilia	Feces
Klismaphilia	Enemas
Urophilia	Urine
Paraphilia not otherwise specified	

declines with age (Abel and Rouleau, 1990). While paraphiliacs may have a favored unconventional sexual outlet, a number of studies have reported that the presence of a single reported paraphilia tends to predict the presence of multiple (two to five) paraphilic outlets over the course of a lifetime (Rooth, 1973; Buhrich and Beaumont, 1981; Freund, et al., 1983; Abel et al., 1988). These studies suggests that there is a diathesis or vulnerability for sexual expression through multiple unconventional sexual behaviors.

The three most common paraphilias presenting for treatment at specialized treatment facilities are exhibitionism, pedophilia, and voyeurism. Although a specific paraphilia might predominate at a single point in time, longitudinally other paraphilic outlets may establish precedence, leading to serial predominant paraphilic proclivities. Paraphilic arousal may wax and wane, may be either ego-syntonic or ego-dystonic, and is more likely to occur or intensify during periods of "stress". Paraphiliacs may describe their sexual behavior as obligatory, repetitive, and stereotyped. Many will report engaging in time-consuming sexual behavior (i.e. sexual fantasizing, urges, and activities) on at least a daily basis over prolonged periods of time.

Many men with paraphilias are married, but some utilize unconventional sexual fantasy for arousal when engaged in socially conventional sexual activities (e.g. an intended romantic, sexual encounter with a spouse or lover). In such instances, it is not uncommon for paraphilic men to report situational impotence, loss of conventional sexual desire, and/or dysphoria if they try to suppress paraphilic fantasies. Reliance on unconventional fantasy or activity with a spouse or lover may precipitate extramarital encounters, reliance on masturbation for sexual activity, and/or marital dysfunction.

RAPE, PARAPHILIAS, AND SEXUAL IMPULSIVITY

Although rape, like pedophilia, is synonymous with sexual aggression and impulsivity, it is not designated as paraphilic in our current diagnostic taxonomy because the consideration of rape as a paraphilic disorder has been controversal (Abel and Rouleau, 1990). In part, this controversy stems from studies reporting rape fantasies and arousal to forced sexual behavior as common amongst "normal" men (Malamuth, 1981; Baxter et al., 1986) and from reports that college age men would be more likely to commit rape if assured protection against being caught or prosecuted (Malamuth, 1981; Briere and Malamuth, 1983). In addition, some studies of rapists utilizing penile plethysmography demonstrate lower sexual arousal in response to depictions of rape than in response to conventional sexual stimuli (Baxter et al., 1984, 1986). These reports collectively suggest that rapists cannot be readily distinguished from "normal" men.

In contrast, some rapists will acknowledge multiple paraphilias, report repetitive sexually arousing rape fantasies, and demonstrate paraphilic (i.e. deviant and preferential) sexual arousal to depictions of nonconsensual sex if evaluated during plethysmography (Abel and Rouleau, 1990). Abel et al. (1985) solicited data from 411 paraphiliacs and found that rapists and pedophiles reported the largest number of associated paraphilias. Of the 89 rapists, 50% were pedophilic, 29% exhibitionists, 20% voyeurs, and 11% were sexual sadists. Bradford et al. (1992) reporting on 443 male sex offenders attending a forensic clinic, confirmed that sex offenders, incuding rapists, have multiple paraphilias. Rapists most commonly reported voyeurism (46%), frotteurism (30%), and pedophilia (30%). When revising DSM-III, the task force on paraphilias proposed that, on the basis of the scientific evidence, a distinct diagnostic paraphilic category, paraphilic coercive disorder, be adopted to characterize that group of rapists with onset of paraphilic rape fantasies prior to the age of 21, a high frequency of other paraphilias, and rape urges and activities subsequent to other paraphilic acts. This diagnostic categorization, however, was not approved by the Board of Directors of the American Psychiatric Association (Abel, 1989).

PARAPHILIA-RELATED DISORDERS

The distinction between "normal" and "deviant" sexual behavior is determined by cultural and historical context (Marmor, 1971). This distinction, however, is one of the primary determinants for the contemporary psychiatric definition of paraphilic sexuality (e.g. the DSM-IV). Inasmuch as sexual behaviors which are now considered "normal" have been considered "deviant" in the recent past, this dimensional criterion of paraphilic sexuality may lead to an overly exclusive boundary for sexual impulse disorders.

Masturbation, currently considered as a healthy expression of sexual behavior, was considered socially deviant in late 19th and early 20th century Western Europe and the USA (Hare, 1962). Homosexuality was considered a paraphilia as well, until it was deleted from the third edition of the American Psychiatric Association's diagnostic manual (1980). This deletion was the result of contemporary community-based nonpatient sample studies that failed to demonstrate distinctive differences in psychopathology between homosexual and heterosexual males (Saghir and Robins, 1973; Marmor, 1981). Some sexual behaviors that were considered as "normal" expressions in other cultures earlier in human history are considered as contemporary paraphilias. For example, homosexual pedophilia was practiced between men and adolescent boys during the Classical Greek period (Greenberg, 1988). Last, there are current sexual behaviors which blur the distinction between "normal" and "deviant" in contemporary American culture. Pornography use, for example, is a culturally sanctioned adult sexual activity, but repetitive indulgence or distribution of child pornography can lead to arrest and incarceration. Telephone scatologia, the victimization of unsuspecting women by male obscene telephone callers, is a paraphilia, but telephone sex, one component of which generally includes sexually explicit, if not obscene, language, is a culturally condoned "nonparaphilic" sexual behavior because it does not include victimization or unwilling participation.

Since cultural and historical factors can determine the "deviance" of a particular sexual behavior, we must consider that certain contemporary culturally sanctioned sexual activities might become "paraphilic-like" — repetitive, impulsive, and accompanied by intrusive sexual fantasies and urges, and by impairment of reciprocal affectionate relationships. These behaviors, currently designated as nonparaphilic sexual addictions (DSM-III-R, American Psychiatric Association, 1987, p. 296) are without a diagnostic appellation in the proposed DSM-IV (American Psychiatric Association, 1994). To achieve congruence with the qualities and boundaries of paraphilia, I suggest the following definition for paraphilia-related disorders (Kafka and Prentky, 1992a; Kafka, 1994a):

1. Over a period of at least 6 months, the person has experienced recurrent intense sexual urges and sexually arousing fantasies involving culturally normative aspects of sexual expression which increase in frequency or intensity so as to significantly interfere with the expression of the capacity for reciprocal, affectionate sexual activity.
2. The person has acted on those urges, or is markedly distressed by them.

The common paraphilia-related disorders are listed in Table 2.

Sexually aggressive as well as nonviolent paraphiliacs can report concurrent paraphilia-related disorders (Breitner, 1973; Gagne, 1981; Carnes, 1983; Prentky et al., 1989a; Levine et al., 1990) and these "nonparaphilic" behaviors may present with a pattern of sexual frequency, intensity, and psychosocial impairment which does not clearly distinguish them from nonviolent paraphilias (Carnes, 1989; Kafka and Prentky, 1992a). Analogous with paraphilias, the presence of a single paraphilia-related disorder predicts the probable presence of several of these disorders, longitudinally diagnosed, in the same individual (Carnes, 1989; Kafka and Prentky, 1992a, 1994b). A recent report examining Axis I comorbidity in men with paraphilias, in comparison with men with only paraphilia-related behaviors, failed to distinguish statistically distinct patterns of comorbidity between the groups (Kafka and Prentky, 1994b). Paraphilia-related disoders as well as paraphilias both appear to be ameliorated by the serotonin (5-hydroxytryptamine, 5-HT) reuptake inhibitor and sertraline (Kafka, 1994c), fluoxetine (Kafka and Prentky, 1992). These data lend credence to the concept that sexual impulsivity is pleomorphic and can include a diverse range of sexual behaviors, both "normal" and "deviant" in content.

Table 2 The paraphilia-related disorders

Disorder	Definition and references
Compulsive masturbation	Masturbation is a primary sexual outlet even during a stable intimate relationship (Marcus and Francis, 1975; Carnes, 1983, 1989; Earle and Crow, 1989)
Protracted promiscuity	A pattern of sexual conquests involving a succession of people who exist only as things to be used (Krafft-Ebbing, 1886; Hirshfeld, 1948; Money, 1986; American Psychiatric Association, 1987, p. 296)
Pornography dependence	An ego-dystonic, repetitive pattern of use of pornographic materials (e.g. magazines, videos) (Carnes, 1983, 1989; Earle and Crow, 1989; Reinisch, 1990)
Telephone sex	An ego-dystonic dependence on telephone sex, which may include significant debt (Carnes, 1983, 1989; Earle and Crow, 1989; Kafka, 1991a)
Sexual accessories	Ego-dystonic, repetitive use of dildos or foreign objects inserted as preferential for sexual arousal or the repetitive, ego-dystonic use of drugs exclusively for sexual arousal (e.g. nitrate inhalants, cocaine) (Agnew, 1986; Boffum et al., 1988)
Severe sexual desire incompatability	An ongoing romantic affiliation in which excessive sexual desire in one partner produces sexual demands on the other partner (who does not suffer from hypoactive sexual desire) that markedly interfere with the capacity to sustain the relationship (Krafft-Ebbing, 1886; Hirshfeld, 1948; Friedman, 1977)
Paraphilia-related disorder not otherwise specified	

In comparison with paraphilic disorders, there is even less systematic research and empirical data examining the clinical characteristics of men and women with paraphilia-related disorders. In my clinical research, the three most common paraphilia-related disorders in men are compulsive masturbation, protracted promiscuity, and dependence on pornography (Kafka and Prentky, 1992a, 1994b; Kafka, 1994a). In women, the three most prevalent forms of sexual impulsivity may be protracted promiscuity, compulsive masturbation, and sexual masochism. Despite the lack of corroborated empirical data, my clinical observation is that many of the same qualities attributed to paraphilic arousal and activity are applicable to paraphilia-related disorders.

SEXUAL IMPULSIVITY AND PSYCHIATRIC COMORBIDITY

Many of the studies examining comorbid psychiatric disorders in sexually aggressive paraphiliacs report symptoms or symptom clusters derived from personality inventories, most commonly the Minnesota Multiphasic Personality Index (MMPI) (McCreary, 1975; Anderson et al., 1979; Kalichman, 1990; Langevin et al., 1990a,b; Grossman et al., 1990). Some of these studies, however, do not identify syndromes as defined by the DSM-III and DSM-IV. Axis I disorders identified include psychoactive substance abuse, especially alcohol (Rada, 1975a; Mio et al., 1986; Langevin and Langs, 1990c), conduct and attention deficit disorder (Kavoussi et al., 1988; Hunter and Goodwin, 1992), mixed anxiety–depression (Wise et al., 1991; Fagan et al., 1991), social anxiety with concomitant social skill deficits (Baxter et al., 1984; Levin and Stava, 1987; Marshall, 1989), and depressive symptoms (Kavoussi et al., 1988; Grossman et al., 1990; Becker et al., 1991). In contrast, psychoses are not commonly diagnosed in sexually aggressive men (Groth and Burgess, 1977).

The Axis II disorder most frequently described in sexually aggressive paraphiliacs is antisocial personality disorder (Henn et al., 1976; Virkkunen, 1985). The base rate of psychopathy in sex offenders can vary considerably, however, across studies. Other studies of Axis II personality disorders in sexually aggressive men suggest that they are a heterogeneous group (Rosenberg and Knight, 1988).

Developmental factors are presumed to be significant determinants differentiating sexually aggressive paraphiliacs from those whose sexual impulsivity does not include sexual assault. In sexual aggressors, a history of physical/sexual abuse (Hanson and Slater, 1988), paternal alcoholism and antisocial personality (Langevin et al., 1984), and family instability with inconsistent limit setting (Rada, 1978a; Prentky et al., 1989b) are hypothesized to contribute to persistent low self-esteem (Groth, 1979; Marshall, 1989), low social and interpersonal competence (Marshall, 1989; Knight et al., 1983), and a lifestyle characterized by impulsivity (Prentky and Knight, 1986, 1991), including alcohol abuse.

Studies of comorbid Axis I and Axis II psychiatric disorders in nonoffending paraphiliacs are very limited. Several authors have anecdotally commented on the "thrill-seeking" characteristics of sexually impulsive men (Stoller, 1975; Carnes, 1983; Wise et al., 1991), an observation consistent with the notion that impulsivity is associated with risk-taking behaviors. Person (1989) notes that, as a general characteristic, paraphiliacs who present for treatment are "depression prone".

Perhaps the best studied group of nonoffending paraphiliacs are fetishistic transvestites. This group has been found to report a high incidence of anxiety, depression, impulsivity, interpersonal sensitivity, and social alienation as measured by (non DSM-III-R related) symptom rating scales (Wilson and Gosselin, 1980; Fagan et al., 1988; Wise et al., 1991). In the report by Wise et al. (1991), the transvestites did not differ from the comparison group of other paraphiliacs in these characteristics.

Studies regarding psychiatric disorders associated with paraphilia-related disorders suggest comorbidity with physical and sexual abuse (Carnes, 1991), substance abuse (Carnes, 1991), impulsivity ("behavioral addictions", e.g. overeating, gambling, and overworking; Carnes, 1991), and depression (Carnes, 1983; Kafka, 1991a; Kafka and Prentky, 1992b, 1994b).

EPIDEMIOLOGY

Determining the base rate of prevalence of the paraphilias has thus far presented insurmountable problems. In clinics that specialize in the characterization and treatment of these disorders, the overwhelming majority (95%) of people with paraphilias are men. Because these sexual behaviors are socially deviant and stigmatized, paraphiliacs are reluctant to report them or to initiate seeking treatment. Shame, guilt, secrecy, and the potential for legal complications are powerful factors that mitigate full disclosure even in situations where strict confidentiality has been guaranteed. There have been a few studies which have tried to determine the incidence of paraphilic fantasies and behavior in a "normal" sample of men. For example, Crepault and Couture (1980) reported that in 94 French-Canadian men, 61% reported pedophilic fantasy, 54% reported voyeuristic fantasy, and 33% reported rape fantasies. Templemann and Stinnett (1991) evaluated the sexual histories and sexual arousal patterns of 60 college males from a rural area. Sixty-five percent of the sample had engaged in some form of sexual misconduct in the past, including frottage, obscene phone calls, "date rape", and sexual contacts with children. In a study which included a control group of 60 men in comparison with a sample of over 220 sex offenders, Fedora et al. (1992), using penile plethysmography, reported that 28% of the control group evinced a paraphilic response to a variety of visual stimuli, ranging from 3% (fetishistic transvestism) to 17% (pedophilic arousal). In these studies, these arousal patterns, however, do not imply any repetitive paraphilic sexual behaviors.

Although the number of men presenting for treatment of paraphilic behaviors is small, the number of people who have been victimized by paraphilic activity is substantial. Abel et al. (1988) reported that the ratio of arrest to self-reported commission of the paraphilic acts of rape and child molestation was 1:30. The ratio of arrest to the reported commission of less violent paraphilias (e.g. exhibitionism and voyeurism) is approximately 1:150. The large commercial market for paraphilic pornography and paraphernalia implies that these disorders are more prevalent than is commonly indicated by the data available from specialized treatment agencies.

There has been no methodology to establish the base-rate prevalence of paraphilia-related disorders, behaviors which, arguably, may be more common than paraphilias since the former are frequently present (but not necessarily given adequate consideration) in paraphiliacs and also occur exclusive of paraphilic arousal and behavior.

THEORIES REGARDING THE ETIOLOGY OF SEXUAL IMPULSIVITY

PSYCHODYNAMIC AND DEVELOPMENTAL THEORIES

Sigmund Freud, in his seminal psychoanalytical work *Three Essays on Sexuality* (1905), identified sexual perversions (i.e. paraphilias) as sexual behaviors which interfered with, or digressed from, the primary "instinctual" aim — adult heterosexual perpetuation of the species. Sexual perversions were conceptualized as remnants of infantile (i.e. prepubertal and early childhood) sexual instincts, activated and elaborated primarily because of developmental vicissitudes related to the castration complex in boys.

Psychoanalytical case reports have provided elaborations of Freud's original psychoanalytical concepts and additional theories suggesting that pre-Oedipal conflicts, the vicissitudes of the aggressive drive and its associated defenses, disturbance in pre-Oedipal mother–child bonding, the Oedipal period and superego formation, separation–individuation anxiety, repression of nuclear conflicts, a desire to merge with pre-Oedipal mother, and a primary disturbance of gender identity are etiological crucibles for anomalous sexual behaviors (Gillespie, 1956; Socarides, 1988). Robert Stoller, a psychoanalyst, and John Money, a biologically oriented investigator of human sexuality, both view paraphilias as a fusion of rage, vengeance, and sexual expression derived and elaborated from early developmental traumas (Stoller, 1975; Money, 1986). Despite considerable theoretical formulations, the psychoanalytical and developmental approach to the etiological explanation of paraphilic activities is lacking in scientific validation. There are no large case series, no controlled studies, and novel theoretical explanatory constructs are frequently based on small samples or single cases. In addition, there are no long-term follow-up studies of paraphiliacs treated by psychoanalysis (Person, 1989). The central role of the castration complex in psychoanalytic explanations of the etiology of sexual perversions lacks scientific data to either support or soundly refute it (Kline, 1987).

BEHAVIORAL THEORY

A classical or operant behavioral theory regarding the etiology of paraphilias would posit that sexual fantasy and activity contains a learned element that can be deliberately or accidentally conditioned. Repetitive sexual fantasy acquired through early sexual experience, paired with the practice of repetitive masturbation, for example, would serve to positively reinforce the conditioning process (McGuire, 1965). While classical conditioning (Rachman and Hodgson, 1968; Langevin and Martin, 1975) and operant conditioning techniques (Quinn et al., 1983) may induce erotic arousal to unconditioned stimuli, the application of these models to the etiology of paraphilias remains to be demonstrated. The most comprehensive, contemporary, and integrated behavioral conditioning formulation for deviant sexuality has been proposed by Laws and Marshall (1990). Behavioral or conditioning theory alone, however, does not provide a sufficient explanation for why only certain men appear to be vulnerable to a paraphilic diathesis.

BIOLOGICAL CORRELATES OF SEXUAL IMPULSIVITY

Contemporary biological investigators have noted an association between male variant sexuality and temporal lobe disorders (Langevin, 1990). The temporal lobe, an integral component of the limbic system of the mammalian brain, appears critical to the regulation of mood, the modulation of anxiety, the integration of the appetitive drives (sex, appetite, and sleep) and the modulation of aggression. Damage or dysfunction associated with the temporal lobes can be associated with alterations of sexual behavior, including hypersexuality (Cummings, 1985). Specific lesions involving temporal lobe epilepsy or temporal lobe damage, cited in case examples of paraphilias, do not predominate in larger samples.

Neuroanatomical and neuropsychological study of the sexually aggressive paraphilic offender, with specific attention to temporal lobe and limbic structures, has been most recently emphasized by Langevin and associates (Langevin, 1990). Since sex offenders are a heterogeneous group with a diversity of paraphilic behaviors, it would at first appear unlikely that a specific neuropsychological profile or neuroanatomical lesion would be uncovered. It is possible, however, that subgroups of sexually aggressive paraphiliacs might have deficits that distinguish their violent or sadistic propensities (Hucker et al., 1988).

Another line of biological investigation exploring the etiology of paraphilias has been to study testosterone, the sex hormone that influences both sexual and aggressive behavior in males. Some studies have suggested a correlation between elevated serum testosterone and violent sexual aggression (Rada et al., 1976, 1983), but the majority of studies reveal that plasma testosterone is within normal limits in all but a subgroup of the most violent paraphiliacs (Hucker and Bain, 1990). Several prominent contemporary investigators have not found any distinctive hormonal profile in either violent or nonviolent paraphilic males (Berlin, 1983; Bradford and McLean, 1984; Lang et al., 1989). There have been no studies of neuropsychological or hormonal correlates for paraphilia-related disorders.

MONOAMINES, SEXUAL BEHAVIOR, AND SEXUAL IMPULSIVITY

Research regarding mammalian sexual behavior and monoamine neuro-transmitters offers some potentially valuable data which might help to elucidate a biological substrate for sexual behaviors, including sexual impulsivity in humans. Taken together, the data to be presented suggest that decreased central (i.e. brain) 5-HT may disinhibit or promote sexual behavior and, conversely, enhancing central 5-HT activity may inhibit sexual behavior in some mammalian species (Tucker and File, 1983). In addition, data will be presented that suggests that decreased central dopaminergic neurotransmission will reduce motivated as well as drive behavior, including male sexual behavior (Everitt, 1983; Segraves, 1989), and conversely pharmacological enhancement of dopaminergic neurotransmission may augment male sexual behaviors (Gessa and Tagliamonte, 1975; Segraves, 1988).

The depletion of central serotonin in rats, by the administration of p-chlorophenlyalanine (PCPA), a selective 5-HT biosynthesis inhibitor, appears to increase measures of sexual excitement and mounting behavior and provided a model of "compulsive" sexual behavior (Sheard, 1969; Tagliamonte et al., 1969). Serotonin blocking agents, cyproheptadine and methysergide, both facilitate sexual activity in male rats, while the direct application of 5-HT in the brain inhibits sexual behavior (Menendez-Abraham et al., 1988). As was reported in rats, use of PCPA in cats has a similar disinhibiting effect on sexual behavior (Ferguson et al., 1970). Conversely, treatment of female rhesus monkeys with clomipramine, a potent enhancer of 5-HT neurotransmission, markedly decreases sexual receptivity in the presence of male rhesus monkeys. These changes in sexual behavior were correlated with increased cerebrospinal fluid levels of the metabolites of 5-HT (Everitt, 1980).

Laboratory studies of rats have demonstrated that the effect of mono-amines on sexual behavior can be as profound as the effect of the depletion of "sex" hormones. For example, sexual behavior in castrated male rats can be restored with a very low dose of testosterone in combination with a pharmacological agent that reduces the availability of central 5-HT, but low-dose testosterone alone fails to restore sexual activity (Sodersten et al., 1976).

The neuromodulation of sexual desire in men and women is poorly understood in comparison to laboratory mammals. As is the case for nonhuman primates, it appears that diminished central 5-HT may increase sexual desire and performance in the human species as well (Segraves, 1989). The use of PCPA in human males has been limited and has produced inconclusive results. Sicuteri (1974) reported that PCPA in combination with testosterone was better than either compound alone in enhancing the sexual fantasies and reported erections in a group of 20 men with migraine headaches and low sexual desire. He also reported that the

PCPA–testosterone effect can be replicated by the administration of an monoamine oxidase inhibitor (phenelzine) with PCPA, and without testosterone (Sicuteri et al., 1976). In contrast, Cremata and Koe (1966) and Benkert et al. (1976) each administered *l*-PCPA to six male subjects in sufficient dose to cause statistically significant reduction in urinary 5-hydroxyindoleacetic acid (5-HIAA), the primary metabolite of 5-HT. No effect was reported for sexual arousal or behavior.

The serotonin reuptake inhibitors, clomipramine and fluoxetine, increase postsynaptic serotonergic effects and have been reported to produce a high frequency of sexual dysfunction "side effects", including loss of sexual desire and impaired sexual response (ejaculatory delay, erectile dysfunction, and anorgasmia) (Jacobsen, 1992). Since chronic loss of libido, characterized in DSM-IV as hypoactive sexual desire disorder co-occurs with sexual response disorders (e.g. impotence), it could be that enhancement or alteration of central 5-HT by selective seron
onergic agents can reproduce naturally occurring sexual dysfunctions. These reports support the observation that in humans increased central 5-HT neurotransmission reduces or inhibits sexual desire and associated sexual behaviors.

In the male rat, central dopamine receptor blockade can abolish all sexual behavior, including ejaculation, intromission, and mounting (Malmnas, 1973; Baum and Starr, 1980). Conversely, dopaminergic agonists, such as apomorphine and *l*-DOPA enhance male sexual activity (Paglietti et al., 1978).

In humans, neuroleptic medications that block central dopaminergic receptors have been reported to diminish sexual desire and have been used to reduce paraphilic behaviors (Bartholomew, 1968; Tennant et al., 1974). Conversely, some investigators have reported increased sexual desire, measured by self-report of fantasies, erections or activities in men treated with dopamine agonists, such as levodopa (Bowers et al., 1971; O'Brian et al., 1971; Sathananathan et al., 1973) and amphetamine (Bell and Trethowen, 1961; Angrist and Gershon, 1976), but not bromocriptine (Cooper, 1977).

It has been reported that the human "sex" hormones, estradiol, testosterone, and progesterone, can induce alterations in the binding of monoamine neurotransmitters in the limbic system, suggesting that one of the cellular mechanisms of hormone action may be at the level of monoamine receptors—the modulation of 5-HT, dopamine and norepinepherine (noradrenaline) (Everitt, 1983). These studies may help to explain why the studies of hormones in sex offenders and nonviolent paraphilic males, discussed above, have been inconclusive. It is most likely that hormones and monoamine neurotransmitters interact in a dynamic fashion that determines the form and intensity of drive behaviors, including sexual behavior (Sicuteri, 1974; Everitt, 1983). The precise delineation of the inter-relationship of these hormone–monoamine systems may hold exciting clues to further elucidate the biological substrate for sexual behaviors, both normal and, perhaps, pathological.

Since some paraphilias lead to acts of sexual aggression, it is noteworthy that animal (e.g. Berzsenyi et al., 1983) and human studies have consistently pointed to an association between reduced central 5-HT neurotransmission, impulsive behavior, and "irritable" destructive aggression (e.g. Coccaro, 1989; Brown and Linnoila, 1990). Neurobiological studies of impulsivity implicate reduced central 5-HT as an important aspect of their pathophysiology (Stein et al., 1993). These associations, reviewed in other chapters of this volume, may apply to sexual impulse disorders as well.

TREATMENTS FOR SEXUAL IMPULSIVITY AND AGGRESSION

The treatment of paraphilias and paraphilia-related disorders is an area of considerable scientific controversy. Outcome studies of paraphilic sex offenders rely on self-report or recidivism rates, both considered as unreliable measures for sexually aggressive paraphilic activity. Many published reports have used small samples, varying measures of outcome, and relatively short duration for determining outcomes, for example less than 4 years (Kilmann et al., 1982; Furby et al., 1989). While there is currently no standardized methodology for the treatment of sexually aggressive men, the Association for the Treatment of Sexual Abusers (ATSA, PO Box 866, Lake Oswego, OR 97034-0140, USA) has become an international organization that seeks to provide standards of care for the sex offender and standards of training and education for those who treat this group of paraphiliacs.

Sex offenders may require penile plethysmography as part of diagnostic as well as treatment outcome assessment. Plethysmography entails the direct measurement of penile response to explicit verbal as well as visual stimuli. This specialized technique, while not infallible, can provide important clinical information regarding deviant sexual arousal, especially in paraphilic men who acknowledge their sexual aggression (for reviews, see Rosen and Beck, 1988; Maletzky, 1991a; Simon and Schouten, 1991).

INDIVIDUAL PSYCHOTHERAPY

Although the largest extant literature involving rich theoretical formulations regarding paraphilias is psychoanalytical/psychodynamic, there are few data to suggest that, a primary treatment, this type of psychotherapy is likely to be effective specifically to reduce paraphilic arousal or behaviors (Crawford, 1981; Person, 1989). Psychodynamic psychotherapy, however, may help to understand developmental antecedents, reduce anxiety and depression, and improve social adjustment. Especially in the treatment of the sexually aggressive paraphiliacs, multimodal treatment approaches, utilizing behavioral, psychodynamic, group, psychoeducational, and pharmacological treatments are commonly prescribed and tailored to the specific needs of the offender (Crown, 1983; Abel, 1989). The informed individual psychotherapist, regardless of theoretical persuasion, may function as a person to select and integrate different therapeutic interventions, akin to the model of "primary-care therapist", advocated by Khantzian (1986) for the recovering substance abuser.

GROUP PSYCHOTHERAPIES

Professionally facilitated group therapies are a common treatment modality for confronting "denial" in sex offenders and exploring the developmental antecedents which may have contributed to symptom formation. There is a small literature on the usefulness or limitations of professionally facilitated group psychotherapy in sexual offender populations (Mathis and Collins, 1970; Cook et al., 1991), including mentally retarded offenders (Swanson and Garwick, 1990), pedophiles (Hartman, 1965; Resnik and Peters, 1967; van Zessen, 1990), incest offenders (Ganzarain and Buchele, 1990), and adolescent sex offenders (Smets and Cebula, 1987; Laben et al., 1991). These are primarily descriptive papers with little to offer regarding outcome. In recent years, an important strategy common to group psychotherapies with sex offenders has been to include educational material and experience with "victim empathy" (Hildebran and Pithers, 1989). Offenders will read about the effects of sexual assault on victims, may meet with victims who describe the effects of sexual assault in their life, and listen to co-offenders who have also been victimized. Relapse prevention (see later) strategies can commonly include professionally conducted group-therapy components as well.

Men with paraphilia-related disorders have also been treated with group psychotherapy. Quadland (1985) reported favorable outcome in 30 gay/bisexual men enrolled in a semistructured 20 week group-therapy program with a goal of controlling promiscuity. Earle and Crow (1989) and Turner (1990) report the use of group psychotherapy in their outpatient program for "sexual addicts", but no outcome results are discussed. A model for an outpatient group therapy for bisexual men and their wives has been published as well (Wolf, 1987).

Since the formation of Alcoholics Anonymous and the articulation of the 12-step recovery program, self-help groups based on 12-step methodology have been formed for many forms of addictive behaviors, including drugs, sex, food, gambling, kleptomania, and others. These programs can have a profound effect on the process of recovery, especially if the program is zealously adhered to. For example, 12-step recovery programs commonly require daily attendance at a 12-step meeting for the first 3 months of recovery, and successful recovery from alcoholism (Galanter et al., 1990) and bulimia (Malenbaum et al., 1988) is associated with five or more 12-step meetings per week for at least 3 years.

Carnes (1983) articulated the construct of "sexual addiction" and helped to establish and promote the 12-step recovery process for nonviolent sexual impulse disorders. There are now several different 12-step programs for recovering "sex addicts", some of which are distinguished by geographical location or differing philosophies as to what constitutes "recovery" and "abstinence" in the context of sexual behaviors. Naditch and Barton (1990) and Carnes (1991) noted a positive long-term outcome associated with 12-step sexual addiction programs in conjunction with individual psychotherapy in a retrospective survey of men and women recovering from both nonviolent paraphilias and paraphilia-related disorders. The successful application of this model to sex offenders remains to be reported, so this mode of treatment should not be recommended as a primary treatment for sexually aggressive paraphiliacs.

There are additional group support networks that reduce the "deviant" label associated with sexual impulsivity and help the paraphiliac to adjust to and accept his sexual arousal as "nondeviant". Examples of these latter networks include the Til Eulenspleigeal Society (for sexual sadism/masochism) and the Tiffany Club (for transvestites/transsexuals) in the northeast of the USA. These associations, which can represent acceptance of and adaptation to a lifestyle that includes paraphilia, can be helpful to reduce suffering and psychosocial impairment and promote a positive identity formation for some paraphiliacs.

COGNITIVE–BEHAVIOR THERAPIES

One form of relapse prevention is an integrated cognitive–behavioral and group therapy treatment approach that was originally evolved from a theoretical understanding of, and treatment for, addictive disorders such as alcohol abuse, nicotine dependence, and overeating (Marlatt and Gordon, 1980). The techniques developed were based on the clinical observation that habitual behaviors (i.e. addictions and impulse disorders) may respond positively to a variety of short-term interventions, but maintenance of remission was problematic and relapse was a common outcome in follow-up studies of addiction treatments. Several different techniques can (1) identify and modify cognitive distortions and beliefs, (2) sensitize the paraphiliac to recognize and then anticipate high-risk situations, and (3) identify behavioral/affective/cognitive precursors to relapse. Extensive behavior rehearsal of new comprehensive problem-solving techniques as well as social and sexual skills training are implemented as well. Although long-term outcome studies using these techniques with sexually aggressive paraphiliacs still remain to be published, the relapse-prevention model and accompanying cognitive–behavioral and social learning techniques are now becoming commonly employed in specialized sex offender treatment programs in the USA and Canada. Initial outcome data (i.e. recidivism rates) from comprehensive programs utilizing these methodologies are encouraging (Laws, 1989; Pithers and Cumming, 1989; Miner et al., 1990; Pithers, 1990; Marques et al., 1994).

BEHAVIOR THERAPY

Behavior therapy techniques are used frequently in treatment centers specialized in the assessment and treatment of sexually aggressive paraphiliacs. These techniques appear to be applicable to nonviolent paraphilias and paraphilia-related disorders as well. Aversive techniques, for example, can be applied to a wide range of human behaviors, including sexual behaviors, when accompanied by the voluntary consent and understanding of the patient. Maletzky (1991a) provides the most current and practical compendium of current theory and technique for the use of behavior therapy conditioning techniques applied to sexually aggressive paraphiliacs, nonviolent paraphiliacs, and selected examples of cases of paraphilia-related disorders.

The use of highly detailed aversive imagery interrupting the arousal inherent in specific imagined sexually arousing scenarios represents a "palatable" form of aversion therapy when the technique is applied repetitively to produce a conditioning effect between a highly sexually arousing fantasy and a markedly aversive consequence (Cautela, 1966, 1967). The technique can be incorporated into both individual or group therapies. Covert sensitization, however, has not consistently produced sustained gains, at least not with paraphilic sex offenders (Maletzky, 1991b).

Olfactory aversion is designed to reduce unconventional sexual arousal with aversive smells, such as ammonia (Colson, 1972), butyric acid (Levin et al., 1977), or rotting animal or human tissues (Maletzky, 1980). The advantage of olfactory aversion is the immediacy of a powerful noxious odor that can be rapidly introduced during the repetition of conditioned, sexually arousing fantasies. Ammonia aversion utilizes encapsulated ammonia ampules that are portable and can be broken and inhaled, both in conjunction with behavioral homework, in vivo practice, and in situations which trigger sexual impulsivity.

Nonaversive "positive" conditioning techniques, are not as widely established as primary treatments for sexually aggressive paraphiliacs. These techniques, however, may be underutilized and, when prescribed, nonaversive conditioning techniques are commonly combined with other therapeutic approaches, including aversive conditioning techniques (Josiassen et al., 1980). Reconditioning behavioral techniques employ the shifting of either the content, timing, or sequence of events present during unconventional sexual fantasies, urges and activities. The shift is aimed at "fading" the intensity of the conditioned unconventional stimulus and strengthening the presence, proximity, and arousal produced by "conventional" sexual fantasies and activities. Marques (1970) integrated a form of fading during masturbation to slowly replace the deviant fantasy with a more conventional fantasy. A variant of this technique has also been called masturbatory satiation (Marshall, 1979).

McConaghy and Armstrong (1985), reported that imaginal desensitization was as effective as covert sensitization in reducing compulsive sexual behaviors in a group of 20 men with paraphilias and paraphilia-related disorders (promiscuity) at both 1 month and 1 year follow up. Since men with paraphilias report social and interpersonal anxiety, a hierarchical systematic desensitization could be of assistance in reducing interpersonal anxiety and, perhaps, be combined with other learning-based techniques to improve interpersonal relationships and assertiveness.

PSYCHOPHARMACOLOGY AND SEXUAL IMPULSIVITY

Currently, the primary biological agents used in the treatment of aggressive paraphilic disorders are the antiandrogens, medroxyprogesterone acetate and cyproterone acetate (Bradford and Bourget, 1987; Bradford, 1990). While neither drug has been approved by the Food and Drug Administration in the USA for the treatment of paraphilic disorders, both agents are used in Canada and Europe and medroxyprogesterone is available in the USA. Cyproterone acetate, the first orally administered antiandrogen commercially available (in 1961), inhibits androgen effects (e.g. testosterone) at androgen receptors and also has antigonadotropic effects (Liang et al., 1977). Medroxyprogesterone, available both as a depot injection and an oral preparation, lowers serum testosterone by reducing the production of testosterone from its precursors, significantly increasing the metabolic clearance rate of free testosterone, and interfering with the binding of testosterone to a sex hormone binding globulin (Albin et al., 1973). Both drugs have been shown to effectively ameliorate deviant sexual imagery, urges, and activity (Cooper et al., 1972, 1992; Cooper, 1981; Meyer III et al., 1992; Gottesman and Schubert, 1993) but some authors report that antiandrogens can nonselectively reduce all aspects of sexual arousal and performance (Rada, 1978b; Berlin, 1983; Maletzky, 1991c). For this reason, sex offenders may perceive these therapeutic agents as "chemical castration", and treatment compliance may be compromised (Cooper et al., 1992). The use of psychopharmacological agents should not be considered as a primary or sole treatment modality for sexually aggressive paraphiliacs unless no other specialized treatment agencies are available. In general, antiandrogen pharmacotherapy is used in combination with cognitive, behavioral, and group therapies as has been described elsewhere (Maletzky, 1991d).

Prior to the use of antiandrogens, neuroleptic drugs that block central dopamine receptors had been prescribed to reduce deviant sexual arousal. These agents also do not selectively abolish deviant sexual arousal, and currently they are less commonly used for the reduction of paraphilic sexual arousal in the absence of associated psychotic symptomatology.

The use of selective serotonin reuptake inhibitors (SRIs) represents a recent addition to the pharmacotherapy of sexual impulsivity. Fluoxetine (Wong et al., 1975; Lemberger et al., 1978) enhances central synaptic transmission of serotonin (Blier et al., 1990). Recent studies have suggested that fluoxetine may also potentiate putative inhibitory effects of 5-HT on the metabolic production or release of dopamine in neurons in the midbrain and brainstem (Bouchard et al., 1989; Baldessarini and Marsh, 1991). Enhanced central 5-HT neurotransmission and reduced central dopamine neurotransmission both appear to be inhibitory to sexual behavior in humans (Segraves, 1989).

In an open trial of fluoxetine in 20 consecutively evaluated outpatient male respondents to a newspaper advertisement, Kafka and Prentky (1992b) reported that self-reported measures of depression and sexual impulsivity improved during 12 weeks (outcome) of pharmacotherapy. At baseline, the paraphilic (nonaggressive paraphiliacs) and the paraphilia-related subgroups were comparable in most intergroup measures of sexual function. All of the paraphiliacs reported concurrent paraphilia-related disorders as well. Sixteen men completed the pharmacological treatment, and statistically significant mitigating effects of fluoxetine (median dose 40 mg/day) were found in both groups over time for all variables pertaining to depression, paraphilias and paraphilia-related behaviors. Statistically significant reduction of sexual impulsivity was evident by week 4 and conventional sexual behavior was not adversely affected by pharmacotherapy. The efficacy of fluoxetine in paraphilic syndromes has been reported in several case reports as well (Lorefice, 1991; Emmanuel et al., 1991; Kafka, 1991b; Perilstein et al., 1991), although one report (Stein et al., 1992) suggested that sexual obsessions (i.e. obsessive compulsive disorder with sexual symptomatology) were more likely to be ameliorated by SRIs in comparison with paraphilias and paraphilia-related disorders. Additional and methodologically rigorous studies, including double-blind placebo controls, are needed to clarify whether fluoxetine is effective for sexual impulse disorders. I have also treated paraphilias and paraphilia-related disorders with sertraline, another selective SRI available in the USA since 1992 (Kafka, 1994c). Although not as globally effective as fluoxetine, this agent has also mitigated sexual impulsivity disorders in some men, including a small group of men who had only partially responded to fluoxetine pharmacotherapy, or had intolerable side effects from fluoxetine (unpublished data). As is the case for the psychopharmacological therapy of depressive disorders, patients who have a partial response or treatment-limiting side effect from one serotonergic agent merit a treatment trial with a second one (Brown and Harrison, 1992).

A smattering of additional case reports have provided support for the efficacy of other thymoleptic agents to mitigate paraphilias, including electroconvulsive treatment (Eyres, 1960), lithium (Ward, 1975; Bartova et al., 1978; Cesnik and Coleman, 1989), buspirone (Federoff, 1988; Pearson et al., 1992), and the tricyclic antidepressants, especially clomipramine (Clayton, 1993; Rubey et al., 1993) and imipramine (Snaith, 1981; Kafka, 1991a). Kruesi et al. (1992) reported that paraphilias were mitigated equally by both desipramine and clomipramine in a small, double-blind crossover study. The absence of a selective or preferential response to the more 5-HT-specific tricyclic antidepressant (clomipramine) implies that paraphilias may not be an obsessive compulsive spectrum disorder (Coleman, 1987). At least one university-based (University of Minnesota) treatment program for sex offenders has reported using lithium carbonate and fluoxetine as the primary biological treatments for sex offenders (Dwyer and Myers, 1990). Although the data published thus far suggesting that sexual impulse disorders may respond to antidepressant pharmacotherapy do not include double-blind methodology (except for Kruesi et al., 1992), these reports together suggest that paraphilias and paraphilia-related disorders may be affective spectrum disorders (Hudson and Pope, 1990), that is, impulse disorders that share a common pathophysiology with mood disorders and respond to several classes of antidepressants. Further study of antidepressant pharmacotherapy of sexual impulse disorders appears warranted.

REFERENCES

Abel, G. (1989). Paraphilias. In: *Comprehensive Textbook of Psychiatry*, 5th edn, vol. 1 (eds H.I. Kaplan and B.J. Sadock) pp. 1079–1080. William & Wilkins, Baltimore.

Abel, G.G., and Rouleau, J.L. (1990). The nature and extent of sexual assault. In: *Handbook of Sexual Assault: Issues, Theories, and Treatment of the Offender* (eds W.L. Marshall, D.R. Laws, and H.E. Barbaree) pp. 9–20. Plenum Press, New York.

Abel, G.G., Mittleman, M., and Becker, J.V. (1985) Sex offenders: results of assessment and recommendations for treatment. In: *Clinical Criminology: Assessment and Treatment of Criminal Behavior* (eds H.H. Ben-Aron, S. Hucker, and C.D. Webster). M&M Graphics, Toronto.

Abel, G.G., Becker, J.V., Cunningham-Rathner, J., et al. (1988) Multiple paraphilic diagnoses among sex offenders. *Bull. Am. Acad. Psychiatry Law*, 16, 153–168.

Agnew, J. (1986). Hazards associated with anal erotic activity. *Arch. Sex Behav.*, 15, 307–315.

Albin, J., Vittek, J., Gordon, G.G., et al. (1973). On the mechanism of the antiandrogenic effect of medroxyprogesterone acetate. *Endocrinology*, 93, 417–422.

American Psychiatric Association (1980). *Diagnostic and Statistical Manual of Mental Disorders*, 3rd edn. American Psychiatric Press, Washington, D.C.

American Psychiatric Association (1987). *Diagnostic and Statistical Manual*, 3rd edn—revised. American Psychiatric Association, Washington, D.C.

American Psychiatric Association (1994). *Diagnostic and Statistical Manual of Mental Disorder, 4th edition*. American Psychiatric Association, Washington, D.C.

Anderson, W.P., Kunce, J.T., and Rich, B. (1979). Sex offenders: Three personality types. *J. Clin. Psychol.*, 35, 671–676.

Angrist, B.M., and Gershon, S. (1976). Clinical effects of amphetamine and L-dopa on sexuality and aggression. *Compr. Psychiatry*, 17, 715–722.

Baldessarini, R.J., and Marsh, E. (1991). Fluoxetine and side effects [letter]. *Arch. Gen. Psychiatry*, 47, 191–192.

Bartova, D., Nahunek, K., and Svestke, J. (1978). Pharmacological treatment of deviant sexual behavior. *Activ. Nerv. Sup. (Praha)*, 20, 72–74.

Bartholomew, A.A. (1968). A long acting phenothiazine as a possible agent to control deviant sexual behavior. *Am. J. Psychiatry*, 124, 917–922.

Baum, M.J., and Starr, M.S. (1980). Inhibition of sexual behavior by dopamine antagonists or serotonin agonist drugs in castrated male rats given estradiol or dihydrotestosterone. *Pharmacol. Biochem. Behav.*, 13, 47–67.

Baxter, D.J., Marshall, W.L., Barbaree, H.E., et al. (1984). Deviant sexual behavior: Differentiating sex offenders by criminal and personal history, psychometric measures and sexual response. *Crim. Justice Behav.*, 11, 477–501.

Baxter, D.J., Barbaree, H.E., and Marshall, W.L. (1986). Sexual responses to consenting and forced sex in a large sample of rapists and nonrapists. *Behav. Res. Ther.*, 24, 513–520.

Becker, J.V., Kaplan, M.S., Tenke, C.E., and Tartaglini, A. (1991). The incidence of depressive symptomatology in juvenile sex offenders with a history of abuse. *Child Abuse Negl.*, 15, 531–536.

Bell, D.S., and Trethowan, W.H. (1961). Amphetamine addiction and disturbed sexuality. *Arch. Gen. Psychiatry*, 4, 74–78.

Benkert, O., Bender, M., Bidlingmaier, F., and Butnandt, O. (1976). Effect of p-chlorolphenylalanine (PCPA) on pituitary hormones and testosterone in humans. *Arzneimittelforschung*, 26, 1369–1371.

Berlin, F.S. (1983). Sex offenders: A biomedical perspective and a status report on biomedical treatment. In: *The Sexual Aggressor: Current Perspectives on Treatment* (eds J.G. Greer and I.R. Stuart) pp. 83–123. Van Nostrand Reinhold, New York.

Berzsenyi, P., Galateo, E., and Valzelli, L. (1983). Fluoxetine activity of muricidal aggression induced in rats by p-chlorophenylalanine. *Aggress. Behav.*, 9, 333–338.

Blier, P., de Montigny, C., and Chaput, Y. (1990). A role for the serotonin system in the mechanism of action of antidepressant treatments: preclinical evidence. *J. Clin. Psychiatry*, 51(4, suppl.), 14–20.

Boffum, J., Moser, C., and Smith, D. (1988). Street drugs and sexual function. In: *Handbook of Sexology*, vol. 6 (ed. J.M.A. Sitsen). Elsevier Science, New York.

Bouchard, R.H., Pourcher, E., and Vincent, P. (1989). Fluoxetine and extrapyramidal side effects. *Am. J. Psychiatry*, 146, 1352–1353.

Bowers, M.B., Woert, M.V., and Davis, L. (1971). Sexual behavior during L-DOPA treatment for parkinsonism. *Am. J. Psychiatry*, 127, 1691–1693.

Bradford, J.W., and McLean, D. (1984). Sexual offenders, violence and testosterone: A clinical study. *Can. J. Psychiatry*, 29, 335–343.

Bradford, J.M.W. (1990). The antiandrogen and hormonal treatment of sex offenders. In: *Handbook of Sexual Assault* (eds. W.L. Marshall, D.R. Laws, and H.E. Barbaree) pp. 297–310. Plenum Press, New York.

Bradford, J.M.W., and Bourget, D. (1987). Sexually aggressive men. *Psychiatr. J. Univ. Ottawa*, 12, 169–175.

Bradford, J.M.W., Boulet, J., and Pawlak, A. (1992). The paraphilias: A multiplicity of deviant behaviors. *Can. J. Psychiatry*, 37, 104–108.

Breitner, I.E. (1973). Psychiatric problems with promiscuity. *South. Med. J.*, 66, 334–336.

Briere, J., and Malamuth, N. (1983). Self-reported likelihood of sexually aggressive behavior: Attitudinal versus sexual explanations. *J. Res. Personality*, 17, 315–323.

Brown, G.L, and Linnoila, M.I. (1990). CSF serotonin metabolite (5-HIAA) studies in depression, impulsivity, and violence. *J. Clin. Psychiatry*, 51(4, suppl.), 31–41.

Brown, W.A., and Harrison, W. (1992). Are patients who are intolerant to one SSRI intolerant to another? *Psychopharmacol. Bull.*, 28, 253–256.

Buhrich, N., and Beaumont, N. (1981). Comparison of transvestism in Australia and America. *Arch. Sex. Behav.*, 10, 269–279.

Carnes, P. (1983). *Out of the Shadows: Understanding Sexual Addiction*. CompCare, Minneapolis.

Carnes, P. (1989). *Contrary to Love: Helping the Sex Addict*. CompCare, Minneapolis.

Carnes, P. (1991). *Don't Call it Love: Recovery from Sexual Addiction*. Bantam, New York.

Cautela, J.R. (1966). Treatment of compulsive behavior by covert sensitization. *Psychol. Res.*, 16, 33–41.

Cautela, J.R. (1967). Covert sensitization. *Psychol. Rec.*, 20, 459–468.

Cesnik, J.A., and Coleman, E. (1989). Use of lithium carbonate in the treatment of autoerotic asphyxia. *Am. J. Psychother.*, 63, 277–286.

Clayton, A.H. (1993). Fetishism and clomipramine [letter]. *Am. J. Psychiatry*, 150, 673–674.

Coccaro, E.F. (1989). Central serotonin and impulsive aggression. *Br. J. Psychiatry*, 149(8, suppl.), 52–62.

Coleman, E. (1987). Sexual compulsivity: Definition, etiology, and treatment considerations. *J. Chem. Depend. Treat.*, 1, 189–204.

Colson, C.E. (1972). Olfactory aversion for homosexual behavior. *J. Behav. Ther. Exp. Psychiatry*, 3, 185–187.

Cook, D.A.G., Fox, C.A., Weaver, C.M., et al. (1991). The Berkeley Group: Ten years' experience of a group for nonviolent sex offenders. *Br. J. Psychiatry*, 158, 238–243.

Cooper, A.J. (1977). Bromocriptine in impotence. *Lancet*, iii, 567.

Cooper, A.J. (1981). A placebo-controlled trial of the antiandrogen cyproterone acetate in deviant hypersexuality. *Compr. Psychiatry*, 22, 458–465.

Cooper, A.J., Ismail, A.A.A., Phanjoo, A.L., and Love, D.L. (1972). Antiandrogen (cyproterone acetate) therapy in deviant hypersexuality. *Br. J. Psychiatry*, 120, 59–63.

Cooper, A.J., Sandhu, S., Losztyn, S., et al. (1992). A double-blind placebo controlled trial of medroxyprogesterone acetate and cyproterone acetate with seven pedophiles. *Can. J. Psychiatry*, 7, 687–693.

Crawford, D. (1981). Treatment approaches with pedophiles. In: *Adult Sexual Interest in Children* (ed. M. Cook and K. Howells). Academic Press, New York.

Cremata, V.Y., and Koe, B.K. (1966). Clinical–pharmacological evaluation of *p*-chlorophenylalanine: A new serontonin-depleting agent. *Clin. Pharmacol. Ther.*, 7, 768–776.

Crepault, C., and Couture, M. (1980). Men's erotic fantasies. *Arch. Sex. Behav.*, 565–581.

Crown, S. (1983). Psychotherapy of sexual deviation. *Br. J. Psychiatry*, 143, 242–247.

Cummings, J.L. (1985). *Clinical Neuropsychiatry*. Grune & Stratton, New York.

Dwyer, S.M., and Myers, S. (1990). Sex offender treatment: A six month to ten year follow-up study. *Ann. Sex Res.*, 3, 305–318.

Earle, R., and Crow, G. (1989). *Lonely all the Time: Recognizing, Understanding and Overcoming Sex Addiction, for Addicts and Codependents.* Pocket Books, New York.

Emmanuel, N.P., Lydiard, R.B., and Ballenger, J.C. (1991). Fluoxetine treatment of voyeurism [letter]. *Am. J. Psychiatry*, 148, 950.

Everitt, B.J. (1980). Alterations in the sexual behavior and 5-hydroxyindoleacetic acid in the cerebrospinal fluid of female rhesus monkeys treated with clomipramine. *Postgrad. Med. J.*, 56 (suppl.), 53–57.

Everitt, B.J. (1983). Monoamines and the control of sexual behavior. *Psychol. Med.*, 13, 715–720.

Eyres, A. (1960). Transvestism: Employment of somatic therapy with subsequent improvement. *Dis. Nerv. Syst.*, 21, 52–53.

Fagan, P.J., Wise, T.N., Schmidt, C.W., et al. (1991). A comparison of five-factor personality dimensions in males with sexual dysfunction and males with paraphilia. *J. Pers. Assess.*, 57, 434–448.

Federoff, J. (1988). Buspirone hydrochloride in the treatment of transvestic fetishism. *J. Clin. Psychiatry*, 49, 408–409.

Ferguson, J., Henriksen, S., Cohen, H., et al. (1970). "Hypersexuality" and behavioral changes in cats caused by administration of p-chlorophenylalanine. *Science*, 168, 499–501.

Fedora, O., Reddon, J.R., Morrison, J.W., et al. (1992). Sadism and other paraphilias in normal controls and aggressive and nonaggressive sex offenders. *Arch. Sex. Behav.*, 21, 1–15.

Freud, S. (1905). *Three Essays on Sexuality* (ed. J. Strachey). Avon Books, New York [1962 edition].

Freund, K., Sher, H., and Hucker, S. (1983). The courtship disorders. *Arch. Sex. Behav.*, 12, 369–379.

Friedman, D. (1977). Hypersexuality in the male and female. In: *Handbook of Sexology*, vol. 5 (eds J. Money and H. Mustaph). Elsevier North-Holland, New York.

Furby, L., Weinrott, M.R., and Blackshaw, L. (1989). Sex offender recidivism: A review. *Psychol. Bull.*, 105, 3–30.

Gagne, P. (1981). Treatment of sex offenders with medroxyprogesterone acetate. *Am. J. Psychiatry*, 138, 644–646.

Galanter, M., Talbott, D., Gallegos, K., et al. (1990). Combined Alcoholics Anonymous and professional care for addicted physicians. *Am. J. Psychiatry*, 147, 64–68.

Ganzarain, R., and Buchele, B.J. (1990). Incest perpetrators in group therapy: A psychodynamic perspective. *Bull. Menninger Clin.*, 54, 295–310.

Gessa, G.L., and Tagliamonte, A. (1975). Role of brain serotonin and dopamine in male sexual behavior In: *Sexual Behavior: Pharmacology and Biochemistry* (eds M. Sandler and G.L. Gessa). Raven Press, New York.

Gillespie, W.H. (1956). The structure and aetiology of sexual perversion. In: *Perversions: Psychodynamics and Therapy* (ed. S Lorand and M. Balint) pp. 28–41. Random House, New York.

Groth, A.N. (1979). *Men Who Rape: The Psychology of the Offender*. Plenum Press, New York.

Gottesman, H.G., and Schubert, D.S.P. (1993). Low-dose oral medroxyprogesterone acetate in the management of the paraphilias. *J. Clin. Psychiatry*, 54, 182–187.

Greenberg, D.F. (1988). *The Construction of Homosexuality*, pp. 141–151. University of Chicago Press, Chicago.

Grossman, L.S., and Cavanaugh, J.L. (1990). Psychopathology and denial in alleged sex offenders. *J. Nerv. Ment. Dis.*, 178, 739–744.

Groth, A.N., and Burgess, A.W. (1977). Rape: A sexual deviation. *Am. J. Ortho-psychiatry*, 47, 400–406.

Hanson, R.K., and Slater, S. (1988). Sexual victimization in the history of sexual abusers: A review. *Ann. Sex. Res.*, 1, 485–499.

Hare, E.H. (1962). Masturbatory insanity: The history of an idea. *J. Ment. Sci.*, 108, 1–25.

Hartman, V. (1965). Group psychotherapy with sexually deviant offenders (pedophiles)—the peer group as an instrument of mutual control. *Crim. Law Q.*, 7, 464–479.

Henn, R.A., Herjanic, M., and Vanderpearl, R.H. (1976). Forensic psychiatry: Profiles of two types of sex offenders. *Am. J. Psychiatry*, 133, 694–696.

Hildebran, D., and Pithers, W.D. (1989). Enhancing offender empathy for sexual abuse victims. In: *Relapse Prevention With Sex Offenders* (ed. D.R. Laws) pp. 236–243. Guilford Press, New York.

Hirshfeld, M. (posthumous) (1948). *Sexual Anomalies: The Origins, Nature, and Treatment of Sexual Disorders*. Emerson Books, New York.

Hucker, S.J., and Bain, J. (1990). Androgenic hormones and sexual assault. In: *Handbook of Sexual Assault* (eds W.L. Marshall, D.R. Laws, and H.E. Barbaree) pp. 93–102. Plenum Press, New York.

Hucker, S., Langevin, R., Dickey, R., Handy, L., et al. (1988). Cerebral damage and dysfunction in sexually aggressive men. *Ann. Sex. Res.*, 1, 33–47.

Hudson, J.I., and Pope, H.G. (1990). Affective spectrum disorders: Does antidepressant response identify a family of disorders with a common pathophysiology? *Am. J. Psychiatry*, 147, 552–564.

Hunter, J.A., and Goodwin, D.W. (1992). The clinical utility of satiation therapy with juvenile sex offenders: Variations and efficacy. *Ann. Sex. Res.*, 5, 71–80.

Jacobsen, F.M. (1992). Fluoxetine-induced sexual dysfunction and an open trial of yohimbine. *J. Clin. Psychiatry*, 53, 119–122.

Josiassen, R.C., Fantuzzo, J., and Rosen, R.C. (1980). Treatment of pedophilia using multistage aversion therapy and social skills training. *J. Behav. Ther. Exp. Psychiatry*, 11, 55–61.

Kafka, M.P. (1991a). Successful antidepressant treatment of nonparaphilic sexual addictions and paraphilias in men. *J. Clin. Psychiatry*, 52, 60–65.

Kafka, M.P. (1991b). Successful treatment of paraphilic coercive disorder (a rapist) with fluoxetine hydrochloride. *Br. J. Psychiatry*, 158, 844–847.

Kafka, M.P., and Prentky, R. (1992a). A comparative study of nonparaphilic sexual addictions and paraphilias in men. *J. Clin. Psychiatry*, 53, 345–350.

Kafka, M.P., and Prentky, R. (1992b) Fluoxetine treatment of nonparaphilic sexual addictions and paraphilias in men. *J. Clin. Psychiatry*, 53, 351–358.

Kafka, M.P. (1994a). Paraphilia-related disorders—common, neglected and misunderstood. *Harvard Rev. Psychiatry*, 2, 39–40.

Kafka, M.P., and Prentky, R. (1994b). A preliminary investigation of lifetime Axis I comorbidity in men with paraphilias and paraphilia-related disorders. *J. Clin. Psychiatry* (in press).

Kafka, M.P. (1994c). Sertraline pharmacotherapy for paraphilias and paraphilia-related disorders: an open trial. *Ann. Clin. Psychiatry* (in press).

Kalichman, S.C. (1990). Affective and personality characteristics of MMPI profile subgroups of incarcerated rapists. *Arch. Sex. Behav.*, 19, 443–459.

Kavoussi, R.J., Kaplan, M., and Becker, J.V. (1988). Psychiatric diagnoses in adolescent sex offenders. *J. Am. Acad. Child Adolesc. Psychiatry*, 27, 241–243.

Khantzian, E.J. (1986). A contemporary psychodynamic approach to drug abuse treatment. *Am. J. Drug Alcohol Abuse*, 12, 213–222.

Kilmann, P.R., Sabalis, R.F., Gearing, M.L. and Bukstel, L.H., et al. (1982). The treatment of sexual paraphilias; A review of the outcome research. *J. Sex. Res.*, 18, 193–252.

Kline, P. (1987). Sexual deviation: Psychoanalytic research and theory. In: *Variant Sexuality: Research and Theory* (ed. G.D. Wilson) pp. 150–175. Johns Hopkins University Press, Baltimore.

Knight, R.A., Prentky, R., Schneider, B., and Rosenberg, R. (1983). Linear causal modeling of adaptation and criminal history in sex offenders. In: *Prospective Studies of Crime and Delinquency* (eds K. Van Dusen and S. Mednick). Kluwer-Nijhoff, Boston.

Krafft-Ebbing, R. (1886). *Psychopathia Sexualis: A Medico-Forensic Study* (English edn, 1965). Putnam's Sons, New York.

Kruesi, M.J.P., Fine, S., Valladares, L., et al. (1992). Does paraphilic behavior respond like obsessive–compulsive disorder to pharmacologic intervention or is it more like anxiety and affective disorders?. A double-blind trial of clomipramine versus desipramine. *Arc. Sex. Behav.*, 21, 1–7.

Laben, J.K., Dodd, D., and Sneed, L. (1991). King's theory of goal attainment applied in group therapy for inpatient juvenile sexual offenders, maximum security state offenders, and community parolees, using visual aids issues. *Ment. Health Nurs.*, 12, 51–60.

Lang, R.A., Langevin, R., Bain, J., et al. (1989). Sex hormone profiles in genital exhibitionists. *Ann. Sex. Res.*, 2, 67–75.

Langevin, R. (1990). Sexual anomalies and the brain. In: *Handbook of Sexual Assault* (eds W.L. Marshall, D.R. Laws, and H.E. Barbaree) pp. 103–114. Plenum Press, New York.

Langevin, R., and Langs, R.A. (1990). Substance abuse among sex offenders. *Ann. Sex. Res.*, 3, 397–424.

Langevin, R., and Martin, M. (1975). Can erotic responses be classically conditioned? *Behav. Ther.*, 6, 350–355.

Langevin, R., Bain, J., and Ben Aron, M. (1984). Sexual aggression: Constructing a predictive equation. A controlled pilot study. In: *Erotic Preference, Gender Identity, and Aggression in Men: New Research Studies* (ed. R. Langevin) pp. 39–76, Lawrence Erlbaum, Hillsdale, NJ.

Langevin, R., Wright, P., and Handy, L. (1990a). Use of the MMPI and its derived scales with sex offenders: 1. Reliability and validity studies. *Ann. Sex. Res.*, 3, 245–291.

Langevin, R., Wright, P., and Handy, L. (1990b). Use of the MMPI and its derived scales with sex offenders: 2. Reliability and criterion validity. *Ann. Sex. Res.*, 3, 453–486.

Laws, D.R. (1989). *Relapse Prevention with Sex Offenders*. Guilford Press, New York.

Laws, D.R., Marshall, W.L. (1990). A conditioning theory of the etiology and maintenance of deviant sexual preference and behavior. In: *Handbook of Sexual Assault* (eds W.L. Marshall, D.R. Laws, and H.E. Barbaree) pp. 209–229. Plenum Press, New York.

Lemberger, L., Rowe, H., Carmichael, R., et al. (1978). Fluoxetine, a selective serontonin uptake inhibitor. *Clin. Pharmacol. Ther.*, 23, 421–429.

Levin, S.M., Barry, S.M., Gambero, S., et al. (1977). Variations of covert sensitization in the treatment of pedophilic behavior. A case study. *J. Consult. Clin. Psychol.*, 10, 896–907.

Levin, S.M., and Stava, L. (1987). Personality characteristics of sex offenders: A review. *Arch. Sex. Behav.*, 16, 57–79.

Levine, S.B., Risen, C.B., and Althof, S.E. (1990) Essay on the diagnosis and nature of paraphilia. *J. Sex. Marital Ther.*, 16, 89–102.

Liang, T., Tymoczko, J.L., Chan, K.M.B., et al. (1977). Androgen action: receptors and rapid responses. In: *Androgens and Antiandrogens* (eds L. Martini and M. Motta). Raven Press, New York.

Lorefice, L.S. (1991). Fluoxetine treatment of a fetish [letter]. *J. Clin. Psychiatry*, 52, 41.

McConaghy, N., and Armstrong, M.S. (1985). Expectancy, covert sensitization and imaginal desensitization in compulsive sexuality. *Acta Psychiatr. Scand.*, 72, 176–187.

McCreary, C.P. (1975). Personality profiles of persons convicted of indecent exposure. *J. Clin. Psychol.*, 31, 260–262.

McGuire, R., Carlisle, J., and Young, B. (1965). Sexual deviations as conditioned behavior: A hypothesis. *Behav. Res. Ther.*, 2, 185–190.

Malamuth, N.M. (1981). Rape proclivity among males. *J. Soc. Issues*, 37, 138–157.

Malamuth, N.M., Check, J.V.P., and Briere, J. (1986). Sexual arousal in response to aggression: Ideological, aggressive, and sexual correlates. *J. Pers. Soc. Psychol.*, 50, 330–340.

Malenbaum, R., Herzog, D., Eisenthal, S., et al. (1988). Overeaters Anonymous: Impact on bulimia. *Int. J. Eat. Disord.*, 7, 139–143.

Maletzty, B.M. (1980). Self-referred versus court referred sexually deviant patients: Success with assisted covert sensitization. *Behav. Ther.*, 11, 306–314.

Maletzky, B.M. (1991a). *Treating the Sexual Offender*. Sage Publications, Newbury Park, CA.

Maletzky, B.M. (1991b). Aversive respondent conditioning techniques. In: *Treating the Sexual Offender*, pp 67–95. Sage Publications, Newbury Park, CA.

Maletzky, B.M. (1991c). The use of medroxyprogesterone acetate to assist in the treatment of sexual offenders. *Ann. Sex. Res.*, 4, 117–129.

Maletzky, B.M. (1991d). Somatic therapies. In: *Treating the Sexual Offender*, pp. 177–193. Sage Publications, Newbury Park, CA.

Malmnas, C.O. (1973). Monoaminergic influence on testosterone activated copulatory behavior in castrated male rats. *Acta Physiol. Scand.*, 395 (suppl.), 1–128.

Marcus, I.M., and Francis, J.J. (1975). *Masturbation: From Infancy to Senescence*. International Universities Press, New York.

Marlatt, G.A., and Gordon, J.R. (1980). Determinants of relapse: Implications for the maintenance of behavior change. In: *Behavioral Medicine: Changing Health Lifestyles* (eds P.O. Davidson and S. M. Davidson). Bruner-Mazel, New York.

Marmor, J. (1971). "Normal" and "deviant" sexual behavior. *JAMA*, 217, 165–170.

Marmor, J. (1981). *Homosexual Behavior: A Modern Reappraisal*. Basic Books, New York.

Marques, J. (1970). Orgasmic reconditioning: Changing sexual object choice through controlling masturbation fantasies. *J. Behav. Ther. Exp. Psychiatry*, 1, 263–271.

Marques, J., Day, D.M., Nelson, C., et al. (1994). Effects of cognitive-behavioral treatment on sex offender recidivism: preliminary results of a longitudinal study. *Crimin. Justice Behav.*, 21, 28–54.

Marshall, W.L. (1979). Satiation therapy: A procedure for reducing deviant sexual arousal. *J. Appl. Behav. Anal.*, 12, 377–389.

Marshall, W.L. (1989). Intimacy, loneliness, and sexual offenders. *Behav. Res. Ther.*, 27, 491–503.

Mathis, J.L., and Collins, M. (1970). Progressive phases in the group therapy of exhibitionists. *Int. J. Group Psychother.*, 20, 167–169.

Menendez-Abraham, E., Moran-Viesca, P., Velasco-Plaza, A. et al. (1988). Modifications of the sexual activity in male rats following the administration of antiserotoninergic drugs. *Behav. Brain Res.*, 30, 251–258.

Meyer III, W.J., Cole, C., and Emory, E. (1992). Depoprovera treatment for sex offending behavior: An evaluation of outcome. *Bull. Am. Acad. Psychiatry Law*, 20, 249–259.

Miner, M.H., Marques, J.K., Day, D.M., and Nelson, C. (1990). Impact of relapse prevention in treating sex offenders: Preliminary findings. *Ann. Sex. Res.*, 3, 165–185.

Mio, J.S., Nanjundappa, G., Verleur, D.E., and de Rios, M.D. (1986). Drug abuse and the adolescent sex offender: A preliminary analysis. *J. Psychoactive Drugs*, 18, 65–72.

Money, J. (1986). *Lovemaps: Clinical Concepts of Sexual/Erotic Health and Pathology, Paraphilia, Gender Transposition in Childhood, Adolescence, and Maturity*. Irvington Publishers, New York.

Naditch, M.P., and Barton, S.N. (1990). Outcome study of an inpatient sexual dependence program. *Am. J. Prev. Psychiatry Neurol.*, 2, 27–32.

O'Brien, C.P., DiGiacomo, J.N., Fahn, S., and Schwartz, G.A. (1971). Mental effects of high dose levodopa. *Arch. Gen. Psychiatry*, 24, 61–64.

Paglietti, E., Pellegrini-Quarantotti, B., Merev, G., and Gessa, G.L. (1978). Apomorphine and L-dopa lower ejaculation threshold in the male rat. *Physiol. Behav.*, 20, 559–562.

Pearson, H.J., Marshall, W.L., Barbaree, H.E., and Southmayd, S. (1992). Treatment of a compulsive paraphilic with buspirone. *Ann. Sex. Res.*, 5, 239–246.

Perilstein, R.D., Lipper, S., and Friedman, L.J. (1991). Three cases of paraphilias responsive to fluoxetine treatment. *J. Clin. Psychiatry*, 52, 169–170.

Person, E. (1989). Paraphilias and gender identity disorders. In: *Psychiatry*, vol. 1, revised edn (ed. R. Michels) chapter 46. Basic Books, New York.

Pithers, W.D. (1990). Relapse prevention with sexual aggressors: A method for maintaining therapeutic gain and enhancing external supervision. In: *Handbook of Sexual Assault* (ed. W.L. Marshall, D.R. Laws, and H.E Barbaree) pp. 343–362. Plenum Press, New York.

Pithers, W.D., and Cumming, G.F. (1989). Can relapses be prevented? Initial outcome data from the Vermont Treatment Program for Sexual Aggressors. In: *Relapse Prevention with Sex Offenders* (ed. D.R. Laws) pp. 363–388. Guilford Press, New York.

Prentky, R.A., and Knight, R.A. (1986). Impulsivity in the lifestyle and criminal behavior of sexual offenders. *Crim. Justice Behav.*, 13, 141–164.

Prentky, R.A., and Knight, R.A. (1991). Identifying critical dimensions for discriminating among rapists. *J. Consult. Clin. Psychol.*, 59, 643–661.

Prentky, R.A., Burgess, A.W., Rokous, F., et al. (1989a). The presumptive role of fantasy in serial sexual homicide. *Am. J. Psychiatry*, 146, 887–891.

Prentky, R.A., Knight, R.A., Sims-Knight, J.E. et al. (1989b). Developmental roots of sexual dangerousness. *Dev. Psychopathol.*, 1, 153–169.

Quadland, M.C. (1985). Compulsive sexual behavior: Definition of a problem and an approach to treatment. *J. Sex. Marital Ther.*, 11, 121–132.

Quinn, V.L., Harbison, J., and McAllister, H. (1983). An attempt to shape human penile responses. *Behav. Res. Ther.*, 8, 27–28.

Rachman, S., and Hodgson, R.J. (1968). Experimentally induced "sexual fetishism" replication and development. *Psychol. Rec.*, 18, 25–27.

Rada, R.T. (1975). Alcoholism and forcible rape. *Am. J. Psychiatry*, 132, 444–446.

Rada, R.T. (1978a). *Clinical Aspects of the Rapist*. Grune & Stratton, New York.

Rada, R.T. (1978b). Biologic aspects and organic treatment of the rapist. In: *Clinical Aspects of the Rapist* (ed. R.T. Rada). Grune & Stratton, New York.

Rada, R.T., Laws, D.R., and Kellner, R. (1976). Plasma testosterone and the rapist. *Psychosom. Med.*, 38, 257–268.

Rada, R.T., Laws, D.R., Kellner, R., Stavastava, L., et al. (1983). Plasma androgens in violent and nonviolent sex offenders. *Bull. Am. Acad. Psychiatry Law*, 11, 149–158.

Reinisch, J.M. (1990). *The Kinsey Institute New Report on Sex: What You Must Know to be Sexually Literate*, pp. 152–153. St Martin's Press, New York.

Resnick, H.L., and Peter, J.J. (1967). Outpatient group therapy with convicted pedophiles. *Int. J. Group Psychother.*, 17, 151–158.

Rooth, G. (1973). Exhibitionism, sexual violence and paedophilia. *Br. J. Psychiatry*, 122, 705–710.

Rosen, R., and Beck, G. (1988). *Patterns of Sexual Arousal: Psychophysiology, Processes and Clinical Applications*. Guilford Press, New York.

Rosenberg, R., and Knight, R.A. (1988). Determining male sex offender subtypes using cluster analysis. *J. Quantitative Criminol.*, 4, 383–410.

Rubey, R., Brady, K.T., and Norris, G.T. (1993). Clomipramine treatment of sexual preoccupation [letter]. *J. Clin. Psychopharmacol.*, 13, 158–159.

Saghir, M.T., and Robins, E. (1973). *Male and Female Homosexuality*. Williams & Wilkins, Baltimore.

Sathananathan, G., Angrist, B.M., and Gershon, G. (1973). Response threshold to L-dopa in psychiatric patients. *Biol. Psychiatry*, 7, 139–146.

Segraves, R.T. (1988). Drugs and desire. In: *Sexual Desire Disorders* (eds S.R. Lieblum, and R.C. Rosen) pp. 313–340. Guilford Press, New York.

Segraves, R.T. (1989). Effects of psychotropic drugs on human erection and ejaculation. *Arch. Gen. Psychiatry*, 46, 275–284.

Sheard, M.H. (1969). The effect of *p*-chlorophenylalanine on behavior in rats: Relation to brain serotonin and 5-hydroxyindoleacetic acid. *Brain Res.*, 15, 524.

Sicuteri, F. (1974). Serotonin and sex in man. *Pharm. Res. Commun.*, 4, 403–411.

Sicuteri, F., Del Bene, F., and Fonda, C. (1976). Sex, migraine, and serontonin interrelationships. *Monogr. Neural Sci.*, 3, 94–101.

Simon, W.T., and Schouten, P.G.W. (1991). Plethysmography in the assessment of sexual deviance. *Arch. Sex. Behav.*, 20, 75–91.

Smets, A.C., and Cebula, C.M. (1987). A group treatment program for adolescent sex offenders: Five steps toward resolution. *Child Abuse Negl.*, 11, 247–54.

Snaith, R.P. (1981). Five exhibitionists and a method of treatment. *Br. J. Psychiatry*, 132, 126–130.

Socarides, C.W. (1988). A unitary theory of sexual perversion. In: *The Preoedipal Origin and Psychoanalytic Therapy of Sexual Perversions*, pp. 36–68. International Universities Press, Madison, CT.

Sodersten, P., Larsson, K., Ahlenius, S., and Engel, J. (1976). Sexual behavior in male rats treated with monoamine synthesis inhibitors and testosterone. *Pharmacol. Biochem. Behav.*, 5, 319–327.

Stein, D.J., Hollander, E., Anthony, D.T., et al. (1992). Serotonergic medications for sexual obsessions, sexual addictions, and paraphilias. *J. Clin. Psychiatry*, 53, 267–271.

Stein, D.J., Hollander, E., and Liebowitz, M.R. (1993). Neurobiology of impulsivity and impulse control disorders. *J. Neuropsychiatr. Clin. Neurosci.*, 5, 9–17.

Stoller, R.J. (1975). *Perversion. The Erotic Form Of Hatred*. Pantheon, New York.

Swanson, C.K., and Garwick, G.B. (1990). Treatment for low-functioning sex offenders: Group therapy and interagency coordination. *Ment. Retard.*, 28, 155–161.

Tagliamonte, A., Tagliamonte, P., Gessa, G.L., et al. (1969). Compulsive sexual activity induced by *p*-chlorophenylalanine in normal and pinealectomized rats. *Science*, 166, 1433–1435.

Templemann, T.L., and Stinnett, R.D. (1991). Patterns of sexual arousal and history in a "normal" sample of young men. *Arch. Sex. Behav.*, 20, 137–150.

Tennant, G., Bancroft, J., Cass, J. (1974). The control of deviant sexual behavior by drugs: A double-blind controlled study of haloperidol, chlorpromazine, and placebo. *Arch. Sex. Behav.*, 3, 261–271.

Tucker, J.C., and File, S.E. (1983). Serotonin and sexual behavior. In: *Psychopharmacology and Sexual Disorders* (ed. D. Wheatley) British Association for Psychopharmacology, monograph 4, pp. 22–49. Oxford University Press, Oxford.

Turner, M. (1990). Long-term group psychotherapy as a modality for treating sexual addiction. *Am. J. Prev. Psychiatr. Neurol.*, 2, 23–26.

van Zessen, G. (1990). A model for group counseling with male pedophiles. *J. Homosex.*, 20, 189–198.

Virkkunen, M. (1985). The pedophilic offender with antisocial character. *Acta Psychiatr. Scand.*, 53, 401–405.

Ward, N.G. (1975). Successful lithium treatment of transvestism associated with manic depression. *J. Nerv. Ment. Dis.*, 161, 204–261.

Wilson, G.D., and Gosselin, C. (1980). Personality characteristics of fetishists, transvestites and sadomasochists. *Pers. Indiv. Diff.*, 1, 289–295.

Wise, T.N., Fagan, P.J., Schmidt, C.W., et al. (1991). Personality and sexual functioning of transvestic fetishists and other paraphiliacs. *J. Nerv. Ment. Dis.*, 179, 694–698.

Wolf, T.J. (1987). Group psychotherapy for bisexual men and their wives. *J. Homosex.*, 14, 191–199.

Wong, D.T., Bymaster, F.P., Horng, J.S., et al. (1975). A new selective inhibitor for uptake of serontonin into synaptosomes of rat brain: 3-(p-trifluoromethylphenoxy)-N-methyl-3-phenylpropylamine. *J. Pharmacol. Exp. Ther.*, 193, 804–811.

14 Neurotransmitters and Psychopharmacology of Impulsive Aggression in Children

BENEDETTO VITIELLO* AND DAVID M STOFF‡
*Division of Clinical Research, Child and Adolescent Disorders Research Branch, and ‡Division of Applied and Services Research, Violence and Traumatic Stress Research Branch, National Institute of Mental Health, Rockville, MD, USA

INTRODUCTION

Aggression, defined as behavior aimed at inflicting harm to others or self, is a common occurrence in child psychopathology. It is a frequent component of the disruptive behavior disorders (American Psychiatric Association, 1987), which make up most child psychiatric referrals (Anderson et al., 1987; Costello et al., 1988). In particular, conduct disorder (CD), in which aggression is often present, affects about 9% of boys and 2% of girls under the age of 18 years (American Psychiatric Association, 1987). Impulsivity, on the other hand, is a main component of attention deficit hyperactivity disorder (ADHD), which also has a high prevalence in youth, affecting about 3% of children, with a rate six to nine times higher in boys than in girls (American Psychiatric Association, 1987).

The common coexistence of ADH and CD makes impulsive aggression a frequently encountered problem in child psychiatry. In 30–50% of cases, ADHD and CD are associated (Anderson et al., 1987; Prinz et al., 1981; Stewart et al., 1981; Biederman et al., 1987). This association has an important prognostic value because hyperactive children with conduct disorder are more likely to display impulsive antisocial behaviors as adults (Gittelman et al., 1985; Mannuzza et al., 1989). In parallel, the prognosis of conduct disorder is poorer when it is associated with ADHD (Magnusson and Bergman, 1988). Children with both aggression and ADHD, but not those with only ADHD, have a family history of antisocial behavior (August and Stewart, 1983). Some authors have theorized that impulsivity is an important feature of antisocial behavior, emphasizing the link between impulsive and aggressive behaviors (e.g. Robins, 1978). It has been posited

Impulsivity and Aggression. Edited by E. Hollander and D.J. Stein
© 1995 John Wiley & Sons Ltd

that impulsivity may be viewed as a personality characteristic that predisposes individuals to develop long-term recidivistic antisocial behavior. Impulsivity may represent an underlying "disinhibitory" personality style, which will be expressed as antisocial behavior when it occurs in conjunction with particular environmental risk factors (Gorenstein and Newman, 1980; Moffitt, in press).

These data indicate that the social impact of childhood disorders characterized by impulsive aggression is enormous. Moreover, impulsive self-directed aggression, as observed in suicidal or other sublethal self-injurious behaviors, is also common in adolescence (Brent et al., 1993; Kashden et al., 1993). It often occurs as part of certain disorders of poor impulse control, such as borderline personality disorder, substance abuse, and manic depressive disorder, which first become evident in the second decade of life. All this points to childhood and adolescence as a time when disorders characterized by impulsive aggressive behavior emerge, often to persist into adulthood.

Extensive work has been done in animals to classify different types of aggressive behavior (Moyer, 1976; Eichelman, 1987). A common dichotomy distinguishes between "predatory" (goal-oriented, controlled, accompanied by low autonomic arousal) and "affective" (reactive, impulsive, with high autonomic arousal) aggression. The fact that different neuroanatomical pathways mediate the two types of aggression supports this differentiation (Bandler, 1970; Siegel and Pott, 1988). In comparison, relatively few attempts have been made to categorize and validate different types of aggression in man. In children, some studies have differentiated between "instrumental" (aimed at some reward or advantage for the aggressor) and "hostile" (merely aimed at inflicting harm upon the victim) aggression (Atkins and Stoff, 1993). A similar distinction has been made between "proactive" and "reactive" aggression, the latter being accompanied by cognitive deficits in information processing (Dodge and Coie, 1987). "Predatory" and "affective" clusters were identified and validated in a group of aggressive children and adolescents (Vitiello et al., 1990a). In this study, patients with the affective type of aggression, which is directly related to impulsiveness, were retrospectively found to have been treated with neuroleptics and lithium more often than children with predatory aggression.

The assessment and measurement of aggression in children presents with difficulties similar to those encountered in adults. Aggression is a behavior that is heavily influenced by environmental and situational factors. Several rating scales have been developed to score aggression in naturalistic settings, such as class-room, playground, and home. In children, most of these rating instruments are administered by the parents or teachers: the Child Behavior Checklist (Achenbach, 1978), the Conner's Parent–Teacher Questionnaire (Guy, 1976), the Child Hostility Inventory (Kazdin et al., 1987), the children version of the Buss–Durkee Hostility Inventory (Buss and Durkee, 1957), or the Interview for Antisocial Behavior (Kazdin and Esveldt-Dawson, 1986). In adolescents, self-rated instruments, such as the Buss–Durkee Hostility Inventory, have been used. A children version of the Overt Aggression Scale, to be scored by the clinician, has also been developed (Kafantaris et al., 1991). In an attempt to control the interference from the multiple environmental variables that affect the process of rating aggression in naturalistic settings, several laboratory models have been developed in which children are provoked to react aggressively in "game-like situations" (Peterson, 1971; Amery et al., 1984; Murphy et al., 1992). Even if these models have produced interesting findings, there is often a poor correlation between these laboratory scores of aggression and the traditional ratings obtained in school or at home (Amery et al., 1984; Murphy et al., 1992). This raises concerns about their validity. Similar problems have been encountered in validating the laboratory models of impulsiveness, such as the Continuous Performance Test (Rosvold et al., 1956) or the Matching Familiar Figures Test (Kagan et al., 1964), which have often failed to properly correlate with clinical ratings of impulsive behavior (Block et al., 1974; Vitiello et al., 1990b).

A predisposition to impulsive behaviors implies dysfunction of brain systems modulating and inhibiting action and aggressive behaviors in response to environmental stimuli. The serotonergic and noradrenergic systems have been the most widely studied neurotransmitters involved in mediating impulsive aggressive behavior of children. Preclinical studies suggesting that the serotonergic system mediates behavioral inhibition and the noradrenergic system mediates arousal and orientation to the environment provides the rationale for these neurotransmitter studies in children.

SEROTONIN

CENTRAL INDICES

The concentration of cerebrospinal fluid (CSF) 5-hydroxyindoleacetic acid (5-HIAA), an indirect indicator of central nervous system (CNS) serotonin (5-hydroxytryptamine, 5-HT) level (Stanley et al., 1985), is negatively associated with behavioral dimensions of aggression and impulsivity (Linnoila and Virkunnen, 1992).

The prolactin response to the serotonergic releasing agent fenfluramine is lower in adults who had personality disorders with significant clinical histories of impulsive aggressive behaviors (Coccaro et al., 1989; Chapter 6). This suggests reduced overall brain 5-HT function in adults with impulsive aggressive behaviors.

It has been noted that impulsive aggressive behaviors (putatively associ-ated with indices of reduced 5-HT function) observed during childhood and adolescence are often found to persist into adulthood, as in antisocial personality disorder (Robins, 1966). In addition, indices of central 5-HT function appear to be relatively consistent in individuals over time (Traskman-Bendz et al., 1984). Therefore, it is possible that the low 5-HT–impulsive aggression relationship may be present in children and adoles-cents. Furthermore, studies of aggressive adults with low CSF 5-HIAA levels have found a high level of retrospectively reported problems in childhood (Traskman-Bendz, 1983; Brown et al., 1986).

Studies of central 5-HT function in children and adolescents who have aggressive behavior are just beginning. Reduced CSF 5-HIAA concentra-tions have been reported by Kruesi et al. (1990) in children and adolescents with disruptive behavior disorders (DBDs; the spectrum of diagnoses en-compassing ADHD, ODD (oppositional defiant disorder), and CD, and characterized by a variety of socially inappropriate behaviors, including impulsivity and aggression), compared with children with obsessive compul-sive disorder. In this study, only one measure of aggression (i.e. child's report of aggression toward people) was related to lower CSF 5-HIAA levels out of numerous measures of aggression and impulsivity. At 26-month follow up CSF 5-HIAA concentration significantly predicted the severity of physical aggression, measured by the modified overt aggression scale (Kruesi et al., 1992). Unlike the finding of a blunted prolactin response in aggressive adults (Coccaro et al., 1989), the prolactin response to fenflura-mine challenge neither correlates with measures of aggression in prepubertal DBD children nor differentiates pubertal DBD from normal controls (Stoff et al., 1992). The failure to demonstrate a serotonergic abnormality in aggression or DBD was interpreted as a reflection of limitations of the neuroendocrine challenge test paradigm in children rather than evidence that serotonergic function in the CNS is normal in aggression.

PERIPHERAL INDICES

Less invasive measures of brain 5-HT function have also been investigated in children and adolescents who have aggressive behavior. Given the fact that platelets share many characteristics with brain cells (Da Prada et al., 1988), studies involving platelets may yield important information about brain function. However, there has been some question regarding the validity of this premise (Stoff et al., 1990) and some methodological problems still exist in the measurement of platelet imipramine binding (IB) (e.g. Friedl and Propping, 1983).

The number of IB sites has been shown to be lower in conduct disordered children than normal controls (Stoff et al., 1987) and also inversely correl-ated with Child Behavior Checklist (CBCL) factors related to aggression or externalizing behavior in prepubertal children with predominantly conduct disorder and coexisting attention deficit hyperactivity disorder (Birmaher et al., 1990). It is tempting to speculate that the low B_{max}, which probably reflects a dysfunction of the presynaptic serotonergic system, might be linked to impulsive aggressive behavior. However, Vitiello (1990b) have been unable to replicate the inverse relationship between platelet IB and parent-rated aggression factors in a sample of less severely disturbed DBD children. In this study, low IB B_{max} was associated with some cognitive measures of impulsivity, but this result must be interpreted cautiously because low IB B_{max} was not associated with other cognitive measures of impulsivity (which usually intercorrelate with each other) or with clinical measures of disruptive externalizing behavior. Since IB sites may label the presynaptic 5-HT transporter (Marcusson et al., 1986), it would be worthwhile to measure directly the platelet 5-HT uptake in children with impulsive aggression. The results on 5-HT uptake are mixed because platelet 5-HT uptake does not differentiate prepubertal CD boys with ADHD comorbidity from normal controls (Stoff et al., 1991a and b) and correlates inversely with symptoms of aggression, suicidality, and conduct problems in adolescents (Modai et al., 1989).

Whole-blood 5-HT was found to be higher in CD than internalizing disorders (anxiety and mood disorders) as well as in violent CD compared with nonviolent CD (Pliszka et al., 1988b; Rogeness et al., 1982). Whole-blood 5-HT may be inversely related to CSF 5-HIAA (McBride et al., 1989) and therefore higher whole-blood 5-HT may be related to decreased serotonergic function. Pliszka et al. (1988b) found higher whole-blood 5-HT in aggressive delinquents, and the higher levels correlated positively with aggressive symptoms. In a population of emotionally disturbed inpatients, boys with aggressive CD had significantly higher whole-blood 5-HT than boys without CD (Rogeness et al., 1982), consistent with the finding of Pliszka et al. (1988b), but opposite to the finding of reduced whole blood 5-hydroxyindole levels in institutionalized, mentally retarded patients with aggressive/hyperactive behavior (Greenberg and Coleman, 1976). We (Stoff et al., 1991a and b) conducted a series of studies to indirectly assess brain 5-HT function in prepubertal boys codiagnosed with CD and ADHD by measuring 5-HT related peripheral markers. Our results indicate that peripheral 5-HT related markers in blood (whole-blood 5-HT, plasma-free 5-HT, free/total tryptophan, tryptophan ratio, and platelet 5-HT$_2$ binding) do not differentiate boys with DBD from healthy boys. These blood 5-HT markers are related neither to behavioral ratings of aggression nor to performance on cognitive impulsivity tasks. These results suggest that the 5-HT hypofunction hypothesis has not received as firm support in aggressive children as it has in adults. Central indices of 5-HT function may be more informative in childhood aggression than single venipuncture studies employing peripheral 5-HT markers in blood.

ENZYMES AND CATECHOLAMINES

DOPAMINE-β-HYDROXYLASE

As the noradrenergic system mediates arousal and orientation to the environment, enhanced noradrenergic activity might be expected to increase the likelihood of externally directed aggression. However, studies of dopamine-β-hydroxylase (DBH), the enzyme involved in the conversion of dopamine (DA) to norepinephrine (NE—noradrenaline), in undersocialized aggressive conduct disorder (UACD) are more consistent with a hypothesis of decreased NE function, assuming that low DBH activity reflects reduced noradrenergic (NA) function. Rogeness et al. (1982) found that subjects with UACD had lower plasma DBH activity. The finding of lower DBH in UACD was replicated in one study of outpatients (Bowden et al., 1988) but not in another (Pliszka et al., 1988a). Lowered DBH has been found not only in UACD but also in autistic children and children who are psychotic and in emotionally disturbed boys diagnosed with borderline personality disorder (BPD). Patients with BPD are particularly impulsive and aggressive, and data from adults suggest that these patients may have reduced brain 5-HT function (Coccaro et al., 1989). The UACD group of boys with near-zero DBH demonstrated more schizotypal, schizophrenic, and borderline symptoms, particularly brief psychotic episodes, than did the conduct disordered, socialized boys with DBH levels greater than six (Rogeness et al., 1986). However, the wide range of DBH activity in normal populations makes it unreliable as a marker or indicator with pathognomonic significance (Cohen et al., 1983). Nonetheless, DBH activity may correlate with NE function in some subjects. When subjects with high DBH activity were compared with subjects with low DBH activity, the low DBH subjects had urinary catecholamine (CA) measures consistent with decreased NE function. When subjects with low DBH activity were compared with subjects with high DBH activity, subjects with low activity had more conduct and attention deficit symptoms and fewer anxiety and depressive symptoms (Rogeness et al., 1986, 1988, 1990).

MONOAMINE OXIDASE

There is no consistent relationship between platelet monoamine oxidase (MAO), the enzyme that metabolizes the monoamine neurotransmitters, and the primary diagnostic status of CD or comorbidity (Bowden et al., 1988; Pliszka et al., 1988a; Rogeness et al., 1982). The finding that platelet MAO activity was positively associated with impulsive errors on laboratory tasks (Stoff et al., 1989) is intriguing but puzzling in light of a lack of association of MAO activity and clinical measures in that study and in some others. Stoff et al. (1989) speculated that elevated platelet MAO activity may lead to impulsivity in children by decreasing intracellular concentrations of 5-HT. This finding is also consistent with the serotonergic hypothesis of impulsive aggression as seen in adults (Linnoila and Virkunnen, 1992), and with the finding that treatment with MAO inhibitors is effective in children with ADHD (Zametkin et al., 1985). However, while it is true that one type of MAO (Type A) preferentially catalyzes both NE and 5-HT, human platelet MAO behaves as the other type, i.e. Type B (Weinshilboum, 1983). This complicates the interpretation of studies using platelet MAO. The relationship of platelet MAO to child diagnostic variables remains speculative at present. A recent provocative finding suggests a genetic basis to impulsive aggression, in that a genetic mutation that causes a selective deficiency of the MAO Type A activity was found to be associated with violent aggression in some male members of a Dutch family (Brunner et al., 1993).

CATECHOLAMINES AND THEIR METABOLITES

Correlations have been shown between possible measures of NA function and conduct symptoms. Plasma 5-methoxy-4-hydroxyphenylglycol (MHPG) correlated negatively with conduct symptoms in one study (Rogeness et al., 1987) and CSF MHPG correlated negatively with only one measure of aggressive symptoms in another (Kruesi et al., 1990). In the studies by Kruesi et al. (1990, 1992), there was essentially no relationship between any of a large number of measures of impulsivity and aggression and CSF levels of homovanillic acid (HVA) and MHPG in a mixed psychiatric sample. Two recent studies by Rogeness et al. (1988, 1990) suggest that ratios are more sensitive discriminators of differences in CA metabolism than are simple metabolite levels. Both studies compared child psychiatric patients selected for very low levels of DBH with those selected for high DBH levels. Rogeness et al. (1988) found that these groups did not differ significantly in urinary levels of any of the CAs or CA metabolites, but later they found that only vanillylmandelic acid (VMA) discriminated the groups at the conventional significance level (Rogeness et al., 1990). However, in both studies the MHPG : VMA ratio in urine, a possible measure of the ratio of intracellular to extracellular metabolism of NE, significantly differed between the groups. In their 1988 report Rogeness et al. found that the MHPG : VMA ratio within the low DBH group was related significantly to Conners Conduct and antisocial factors, but not to anxiety or impulsive/ hyperactive factors. These findings were interpreted as being consistent with decreased NA function and decreased tissue release of NA among the subgroup of CD children with very low DBH activity.

CLINICAL PSYCHOPHARMACOLOGICAL STUDIES

The concept of an underlying biological contribution to impulsive aggressive behaviors raises the possibility that pharmacological interventions might have an impact on the amelioration of these behaviors. Nonetheless, treatment modalities must be multifactorial and include social, behavioral, cognitive, and pharmacological interventions (Kazdin, 1987). In this review we will limit our focus to the currently available pharmacological tools for impulsive aggression in childhood.

Stimulants have been used with success in controlling aggression in children with ADHD. Both d-amphetamine (Amery et al., 1984) and methylphenidate (Klorman et al., 1988) have been found to be effective. The anti-aggressive effects of the stimulants are dose related, with higher doses of methylphenidate (≥ 0.6 mg/kg) being more effective than lower doses (0.3 mg/kg) (Hinshaw et al., 1984, 1989; Gadow et al., 1990). Thus, the dose required to control aggression is generally higher than the optimal dose for increasing attention and cognitive performance (Sprague and Sleator, 1977). The reports on the anti-aggressive effects of stimulants are, however, not entirely consistent. Age, environment, level of maturation of the central nervous system, and global intelligence, all may play a role in the response of aggression to stimulants. Aggressive mentally retarded children improved on 0.3 mg/kg of methylphenidate, but worsened on 0.6 mg/kg (as reviewed by Campbell et al., 1992). This seems to be consistent with animal data, which show that low to moderate doses of stimulants generally decrease aggression and higher doses increase it (Allen et al., 1975). In contrast, an opposite biphasic effect was observed with d-amphetamine on the aggression of normal adults in a laboratory paradigm (Cherek et al., 1986). In this study, amphetamine doses of 5 and 10 mg increased aggression, while 20 mg decreased it. It is possible that stimulants act by decreasing impulsiveness and increasing concentration, rather than by a direct suppression of aggression, and therefore their response is highly contingent on situational factors. Because of their relative safety and common use in pediatric age, stimulants can be considered the drug of choice for impulsive aggression in children. However, their efficacy seems to be limited to mild to moderate levels of aggression.

For more severe aggression, lithium carbonate has been found to be effective in children and adolescents (Siassi, 1982; Campbell et al., 1984a and b). Lithium has been known to decrease aggression in adults (Sheard, 1971). It was first reported effective in severely mentally retarded adolescents (Dostal and Zvolsky, 1970). It also decreases aggression in non-retarded children, at serum levels of 0.3–1.5 mEq/l (average 0.9 mEq/l) (Campbell et al., 1984a and b). Lithium offers advantages over the neuroleptics, in that does not seem to impair cognition (Platt et al., 1984) and chronic use does not have a risk of tardive dyskinesia. Its mechanism of action is not known, but it may be related to enhancement of serotonin metabolism. Carbamazepine, another drug with anti-manic properties like lithium, is effective in decreasing aggression, particularly impulsive aggression that assumes characters of explosiveness. Several anecdotal reports and an open trial (Kafantaris et al., 1992) supports its effectiveness. The anti-aggressive effects of carbamazepine correlate well with its ability to control temporal lobe seizures and to specifically suppress amygdala focal seizures (Albright and Burnham, 1980). This further supports the involvement of these cortical areas in the manifestation of aggression.

Neuroleptics are effective in controlling aggression at fairly low doses (Joshi et al., 1988). Their use has decreased since attention was brought to the risk of tardive dyskinesia in the pediatric age group.

Other anti-aggressive agents include β-blockers and α_2-agonists. Propranolol controls aggression in children with brain damage (Williams et al., 1982; Kuperman and Stewart, 1987). Its mechanism of action is not clear, and it is perplexing that nadolol, a β-blocker that does not pass the blood–brain barrier, is equally effective in curbing aggression (Polakoff et al., 1986). Clonidine, an α_2-agonist, has been reported to decrease aggression in 15 boys (Kemph et al., 1993). This effect may be accompanied by an increase in plasma γ-aminobutyric acid. Its efficacy needs to be confirmed with a controlled study.

Of interest are the attempts to find specific anti-aggressive agents working through the serotonergic receptors. Buspirone, a partial agonist at 5-HT$_{1A}$ receptors (Peroutka, 1985), has been anecdotally reported to decrease aggression in children (Realmuto et al., 1989; Quiason et al., 1991), but no controlled data are available. Recently, a category of specific anti-aggressive agents, the "serenics", has been proposed (Rasmussen et al., 1990). Eltoprazine acts as a serotonergic agonist at the 5HT$_{1B}$ receptor (see Chapter 17) and has been tried in mentally retarded adults (Verhoeven et al., 1992), but no data on its use in children have been reported.

The pharmacological agents employed in the control of aggression constitute a very heterogenous group, which includes drugs with different and possibly opposite mechanisms of action. From a biochemical and pharmacological point of view, it appears difficult to find a common denominator that may explain their efficacy. From a clinical point of view, we can say that all the anti-aggressive agents seem to be active in decreasing impulsivity and mood lability, thus confirming the intrinsic connection between impulsiveness and aggressive behavior.

REFERENCES

Achenbach, T.M. (1978). The Child Behavior Profile: I. Boys aged 6 through 11. *J. Consult. Clin. Psychol.*, 46, 478–488.

Albright, P.S., and Burnham, W.M. (1980). Development of a new pharmacological seizure model: Effects of anticonvulsants on cortical and amygdala-kindled seizures in the rat. *Epilepsia*, 21, 681–689.

Allen, R.P., Safer, D., and Covi, L. (1975). Effects of psychostimulants on aggression. *J. Nerv. Ment. Dis.*, 160, 138–145.

American Psychiatric Association (1987). *Diagnostic and Statistical Manual of Mental Disorders*, 3rd edn—revised. American Psychiatric Association, Washington, D.C.

Amery, B., Minichiello, M.D., and Brown, G.L. (1984). Aggression in hyperactive boys: response to d-amphetamine. *J. Am. Acad. Child Psychiatry*, 23, 291–294.

Anderson, J.C., Williams, S., McGee, R., et al. (1987). DSM-III disorders in preadolescent children: Prevalence in a large sample from the general population. *Arch. Gen. Psychiatry*, 44, 69–76.

Atkins, M.S., and Stoff, D.M. (1993). Instrumental and hostile aggression in childhood disruptive behavior disorders. *J. Abnorm. Child Psychol.*, 21, 165–178.

August, G.J., and Stewart, M.A. (1983). Familial subtypes of childhood hyperactivity. *J. Nerv. Ment. Dis.*, 171, 362–368.

Bandler, R.J. (1970). Cholinergic synapses in the lateral hypothalamus for the control of predatory aggression in the rat. *Brain Res.*, 20, 409–424.

Biederman, J., Munir, K., and Knee, D. (1987). Conduct disorder and oppositional disorder in clinically referred children with attention deficit disorder: a family study. *J. Am. Acad. Child Adolesc. Psychiatry*, 26, 724–727.

Birmaher, B., Stanley, M., Greenhill, L., Twomey, J., Gavrilescu, A., and Rabinovich, H. (1990). Platelet imipramine binding in children and adolescents with impulsive behavior. *J. Am. Acad. Child Adolesc. Psychiatry*, 29, 914–918.

Block, J., Block, J.H., and Harrington, D. (1974). Some misgivings about the Matching Familiar Figures Test as a measure of reflection-impulsivity. *Dev. Psychol.*, 10, 611–632.

Bowden, C.L., Deutsch, C.K., and Swanson, J.M. (1988). Plasma dopamine-β-hydroxylase and platelet monoamine oxidase in attention deficit disorder and conduct disorder. *J. Am. Acad. Child Adolesc. Psychiatry*, 27, 171–174.

Brent, D.A., Johnson, B., Bartle, S., et al. (1993). Personality disorder, tendency to impulsive violence, and suicidal behavior in adolescents. *J. Am. Acad. Child Adolesc. Psychiatry*, 32, 69–75.

Brown, G.L., Kline, W.J., Goyer, P.F., Minichiello, M.D., Kruesi, M.J.P., and Goodwin, F.K. (1986). Relationship of childhood characteristics to cerebrospinal fluid 5-hydroxyindoleacetic acid in aggressive adults. In: *Biological Psychiatry* (eds C. Shagass, R.C. Josiassen, W.H. Bridger, K.J. Weiss, D. Stoff, and Simpson) pp. 177–179. Elsevier Science Publishing, New York.

Brunner, H.G., Nelen, M., Breakefield, X.O., Ropers, H.H., and van Oost, B.A. (1993). Abnormal behavior associated with a point mutation in the structural gene for monoamine oxidase. *Science*, 262, 578–580.

Buss, A.H., and Durkee, A. (1957). An inventory for assessing different kinds of hostility. *J. Consult. Psychol.*, 21, 343–348.

Campbell, M., Small, A.M., Green, W.H., et al. (1984a). Behavioral efficacy of haloperidol and lithium carbonate. *Arch. Gen. Psychiatry*, 41, 650–656.

Campbell, M., Small, A.M., Green, W.H., et al. (1984b). Behavioral efficacy of haloperidol and lithium carbonate: A comparison in hospitalized aggressive children with conduct disorder. *Arch. Gen. Psychiatry*, 41, 650–656.

Campbell, M., Gonzales, N.M., and Silva, R.R. (1992). The pharmacologic treatment of conduct disorders and rage outbursts. *Psychiatr. Clin. North Am.*, 15, 69–85.

Cherek, D.R., Steinberg, J.L., Kelly, T.H., and Robinson, D.E. (1986). Effects of D-amphetamine on human aggressive behavior. *Psychopharmacology*, 88, 381–386.

Coccaro, E.F., Siever, L.J., Klar, H.M., et al. (1989). Serotonergic studies in patients with affective and personality disorders: Correlates with suicidal and impulsive aggressive behavior. *Arch. Gen. Psychiatry*, 46, 587–599.

Cohen, D.J., Shawywitz, S.E., Young, J.G., and Shaywitz, B.A. (1983). Borderline symptoms and attention deficit disorders of childhood: clinical and neurochemical perspectives. In: *The Borderline Child* (ed. K.S. Robson) pp. 197–221. McGraw-Hill, New York.

Costello, E.J., Costello, A.J., Edelbrock, C., et al. (1988). Psychiatric disorders in pediatric primary care. *Arch. Gen. Psychiatry*, 45, 1107–1116.

Da Prada, M., Cesura, A.M., Launay, J.M., and Richards, J.J. (1988). Platelets as a model for neurones? *Experientia*, 44, 115–126.

Dodge, K.A., and Coie, J.D. (1987). Social information processing factors in reactive and proactive aggression in children's peer groups. *J. Pers. Soc. Psychol.*, 53, 1146–1158.

Dostal, T., and Zvolsky, P. (1970). Antiaggressive effect of lithium salts in severe mentally retarted adolescents. *Int. Pharmacopsychiatr.*, 5, 203–207.

Eichelman, B. (1987). Neurochemical and psychopharmacologic aspects of aggressive behavior. In: *Psychopharmacology: The Third Generation of Progress* (ed. H. Meltzer) pp. 697–704. Raven Press, New York.

Friedl, W., and Propping, P. (1983). ^{3}H-Imipramine binding in human platelets: Influence of varying proportions of intact platelets in membrane. *Psychopharmacology*, 80, 96–100.

Gadow, K.L., Nolan, E.E., Sverd, J., Sprafkin, J., and Paolicelli, L. (1990). Methylphenidate in aggressive-hyperactive boys: I. Effects on peer aggression in public school settings. *J. Am. Acad. Child Adolesc. Psychiatry*, 29, 710–718.

Gittelman, R., Mannuzza, S., Shenker, R., and Bonagura, N. (1985). Hyperactive boys almost grown up: I. Psychiatric status. *Arch. Gen. Psychiatry*, 42, 937–947.

Gorenstein, E.E., and Newman, J.P. (1980). Disinhibitory psychopathology: A new perspective and model for research. *Psychol. Rev.*, 87, 301–315.

Greenberg, A.S., and Coleman, M. (1976). Depressed 5-hydroxyindole levels associated with hyperactive and aggressive behavior. *Arch. Gen. Psychiatry*, 33, 331–336.

Guy, W. (1976). *ECDEU Assessment Manual for Psychopharmacology*, revised. DHEW Pub. No. (ADM) 76-338. National Institute of Mental Health, Rockville, MD.

Hinshaw, S.P., Henker, B., and Whalen, C.K. (1984). Self-control in hyperactive boys in anger-inducing situations: Effects of cognitive-behavioral training and of methylphenidate. *J. Abnorm. Child Psychol.*, 12, 55–77.

Hinshaw, S.P., Henker, B., Whalen, C.K., Erhardt, D., and Dunnington, R.E. (1989). Aggressive, prosocial, and nonsocial behavior in hyperactive boys: Dose effects of methylphenidate in naturalistic settings. *J. Consult. Clin. Psychol.*, 57, 636–643.

Joshi, P.T., Capozzoli, J.A., and Coyle, J.T. (1988). Low dose neuroleptic therapy for children with childhood-onset pervasive developmental disorder. *Am. J. Psychiatry*, 145, 335–338.

Kafantaris, V., Lee, D., Magee, H., Winny, G., Samuel, R., and Campbell, M. (1991). The Overt Aggression Scale in a child psychiatry inpatient unit: A pilot study. Scientific Proceedings of the 38th Annual Meeting of the American Academy of Child and Adolescent Psychiatry, San Francisco, CA, p. 76.

Kafantaris, V., Campbell, M., Padron-Gayol, M.V., Small, A.M., Locascio, J.J., and Rosenberg, C.R. (1992). Carbamazepine in hospitalized aggressive conduct disorder children: An open pilot study. *Psychopharmacol. Bull.*, 28, 193–199.

Kagan, J., Rosman, B.L., Day, D., et al. (1964). Information processing in the child: significance of analytic and reflective attitudes. *Psychol. Monogr.*, 78, no. 578.

Kashden, J., Fremouw, W.J., Callahan, T.S., and Franzen, M.D. (1993). Impulsivity in suicidal and nonsuicidal adolescents. *J. Abnorm. Child Psychol.*, 21, 339–353.

Kazdin, A.E. (1987). Treatment of antisocial behavior in children: current status and future directions. *Psychol. Bull.*, 102, 187–203.

Kazdin, A.E., and Esveldt-Dawson, K. (1986). The Interview for Antisocial Behavior: Psychometric characteristics and concurrent validity with child psychiatric inpatients. *J. Psychopathol. Behav. Assess.*, 8, 289–303.

Kazdin, A.E., Rodgers, A., Colbus, D., and Siegel, T. (1987). Children's Hostility Inventory: Measurement of aggression and hostility in psychiatric inpatient children. *J. Clin. Child Psychol.*, 16, 120–128.

Kemph, J.P., DeVane, C.L., Levin, G.M., Jarecke, R., and Miller, R.L. (1993). Treatment of aggressive children with clonidine: Results of an open pilot study. *J. Am. Acad. Child Adolesc. Psychiatry*, 32, 577–581.

Klorman, R., Brumaghim, J.T., Salzman, L.F., et al. (1988). Effects of methylphenidate on attention deficit hyperactivity disorders with and without aggressive/noncompliant features. *J. Abnorm. Psychol.*, 97, 413–422.

Kruesi, M.J.P., Rapoport, J.L., Hamburger, S., et al. (1990). Cerebrospinal fluid monoamine metabolites, aggression, and impulsivity in disruptive behavior disorders of children and adolescents. *Arch. Gen. Psychiatry*, 47, 419–426.

Kruesi, M.J.P., Hibbs, E.D., Zahn, T.P., et al. (1992). A 2-year prospective follow-up study of children and adolescents with disruptive behavior disorders: Prediction by cerebrospinal fluid 5-hydroxyindoleacetic acid, homovanillic acid and autonomic measures? *Arch. Gen. Psychiatry*, 49, 429–435.

Kuperman, S., and Stewart, M.A. (1987). Use of propranolol to decrease aggressive outbursts in younger patients. *Psychosomatics*, 28, 315–319.

Linnoila, M., and Virkunnen, M. (1992). Aggression, suicidality and serotonin. *J. Clin. Psychiatry*, 53 (10, suppl.), 46–51.

McBride, P.A., Anderson, G.M., Hertzig, M.E., et al. (1989). Serotonergic responsivity in male young adults with autistic disorder. *Arch. Gen. Psychiatry*, 46, 2123–221.

Magnusson, D., and Bergman, L.R. (1988). Individual and variable-based approaches to longitudinal research on early risk factors. In: *Studies of Psychosocial Risk* (ed. M. Rutter). Cambridge University Press, New York.

Mannuzza, S., Gittelman Klein, R., Horowits Konig, P., and Giampino, T.L. (1989). Hyperactive boys almost grown up: IV. Criminality and its relationship to psychiatric status. *Arch. Gen. Psychiatry*, 46, 1073–1079.

Marcusson, J.O., Baeckstroem, I., and Ross, S.B. (1986). Single-site model of the neuronal 5-hydroxytryptamine uptake and imipramine binding site. *Mol. Pharmacol.*, 30, 121–128.

Milich, R., and Loney, J. (1979). The role of hyperactive and aggressive symptomatology in predicting outcome among hyperactive children. *J. Pediatr. Psychol.*, 4, 93–112.

Modai, I., Apter, A., Meltzer, M., Tyano, S., Walevski, A., and Jerushalmy, Z. (1989). Serotonin uptake by platelets of suicidal and aggressive adolescent psychiatric inpatients. *Neuropsychobiology*, 21, 9–13.

Moffitt, T.E. (in press). Life-course-persistent and adolescence-limited antisocial behavior. *Psychological Review*.

Moyer, K.E. (1976). *The Psychobiology of Aggression*, Harper & Row, New York.

Murphy, D.A., Pelham, W.E., and Lang, A.R. (1992). Aggression in boys with attention deficit–hyperactivity disorder: Methylphenidate effects on naturalistically observed aggression, response to provocation, and social information processing. *J. Abnorm. Child Psychol.*, 29, 451–466.

Peroutka, S. (1985). Selective interaction of novel anxiolytics with 5-hydroxytryptamine-1A receptors. *Biol. Psychiatry*, 20, 971–979.

Peterson, R. (1971). Aggression as a function of retaliation and aggressive level of target and aggressor. *Dev. Psychol.*, 5, 161–166.

Platt, J.E., Campbell, M., Green, W.H., and Grega, D.M. (1984). Cognitive effects of lithium carbonate and haloperidol in treatment resistant aggressive children. *Arch. Gen. Psychiatry*, 41, 657–662.

Pliszka, S.R., Rogeness, G.A., and Medrano, M.A. (1988a). DBH, MHPG, and MAO in children with depressive, anxiety, and conduct disorders: Relationship to diagnosis and symptoms. *Psychiatr. Res.*, 24, 35–44.

Pliszka, S.R., Rogeness, G.A., Renner, P., Sherman, J., and Broussard, T. (1988b). Plasma neurochemistry in juvenile offenders. *J. Am. Acad. Child Adolesc. Psychiatry*, 27, 588–594.

Polakoff, S.A., Sorgi, P.J., and Ratey, J.J. (1986). The treatment of impulsive and aggressive behavior with nadolol. *J. Clin. Psychopharmacol.*, 6, 125–126.

Prinz, R.J., Connor, P.A., and Wilson, C.C. (1981). Hyperactive and aggressive behaviors in childhood: Intertwined dimensions. *J. Abnorm. Child Psychol.*, 9, 191–202.

Quiason, N., Ward, D., and Kitchen, T. (1991). Buspirone for aggression. *J. Clin. Psychiatry*, 30, 1026.

Rasmussen, D.L., Olivier, B., Raghoebar, M., and Mos, J. (1990). Possible clinical applications of serenics and some implications of their preclinical profile for their clinical use in psychiatric disorders. *Drug Metab. Drug Interact.*, 8, 156–186.

Realmuto, G.M., August, G.J., and Garfinkel, B.D. (1989). Clinical effect of buspirone in autistic children. *J. Clin. Psychopharmacol.*, 9, 122–125.

Robins, L.N. (1966). *Deviant Children Grown Up*. Williams & Wilkins, Baltimore, MD.

Robins, L.N. (1978). Sturdy predictors of adult antisocial behavior, replications from longitudinal studies. *Psychol. Med.*, 8, 611–622.

Rogeness, G.A., Hernandez, J.M., and Macedo, C.A. (1982). Biochemical differences in children with conduct disorder socialized and undersocialized. *Am. J. Psychiatry*, 139, 307–311.

Rogeness, G.A., Hernandez, J.M., Macedo, C.A., Amrung, S.A., and Hoppe, S.K. (1986). Near-zero plasma dopamine-β-hydroxylase and conduct disorder in emotionally disturbed boys. *J. Am. Acad. Child Psychiatry*, 25, 521–527.

Rogeness, G.A., Javors, M.A., Maas, J.W., Macedo, C.A., and Fischer, C. (1987). Plasma dopamine-β-hydroxylase, HVA, MHPG and conduct disorder in emotionally disturbed boys. *Biol. Psychiatry*, 22, 1158–1162.

Rogeness, G.A., Maas, J.W., Javors, M.A., Macedo, C.A., Harris, W.R., and Hoppe, S.K. (1988). Diagnoses, catecholamine metabolism, and plasma dopamine-β-hydroxylase. *J. Am. Acad. Child Adolesc. Psychiatry*, 27, 121–125.

Rogeness, G.A., Javors, M.A., Maas, J.W., and Macedo, C.A. (1990). Catecholamines and diagnosis in children. *J. Am. Acad. Child Adolesc. Psychiatry*, 29, 234–241.

Rosvold, H.F., Mirsky, A.F., Sarason, I., et al. (1956). Continuous performance test of brain damage. *J. Consult. Clin. Psychol.*, 20, 343–350.

Sheard, M.H. (1971). Effect of lithium on human aggression. *Nature*, 230, 113–114.

Siegel, A., and Pott, C.B. (1988). Neural substrates of aggression and flight in the cat. *Prog. Neurobiol.*, 31, 261–283.

Siassi, I. (1982). Lithium treatment of impulsive behavior in children. *J. Clin. Psychiatry*, 43, 482–484.

Sprague, R.L., and Sleator, E.K. (1977). Methylphenidate in hyperkinetic children: Differences in dose effects on learning and social behavior. *Science*, 198, 1274–1276.

Stanley, M., Traskman-Bendz, L., and Dorovini-Zis, K. (1985). Correlations between aminergic metabolites simultaneously obtained from human CSF and brain. *Life Sci.*, 37, 1279–1286.

Stewart, M.A., Cummings, C., Singer, S., et al. (1981). The overlap between hyperactive and aggressive children. *J. Child Psychol. Psychiatry*, 22, 35–45.

Stoff, D.M., Pollock, L., Vitiello, B., Behar, D., and Bridger, W.H. (1987). Reduction of ³H-imipramine binding sites on platelets of conduct-disordered children. *Neuropsychopharmacology*, 1, 55–62.

Stoff, D.M., Friedman, E., Pollock, L., Vitiello, B., Kendall, P.C., and Bridger, W.H. (1989). Elevated platelet MAO is related to impulsivity in disruptive behavior disorders. *J. Am. Acad. Child Adolesc. Psychiatry*, 28, 754–760.

Stoff, D.M., Goldman, W., Bridger, W.H., Jain, A.K., and Pylpiw, A. (1990). No correlation between platelet imipramine binding and CSF 5-HIAA in neurosurgical patients. *Psychiatr. Res.*, 33, 323–326.

Stoff, D.M., Cook, E., Perry, B., et al. (1991a). Blood serotonin (5HT) indices in children. *Biol. Psychiatry*, 29 (suppl.), 523.

Stoff, D.M., Ieni, J., Friedman, E., Bridger, W.H., Pollock, L., and Vitiello, B. (1991b). Platelet ³H-imipramine binding, serotonin uptake, and plasma alpha₁ acid glycoprotein in disruptive behavior disorders. *Biol. Psychiatry*, 29, 494–498.

Stoff, D.M., Pasatiempo, A.P., Yeung, J., Cooper, T.B., Bridger, W.H., and Rabinovich, H. (1992). Neuroendocrine responses to challenge with *d,l*-fenfluramine and aggression in disruptive behavior disorders of children and adolescents. *Psychiatr. Res.*, 43, 263–276.

Traskman-Bendz, L. (1983). CSF 5-HIAA and family history of psychiatric disorder. *Am. J. Psychiatry*, 140, 1257.

Traskman-Bendz, L., Asberg, M., Bertilsson, L., et al. (1984). CSF monoamine metabolites of depressed patients during illness and after recovery. *Acta Psychiatr. Scand.*, 69, 333–342.

Verhoeven, W.M.A., Tuinier, S., Sijben, N.A.S., et al. (1992). Eltoprazine in mentally retarded self-injurious patients. *Lancet*, 340, 1037–1038.

Vitiello, B., Behar, D., Hunt, J., Stoff, D., and Ricciuti, A. (1990a). Subtyping aggression in children and adolescents. *J. Neuropsychiatry Clin. Neurosci.*, 2, 189–192.

Vitiello, B., Stoff, D., Atkins, M., and Mahoney, A. (1990b). Soft neurological signs and impulsivity in children. *Dev. Behav. Pediatr.*, 11, 112–115.

Weinshilboum, R.M. (1983). Biochemical genetics of catecholamines in man. *Mayo Clin. Proc.*, 58, 319–330.

Williams, D.T., Mehl, R., Yudofsky, S., et al. (1982). The effects of propranolol on uncontrolled rage outbursts in children and adolescents with organic brain dysfunction. *J. Am. Acad. Child Psychiatry*, 21, 129–135.

Zametkin, A., Rapoport, J.L., Murphy, D.L., Linnoila, M., and Ismond, D. (1985). Treatment of hyperactive children with monoamine oxidase inhibitors. *Arch. Gen. Psychiatry*, 42, 962–966.

15 Organic Mental Disorders and Impulsive Aggression

JONATHAN M SILVER* AND STUART C YUDOFSKY‡
*Columbia-Presbyterian Medical Center, College of Physicians and Surgeons, Columbia University, New York, NY, USA
‡Department of Psychiatry and Behavioral Sciences, Baylor College of Medicine, Houston, TX, USA

INTRODUCTION

Explosive behavior and violent behavior have long been associated with neuropsychiatric disorders such as traumatic brain injury (TBI), senile dementia of the Alzheimer's type (SDAT), and mental retardation (Silver and Yudofsky, 1987a), and it can occur with focal brain lesions as well as with diffuse damage to the central nervous system (CNS) (Elliott, 1992). For those patients who suffer brain injury, irritability and aggressiveness are a major source of disability to the victim and of stress to their families. These episodes range in severity from irritability to outbursts that result in damage to property or assaults on others. In severe cases, affected individuals cannot remain in the community or with their families, and often are referred to long-term psychiatric or neurobehavioral facilities. Among a sample of outpatients with SDAT, Reisberg et al. (1987) reported that 48% exhibited agitation, 30% violent behavior, and 24% verbal outbursts, which together accounted for the most common of all behavioral symptomatologies in this population. Chandler and Chandler (1988) reported that the most common behavioral problems in a sample of 65 nursing-home residents was agitation and aggression, which affected 48% of their sample.

Aggression is highly prevalent in both the acute and chronic recovery stages from TBI. In the acute recovery period, 35–96% of patients are reported to have exhibited agitated behavior (Levin and Grossman, 1978; Rao et al., 1985). After the acute recovery phase, irritability or bad temper is common. There has been only one prospective study of the occurrence of agitation and restlessness that has been monitored by an objective rating instrument, the Overt Aggression Scale (OAS): Brooke et al. (1992) found that out of 100 patients with severe TBI (Glasgow Coma Scale score less than 8, more than 1 hour of coma, and more than 1 week of hospitalization), only 11 patients exhibited agitated behavior. Only three patients manifested

Impulsivity and Aggression. Edited by E. Hollander and D.J. Stein
© 1995 John Wiley & Sons Ltd

these behaviors for more than 1 week. However, 35 patients were observed to be restless, but not agitated. In follow-up periods ranging from 1 to 15 years after injury, these behaviors occur in 31–71% of patients who have experienced severe TBI.

Studies of the emotional and psychiatric syndromes associated with epilepsy have documented an increase in hostility, irritability, and aggression interictally (Mendez et al., 1986; Robertson et al., 1987). Weiger and Bear (1988) describe interictal aggression in patients with temporal lobe epilepsy. They have observed that interictal aggression is characterized by behavior that is justified on moral or ethical grounds and may develop over protracted periods of time. This aggressive behavior is distinguished from the violent behavior that occurs during the ictal or postictal period, which is characterized by its nondirected quality and the presence of an altered level of consciousness. Even in patients with temporal lobe epilepsy, there are many factors that influence aggression. In a retrospective survey of aggressive and nonaggressive patients with temporal lobe epilepsy, Herzberg and Fenwick (1988) found that aggressive behavior was associated with early onset of seizures, a long duration of behavioral problems, and the male gender. There was no significant correlation of aggression with electroencephalography (EEG) or computerized tomography (CT) scan abnormalities or a history of psychosis. These findings are consistent with those of Stevens and Hermann (1981), who critically examined the scientific literature on the association between temporal lobe epilepsy and violent behavior, and concluded that the significant factor predisposing to violence is the site of the lesion, particularly damage or dysfunction in the limbic areas of the brain.

Those patients who have mental retardation and require institutionalization frequently exhibit aggressive behaviors. In a group of severely or profoundly mentally retarded individuals, approximately 33% were irritable and 20% were injurious to themselves (Reid et al., 1984). In a survey of patients in community residences or institutions for the mentally retarded, 30–40% of the residents had either disruptive behaviors or injury to self, others, or property (Hill et al., 1985).

ORGANIC AGGRESSIVE SYNDROME

Aggressive outbursts that result from organic brain dysfunction have typical characteristics (Table 1). Because of the high prevalence and significant disability associated with this syndrome, we have proposed a specific diagnostic category of organic aggressive syndrome (Table 2) (Silver and Yudofsky, 1987a; Yudofsky and Silver, 1985; Yudofsky et al., 1989).

The diagnostic category in DSM-IV is "personality change due to a general medical condition" (American Psychiatric Association, 1994) (Table 3). Patients with aggressive behavior would be specified as "aggressive

Table 1 Characteristic features of organic aggression syndrome*

Feature	Comments
Reactive	Triggered by modest or trivial stimuli
Nonreflective	Usually does not involve premeditation or planning
Nonpurposeful	Aggressive serves no obvious long-term aims or goals
Explosive	Build up is NOT gradual
Periodic	Brief outbursts of rage and aggression; punctuated by long periods of relative calm
Ego-dystonic	After outbursts, patients are upset, concerned, embarrassed as opposed to blaming others or justifying behavior

Reprinted from Yudofsky, S.C., Silver, J.M., Hales, R.E.: "Pharmacologic Management of Aggression in the Elderly." *Journal of Clinical Psychiatry*, 51 (Suppl. 10), 22–28, 1990. Copyright 1990, Physicians Postgraduate Press. Used with permission.

Table 2 Diagnostic criteria for proposed organic aggressive syndrome

Persistent or recurrent aggressive outbursts, whether of a verbal or physical nature

The outbursts are out of proportion to the precipitating stress or provocation

Evidence from history, physical examination, or laboratory tests of a specific organic factor that is judged to be etiologically related to the disturbance

The outbursts are not primarily related to the following disorders: paranoia, mania, schizophrenia, narcissistic personality disorder, borderline disorder, conduct disorder, or antisocial personality disorder

*From Yudofsky et al. (1989) with permission.

type". We believe it is an egregious error to categorize rage outbursts as a "personality change", just as psychotic and affective symptomatologies are not considered personality. The specific category of organic aggressive syndrome gives appropriate credence to the true specificity of this disorder, and would result in accurate diagnosis of, specific treatment of, and increased research into this condition.

NEUROANATOMY AND NEUROPHYSIOLOGY OF AGGRESSION

Many areas of the brain are involved in the production and mediation of aggressive behavior, and lesions at different levels of neuronal organization can elicit specific types of aggressive behavior (Ovsiew and Yudofsky, 1993). Table 4 summarizes the roles of key regions of the brain in mediating

Table 3   DSM IV criteria for personality change due to a general medical condition*

A.	A persistent personality disturbance that represents a change from the individual's previous characteristic personality pattern
B.	There is evidence from the history, physical examination, or laboratory findings that the disturbance is the direct physiological consequence of a general medical condition
C.	The disturbance is not better accounted by another mental disorder (including other mental disorders due to a general medical condition)
D.	The disturbance does not occur exclusively during delirium and does not meet criteria for a dementia
E.	The disturbance causes clinically significant distress or impairment in social, occupational, or other important areas of functioning

Specify type:
  Labile type: if the predominant feature is affective lability
  Disinhibited type: if the predominant feature is poor impulse control as
    evidenced by sexual indiscretions, etc.
  Aggressive type: if the predominant feature is aggressive behavior
  Apathetic type: if the predominant feature is marked apathy and indifference
  Paranoid type: if the predominant feature is suspiciousness or paranoid
  ideation
  Other type: if the predominant feature is not one of the above, (e.g.,
  personality changes associated with a seizure disorder)
  Combined type: if more than one feature predominates in the clinical picture
  Unspecified

*Reprinted from American Psychiatric Association: Diagnostic and Statistical Manual of Mental Disorders, 4th Edition. Washington, DC, American Psychiatric Association, 1994. Used with permission.

Table 4   Neuropathology of aggression*

Locus	Activity
Hypothalamus	Orchestrates neuroendocrine response via sympathetic arousal Monitors internal status
Limbic system	
Amygdala	Activates and/or suppresses hypothalmus Input from neocortex
Temporal cortex	Associated with aggression in both ictal and interictal status
Frontal neocortex	Modulates limbic and hypothalamic activity Associated with social and judgment aspects of aggression

*From J.M. Silver, P.E. Hales, and S.C. Yudofsky (1992), Neuropsychiatric aspects of traumatic brain injury, in *American Psychiatric Press Textbook of Neuropsychiatry*, 2nd edn (eds S.C. Yudofsky and R.E. Hales) pp. 363–395. American Psychiatric Press, Washington, D.C.

aggression. The regulation of the neuroendocrine and autonomic response is controlled by the hypothalamus, which is involved in "flight or fight" reactions. Investigations in animals have shown that lesions in the ventro-medial hypothalamus result in nondirected rage with stereotypical behavior (i.e. scratching, biting, etc.). This area of the brain may be vulnerable to injury from diffuse axonal injury, and, therefore, would be associated with other deficits, such as cognitive slowing and slurred speech.

The limbic system, especially the amygdala, is responsible for mediating impulses from the prefrontal cortex and hypothalamus, and it adds emotional content to cognition and associating biological drives to specific stimuli (i.e. searching for food when hungry) (Halgren, 1992). Activation of the amygdala, which can occur in seizure-like states or in kindling, may result in enhanced emotional reactions, such as outrage at personal slights. Damage to the amygdaloid area has resulted in violent behavior (Tonko-nogy, 1991). Injury to the anterior temporal lobe, which is a common site for contusions, has been associated with the "dyscontrol syndrome". Some patients with temporal lobe epilepsy exhibit emotional lability, impairment of impulse control, and suspiciousness (Garyfallos et al., 1988).

The most recent region of the brain to evolve, the neocortex, coordinates timing and observation of social cues, often prior to the expression of associated emotions. Due to the location of prominent bony protuberances in the base of the skull, this area of the brain is highly vulnerable to traumatic injury. Lesions in this area give rise to disinhibited anger after minimal provocation, characterized by an individual showing little regard for the consequences of the affect or behavior. Patients with violent behavior have been found to have a high frequency of frontal lobe lesions (Heinrichs, 1989). Frontal lesions may result in the sudden discharge of limbic and/or amygdala-generated affects—affects that are no longer modulated, proc-essed, or inhibited by the frontal lobe. In this condition, the patient over-responds with rage and/or aggression upon thoughts or feelings that would have ordinarily been modulated, inhibited, or suppressed by the individual. In summary, prefrontal damage may cause aggression by a secondary process involving lack of inhibition of the limbic areas.

Aggressive behavior may result from neuronal excitability of limbic system structures. For example, subconvulsive stimulation (i.e. kindling) of the amygdala leads to permanent changes in neuronal excitability (Post et al., 1982). Epileptogenic lesions in the hippocampus in cats, induced by the injection of the excitotoxic substance kainic acid, result in interictal defen-sive rage reactions (Engel et al., 1991). During periods in which the cat experiences partial seizures, the animal exhibits heightened emotional reac-tivity and lability. In addition, defensive reactions can be elicited by excit-atory injections to the midbrain periacqueductal gray region. Hypothalamus-induced rage reactions can be modulated by amygdaloid kindling.

ASSESSMENT OF AGGRESSION IN PATIENTS WITH TRAUMATIC BRAIN INJURY

DIFFERENTIAL DIAGNOSIS

Patients who exhibit aggressive behavior require a thorough assessment. Multiple factors may play a significant role in the production of their aggressive behaviors. It is important to assess systematically the presence of concurrent neuropsychiatric disorders, because this may guide subsequent treatment. Thus, the clinician must diagnose psychosis, depression, mania, mood lability, anxiety, seizure disorders, and other concurrent neurological conditions (Table 5).

It must be determined whether or not the aggressivity and impulsivity of the individual antedated, was caused by, or was aggravated by the brain injury. A prior history of neuropsychiatric problems, including learning disabilities, attentional deficits, behavioral problems, personality disorders, and/or drug and alcohol use, will influence the development of aggression after brain damage. Because previous impulse dyscontrol and lability is exacerbated by brain injury, traits will intensify after damage to the prefrontal areas and other brain regions that inhibit pre-existing aggressive impulses. Many patients are able to differentiate between the aggressivity exhibited before brain injury and their current dyscontrol.

Drug effects and side effects commonly result in disinhibition or irritability (Table 6). By far the most common drug associated with aggression is alcohol, both during intoxication and withdrawal. Stimulating drugs, such as

Table 5 Common etiologies of organically induced aggression*

A.	Traumatic brain injury
B.	Stroke and other cerebrovascular disease
C.	Medications, alcohol and other abused substances, over-the-counter drugs
D.	Delirium (hypoxia, electrolyte imbalance, anesthesia and surgery, uremia, etc.)
E.	Alzheimer's disease
F.	Chronic neurological disorders: Huntington's disease, Wilson's disease, Parkinson's disease, multiple sclerosis, systemic lupus erythematosis
G.	Brain tumors
H.	Infectious diseases (encephalitis, meningitis)
I.	Epilepsy (ictal, postictal, and interictal)
J.	Metabolic disorders: hyperthyroidism or hypothyroidism, hypoglycemia, vitamin deficiencies, porphyria

*Reprinted from Yudofsky, S.C., Silver, J.M., Hales, R.E.: "Pharmacologic Management of Aggression in the Elderly." *Journal of Clinical Psychiatry* 51 (Suppl. 10); 22–28, 1990. Copyright 1990, Physicians Postgraduate Press. Used with permission.

Table 6 Medications and drugs associated with aggression*

A.	Alcohol-intoxication and withdrawal states
B.	Hypnotic and antianxiety agents (barbiturates, benzodiazepines): intoxication and withdrawal states
C.	Analgesics—opiates and other narcotics—intoxication and withdrawal states
D.	Steroids (prednisone, cortisone, and anabolic steroids)
E.	Antidepressants—especially in initial phases of treatment
F.	Amphetamines and cocaine—aggression associated with manic excitement in early stages of abuse and secondary to paranoid ideation in later stages of use
G.	Antipsychotics—high potency agents that lead to akathisia
H.	Anticholinergic drugs (including over-the-counter sedatives) associated with delirium and central anticholinergic syndrome

*Reprinted from Yudofsky, S.C., Silver, J.M., Hales, R.E.: "Pharmacologic Management of Aggression in the Elderly." *Journal of Clinical Psychiatry* 51 (Suppl. 10); 22–28, 1990. Copyright 1990, Physicians Postgraduate Press. Used with permission.

cocaine and amphetamines, as well as the stimulating antidepressants, commonly produce severe anxiety and agitation in patients with or without brain lesions. Antipsychotic medications often increase agitation through anticholinergic side effects, and agitation and irritability usually accompany severe akathisia. Many other drugs may produce confusional states, especially anticholinergic medications that cause agitated delirium (Beresin, 1988). Drugs such as the tricyclic antidepressants (e.g. amitriptyline, imipramine, and doxepin) and the aliphatic phenothiazine antipsychotic drugs (e.g. chlorpromazine and thioridazine) are well known to have potent anticholinergic effects. However, other drugs that are usually not considered to have these effects do have anticholinergic properties. These drugs include digoxin, ranitidine, cimetidine, theophylline, nifedipine, codeine, and furosemide (Tune et al., 1992).

DOCUMENTATION OF AGGRESSIVE BEHAVIOR

Before therapeutic intervention is initiated to treat violent behavior, the clinician should document the baseline frequency of these behaviors. There are spontaneous day-to-day and week-to-week fluctuations in aggression that cannot be validly interpreted without prospective documentation. In our study of over 4000 aggressive episodes in chronically hospitalized patients, hospital records failed to document 50–75% of episodes (Silver and Yudofsky, 1987b 1991). This study and others also indicated that aggression—like certain mood disorders—may have cyclical exacerbations. It is essential that the clinician establish a treatment plan that uses objective documentation of aggressive episodes to monitor the efficacy of interventions, and to designate specific time frames for the initiation and discontinuation of pharmacotherapy of acute episodes as well as the initiation of pharmacotherapy for chronic aggressive behavior.

Many of the scales designed to measure rage, anger, and violence are self-report questionnaires of angry feelings, violent thoughts, or reactions to

---

OVERT AGGRESSION SCALE (OAS)
Stuart Yudofsky, M.D., Jonathan Silver, M.D., Wynn Jackson, M.D., and Jean Endicott, Ph.D.
IDENTIFYING DATA

Name of Patient	Name of Rater
Sex of Patient: 1 Male 2 Female	Date / / (mo da yr) Shift: 1 Night 2 Day 3 Evening

☐ No aggressive incident(s) (verbal or physical) against self, others, or objects during the shift. (check here)

AGGRESSIVE BEHAVIOR (check all that apply)

VERBAL AGGRESSION	**PHYSICAL AGGRESSION AGAINST SELF**
☐ Makes loud noises, shouts angrily	☐ Picks or scratches skin, hits self, pulls hair, (with no or minor injury only)
☐ Yells mild personal insults, e.g., "You're stupid!"	☐ Bangs head, hits fist into objects, throws self onto floor or into objects, (hurts self without serious injury)
☐ Curses viciously, uses foul language in anger, makes moderate threats to others or self	☐ Small cuts or bruises, minor burns
☐ Makes clear threats of violence towards others or self, (I'm going to kill you.) or requests to help to control self	☐ Mutilates self, makes deep cuts, bites that bleed, internal injury, fracture, loss of consciousness, loss of teeth

PHYSICAL AGGRESSION AGAINST OBJECTS	**PHYSICAL AGGRESSION AGAINST OTHER PEOPLE**
☐ Slams door, scatters clothing, makes a mess	☐ Makes threatening gesture, swings at people, grabs at clothes
☐ Throws objects down, kicks furniture without breaking it, marks the wall	☐ Strikes, kicks, pushes, pulls hair, (without injury to them)
☐ Breaks objects, smashes windows	☐ Attacks others causing mild-moderate physical injury (bruises, sprain, welts)
☐ Sets fire, throws objects dangerously	☐ Attacks others causing severe physical injury (broken bones, deep lacerations, internal injury)

Time incident began: __ __ : __ __ am/pm	Duration of incident: __ __ : __ __ (hours/minutes)

INTERVENTION (check all that apply)

☐ None ☐ Talking to patient ☐ Closer observation ☐ Holding patient	☐ Immediate medication given by mouth ☐ Immediate medication given by injection ☐ Isolation without seclusion (time out) ☐ Seclusion	☐ Use of restraints ☐ Injury requires immediate medical treatment for patient ☐ Injury requires immediate treatment for other person

COMMENTS

New York State Psychiatric Institute and Department of Psychiatry, College of Physicians and Surgeons, Columbia University, 722 West 168th Street, New York, NY 10032

Figure 1   The Overt Aggression Scale. Reprinted from Yudofsky, S.C., Silver, J.M., Jackson, W. et al.: "The Overt Aggression Scale for the Objective Rating of Verbal and Physical Aggression." *American Journal of Psychiatry* 143: 35–39, 1986. Used with permission.

anger-provoking situations (Buss and Durkee, 1957; Novaco, 1976). However, patients whose cognitive abilities or frustration tolerance are impaired by brain injury cannot reliably complete questionnaires. Further, many patients have impaired insight into their behavior, and thus do not reliably recall or to admit to past violent events.

The OAS is an operationalized instrument of proven reliability and validity that can be used for easily and effectively rating aggressive behavior in patients with a wide range of disorders (Yudofsky et al., 1986; Silver and Yudofsky, 1987b, 1991) (Figure 1). The OAS comprises items that assess verbal aggression, physical aggression against objects, physical aggression against self, or physical aggression against others. Each category of aggression has four levels of severity that are defined by objective criteria. An aggression score can be derived, which equals the sum of the most severe ratings of each type of aggressive behavior over a particular time course. Aggressive behavior can be monitored by staff or family members using the OAS.

TREATMENT

Aggressive and agitated behaviors may be treated in a variety of settings, ranging from the acute brain injury unit in a general hospital, to a "neurobehavioral" unit in a rehabilitation facility, to nursing homes, to residential facilities for mentally retarded individuals, and to outpatient environments, including the home setting. A multifactorial, multidisciplinary, collaborative approach to treatment is necessary in most cases. The continuation of family treatments, psychopharmacological interventions, and insight-oriented psychotherapeutic approaches is often required.

PHARMACOTHERAPY

Although there is no medication that is approved by the US Food and Drug Administration (FDA) specifically for the treatment of aggression, medications are widely used (and commonly misused) in the management of patients with acute or chronic aggression. After diagnosis and treatment of underlying causes of aggression (e.g. brain tumor), and evaluation and documentation of aggressive behaviors, the use of pharmacological interventions can be considered in two categories: (1) the use of the sedating effects of medications, as required in acute situations, so that the patient does not harm himself or others; and (2) the use of nonsedating antiaggressive medications for the treatment, when necessary, for chronic aggression. The clinician must be aware that patients may not respond to just one medication, but may require combination treatment, as is done in the pharmacotherapy of refractory depression.

Acute aggression and agitation

Agitation, irritability, rage, and/or violence may occur during the early phases of recovery after traumatic brain injury. In the treatment of agitation and for treating acute episodes of aggressive behavior, medications that are sedating, such as antipsychotic drugs or benzodiazepines, may be indicated. However, as these drugs are not specific in their ability to inhibit aggressive behaviors, there may be detrimental effects on arousal and cognitive function. In addition, due to the potential for interference with respiratory and temperature regulation, these drugs should be administered only under careful medical supervision. Therefore, the use of sedation-producing medications must be time limited to avoid the emergence of seriously disabling side effects, ranging from oversedation to tardive dyskinesia.

Chronic aggression

If a patient continues to exhibit periods of agitation or aggression beyond several weeks, the use of specific anti-aggressive medications should be initiated to prevent these episodes from occurring. The choice of medication may be guided by the underlying hypothesized mechanism of action (i.e. effects on serotonin system, adrenergic system, kindling, etc.), or by consideration of the predominant clinical features. As no medication has been approved by the US FDA for the treatment of aggression, the clinician must use medications that may be anti-aggressive but have actually been approved for other uses (i.e. for seizure disorders, depression, hypertension, etc.).

Table 7 summarizes our recommendations for the utilization of various classes of medication in the treatment of aggressive disorders. The scientific literature of the pharmacotherapy of aggression has been reviewed in detail elsewhere (Silver and Yudofsky, 1994; Yudofsky et al., in press). In treating aggression, the clinician, when possible, should diagnose and treat underlying disorders, and utilize, when possible, anti-aggressive agents specific for those disorders. When there is partial response after a therapeutic trial with a specific medication, adjunctive treatment with a medication that has a different mechanism of action should be instituted. For example, a patient with partial response to β-blockers can have additional improvement with the addition of an anticonvulsant or a serotonergic antidepressant.

Anti-hypertensive medications (β-blockers)

Since the first report of the use of β-adrenergic receptor blockers in the treatment of acute aggression in 1977, over 25 papers have appeared in the neurological and psychiatric literature reporting experience of β-blockers in over 200 patients with aggression (Silver and Yudofsky, 1988; Yudofsky et al., 1987). Most of these patients had been unsuccessfully treated with

Table 7 Psychopharmacological treatment of chronic aggression*

Agent	Indications	Special clinical considerations
Antipsychotics	Psychotic symptoms	Oversedation and multiple side effects
Benzodiazepines	Anxiety symptoms	Paradoxical rage
Anticonvulsants Carbamazepine (CBZ) Valproic acid (VPA)	Seizure disorder	Bone marrow suppression CBZ and hepatoxicity (CBZ and VPA)
Lithium	Manic excitement or bipolar disorder	Neurotoxicity and confusion
Buspirone	Persistent, underlying anxiety and/or depression	Delayed onset of action
Propranolol (and other β-blockers)	Chronic or recurrent aggression	Latency of 4–6 weeks
Serotonergic Antidepressants	Depression or mood lability with irritability	May need usual clinical doses

*Reprinted from Yudofsky, S.C., Silver, J.M., Schneider, S.E.: "Pharmacologic Treatment of Aggression." *Psychiatric Annals* 17: 397–407, 1987. Used with permission.

antipsychotics, minor tranquilizers, lithium, and/or anticonvulsants before treatment with β-blockers. The β-blockers that have been investigated in controlled prospective studies include propranolol (a lipid-soluble, non-selective receptor antagonist; Greendyke et al., 1986; Mattes, 1988), nadolol (a water soluble, nonselective receptor antagonist; Alpert et al., 1990; Ratey et al., 1992), and pindolol (a lipid-soluble, nonselective β-receptor antagonist with partial sympathomimetic activity; Greendyke et al., 1986, 1989). A list of β-blockers and their pharmacological properties is shown in Table 8. All β-blockers are $β_1$-antagonists. A growing body of preliminary evidence suggests that β-adrenergic receptor blockers are effective agents for the treatment of aggressive and violent behaviors, particularly those related to organic brain syndrome. Guidelines for the use of propranolol are listed in Table 9. When a patient requires once-a-day medication because of compliance difficulties, a long-acting preparation of propranolol (i.e. Inderal LA) or nadolol (Corgard) can be utilized in once-daily regimens. When patients develop bradycardia that prevents prescribing therapeutic dosages of propranolol, pindolol (Visken) can be substituted, using one-tenth the dosage of propranolol. Pindolol's intrinsic sympathomimetic activity stimulates the β-receptor and restricts the development of bradycardia.

Table 8   Pharmacological characteristics of β-adrenergic receptor antagonists*

Drug (trade name)	Potency (Pro = 1)[†]	Local anesthetic activity	ISA[‡]	Lipid solubility	Plasma half life (hrs)
Nonselective (β_1 and β_2) antagonists					
Alprenolol (Aptine)	0.3–1.0	+	+ +	+ +	2–3
Nadolol (Corgard)	0.5	0	0	0	14–18
Pindolol (Visken)	5–10	±	+ +	+	3–4
Propranolol (Inderal)	1.0	+ +	0	+ +	3–5
Sotalol (Sotalex)	0.3	0	0	0	5–12
Timolol (Blockadren)	5–10	0	±	0	4
Selective (β_1) antagonists					
Acebutalol (Sectral)	0.3	+	+	0	3
Atenolol (Tenormin)	1.0	0	0	0	6–8
Metoprolol (Lopressor)	0.5–2.0	±	0	+	3–4

*Data from Hoffman and Lefkowitz (1990) and American Medical Association Division of Drugs (1986)
[†]propanolol is equivalent to 1
[‡]intrinsic sympathomimetic activity

The mechanism of action of β-blockers in the treatment of aggression is not known. While some investigators have hypothesized a peripheral (e.g. nonbrain) site of action secondary to decreased afferent input to the brain (Ratey et al., 1992), even "nonlipid-soluble" β-adrenergic antagonists, when used over several days, gain access to the CNS (Gengo et al., 1988). Considering the presence of β-receptors in the CNS, and the fact that when these agents have anti-aggressive effects when administered to animals intraventricularly (Leavitt et al., 1989), we believe that there is a central site of action.

The major side effects of β-blockers when used to treat aggression, are a lowering of blood pressure and pulse rate. Peripheral β-receptors are fully inhibited after doses of 300–400 mg/day are administered, so further decreases in these parameters usually do not occur even when doses are increased to much higher levels. Despite reports of depression with the use of β-blockers, controlled trials and our experience indicate that it is a rare occurrence (Yudofsky, 1992). Because the use of propranolol is associated with significant increases in plasma levels of thioridazine, which has an absolute dosage ceiling of 800 mg/day, the combination of these two medications should be avoided whenever possible (Silver et al., 1986).

BEHAVIORAL TREATMENT

It is clear that aggression can be caused and influenced by a combination of environmental and biological factors. Because of the dangerous and unpredictable nature of aggression, care-givers, both in institutions and at home, have intense and sometimes injudicious reactions to aggression when it

Table 9   Clinical use of propranolol*

---

1. Conduct a thorough medical evaluation

2. Exclude patients with the following disorders: bronchial asthma, chronic obstructive pulmonary disease, insulin-dependent diabetes mellitus, congestive heart failure, persistent angina, significant peripheral vascular disease, hyperthyroidism

3. Avoid sudden discontinuation of propranolol (particularly in patients with hypertension)

4. Begin with a single test-dose of 20 mg per day in patients for whom there are clinical concerns with hypotension or bradycardia; increase dose of propranolol by 20 mg per day every 3 days

5. Initiate propranolol on a 20 mg t.i.d. schedule for patients without cardiovascular or cardiopulmonary disorder

6. Increase the dosage of propranolol by 60 mg per day every 3 days

7. Increase medication unless the pulse rate is reduced below 50 b.p.m., or systolic blood pressure is less than 90 mmHg

8. Do not administer medication if severe dizziness, ataxia, or wheezing occurs; reduce or discontinue propranolol if such symptoms persist

9. Increase dose to 12 mg/kg or until aggressive behavior is under control

10. Doses of greater than 800 mg are not usually required to control aggressive behavior

11. Maintain the patient on the highest dose of propranolol for at least 8 weeks prior to concluding that the patient is not responding to the medication; some patients, however, may respond rapidly to propranolol

12. Utilize concurrent medications with caution; monitor plasma levels of all antipsychotic and anticonvulsive medications

---

*Reprinted from Yudofsky, S.C., Silver, J.M., Schneider, S.E.: "Pharmacologic Treatment of Aggression." *Psychiatric Annals* 17: 397–407, 1987. Used with permission.

occurs. Behavioral treatments have been shown to a highly effective in treating patients with organic aggression and may be useful when combined with pharmacotherapy. Behavioral strategies, including a token economy, aggression replacement strategies, and decelerative techniques may reduce aggression in the inpatient setting, and can be combined effectively with pharmacological treatment (Table 10). This subject has been reviewed by Corrigan et al. (1993).

CONCLUSIONS

Aggressive behavior in the presence of brain damage is common and can be highly disabling. Aggression often significantly impedes appropriate rehabilitation and reintegration into the community. There are many neurobio-

Table 10   Behavioral treatment of aggression*

Strategy	Indication	Special considerations
Token economy	Provides both proactive and reactive strategies for aggressive behaviors	A strict format for implementing contingency management
Aggression replacement		
Differential reinforcement schedules	Replaces punishing contingency for previolent behavior	Differential reinforcement of other behaviors is resource intensive; differential reinforcement of incompatible behaviors requires identification of suitable interfering behaviors
Assertiveness training	Effective for patients who become angry when their needs are not met	Patients must work well in skills training groups
Activity programming	Diminishes opportunities for unstructured, frustrating interactions	Activities that patients find reinforcing should be identified
Decelerative techniques		
Social extinction	Effective with previolent patients who respond to social reinforcements	May not work with schizoid
Contingent observation	Effective with previolent patients who respond to social reinforcements	Patients must be sufficiently organized to accurately perceive models
Self-controlled time-out	Effective with violent patients immediately after incidents	May diminish risky attempts to seclude or restrain
Overcorrection	Effective with relatively docile patients	Stop if patient struggles with guided practice
Contingent restraint	Effective with violent patients who do not comply with self-controlled time out and are resistant to guided practice	Decreases inadvertent reinforcement of behaviors that co-vary with seclusion and restraint

*From Corrigan, P.W., Yudofsky, S.C., and Silver, J.M. (1993). Pharmacological and behavioral treatments aggressive psychiatric inpatients. *Hosp. Community Psychiatrics*, 44, 125–133, copyright 1993, American chiatric Association, with permission.

logical factors that can lead to aggressive behavior. After appropriate evaluation and assessment of possible etiologies, treatment begins with the documentation of the aggressive episodes. Psychopharmacological strategies are divided into the treatment of acute aggression and the need for preventing episodes in the patient with chronic aggression. While the treatment of acute aggression involves the judicious use of sedation, the treatment of chronic aggression is guided by underlying diagnoses and symptomatologies. Behavioral strategies remain an important component in the comprehensive treatment of aggression. In this manner, aggression can be controlled with minimal adverse cognitive sequelae.

REFERENCES

Alpert, M., Allan, E.R., Citrome, L., et al. (1990). A double-blind, placebo-controlled study of adjunctive nadolol in the management of violent psychiatric patients. *Psychopharmacol. Bull.*, 28, 367–371.

American Medical Association (AMA) Division of Drugs. (1986). *AMA Drug Evaluations*, 6th edn. American Medical Association, Chicago.

American Psychiatric Association. (1994). *Diagnostic and Statistical Manual of Mental Disorders, fourth edition.* American Psychiatric Association, Washington, D.C.

Beresin, E. (1988). Delirium in the elderly. *J. Geriatr. Psychiatry Neurol.*, 1, 127–143.

Brooke, M.M., Questad, K.A., Patterson, D.R., et al. (1992). Agitation and restlessness after closed head injury: A prospective study of 100 consecutive admissions. *Arch. Phys. Med. Rehabil.*, 73, 320–323.

Buss, A.H., and Durkee, A. (1957). An inventory for assessing different kinds of hostility. *J. Consult. Psychol.*, 21, 343–349.

Chandler, J.D., and Chandler, J.E. (1988). The prevalence of neuropsychiatric disorders in a nursing home population. *J. Getriar. Psychiatry Neurol.*, 1, 71–76.

Corrigan, P.W., Yudofsky, S.C., and Silver, J.M. (1993). Pharmacological and behavioral treatments for aggressive psychiatric inpatients. *Hosp. Community Psychiatry*, 44, 125–133.

Elliott, F.A. (1992). Violence: The neurologic contribution: An overview. *Arch. Neurol.*, 49, 595–603.

Engel, J. Jr, Bandler, R., Griffith, N.C., et al. (1991). Neurobiological evidence for epilepsy-induced interictal disturbances. In: *Advances in Neurology*, vol. 55, *Neurobehavioral Problems in Epilepsy.* (eds D. Smith, D. Treiman, and M. Trimble). Raven Press, New York.

Garyfallos, G., Manos, N., Adamopoulou, A. (1988). Psychopathology and personality characteristics of epileptic patients: epilepsy, psychopathology, and personality. *Acta. Psychiatr. Scand.*, 78, 87–95.

Gengo, F.M., Fagan, S.C., de Padova, A., et al. (1988). The effect of β-blockers on mental performance in older hypertensive patients. *Arch. Intern. Med.*, 148, 779–784.

Greendyke, R.M., and Kanter, D.R. (1986). Therapeutic effects of pindolol on behavioral disturbances associated with organic brain disease: A double-blind study. *J. Clin. Psychiatry*, 47, 423–426.

Greendyke, R.M., Kanter, D.R., Schuster, D.B., et al. (1986). Propranolol treatment of assaultive patients with organic brain disease: A double-blind crossover, placebo-controlled study. *J. Nerv. Ment. Dis.*, 174, 290–294.

Greendyke, R.M., Berkner, J.P., Webster, J.C., et al. (1989). Treatment of behavioral problems with pindolol. *Psychosomatics*, 30, 161–165.

Halgren, E. (1992). Emotional neurophysiology of the amygdala within the context of human cognition. In: *The Amygdala: Neurobiological Aspects of Emotion,*

Memory, and Mental Dysfunction (ed J.P. Aggleton) pp. 191–228. Wiley-Liss, New York.

Heinrichs, R.W. (1989). Frontal cerebral lesions and violent incidents in chronic neuropsychiatric patients. *Biol. Psychiatry*, 25, 174–178.

Herzberg, J.L., and Fenwick, P.B.C. (1988). The aetiology of aggression in temporal-lobe epilepsy. *Br. J. Psychiatry*, 153, 50–55.

Hill, B.K., Balow, E.A., and Bruininks, R.H. (1985). A national study of prescribed drugs in institutions and community residential facilities for mentally retarded people. *Psychopharmacol. Bull.*, 21, 279–284.

Hoffman, B.B., and Lefkowitz, R.J. (1990). Adrenergic receptor antagonists. In: *Goodwin and Gilman's The Pharmacological Basis of Therapeutics*, 8th edn (eds A.G. Gilman, T.W. Rall, A.S. Neiw, et al.). Pergamon Press, New York.

Leavitt, M.L., Yudofsky, S.C., Maroon, J.C., et al. (1989). Effect of introventricular nadolol infusion on shock-induced aggression in 6-OHDA lesioned rats. *J. Neuropsychiatry. Clin. Neurosci.*, 1, 167–172.

Levin, H.S., and Grossman, R.G. (1978). Behavioral sequelae of closed head injury: A quantitative study. *Arch. Neurol.*, 35, 720–727.

Mattes, J.A. (1988). Carbamazepine vs propranolol for rage outbursts. *Psychopharmacol. Bull.*, 24, 179–182.

Mendez, M.F., Cummings, J.L., and Benson, D.F. (1986). Depression in epilepsy: Significance and phenomenology. *Arch. Neurol.*, 43, 766–770.

Novaco, R.W. (1976). *Anger Control: The Development and Evaluation of an Experimental Treatment*. Lexington Books, Lexington, MA.

Ovsiew, F., and Yudofsky, S.C. (1993). Aggression: A neuropsychiatric perspective. In: *Rage, Poser, and Aggression* (eds S. Roose, and R.D. Glick). Yale University Press, New Haven, CT.

Post, R.M., Uhde, T.W., Putnam, F.E., et al. (1982). Kindling and carbamazepine in affective illness. *J. Nerv. Ment. Dis.*, 170, 717–731.

Rao, N., Jellinek, H.M., and Woolston, D.C. (1985). Agitation in closed head injury: Haloperidol effects on rehabilitation outcome. *Arch. Phys. Med. Rehabil.*, 66, 30–34.

Ratey, J.J., Sorgi, P., O'Driscoll, G.A., et al. (1992). Nadolol to treat aggression and psychiatric symptomatology in chronic psychiatric inpatients: A double-blind, placebo-controlled study. *J. Clin. Psychiatry*, 53, 41–46.

Reid, A.H., Ballinger, B.R., Heather, B.B., et al. (1984). The natural history of behavioral symptoms among severely and profoundly mentally retarded patients. *Br. J. Psychiatry*, 145, 289–293.

Reisberg, B., Borenstein, J., Salob, S.P., et al. (1987). Behavioral symptoms in Alzheimer's disease: Phenomenology and treatment. *J. Clin. Psychiatry*, 48 (5, suppl.), 9–15.

Robertson, M.M., Trimble, M.R., and Townsend, H.R.A. (1987). Phenomenology of depression in epilepsy. *Epilepsia*, 28, 364–372.

Silver, J.M., and Yudofsky, S.C. (1987a). Aggressive behavior in patients with neuropsychiatric disorders. *Psychiatr. Ann.*, 17, 367–370.

Silver, J.M., and Yudofsky, S.C. (1987b). Documentation of aggression in the assessment of the violent patient. *Psychiatr. Ann.*, 17, 375–384.

Silver, J.M., and Yudofsky, S.C. (1988). Psychopharmacology and electroconvulsive therapy. In: *Textbook of Psychiatry* (eds J.A. Talbott, R.E. Hales, and S.C. Yudofsky) pp. 767–853. American Psychiatric Press, Washington, D.C.

Silver, J.M., and Yudofsky, S.C. (1991). The Overt Aggression Scale: Overview and clinical guidelines. *J. Neuropsychiatry Clin. Neurosci.*, 3 (suppl.), 22–29.

Silver, J.M., and Yudofsky, S.C. (1994). Aggressive Disorders. In: *Neuropsychiatry of Traumatic Brain Injury* (eds J.M. Silver, S.C. Yudofsky, and R.E. Hales).

American Psychiatric Press, Washington, D.C.

Silver, J.M., Yudofsky, S.C., Kogan, M., et al. (1986). Elevation of thioridazine plasma levels by propranolol. *Am. J. Psychiatry*, 143, 1290–1292.

Stevens, J.R., and Hermann, B.P. (1981). Temporal lobe epilepsy, psychopathology, and violence: the state of the evidence. *Neurology*, 31, 1127–1132.

Tonkonogy, T.M. (1991). Violence and temporal lobes lesion: Head CT and MRI data. *J. Neuropsychiatry Clin. Neurosci.*, 3, 189–196.

Tune, L., Carr, S., Hoag, E., et al. (1992). Anticholinergic effects of drugs commonly prescribed for the elderly: Potential means for assessing risk of delirium. *Am. J. Psychiatry*, 149, 1393–1394.

Weiger, W.A., and Bear, D.M. (1988). An approach to the neurology of aggression. *J. Psychiatr. Res.*, 22, 85–98.

Yudofsky, S.C. (1992). β-Blockers and depression: The clinician's dilemma. *JAMA*, 267, 1826–1827.

Yudofsky, S.C., and Silver, J.M. (1985). Psychiatric aspects of brain injury: Trauma, stroke, and tumor. In: *Psychiatry Update 1985* (eds R.E. Hales and A.J. Frances) pp. 142–158. American Psychiatric Press, Washington, D.C.

Yudofsky, S.C., Silver, J.M., Jackson, W., et al. (1986). The Overt Aggression Scale for the objective rating of verbal and physical aggression. *Am. J. Psychiatry*, 143, 35–39.

Yudofsky, S.C., Silver, J.M., and Schneider, S.E. (1987). Pharmacologic treatment of aggression. *Psychiatr. Ann.*, 17, 397–407.

Yudofsky, S.C., Silver, J., and Yudofsky, B. (1989). Organic personality disorder, explosive type. In: *Treatment of Psychiatric Disorders* (ed. T.B. Karasu). American Psychiatric Press, Washington, D.C.

Yudofsky, S.C., Silver, J.M., and Hales, R.E. (1990). Pharmacologic management of aggression in the elderly. *J. Clin. Psychiatry*, 51 (10, suppl.), 22–28.

Yudofsky, S.C., Silver, J.M., and Hales, R.E. (in press). Pharmacologic treatment of aggressive disorders. In: *American Psychiatric Press Textbook of Psychopharmacology* (eds C.B. Nemeroff and A.F. Schatzberg). American Psychiatric Press, Washington, D.C.

Part VI

TREATMENT STRATEGIES

16 Pharmacotherapy of Impulsivity, Aggression, and Related Disorders

PAUL MARKOVITZ

Mood and Anxiety Research Center, Case Western Reserve University, Beachwood, OH, USA

INTRODUCTION

Earlier chapters have reviewed the phenomenology and neurobiology of impulsivity and aggression. The purpose of this chapter will be to review the clinical literature on treatment of impulsivity and aggression. The occurrence of these behaviors is extremely broad, and certain areas will not be reviewed. Excluded areas include brain injured/diseased patients who were previously well, patients with epilepsy, and patients with drug-induced aggression or impulsivity. These have been reviewed elsewhere (Mattes, 1986; Jenkins et al., 1987; Conacher, 1988), and their inclusion seemed out of context with the original purpose of this book.

Much of this chapter will focus on newer studies, particularly those involving serotonin reuptake inhibitors (SRIs). Many individual behaviors, including aggression, impulsivity, depression, anxiety, obsessionality, suicidality, self-injury, eating disorders, somatic disorders, and some personality disorders have been linked to irregularities of the serotonin (5-hydroxytryptamine, 5-HT) system (van Praag and Korf, 1971; Asberg et al., 1976; Linnoila et al., 1983; Blundell, 1984; Brown and Goodwin, 1986; Roy et al., 1986; van Praag et al., 1986; Zohar et al., 1987; Kahn and van Praag, 1988; Coccaro et al., 1990; Brewerton et al., 1992). If these behaviors arise directly from dysfunction of the 5-HT system or some event resulting in anomalies of 5-HT levels, it is logical that some or all of the behaviors will occur comorbidly since each behavior shares the same neurobiological cause. Thus, discussing aggression or impulsivity as discrete behaviors can be misleading. These behaviors exist within a context of other behaviors mediated by a similar neurochemistry. Because selective SRIs increase the level of 5-HT in the central nervous system (CNS) (Schmidt et al., 1988), they are good candidates for treating impulsivity and aggression existing in contexts linked to hyposerotonergic function.

Impulsivity and Aggression. Edited by E. Hollander and D.J. Stein
© 1995 John Wiley & Sons Ltd

BORDERLINE PERSONALITY DISORDER

Most psychiatric medications have been used to target some of the behaviors accompanying borderline personality disorder (BPD). Frequently, the purpose is to control the aggression, hostility, impulsivity, and lability of mood accompanying the illness.

LITHIUM

The use of lithium in BPD is based on its ability to stabilize mood swings in manic depressive disorder, and researchers reasoned it might stabilize the affective instability and impulsivity in BPD. Lithium, however, has not been studied very extensively in BPD or related entities, and the trials done show only modest benefit. Rifkin et al. (1972b) looked at patients with emotionally unstable character disorder (EUCD) and found behavioral improvement in 14 of 21 patients during lithium treatment, whereas only four patients showed improvement on placebo. Behaviors targeted in the study were reductions in mania and depression. The authors noted that increased social intrusiveness, anger, and over-reaction to stressors were associated with depressive and hypomanic/manic episodes. This study did not report on impulsivity or aggression directly, but it did show a significant reduction in depressive and hypomanic episodes. An illustrative case report in the study indicated a reduction in impulsivity coinciding with reductions in depressive and manic episodes, suggesting that lithium was helpful. A prospective open study (Rifkin et al., 1972a) of 31 patients with EUCD indicated that 30% of patients improved on lithium, 40% had an unchanged course, and 30% worsened. Goldberg (1989) is replicating the study by Rifkin et al., in patients specifically diagnosed with BPD, and his preliminary data confirm the beneficial effects of lithium.

A closer examination of these results, however, indicates that lithium therapy is only partially effective. Mood swings continue on lithium, albeit with decreased intensity. Also, most patients do not like the side effects accompanying lithium. Diarrhea, weight gain, mental lethargy, tremor, and polyuria are all common problems, and many patients discontinue lithium because of these side effects (Rifkin, 1972b).

NEUROLEPTICS

Neuroleptics have been the group of medications most studied in controlled trials investigating pharmacological treatment of BPD. The use of these agents was based on their theoretical ability to dampen aggressive outbursts and decrease psychotic thinking. Investigators initially noted the beneficial effects of low-dose neuroleptic regimens in the treatment of BPD in trials without placebo control (Brinkley et al., 1979; Leone, 1982; Serban and

Siegel, 1984). Two double-blind placebo-controlled trials were then published simultaneously. Goldberg et al. (1986) documented the efficacy of low-dose thiothixene (average dose 8.7 mg/day) in BPD patients with concomitant brief psychotic episodes. Psychosis, obsessionality, phobic anxiety, and ideas of reference were reduced in this group. Nonpsychotic patients showed little benefit. The neuroleptic did not reduce anger or hostility as measured by the Hopkins Symptom Checklist–90 (HSCL-90). No longitudinal studies of any type were conducted by this group.

Soloff et al. (1986a) showed similar efficacy in the acute treatment of BPD patients treated with haloperidol (7.2 mg/day average dose). Benefits were more robust than in the study by Goldberg et al., and included improvement in all 10 of the HSCL-90 factors, including a reduction in hostility and improved interpersonal sensitivity. The study also showed neuroleptic treatment to be as effective as amitriptyline in treating depression and better than amitriptyline in treating behavioral dyscontrol and anger. Longitudinal studies, however, have shown that the gains on haloperidol are transient (Cornelius et al., 1993). Patients treated with haloperidol had a much higher drop-out rate than placebo (64 vs 28%), without any difference in outcome except for a modest reduction in irritability as measured by the Buss–Durkee Hostility Inventory. The authors felt that the use of neuroleptics in borderline patients is of limited value.

Cowdry and Gardner (1988) saw an improvement in anxiety, rejection sensitivity, and suicidality on trifluoperazine, but no change in behavioral dyscontrol. They felt that trifluoperazine was marginally beneficial overall.

While neuroleptics may acutely aid some individuals with BDP, they fail to relieve most of the anxiety, obsessiveness, and depression accompanying the illness. They are statistically no better than placebo in the reduction of hostility, anger, and aggression. Neuroleptics are poorly tolerated in BPD, as witnessed by the high drop-out rates of neuroleptic-medicated patients in controlled acute studies (39% in the study by Soloff et al., and 54% in the study by Goldberg et al.), and in longitudinal studies (64% in the study by Cornelius et al.). Neuroleptics have the ominous side effect of tardive dyskinesia, along with lethargy, weight gain, mental slowing, and akathisia. The use of neuroleptics in the BPD population is limited. Those patients who have the target symptoms of psychotic thinking described by Goldberg et al. (1986) may benefit acutely, but not longitudinally. The theoretical ability of these agents to control impulsivity and aggression is not supported by the available reports of controlled trials.

ANTICONVULSANTS

Reports of efficacy of anticonvulsants first appeared in 1967. Jonas (1967) used phenytoin to treat patients with pseudoneurotic schizophrenia and noted an improvement in their condition. Stephens and Shaffer (1970) used phenytoin to help decrease the anxiety, irritability and anger of outpatients who had many borderline characteristics. Cowdry and Gardner (Gardner and Cowdry, 1986a; Cowdry and Gardner, 1988) showed the beneficial effects of carbamazepine in BPD in a double-blind placebo-controlled trial. Carbamazepine proved the most beneficial of the four medications they studied, and 11 of 15 patients opted to remain on or return to carbamazepine therapy at the study's conclusion. For the group as a whole, impulsiveness decreased markedly on carbamazepine. Even when behavioral dyscontrol did occur, the authors noted it to be less severe than while on placebo. Three patients, however, noted the development of severe melancholic depression while on carbamazepine (Gardner and Cowdry, 1986b).

Carbamazepine may be an effective medication for treating affective instability and behavioral dyscontrol that accompanies BPD but a poor choice for patients with depressive episodes. The potential induction of melancholia (Gardner and Cowdry, 1986b) in a group prone to suicidality is far from ideal. Carbamazepine therapy is often accompanied by lethargy (Elphick, 1989), which can also be a presenting complaint in patients with BPD. Allergic and dermatological reactions to carbamazepine can occur in as many as 15% of cases (Elphick, 1989). As with the prior treatments, carbamazepine partially controls only some of the aberrant behavioral sequelae accompanying BPD (Gardner and Cowdry, 1989), although it is statistically effective in reducing impulsivity.

There are case reports of benzodiazepines having some efficacy (Vilkin, 1972; Faltus, 1984). The only controlled trial involved alprazolam (Cowdry and Gardner, 1988), and the medication was found to worsen suicidality and was no better or worse than placebo in all other ratings. Alprazolam has been associated with an increase in the frequency and seriousness of behavioral dyscontrol (Gardner and Cowdry, 1985). Some patients noted alprazolam to be beneficial in mood improvement, but this was offset in the clinician's view by the worsening impulsivity. Current data are sparse but suggest that benzodiazepines are probably best avoided in BPD.

ANTIDEPRESSANTS

The use of antidepressants in the treatment of pseudoneurotic schizophrenia, a precursor to BPD, stemmed from the frequent findings of comorbidity depression and anxiety. Hedberg et al. (see Hedberg, 1971) showed that institutionalized pseudoneurotic schizophrenics did best on tranylcypromine, as opposed to neuroleptics or no medication. No quantification of benefit was made. Liebowitz, Klein, Quitkin, and colleagues were working along similar lines in treating atypical depression, hysteroid dysphoria, and EUCD with tranylcypromine or phenelzine (Liebowitz and Klein, 1981; Liebowitz et al., 1988; Quitkin et al., 1988, 1990; Parsons et al., 1989). These three entities include many individuals with BPD. In these latter five studies, 50%

of the individuals had improvement with monoamine oxidase inhibitor (MAOI) therapy. The overall benefit of MAOIs in atypical depression, hysteroid dysphoria, and EUCD has been well studied. The different diagnostic groups represent variations on a theme, as many of the patients fulfilling criteria for the aforementioned illnesses also meet criteria for BPD (Parsons et al., 1989). The benefits of MAOI therapy are limited, and there is little data to suggest a diminution of impulsivity in any of the studies. Cowdry and Gardner (1988), in a double-blind study, used tranylcypromine in 16 patients with BPD and demonstrated marked improvement in mood, but little change in behavioral dyscontrol. Cornelius et al. (1993) used phenelzine in BPD longitudinally, and found little benefit over placebo. They felt that the improvements noted in irritability, energy, and depression were modest and unremarkable.

MONOAMINE OXIDASE INHIBITORS

In BPD, MAOI treatment is problematic. First, only 50% of the patients receive any clinical benefit from the treatment. Those that do benefit must tolerate the side effects of hypotension, possible hypertension, weight gain, agitation, poor sleep, and relapse of their illness. Second, in an illness in which overdosing on psychotropics is a common method of suicide, MAOIs are a particularly lethal medication. Patients with BPD often abuse alcohol and substances (cocaine, amphetamines, etc.), and the use of many of these agents with MAOIs can prove lethal. Lastly, the MAOIs do not decrease the behavioral dyscontrol or impulsivity seen with the illness.

TRICYCLIC ANTIDEPRESSANTS

Tricyclic antidepressants have also been extensively studied in BPD. They were selected primarily to treat the dysphoria accompanying the illness, and researchers reasoned that the depressive aspect of BPD might be amenable to tricyclic antidepressant therapy. Fink et al. (1964) were the first to show the advantages of imipramine in the treatment of patients who would probably have a diagnosis of BPD using current inclusion criteria. Klein (1967, 1968) continued these studies and showed many pseudoneurotic schizophrenics benefited from a course of imipramine. Likewise, many patients assessed to have emotionally unstable character disorder also showed improvement on imipramine (Klein, 1967, 1968). A subset of these patients, however, showed an increase in anger, hostility, and aggression while taking imipramine (Klein, 1968). Soloff et al. (1986a) confirmed the above findings in a well-controlled study, showing some mood improvement on amitriptyline and further showing that behavioral dyscontrol was unchanged for the group as a whole. Soloff et al. (1986b) also found that a subset of patients showed an increase in hostility on amitriptyline.

The tricyclics share many of the problems found with MAOIs. They are only partially effective in improving the depressive component of BPD and impact minimally on the behavioral symptoms of the illness. Side effects of the medication include weight gain and lethargy, two of the presenting complaints in many BPD patients. Tricyclics are a particularly lethal medication to prescribe for patients unable to control impulses to overdose. Because a significant number of these patients show worsening hostility on tricyclics, this side effect alone clearly limits the use of tricyclics.

SEROTONIN REUPTAKE INHIBITORS

Fluoxetine has been the best studied of the SRIs for treatment of impulsive and aggressive symptoms alone or in the context of psychiatric illnesses encompassing these symptoms. Borderline personality disorder is associated with impulsive (hypersexuality, spending sprees, and reckless driving) and aggressive behaviors (towards self and others), depression, panic, obsessionality, suicidality, self-injury, somatization, eating disorders, and anxiety. These behaviors have all been linked to aberrant 5-HT function in the CNS. Thus, using an SRI in patients with BPD seems logical.

Fluoxetine Open Trials

Four recent open trials of fluoxetine in BPD suggest that this SRI may be beneficial in the treatment of BPD. Norden (1989) reported that 5–40 mg/day of fluoxetine relieved many of the anxiety and depressive symptoms accompanying BPD. Nine of 12 BPD patients (75%), were judged to be very much improved ($n = 6$) or much improved ($n = 3$). Trial length varied from 5 to 26 weeks. Depression and impulsivity improved the most. These benefits were still evident at 6 months in two patients. Compliance with treatment and side effects were not reported.

Coccaro et al. (1990) reported on three patients with impulsive aggressive behavior sequentially receiving 20, 40, and 60 mg/day of fluoxetine for 2 weeks. Two of the three patients were felt to be primarily borderline, and one of the patients was felt to be primarily antisocial. All three showed reduction in impulsive aggressive behavior during the trial. Two of the patients showed a temporal exacerbation of irritability, aggression, and verbal hostility when life stressors arose. The authors felt the trial of fluoxetine in these three patients was successful. Side effects and compliance were not discussed.

Markovitz et al. (1991a) reported on 22 BPD patients treated with 80 mg/day of fluoxetine for 12 weeks. This study reported significant decreases in the frequency of self-injurious behavior as well as improvement in the items included in the HSCL (Lipman et al., 1979). Twelve patients were reported to be self-injurious at the start of the study. All 12 of the patients cut themselves with either razor blades, glass, or knives. The week was divided into 14 12-h periods (midnight to noon and noon to midnight), and patients were either positive or negative for self injury during these periods. Neither the number of episodes of self-injury nor severity of the action were assessed, only the presence or absence of the behavior. The 12 patients averaged four periods of self-injurious behavior per week. At the conclusion of the study, only two individuals were still self-injurious, with a decrease in the incidence of such events to only once per month. This study also noted improvement in anxiety, hostility, obsessiveness, depression, psychosis, and interpersonal skills. The HSCL was reduced from 197.3 ± 60.1 to 69.5 ± 44.7, and the presence or absence of depression did not effect outcome. Neither side effects of the treatment nor compliance were discussed.

A study by Cornelius et al. (1991) reported benefit from 20–40 mg/day of fluoxetine in five BPD patients. Improvement in overall functioning and dysphoria were found. In contrast with the results of Markovitz et al. (1991a), they noted that hostility and psychotic symptomatology did not decrease. It should be noted that the dose of fluoxetine was 20–40 mg/day compared with the 80 mg/day dose used in the study by Markovitz et al., and it is possible that higher levels of fluoxetine are required to eliminate certain symptoms. As with the other studies, side effects and compliance with treatment were not discussed.

Sertraline Open Trials

I have also investigated the use of sertraline in the treatment of BPD. Twenty-three patients were begun on 50 mg/day of sertraline, and the dosage was increased by 50 mg every 3 days to 200 mg/day. Twelve of the 23 patients had failed to respond to 80 mg/day of fluoxetine because of lack of efficacy ($n = 7$) or side effects ($n = 5$). After 12 weeks, 11 of 23 patients (48%) showed improvement as assessed by decreased self-injurious behavior, anxiety, depression, and suicidality. Five of these patients had failed to respond to fluoxetine. It was noted that the patients who had benefited from sertraline had at least one of two behaviors predictive of a positive response. First, a reduction in appetite for sweets and carbohydrates became apparent in individuals with carbohydrate craving. Second, some patients developed a fine myoclonic tremor of the fingers which waxed and waned over 3 weeks before resolving.

The 12 patients not showing any responsivity to the sertraline had their dosage increased by 100 mg/day every week until they had diminished appetite and/or developed a fine myoclonic tremor. Once either of these side effects developed, dosage escalation was stopped and the patients were followed for another 12 weeks. Six of the 12 patients showed significant responsivity based on decreases in self-injurious behavior, anxiety, depression, and suicidality. These data suggest that there may be a certain serum/CNS level of medication necessary to respond, and that this level is attained when appetite decreases and/or a fine myoclonic tremor develops. The data also suggest that failure to respond to one SRI should not rule out use of another, if the presenting symptoms point to behaviors associated with 5-HT dysregulation. Further studies are needed to resolve this question. It is also possible that some individuals take longer than 12 weeks to respond to sertraline. All 23 of the aforementioned sertraline-treated patients were followed over a 12-month period, and the acute efficacy of the medication was maintained longitudinally. The results are summarized in Table 1.

Not all open studies have found improvement with SRIs. King et al. (1991) reported on the emergence of self-destructive behavior in six of 42 patients treated with fluoxetine for obsessive compulsive disorder and/or Tourette's syndrome. The data suggested a temporal relationship between fluoxetine use and the emergence of self-injurious behavior or thoughts. Four of the six subjects had previous risk factors for this action, including suicidal ideation, self-injury, and depression. Since all three of the aforementioned symptoms have been linked to dysregulation of the 5-HT system, it is possible that the fluoxetine was ineffectual in these children and adolescents, and that the self-destructive behavior simply re-emerged in four patients and emerged as part of the evolution of the illness in the other two patients. Hawthorne and Lacey (1992) described a patient meeting criteria for BPD and being treated for bulimia, who developed self-injurious behavior following initiation of fluoxetine therapy. Two of the patients described by Teicher et al. (1990) had BPD, too, and the emergence of suicidality may well have been a natural evolution of the illness in patients in whom fluoxetine just was not effective.

Fluoxetine Double blind trial

These open studies were followed by a double-blind placebo-controlled trial of fluoxetine by Markovitz et al. (1991b). The interim analysis of the trial involved only 17 patients (nine on fluoxetine and eight on placebo), but

Table 1 One-year efficacy of sertraline in 23 patients with borderline personality disorder

	0 weeks	52 weeks
Beck Depression Index	25.5 ± 10.1	11.3 ± 10.4
Self-injurious patients	11	2
Self-injury episodes/week	4.2 ± 3.8	0.3 ± 0.3
Sertraline daily dosage (mg)	—	321.7 ± 141.3

confirmed the findings of the earlier open study. Inclusion criteria included a diagnosis of BPD by the Structured Clinical Interview for DSM-III-R personality disorders (SCID-II) (Spitzer et al., 1987), a Gunderson's Diagnostic Interview for Borderline Personality Disorder score of 7 or higher (Gunderson et al., 1981), and unanimous consensus on the diagnosis by two blinded clinicians and two raters.

The patients were randomly assigned to fluoxetine or placebo, and remained on this regimen for 14 weeks. Medication was initiated as one capsule per day (0 or 20 mg fluoxetine) and increased by one capsule every week to four capsules per day at the end of 3 weeks (0 or 80 mg fluoxetine). Improvement was monitored by changes in the HSCL, Hamilton Anxiety Scale (HAM-A; Hamilton, 1959), Hamilton Depression Scale (HAM-D; Hamilton, 1960), Beck Depression Index (BDI; Beck et al., 1961), and Global Assessment Scale (GAS; Spitzer et al., 1976). Patients were required to complete at least 3 weeks on medication for inclusion in data analysis. Drop outs after 3 weeks but prior to 14 weeks and their final rating scores carried through for each subsequent time point. Seven of nine patients on fluoxetine completed the entire study, and seven of eight patients on placebo completed all 14 weeks of the trial. There was a statistically significant improvement ($p \leq 0.05$) in the fluoxetine group compared with placebo on all of the aforementioned rating instruments (Figure 1). Interestingly, all of the rating instruments were continuing to show increasing improvement at 14 weeks in patients on fluoxetine, suggesting the trial may not have been long enough.

Comorbidity

Axis I diagnoses were evaluated in the study and showed notable comorbidity (Table 2). This comorbidity parallels that seen in earlier studies of BPD (Fyer et al., 1988) and is consistent with the premise that an aberration of neurochemistry will lead to more than one type of pathological behavior. While it could be argued that the BPD might arise as a behavioral sequelae of the Axis I disorder(s) (Liebowitz et al., 1979; Hirschfield et al., 1983, 1989; Reich et al., 1986; Joffe and Regan, 1988), it is significant that all of the comorbid diagnoses have been linked to anomalies of the 5-HT system, or symptoms responding to SRI. As reviewed above, comorbid behaviors arising in BPD should be expected if these behaviors, as well as the BPD, arose from a common lesion. All of the "diagnoses" are behaviors, some of which may be preferentially expressed in any individual but all of which probably arise from a common origin.

Many of the diagnoses noted in Table 2 are also symptoms of BPD, for example bulimia, drug abuse, depression, mania, and alcohol abuse. All 10 of the patients with depression had at least two features of atypical depression using Columbia criteria (Quitkin et al., 1990), and these symptoms

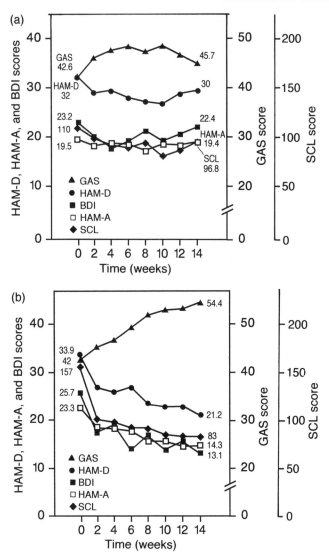

Figure 1 Comparison of Global Assessment Score (GAS), Hamilton Depression Scale (HAM-D), Beck Depression Index (BDI), Hopkins Symptom Checklist (SCL), and Hamilton Anxiety Scale (HAM-A) scores during a 14-week trial of placebo (a; $n = 8$) and fluoxetine 80 mg/day (b; $n = 9$) in patients with borderline personality disorder [from Markovitz et al. (1991b) with permission].

overlap significantly with BPD. Six patients had a clinical diagnosis of manic depressive disorder by history, and the overlap between manic depression and BPD is marked (Akiskal et al., 1983, 1985; Blacker et al., 1992). Interestingly, two recent studies support the efficacy of fluoxetine in the

Table 2 Comorbid Axis I diagnoses in 17 patients included in a trial of fluoxetine vs placebo in borderline personality disorder

	DSM-III-R Comorbidity ($n = 17$)	
	Current	Lifetime
Major depression	10	10
Bipolar disorder		
Type I	2	2
Type II	4	5
Dysthymia	1	11
Generalized anxiety disorder	9	15
Obsessive compulsive disorder	6	8
Panic disorder	4	7
Drug abuse, use, dependence	4	6
Alcoholism	3	7
Somatization	2	2
Anorexia/bulimia	3	3
Phobic disorder	2	4
Average diagnoses per patient	3.0	4.7

Table 3 Comorbid Axis II diagnoses in 17 patients included in a trial of fluoxetine vs placebo in borderline personality disorder

	Axis II comorbidity ($n = 17$)	
	n	%
Borderline	17	100
Self-defeating	14	82
Paranoid	14	82
Compulsive	12	71
Avoidant	11	65
Dependent	11	65
Histrionic	10	59
Passive aggressive	10	59
Schizotypal	9	53
Narcissistic	6	35
Antisocial	6	35
Schizoid	0	0
Diagnoses per patient	7.0	

treatment of depressed bipolar patients (Cohn et al., 1989; Simpson and DePaulo, 1991). The overlap of BPD symptoms with other Axis I diagnoses supports the contention of van Praag et al. (1987) that our current nosology is limited. Their data (van Praag et al., 1987; Apter et al., 1990, 1993) support biological treatment, on the basis of symptom clusters theoretically arising from a common cause. For example, manic behavior by itself should not dictate treatment. The manic behavior might be more logically viewed as an impulsive episode if there is comorbid obsessive compulsive disorder, suicidality, bulimia, rejection sensitivity, or self-injurious behavior. Borderline personality disorder would be a behavioral symptom arising as a sequela of a lesion associated with an abnormal 5-HT state (van Praag et al., 1986).

Axis II diagnoses in our study were obtained from the SCID-II. As can be seen in Table 3, comorbidity is common. Similar levels of comorbidity were seen in Norden's (1989) study. Since these studies selected for the presence of Axis II pathology (BPD) as an entry requirement, both might have a built-in bias for an increased incidence of Axis II behavior. Studies investigating other behaviors, for example suicide (Marttunen et al., 1991), impulsivity (Virkkunen et al., 1989), disruptive behavior (Kruesi et al., 1990), and depression (Shea et al., 1990), also found high levels of Axis II comorbidity. A recent review corroborates these findings for many Axis II disorders (Gitlin, 1993).

Also of interest in the interim analysis of fluoxetine versus placebo in BPD was the prevalence of Axis III disorders (Table 4). Somatic complaints have long been noted in psychiatric conditions, and they could represent another physical manifestation of neurochemistry. These syndromes would be expected to occur more frequently if they, too, were associated with 5-HT dysfunction.

Considering its prevalence, premenstrual syndrome (PMS) has been poorly studied biologically, but there are data supporting a 5-HT dysregulation (Taylor et al., 1984; Rapkin et al., 1987; Wurtman, 1990). The success of fluoxetine in treating the disorder (Stone et al., 1990; Rickels et al., 1990; Woods et al., 1992), has been documented, but not all SRIs have proved efficacious in PMS. A fluvoxamine trial failed to show an advantage over placebo (Veeninga et al., 1990). In the interim analysis of the study by Markovitz et al. (1991b) comparing fluoxetine and placebo in BPD, seven of the 12 women with PMS were randomized to fluoxetine treatment. Six of the seven completed the trial, and five had complete resolution of their

Table 4 Axis III comorbidity in 17 patients included in a trial of fluoxetine vs placebo in borderline personality disorder

	Axis III comorbidity ($n = 17$)	
	n	%
Premenstrual syndrome ($n = 13$)	12	92
Headaches/migraines	8	47
Irritable bowel syndrome	7	41
Fibrocytis	6	35
Neurodermatitis	5	29
Sleep apnea	5	29

PMS. None of the women randomized to placebo noted improvement in PMS symptomatology.

Migraines and severe headaches were also prevalent in BPD patients studied by Markovitz et al. (1991b). The eight (47%) patients with this symptom were randomized to fluoxetine ($n = 4$) or placebo ($n = 4$) treatment. None of the patients receiving placebo noted improvement in frequency or intensity of migraines/headaches. Three of the patients randomized to fluoxetine noted complete resolution of this symptom. Similar results were found in another center where headaches alone were treated (Diamond and Freitag, 1989). The success of sumatriptan (a 5-HT1$_D$ receptor agonist) in relieving migraines suggests a 5-HT-mediated component to this symptom in some individuals (Doenicke et al., 1988).

Irritable bowel syndrome may be linked to irregularities of the 5-HT system, either directly or indirectly (Talley, 1992), and has been found clinically with other diagnoses associated with 5-HT anomalies (Hudson and Pope, 1990). The number of patients in the study by Markovitz et al. (1991b, and see earlier) was too low to compare efficacy between groups.

Some forms of fibromyalgia are related to hyposerotonin function, based on serum tryptophan levels (Russell et al., 1989; Yunus et al., 1992), 5-HT levels (Russell et al., 1992), and [^{3}H]imipramine binding in platelets (Russell et al., 1992). A variety of other 5-HT-associated symptoms (e.g. sleep disturbances, migraines, and anxiety) are found in much higher than expected frequency in patients with fibromyalgia (Moldofsky, 1982, 1989). Geller (1989) noted the efficacy of fluoxetine in the treatment of fibromyalgia in an uncontrolled setting.

Dermatological problems arising with anxiety or depression—psychogenic pruritus, urticaria, alopecia areata, etc.—have been noted in the literature. Hendricks et al. (1991) noted improvement in patients with psychocutaneous disorders treated with fluvoxamine in a double-blind placebo-controlled trial. The medication did not, however, prove statistically better than placebo. Patients responding to fluoxetine treatment in the study by Markovitz et al. (1991b, and see earlier) showed resolution of neurodermatitis, but the number of patients with this symptom was too low for statistical analysis of the data.

Sleep disturbances share many of the symptoms of depression, and studies have found a serotonergic dysregulation associated with sleep dysfunction (Moldofsky, 1989). Repeat polysomnographic data are not available from the double-blind study of fluoxetine in BPD, but other centers have shown efficacy in treating sleep apnea with fluoxetine (Hanzel et al., 1991).

It should not be inferred that each of these medical entities are always caused by an abnormality of 5-HT or something linked to 5-HT levels. If these symptoms are found within the context of other Axis I and II behaviors linked to 5-HT dysregulation, however, parsimony of diagnosis suggests that all the behaviors arise from a common cause.

Summary

Overall, open and controlled studies of fluoxetine, sertraline, and fluvoxamine suggest these medications are of benefit to patients with impulsivity and aggression within the context of BPD. Comorbid symptoms also resolve for many of these patients. In the study by Markovitz et al. (1991b, and see earlier) somatic symptomatology waxed and waned in conjunction with Axis I and II behavior exacerbations, intimating a common cause. Further studies are needed to assess further which behaviors are associated with responsivity to SRI, appropriate dosage, and longitudinal efficacy of these agents.

Clomipramine

No studies investigating clomipramine in BPD are available. While the potent SRI properties of clomipramine suggest it may have efficacy in some patients, there are reasons to use it cautiously. First, because suicidality often accompanies impulsive behaviors (Virkkunen et al., 1989), the risk of suicide via overdose must be considered. Clomipramine is a very toxic agent in overdose. Second, clomipramine is a tricyclic, and shares most of the properties of other tricyclic agents. Amitriptyline has been shown by Soloff et al. (1986b) to be ineffectual in BPD and potentially can worsen symptoms of the illness. The behaviors elicited by amitriptyline and described by Soloff et al., are very much like those discussed in clomipramine-induced manic behavior in unipolar depressives (van Scheyen and van Kammen, 1979). It is impossible to tell from the data presented by van Scheyen and van Kammen (1979) whether their subjects had atypical depression. Because atypical depression is often comorbid with borderline personality disorder (Parsons et al., 1989), many of these manic patients may have been borderline patients, too, who had a reaction like those described by Soloff et al. As Soloff et al., have shown that amitriptyline is potentially dangerous in borderline patients, and van Scheyen et al., indicated that these manic-like behaviors occur more frequently with clomipramine than amitriptyline (six manic inductions on clomipramine, and one on amitriptyline), the use of clomipramine in disorders of impulsivity and aggression should be approached with caution. Alarcon et al. (1991) described two cases of clomipramine-induced aggression and paranoia in obsessive compulsive adolescents, underscoring this point. One of the individuals clearly showed features of borderline personality disorder comorbid with obsessive compulsive disorder, and insufficient data were presented on the other case to assess Axis II pathology.

Clomipramine may have a role in some patients with disorders involving aggression and impulsivity, but little of the data supports its use. Because other agents are less lethal in overdose and less likely to induce manic-like/impulsive behaviors, the use of clomipramine should be pursued prudently.

SEXUAL IMPULSIVITY AND AGGRESSION

Treatment of impulsive sexual episodes with fluoxetine was initially noted in a series of case reports (Emmanuel et al., 1991; Kafka, 1991; Lorefice, 1991; Perilstein et al., 1991). Kafka followed up his single case report with an open trial of fluoxetine in 20 men with a variety of sexual addictions (Kafka and Prentky, 1992). Comorbidity, as with the BPD studies, was highly prevalent. Nineteen of the men (95%) had dysthymia and 16 (80%) were clinically depressed. There was a marked improvement in sexual addictions, as well as mood and anxiety symptoms, with fluoxetine treatment. No controlled trials are yet available. The use of SRI in hypersexuality states is consistent with behavioral studies correlating increased sex drive and decreased 5-HT levels (Green and Grahame-Smith, 1975).

Stein and co-workers reported on 13 patients with sexual obsessions ($n = 3$), sexual addictions ($n = 5$), and paraphilias ($n = 5$) treated openly with fluoxetine ($n = 12$), clomipramine ($n = 4$), fluvoxamine ($n = 1$), and fenfluramine ($n = 1$). Comorbidity was highly prevalent in this study in the subjects discussed. Nine patients had obsessive compulsive disorder (69%) and three had major depression (23%). With any of the SRIs, improvement in paraphilics and in nonparaphilic sexual addictions was minimal. Sexual obsessions, however, showed improvement in two of three patients. An interesting finding of the study was that depression or obsessive compulsive behavior could improve without any change in sexual symptoms. The reasons for this are unclear and need further study.

Kruesi and collaborators looked at 15 paraphiliacs in a double-blind crossover study of desipramine versus clomipramine. Comorbidity was common, with nine of 15 patients (60%) meeting Research Diagnostic Criteria (RDC) criteria for depression or dysthymia, eight of 15 were substance abusers (53%), six of 15 had an anxiety disorder (40%), and four had antisocial personality disorder (27%). Only three of the patients (20%) had only paraphilia as their diagnosis. Eight of the subjects were able to complete both arms of the study, and there was no difference in responsiveness between clomipramine or desipramine. On the basis of this response, the authors felt that paraphilias may have a biological etiology different from obsessive compulsive disorder. It is difficult to draw this conclusion, however, on the basis of nonresponse to clomipramine. First, the duration of the trial was very short, and behaviors on each medication were assessed at week 5. Many clinicians feel that at least 10 weeks on clomipramine are required to assess outcome in obsessive compulsive disorder. Second, the dose of clomipramine was low (mean maximal daily dose 162.5 mg). Finally, failure to respond to a drug does not define an illness. While patients did better on both desipramine and clomipramine, lack of preferential response to the latter only implies that neither drug is better than the other, and both are better than placebo. The positive results seen with fluoxetine in open trials of paraphilia suggest that this medication should be studied further and that it has potential in the treatment of paraphilias.

IMPULSIVITY AND AGGRESSION IN THE DEVELOPMENTALLY DISABLED

Autistic disorder and mental retardation are frequently associated with impulsive outbursts manifested as emotional lability, obsessionality, agitation, rage episodes, and aggression toward self and others. A series of cases have been reported in the literature and indicated decreases in self-injury, aggression, impulsivity, and obsessionality associated with mental retardation and autistic disorder in individuals treated with fluoxetine or fluvoxamine (McDougle et al., 1990; Markowitz, 1990; Mehlinger et al., 1990; Ghaziuddin et al., 1991; Hamdan-Allen, 1991; Todd, 1991). Markowitz followed up on his initial report with a larger open study using 20–40 mg of fluoxetine daily in 21 severely to profoundly mentally retarded persons with aggression and self-injurious behavior (Markowitz, 1992). Marked improvement occurred in 13 individuals (62%), and moderate to mild improvement in six (29%). Measurement of decreases in aggression, self-injury, agitation, and emotional lability all indicated benefit from fluoxetine treatment. Markowitz discussed the possibility of higher fluoxetine doses resulting in more improvement in those patients with an incomplete response. Follow up in the study ranged from 6 to 12 months, and treatment benefits continued over this period. The study was open, and controlled trials are needed to quantify the benefit of SRI in this population. Other areas yet to be addressed include appropriate dosage, behaviors amenable to treatment, and longitudinal efficacy.

Clomipramine has not been well studied in impulsivity or aggression in developmentally disabled individuals. Garber and coworkers reported on 11 consecutive developmentally disabled patients presenting with chronic stereotypical and self-injurious behaviors. Ten of the patients showed acute decreases in stereotypical behaviors and/or self-injury on clomipramine, suggesting that this medication may prove beneficial in this group of patients. Gordon et al. (1992) reported on seven patients treated in a double-blind study with either desipramine or clomipramine and then crossed to the other medication after 5 weeks. The clomipramine-treated group showed close to 50% improvement in Children's Psychiatric Rating Scale Scores, whereas the desipramine-treated group showed no improvement. This study is encouraging, but is small and further controlled studies are needed.

Jaselskis et al. (1992) investigated the use of clonidine in eight hyperactive and impulsive children with autistic disorder. The trial was a crossover study in which patients were begun on clonidine or placebo, treated for 6 weeks, tapered during week 7, and begun on the alternative treatment during weeks 8–13. Clonidine showed a modest improvement over placebo, with a 33% decrease in irritability being the major finding. Six of the eight patients were continued on clonidine after the study was concluded, and four relapsed to their preclonidine levels of irritability and hyperactivity. Sedation and decreased blood pressure were problematical in the majority of patients, and the usefulness of this agent seems limited.

Lithium has been shown to be beneficial in a subset of children with rage, aggression, and irritability (DeLong, 1978). Most of the children described would now be labelled conduct disorder or attention deficit disorder. Benefits were described in four children previously shown to benefit from lithium therapy who were given lithium or placebo blindly for 3 weeks and then crossed over to the alternative treatment. Actual clinical benefit was difficult to assess, although the lithium-treated group did improve.

A study of mentally retarded patients with repeated uncontrolled aggression and self-injury (Craft et al., 1987) suggested that lithium could benefit some patients. Forty-two patients were involved in this double-blind placebo-controlled trial, and 73% of the lithium-treated patients improved, compared with 30% of placebo-treated patients. While the results were statistically significant, it is not clear what meaningful results occur in clinical practice. Further controlled studies are needed in both of these populations to determine whether the changes seen meaningfully improve quality of life.

Use of propranolol was initially described in a single case report (Yudofsky et al., 1981). The case described was a 22-year-old retarded woman who showed meaningful improvement on propranolol at 510 mg/day. A larger series of cases by the same group (Williams et al., 1982) documented the efficacy of propranolol in a diagnostically diverse population sharing the problem of rage outbursts. Comorbid diagnoses included conduct disorder (83%), intermittent explosive disorder (10%), attention deficit disorder (70%), mental retardation (43%), and pervasive developmental disorder (7%). Doses of propranolol ranged from 50 to 1600 mg/day, with an average dose of 160 mg/day. During the study, 33% of the patients had marked improvement, and 46% had moderate improvement. The majority of patients were on other psychotropic medications and it is difficult to assess how much these contributed to recovery. While the reduction in aggression was impressive, controlled trials are needed to quantify the potential usefulness of propranolol in controlling rage and aggression. Mattes et al. (1984) presented preliminary data comparing propranolol with carbamazepine, but no placebo group was included. Both drugs were described as beneficial.

A series of case reports have indicated that carbamazepine could be helpful in aggression and rage control (Monroe, 1975; Neppe, 1982; Luchins, 1983; Mattes, 1984). In all cases, there was significant diagnostic overlap. Mattes (1984) studied 34 patients, with seven different diagnostic groups represented, and each patient had over two diagnoses (74 diagnoses for the group). This again suggests the heterogeneity of behaviors associated with aggression, and problems of selecting a homogeneous group for study. Clearly, however, in all of these reports, carbamazepine decreased rage outbursts significantly. Controlled trials are needed to define patient characteristics suggestive of a positive response, to quantify the level of improvement, and to document the longitudinal efficacy of carbamazepine in various groups.

IMPULSIVITY AND AGGRESSION IN PRISONERS

Sheard et al. (1976) studied aggression in prisoners, and the acute effects of lithium on impulse control problems. In this double-blind placebo-controlled trial, 31 patients on placebo were compared with 28 patients on lithium. The lithium-treated group showed an almost complete elimination of major infractions, but minor infractions increased, suggesting a decrease in the intensity of aggressive drive. The placebo group showed no changes compared with their baseline. Tupin et al. (1973) followed up on an earlier study by Sheard with an open trial of lithium lasting an average of just under 10 months. Their results corroborated those of Sheard, and documented decreases in violent infractions. Interestingly, the change in nonviolent infractions was much less pronounced. Other measures pointing to improvement included reduction of security classification (less need for surveillance), patient reports of less anger, and improved global ratings by the hospital psychiatric staff. Psychiatric diagnoses were not presented in either study, and it is unclear what pretreatment pathology existed. Overall, these results support the benefits of lithium in aggression and impulsivity documented in many of the studies reviewed earlier.

DISCUSSION

Impulsivity and aggression are commonly comorbid. Neither behavior exists as a discrete clinical entity, but instead each is a trait within the context of other psychiatric diagnoses. It is most likely that the behaviors can arise from a myriad of neurochemical anomalies (reviewed in earlier chapters). The more common clustering of aggression and impulsivity (e.g. BPD) may arise predominantly from one lesion that gives rise to the vast number of cases. This lesion should preferentially respond to one treatment that addresses the deficit. Virtually all medications available to psychiatrists have been utilized in the treatment of impulsivity and aggression. Carbamazepine, lithium, and the SRIs seem to provide the highest degree of improvement, although all other agents discussed have proven efficacious in some patients.

Van Praag (1986) has discussed using impulsivity and aggression in defining psychiatric illnesses because of their strong correlation with 5-HT anomalies in the CNS. If the correlation is correct, it is logical to try to ameliorate the behavior by increasing 5-HT function in the CNS, and the SRIs are proficient in doing this. Lithium and carbamazepine have both been shown to have a positive effect on 5-HT function too, and this may account for their efficacy in treating impulsivity and aggression.

The available data suggest that impulsivity and/or aggression can be reduced or even eliminated through the use of carbamazepine, lithium or SRI. More specifically, in those individuals also having comorbid symptomatology correlated with hyposerotonergic function, the success of treatment with SRIs seems to be even higher. Not only are obsessionality, depression, panic, and self-injury associated with low 5-HT and a positive response, but physical manifestations of 5-HT dysfunction such as migraines, irritable bowel syndrome, neurodermatitis, PMS, sleep apnea, and fibromyalgia also respond. Van Praag's (1986, 1987) data suggest that the presence of impulsivity and aggression is common, correlated with decreased 5-HT function, and may be a behavior representative of the primary neurochemical problem. The SRIs increase 5-HT function and this may be the mode by which they mediate their effects in the CNS.

This cause-and-effect idea must be viewed cautiously. It may be that 5-HT function is only a step in a cascade of events leading to impulsivity and aggression. Likewise, it may represent a neurochemical problem but have nothing to do with the mode of action of the drugs used. The lack of objective measures to validate the chemical basis for the treatment chosen results in the substitution of one nosological hierarchy for another. While the clinical treatment of symptom clusters linked chemically and behaviorally is logical, too much subjectivity remains. Nevertheless, SRIs have proved the most successful in treating impulsivity and aggression, behaviors that are poorly responsive to other pharmacological agents and psychological interventions. The available studies are encouraging and suggest many areas for research and for potential applications of the SRIs in psychiatry.

REFERENCES

Akiskal, H.S., Hirschfeld, R.M.A., and Yerevanian, B.I. (1983). The relationship of personality to affective disorders: A critical review. *Arch. Gen. Psychiatry*, 40, 801–810.

Akiskal, H.S., Chen, S.E., Davis, G.C., Puzantian, V.R., Kashgarian, M., and Bolinger, J.M. (1985). Borderline: An adjective in search of a noun. *J. Clin. Psychiatry*, 46, 41–48.

Alarcon, R.D., Johnson, B.R., and Lucas, J.P. (1991). Paranoid and aggressive behavior in two obsessive–compulsive adolescents treated with clomipramine. *J. Am. Acad. Child Adolesc. Psychiatry*, 30, 999–1002.

Apter, A., van Praag, H.M., Plutchik, R., Sevy, S., Korn, M., and Brown, S.L. (1990). Interrelationships among anxiety, aggression, impulsivity, and mood: A serotonergically linked cluster? *Psychiatry Res.*, 32, 191–199.

Apter, A., Plutchik, R., and van Praag, H.M. (1993). Anxiety, impulsivity and depressed mood in relation to suicidal and violent behavior. *Acta Psychiatr. Scand.*, 87, 1–5.

Asberg, M., Traskman, L., and Thoren, P. (1976). 5-HIAA in the cerebrospinal fluid: A biochemical suicide predictor? *Arch. Gen. Psychiatry*, 33, 1193–1197.

Beck, A.T., Ward, D.H., Mendelson, M., Mock, J., and Erbaugh, J. (1961). An inventory for measuring depression. *Arch. Gen. Psychiatry*, 4, 561–571.

Blacker, D., and Tsuang, M.T. (1992). Contested boundaries of bipolar disorder and the limits of categorical diagnosis in psychiatry. *Am. J. Psychiatry*, 149, 1473–1483.

Blundell, J.E. (1984). Serotonin and appetite. *Neuropharmacology*, 23, 1537–1551.

Brewerton, T.D., Mueller, E.A., Lesem, M.D., et al. (1992). Neuroendocrine responses to *m*-chloro-phenylpiperazine and L-tryptophan in bulimia. *Arch. Gen. Psychiatry*, 49, 852–861.

Brinkley, J.R., Beitman, B.D., and Friedel, R.O. (1979). Low dose neuroleptic regimens in the treatment of borderline patients. *Arch. Gen. Psychiatry*, 36, 319–326.

Brown, G.L., and Goodwin, F.K. (1986). Cerebrospinal fluid correlates of suicide attempts and aggression. *Ann. N. Y. Acad. Sci.*, 487, 175–188.

Coccaro, E.F., Astill, J.L., Herbert, J.L., and Schut, A.G. (1990). Fluoxetine treatment of impulsive aggression in DSM-III-R personality disorder patients. *J. Clin. Psychopharmacol.*, 10, 373–375.

Coccaro, E.F., Siever, L.J., Klar, H.M., et al. (1989). Serotonergic studies in patients with affective and personality disorder: correlates with suicidal and impulsive aggressive behavior. *Arch. Gen. Psychiatry*, 46, 587–599 [and correction (1990), vol. 47, 124].

Cohn, J.B., Collins, G., Ashbrook, E., and Wernicke, J.F. (1989). A comparison of fluoxetine, imipramine, and placebo in patients with bipolar depressive disorder. *Int. Clin. Psychopharmacol.*, 4, 314–322.

Conacher, G.N. (1988). Pharmacotherapy of the aggressive adult patient. *Intl. J. Law Psychiatry*, 11, 205–212.

Cornelius, J.R., Soloff, P.H., Perel, J.M., and Ulrich, R.F. (1991). A preliminary trial of fluoxetine in refractory borderline patients. *J. Clin. Psychopharmacol.*, 11, 116–120.

Cornelius, J.R., Soloff, P.H., Perel, J.M., and Ulrich, R.F. (1993). Continuation pharmacotherapy of borderline personality disorder with haloperidol and phenelzine. *Am. J. Psychiatry*, 150, 1843–1848.

Cowdry, R.W., and Gardner, D.L. (1988). Pharmacotherapy of borderline personality disorder. *Arch. Gen. Psychiatry*, 45, 111–119.

Craft, M., Ismail, I.A., Krishnamurti, D., et al. (1987). Lithium in the treatment of aggression in mentally handicapped patients: A double blind trial. *Br. J. Psychiatry*, 150, 685–689.

DeLong, G.R. (1978). Lithium carbonate treatment of select behavior disorders in children suggesting manic–depressive illness. *J. Pediatr.*, 93, 689–694.

Diamond, S., and Freitag, F.G. (1989). The use of fluoxetine in the treatment of headache. *Clin. J. Pain*, 5, 200–201.

Doenicke, A., Brand, J., and Perrin, V.L. (1988). Possible benefit of GR43175, a novel 5-HT1-like receptor agonist, for the acute treatment of severe migraine. *Lancet*, i, 8598, 1309–1312.

Elphick, M. (1989). Clinical issues in the use of carbamazepine in psychiatry. *Psychol. Med.*, 19, 591–604.

Emmanuel, N.P., Lydiard, R.B., and Ballenger, J.C. (1991). Fluoxetine treatment of voyeurism [letter]. *Am. J. Psychiatry*, 148, 950.

Faltus, F.J. (1984). The positive effect of alprazolam in the treatment of three patients with borderline personality disorder. *Am. J. Psychiatry*, 141, 802–803.

Fink, M., Pollack, M., and Klein, D.F. (1964). Comparative studies of chlorpromazine and imipramine: I. Drug discriminating patterns. *Neuropsychopharmacology*, 3, 370–372.

Fyer, M.R., Frances, A.J., Sullivan, T., Hurt, S.W., and Clarkin, J. (1988). Comorbidity of borderline personality disorder. *Arch. Gen. Psychiatry*, 45, 348–352.

Garber, H.J., McGonigle, J.J., Slomka, G.T., and Monteverae, E. (1992). Clomipramine treatment of stereotypic behaviors and self-injury in patients with developmental disabilities. *J. Am. Acad. Child Adolesc. Psychiatry*, 31, 1157–1160.

Gardner, D.L., and Cowdry, R.W. (1985). Alprazolam-induced dyscontrol in borderline personality disorder. *Am. J. Psychiatry*, 142, 98–100.

Gardner, D.L., and Cowdry, R.W. (1986a). Positive effects of carbamazepine on behavioral dyscontrol in borderline personality disorder. *Am. J. Psychiatry*, 143, 519–522.

Gardner, D.L., and Cowdry, R.W. (1986b). Development of melancholia during carbamazepine treatment in borderline personality disorder. *J. Clin. Psychopharmacol*, 6, 236–239.

Gardner, D.L., and Cowdry, R.W. (1989). Pharmacotherapy of borderline personality disorder: A review. *Psychopharmacol. Bull.*, 25, 515–523.

Geller, S.A. (1989). Treatment of fibrositis with fluoxetine hydrochloride. *Am. J. Med.*, 87, 594–595.

Ghaziuddin, M., Tsai, L., and Ghaziuddin, N. (1991). Fluoxetine in autism with depression. *J. Am. Acad. Child Adolesc. Psychiatry*, 30, 508–509.

Gitlin, M.J. (1993). Pharmacotherapy of personality disorders: conceptual framework and clinical strategies. *J. Clin. Psychopharmacol.*, 13, 343–353.

Goldberg, S.C. (1989). Lithium in the treatment of borderline personality disorder. *Psychopharmacol. Bull.*, 25, 550–555.

Goldberg, S.C., Schulz, S.C., Schulz, P.M., Resnick, R.J., Hamer, R.M., and Friedel, R.O. (1986). Borderline and schizotypal personality disorders treated with low-dose thiothixene vs placebo. *Arch. Gen. Psychiatry*, 43, 680–686.

Gordon, C.T., Rapoport, J.L., Hamburger, S.D., State, R.C., and Mannheim, G.B. (1992). Differential response of seven subjects with autistic disorder to clomipramine and desipramine. *Am. J. Psychiatry*, 149, 363–366.

Green, A.R., and Grahame-Smith, D.S. (1975). 5-Hydroxytryptamine in CNS function. In: *Handbook of Psychopharmacology* (eds L.L. Iverson, S.D. Iverson, and S.H. Snyder) pp. 169–245. Plenum Press, New York.

Gunderson, J.G., Kolb, J.E., Austin, V. (1981). The diagnostic interview for borderline patients. *Am. J. Psychiatry*, 138, 896–903.

Hamdan-Allen, G. (1991). Brief report: Trichotillomania in an autistic male. *J. Autism Dev. Disord.*, 21, 79–82.

Hamilton, M. (1959). A psychiatric rating scale for anxiety. *Br. J. Med. Psychol.*, 32, 50–55.

Hamilton, M. (1960). A psychiatric rating scale for depression. *J. Neurol. Neurosurg. Psychiatry*, 23, 56–62.

Hanzel, D.A., Proia, N.C., and Hudgel, D.W. (1991). Response of obstructive sleep apnea to fluoxetine and protriptyline. *Chest*, 100, 416–421.

Hawthorne, M.E., and Lacey, J.H. (1992). Severe disturbance occurring during treatment for depression of a bulimic patient with fluoxetine. *J. Affect. Disord.*, 26, 205–208.

Hedberg, D.L., Houck, J.H., and Glueck, B.C. (1971). Tranylcypromine-trifluoperazine combination in the treatment of schizophrenia. *Am. J. Psychiatry*, 127, 1141–1146.

Hendricks, B., Van Moffaert, M., Spiers, R., et al. (1991). The treatment of psychocutaneous disorders: A new approach. *Curr. Ther. Res.*, 49, 111–119.

Hirschfeld, R.M.A., Klerman, G.L., Clayton, P.J., Keller, M.B., McDonald-Scott, M.A., and Larkin, B.H. (1983). Assessing personality: Effects of the depressive state on trait assessment. *Am. J. Psychiatry*, 140, 695–699.

Hirschfeld, R.M.A., Klerman, G.L., Lavori, P., Keller, M.B., Griffith, P., and Coryell, W. (1989). Premorbid personality assessments of first onset of major depression. *Arch. Gen. Psychiatry*, 46, 345–350.

Hudson, J.I., and Pope, H.G. (1990). Affective spectrum disorder: Does antidepressant response identify a family of disorders with a common pathophysiology? *Am. J. Psychiatry*, 147, 552–564.

Jaselskis, C.A., Cook, E.H., Fletcher, K.E., and Leventhal, B.L. (1992). Clonidine treatment of hyperactive and impulsive children with autistic disorder. *J. Clin. Psychopharmacol.* 12, 322–327.

Jenkins, S.C., and Maruta, T. (1987). Therapeutic use of propanolol for intermittent explosive disorder. *Mayo. Clin. Proc.*, 62, 204–214.

Joffe, R.T., and Regan, J.J. (1988). Personality and depression. *J. Psychiatr. Res.*, 22, 279–286.

Jonas, A.D. (1967). The diagnostic and therapeutic use of diphenyl-hydantoin in the subictal state and non-epileptic dysphoria. *Int. J. Neuropsychiatry*, 3 (suppl.), 21–29.

Kafka, M.P. (1991). Successful treatment of paraphilic coercive disorder (a rapist) with fluoxetine hydrochloride. *Br. J. Psychiatry*, 158, 844–847.

Kafka, M.P., and Prentky, R. (1992). Fluoxetine treatment of nonparaphilic sexual addictions and paraphilias in men. *J. Clin. Psychiatry*, 53, 351–358.

Kahn, R.S., and van Praag, H.M. (1988). A serotonin hypothesis of panic disorder. *Hum. Psychopharmacol.*, 3, 285–288.

King, R.A., Riddle, M.A., Chappell, P.B., et al. (1991). Emergence of self-destructive phenomena in children and adolescents during fluoxetine treatment. *J. Am. Acad. Child Adolesc. Psychiatry*, 30, 179–186.

Klein, D.F. (1967). Importance of psychiatric diagnosis in prediction of clinical drug effects. *Arch. Gen. Psychiatry*, 16, 118–126.

Klein, D.F. (1968). Psychiatric diagnosis and a typology of clinical drug effects. *Psychopharmacologia*, 13, 359–386.

Kruesi, M.J.P., Fine, S., Valladares, L., Phillips, R.A., and Rapoport, J.L. (1992). Paraphilias: A double blind crossover comparison of clomipramine versus desipramine. *Arch. Sex. Behav.*, 21, 587–593.

Leone, F.N. (1982). Response of borderline patients to loxapine and chlorpromazine. *J. Clin. Psychiatry*, 43, 148–150.

Liebowitz, M.R., and Klein, D.F. (1981). Interrelationship of hysteroid dysphoria and borderline personality disorder. *Psychiatr. Clin. North Am.*, 4, 67–87.

Liebowitz, M.R., Stallone, F., Dunner, D.L., and Fieve, R.H. (1979). Personality features of patients with primary affective disorders. *Acta Psychiatr. Scand.*, 60, 214–224.

Liebowitz, M.R., Quitkin, F.M., Stewart, J.W., et al. (1988). Antidepressant efficacy in atypical depression. *Arch. Gen. Psychiatry*, 45, 129–137.

Linnoila, M., Virkkunen, M., Scheinin, M., Nuutila, A., Rimon, R., and Goodwin, F.K. (1983). Low cerebrospinal fluid 5-hydroxyindoleacetic acid concentration differentiates impulsive from nonimpulsive behavior. *Life Sci.*, 33, 2609–2614.

Lipman, R.S., Covi, L., and Shapiro, A.K. (1979). The Hopkins symptom checklist (HSCL). *J. Affect. Disord.*, 1, 9–24.

Lorefice, L.S. (1991). Fluoxetine treatment of a fetish [letter]. *J. Clin. Psychiatry*, 52, 41.

Luchins, D.J. (1983). Carbamazepine for the violent psychiatric patient. *Lancet*, i, 766.

McDougle, C.J., Price, L.H., and Goodman, W.K. (1990). Fluvoxamine treatment of coincident autistic disorder and obsessive–compulsive disorder: a case report. *J. Autism Dev. Disord.*, 20, 537–543.

Markovitz, P.J., Calabrese, J.R., Schulz, S.C., and Meltzer, H.Y. (1991a). Fluoxetine in borderline and schizotypal personality disorder. *Am. J. Psychiatry*, 148, 1064–1067.

Markovitz, P.J., Calabrese, J.R., Schulz, S.C., Wagner, S., Trevidi, C., and Meltzer, H.Y. (1991b). Presented at the New Clinical Drug Evaluation Meeting, Key Biscayne, Florida.

Markowitz, P.I. (1990). Fluoxetine treatment of self-injurious behavior in the mentally retarded [letter]. *J. Clin. Psychopharmacol.*, 10, 299–300.

Markowitz, P.I. (1992). Effect of fluoxetine on self-injurious behavior in the developmentally disabled: A preliminary study. *J. Clin. Psychopharmacol.*, 12, 27–31.

Marttunen, M.J., Aro, H.M., Henrikson, M.M., and Lonnqvist, J.K. (1991). Mental disorders in adolescent suicide: DSM-III-R axes I and II diagnoses in suicides among 13- to 19-year-olds in Finland. *Arch. Gen. Psychiatry*, 48, 834–839.

Matson, J.L. (1982). Treatment of obsessive–compulsive behavior in mentally retarded adults. *Behav. Modif.*, 6, 551–567.

Mattes, J.A. (1984). Carbamazepine for uncontrolled rage outbursts. *Lancet*, ii, 1164–1165.

Mattes, J.A. (1986). Psychopharmacology of temper outbursts, a review. *J. Nervous and Ment. Disorders*, 174, 464–470.

Mattes, J.A., Rosenberg, J., and Mays, D. (1984). Carbamazepine versus propranolol in patients with uncontrolled rage outbursts: A random assignment study. *Psychopharmacol. Bull.*, 20, 98–100.

Mehlinger, R., Scheftner, W.A., and Pozanski, E. (1990). Fluoxetine and autism. *J. Am. Acad. Child Adolesc. Psychiatry*, 29, 985.

Moldofsky, H. (1982). Rheumatic pain modulation syndrome: The interrelationships between sleep, central nervous system serotonin, and pain. *Adv. Neurol.*, 33, 51–57.

Moldofsky, H. (1989). Sleep and fibrositis syndrome. *Rheum. Dis. Clin. North Am.*, 15, 91–103.

Monroe, R.R. (1975). Anticonvulsants in the treatment of aggression. *J. Nerv. Ment. Dis.*, 160, 119–126.

Neppe, V.M. (1982). Carbamazepine in the psychiatric patient. *Lancet*, ii, 334.

Norden, M.J. (1989). Fluoxetine in borderline personality disorder. *Prog. Neuropsychopharmacol. Biol. Psychiatry*, 13, 885–893.

Parsons, B., Quitkin, F.M., McGrath, P.J., et al. (1989). Phenelzine, impipramine, and placebo in borderline patients meeting criteria for atypical depression. *Psychopharmacol. Bull.*, 25, 524–534.

Perilstein, R.D., Lipper, S., and Friedman, L.J. (1991). Three cases of paraphilias responsive to fluoxetine treatment. *J. Clin. Psychiatry*, 52, 169–170.

Quitkin, F.M., Stewart, J., McGrath, P.J., et al. (1988). Phenelzine versus imipramine in the treatment of probable atypical depression: Defining syndrome boundaries of selective MAOI responders. *Am. J. Psychiatry*, 145, 306–311.

Quitkin, F.M., McGrath, P.J., Stewart, J.W., et al. (1990). Atypical depression, panic attacks, and response to imipramine and phenelzine: Replication. *Arch. Gen. Psychiatry*, 47, 935–941.

Rapkin, A.J., Edelmuth, E., Chang, L.C., Reading, A.E., McGuire, M.T., and Su, T.P. (1987). Whole-blood serotonin in premenstrual syndrome. *Obstet. Gynecol.*, 70, 533–537.

Reich, J., Noyes, R., Coryell, W., and O'Gorman, T.W. (1986). The effect of state anxiety on personality measurement. *Am. J. Psychiatry*, 143, 760–763.

Rickels, K., Freeman, E.W., Sondheimer, S., et al. (1990). Fluoxetine in the treatment of premenstrual syndrome. *Curr. Ther. Res. Clin. Exp.*, 48, 161–166.

Rifkin, A., Levitan, S.J., Galewski, J., and Klein, D.F. (1972a). Emotionally unstable character disorder—A follow-up study. Description of patients and outcome. *Biol. Psychiatry*, 4, 65–79.

Rifkin, A., Quitkin, F., Carrillo, C., Blumberg, A.G., and Klein, D.F. (1972b). Lithium carbonate in emotionally unstable character disorder. *Arch. Gen. Psychiatry*, 27, 519–523.

Roy, A., Virrkunen, M., Guthrie, S., and Linnoila, M. (1986). Indices of serotonin and glucose metabolism in violent offenders, arsonists, and alcoholics. *Ann. N. Y. Acad. Sci.*, 487, 202–220.

Russell, I.J., Michalek, J.E., Vipraio, G.A., Fletcher, E.M., and Wall, K. (1989). Serum amino acids in fibrositis/fibromyalgia syndrome. *J. Rheumatol.*, 19 (suppl.), 158–163.

Russell, I.J., Michalek, J.E., Vipraio, G.A., Fletcher, E.M., Javors, M.A., and Bowden, C.A. (1992). Platelet tritiated imipramine uptake receptor density and serum serotonin levels in patients with fibromyalgia/fibrositis syndrome. *J. Rheumatol.*, 19, 104–109.

Schmidt, M.J., Fuller, R.W., and Wong, D.T. (1988). Fluoxetine, a highly selective serotonin reuptake inhibitor; a review of preclinical studies. *Br. J. Psychiatry*, 153 (suppl. 3), 40–46.

Serban, G., and Siegel, S. (1984). Response of borderline and schizotypal patients to small doses of thiothixene and haloperidol. *Am. J. Psychiatry*, 141, 1455–1458.

Shea, M.T., Pilkonis, P.A., Beckham, E., et al. (1991). Personality disorders and treatment outcome in the NIMH Treatment of Depression Collaborative Research Program. *Am. J. Psychiatry*, 147, 711–718.

Sheard, M.H., Marini, J.L., Bridges, C.L., and Wagner, E. (1976). The effect of lithium on impulsive aggressive behavior in man. *Am. J. Psychiatry*, 133, 1409–1413.

Simpson, S.G., and DePaulo, J.R. (1991). Fluoxetine treatment of bipolar II depression. *J. Clin. Psychopharmacol.*, 11, 52–54.

Soloff, P.H., George, A., Nathan, S., Schulz, P.M., Ulrich, R.F., and Perel, J. (1986a). Progress in pharmacotherapy of borderline disorders. *Arch. Gen. Psychiatry*, 43, 691–697.

Soloff, P.H., George, A., Nathan, R.S., Schulz, P.M., and Perel, J.M. (1986b). Paradoxical effects of amitriptyline on borderline patients. *Am. J. Psychiatry*, 143, 1603–1605.

Spitzer, R.L., Gibbon, M., and Endicott, J. (1976). The global assessment scale: A procedure for measuring overall severity of psychiatric disturbance. *Arch. Gen. Psychiatry*, 33, 766–771.

Spitzer, R.L., Williams, J.B.W., Gibbon, M., and First, M.B. (1990). *Structured Clinical Interview for DSM-III-R Personality Disorders*. American Psychiatric Press, Washington, D.C.

Stein, D.J., Hollander, E., Anthony, D.T., et al. (1992). Serotonergic medications for sexual obsessions, sexual addictions, and paraphilias. *J. Clin. Psychiatry*, 53, 267–271.

Stephens, J.H., and Shaffer, J.W. (1970). A controlled study of the effects of diphenylhydantoin on anxiety, irritability, and anger in neurotic outpatients. *Psychopharmacologia (Berl.)*, 17, 169–181.

Stone, A.B., Pearlstein, T.B., and Brown, W.A. (1990). Fluoxetine in the treatment of premenstrual syndrome. *Psychopharmacol. Bull.*, 26, 331–335.

Talley, N.J. (1992). 5-Hydroxytryptamine agonists and antagonists in the modulation of gastrointestinal motility and sensation: Clinical implications. *Aliment. Pharmacol. Ther.*, 6, 273–289.

Taylor, D.L., Mathew, R.J., Ho, B.T., and Weinman, M.L. (1984). Serotonin levels and platelet uptake during premenstrual tension. *Neuropsychobiology*, 12, 16–18.

Teicher, M.H., Glod, C., and Cole, J.O. (1990). Emergence of intense suicidal preoccupation during fluoxetine treatment. *Am. J. Psychiatry*, 147, 207–210.

Todd, R.D. (1991). Fluoxetine in autism. *Am. J. Psychiatry*, 148, 1089.

Tupin, J.P., Smith, D.B., Clanon, T.L., Kim, L.I., Nugent, A., and Groupe, A. (1973). The long-term use of lithium in aggressive prisoners. *Compr. Psychiatry*, 14, 311–317.

van Praag, H.M., and Korf, J. (1971). Endogenous depressions with and without disturbances in the 5-hydroxytryptamine metabolism: A biochemical classification. *Psychopharmacology*, 19, 148–152.

van Praag, H.M., Plutchik, R., and Conte, H. (1986). The serotonin hypothesis of (auto)aggression. *Ann. N. Y. Acad. Sci.*, 487, 150–167.

van Praag, H.M., Kahn, R.S., Asnis, G.M., et al. (1987). Denosologation of biological psychiatry or the specificity of 5-HT disturbances in psychiatric disorders. *J. Affect. Disord.*, 13, 1–8.

van Scheyen, J.D., and van Kammen, D.P. (1979). Clomipramine-induced mania in unipolar depression. *Arch. Gen. Psychiatry*, 36, 560–565.

Veeninga, A.T., Westenberg, H.G., and Wesuten, J.T. (1990). Fluvoxamine in the treatment of menstrualy related mood disorders. *Psychopharmacology*, 102, 414–416.

Vilkin, M.I. (1972). Comparative chemotherapeutic trial in treatment of chronic borderline patients. *Am. J. Psychiatry*, 120, 1004.

Virkkunen, M., DeJong, J., Bartko, J., and Linnoila, M. (1989). Psychobiological concomitants of history of suicide attempts among violent offenders and impulsive fire setters. *Arch. Gen. Psychiatry*, 46, 604–608.

Williams, D.T., Mehl, R., Yudofsky, S., Adams, D., and Roseman, B. (1982). The effect of propranolol on uncontrolled rage outbursts in children and adolescents with organic brain dysfunction. *J. Am. Acad. Child Psychiatry*, 21, 129–135.

Woods, S.H., Mortola, J.F., Chan, Y.F., Moossazadeh, F., and Yen, S.S. (1992). Treatment of premenstrual syndrome with fluoxetine: A double-blind, placebo-controlled, crossover study. *Obstet. Gynecol.*, 80, 339–344.

Wurtman, J.J. (1990). Carbohydrate craving. Relationship between carbohydrate intake and disorders of mood. *Drugs*, 39 (suppl.), 49–52.

Yudofsky, S., Williams, D., and Gorman, J. (1981). Propranolol in the treatment of rage and violent behavior in patients with chronic brain syndromes. *Am. J. Psychiatry*, 138, 218–220.

Yunus, M.B., Dailey, J.W., Aldag, J.C., Masi, A.T., and Jobe, P.C. (1992). Plasma tryptophan and other amino acids in primary fibromyalgia: A controlled study. *J. Rheumatol.*, 19, 90–94.

Zohar, J., Mueller, E.A., Insel, T.R., Zohar-Kadouch, R.C., and Murphy, D.L. (1987). Serotonergic responsivity in obsessive–compulsive disorder: comparison of patients and healthy controls. *Arch. Gen. Psychiatry*, 44, 946–951.

17 Preclinical and Clinical Studies on the Role of 5-HT$_1$ Receptors in Aggression

MARIANNE MAK*, PAUL DE KONING*, JAN MOS‡, AND BEREND OLIVIER‡§

*Clinical Research Department, Solvay Duphar BV, Weesp, The Netherlands

‡CNS Pharmacology, Solvay Duphar BV, Weesp, The Netherlands

§Psychopharmacology Department, Faculty of Pharmacy, University of Utrecht, Utrecht, The Netherlands

INTRODUCTION

This chapter deals specifically with a serotonergic compound, eltoprazine, and how this drug has been developed and tested clinically. However, this topic will be treated in the wider perspective of the role of serotonin (5-hydroxytryptamine, 5-HT) agonists and antagonists in aggression. First we will present the preclinical data and subsequently the clinical strategy to test and evaluate the potential usefulness of a new psychotropic drug in aggressive patients. In the final section the approach will be evaluated and the relationship between preclinical and clinical data will be discussed.

DEFINITION OF PATHOLOGICAL AGGRESSION

For the development of psychoactive drugs aimed at specifically suppressing aggression, some kind of definition of pathological aggression is needed. What are the essential features of pathological aggression in man? Despite many studies of aggression, both preclinical and clinical, this area of pathological aggression is in desperate need of clear definitions and an overall theory that can be tested and verified. Pathological aggression is not a DSM-III-R disorder with known criteria. A satisfactory knowledge of underlying biological factors is not the starting point for rational research, either preclinical or clinical. Thus, a discussion about the nature and characteristics of pathological aggression is needed before successful attempts can be made to develop animal models and new treatment strategies. It will be clear from the foregoing that the lack of clear definitions of

Impulsivity and Aggression. Edited by E. Hollander and D.J. Stein
© 1995 John Wiley & Sons Ltd

pathological aggression puts considerable limitations on the use of animal models.

The multitude of definitions of "normal" aggression (Moyer, 1968) underlines the complexity of this set of behaviors. Aggression serves many purposes, which, in animals at least, do not necessarily have negative connotations. The variety of situations in which aggression may occur and the differences between species do not make animal studies the primary candidate to reveal definitions concerning *pathological* aggression. The same applies to the concept of impulsivity, which can at best be defined operationally in animals. However, the study of the biology of aggression has revealed some basic characteristics that are shared in many situations. These characteristics may be a useful starting point to consider factors determining aggression in humans. Aggression in animals often occurs in situations of competition. The competition may center around many different items. Huntingford and Turner (1987) mention the immediate biological needs for food, shelter, nesting place, mate, etc. These are usually so obvious that the area of conflict is generally well defined. In human situations it is important to have a clear vision of the area of conflict. Conflict in itself may be unavoidable, but the ways to handle the conflict may vary. Conflict and aggression also include risks like being hurt and losing, so careful judgment of when and how to fight is needed. The functionality of aggression is largely determined by this balance and the subsequent investment in fighting or retreat.

The context in which aggression takes place is an important variable. The perception of threat, the area of conflict, and the ways to resolve the conflict determines the eventual occurrence of aggressive behavior. Moreover, the intensity of aggression, in terms of both the frequency of aggressive acts and the character of the behavior, is of importance. Although this does not immediately lead to a well-established definition of pathological aggression, these variables should be studied carefully.

A faulty perception of the area of conflict may result in nonfunctional aggression. If there is no genuine area of conflict, there is no need for aggression. In many psychiatric patients, perception of reality may not be very accurate and leads to aggression in situations that would not precipitate aggression in people who do not experience "inappropriate" threat. The ways to resolve potential areas of conflict may also determine the functionality of aggression. For example, an impulsive reaction could interfere with more effective, nonaggressive interventions in which both parties run less risks of being damaged. However, perception is quite difficult to measure, in contrast to the intensity of aggression, which is easier to record and is more objective. The complete scoring of aggressive behavior is often possible in laboratory studies of attacks, and scales for human aggression have been developed and are used to quantify the intensity of aggressive responses, for example the Overt Aggression Scale (OAS) of Yudofsky et al. (1986).

Without suggesting that the foregoing is an exhaustive treatment of the subject of defining pathological aggression, it can be concluded that to define the limits of adaptive and maladaptive aggression by simply looking at the characteristics of aggression in humans and animals is not an easy task. The problems are even greater in reality, because comorbidity often distorts the evaluation of adaptive behaviors in humans. If we admit these limitations in the definition of pathological aggression, what can we do with animal models for the study of aggression? How can they be used to test new drugs and how do they relate to the (pathological) human aggression problem?

ANIMAL MODELS

Because human pathological aggression is ill defined, it is impossible to "construct" animal models which are theoretically convincing and have adequate face validity for the behavioral problems in humans. One has to rely on animal models that have sufficient biologically or pharmacologically relevant characteristics. Originally, aggression models were quite artificial. Gradually, emphasis was given to more naturalistic models, as excellently summarized by Miczek (1987), who reviewed the history of animal models in the psychopharmacology of aggression. It is especially in the field of aggression research that ethopharmacological approaches have been of great benefit in the understanding of the neuropharmacology of aggression. Although the ethopharmacological approach has many attractive and convincing advantages, it should be noted that animal models in which aggression is induced by less naturalistic conditions also have their advantages. In a sense, their lack of appropriate contextual relevance could turn into an advantage, because pathological aggression could well appear outside the normal context.

During the development of more naturalistic aggression models, an important distinction arose: the differentiation between offensive and defensive aggressive behavior (Adams, 1979). While offensive agonistic behavior is characterized by the initiative of the aggressor and damage to the opponent (Blanchard et al., 1977a,b; Mos et al., 1984), defensive behavior, in contrast, lacks active approach (initiative) and no wounds (or incidental ones only) are inflicted by the defensive animal. Several models focus (although not exclusively) upon the "offensive" components of agonistic interactions. Other models reflect the more defensive aspects of agonistic behavior. We have used both types of models and the main characteristics have been described elsewhere (Olivier et al., 1990).

Thus, we have chosen to study drug effects in what can be considered as normal, functional aggression models. There is no compelling evidence that what we measure in these models is pathological aggression, even though our experimental set up contains artificial elements. An evolutionary evaluation of the adaptive value of the behavior in these models is also impossible. However, the models can be considered as situations that permit the study of animal behavior in well-known and ethologically understood settings. In these paradigms, the effects of drugs not only on aggressive acts but also on nonaggressive behaviors are studied. In this way, the specificity of anti-aggressive effects can be evaluated by comparing the effects with different behaviors occurring under the same conditions.

A final remark on the use of these models is that they often contain many elements of territoriality. Malmberg (1980) is one of the few authors who has studied territoriality in humans. He has convincingly shown the importance of the concept of territoriality for humans. The aspect of territoriality and pathological aggression deserves more careful study in humans than it has received so far.

PHARMACOLOGICAL DATA

Eltoprazine is a phenylpiperazine derivative (Figure 1) that has remarkable anti-aggressive properties in animal models. It was discovered during research aimed at finding compounds that specifically reduce aggression. A more elaborate description of its pharmacological properties is found elsewhere (Olivier et al., 1990; Schipper et al., 1990). It proved to be a serotonergic agonist and it is of interest to compare the anti-aggressive actions of other 5-HT agonists and antagonists in more detail. Isolation-induced aggression in mice is a suitable model to test many compounds for their intrinsic anti-aggressive activities, although in this model only the suppression of aggression is recorded, which need not be specific but may be caused by sedation as well. Table 1 summarizes for a number of serotonergic compounds the median effective doses (ED_{50}) required to suppress aggression in isolated male mice.

It is clear that 5-HT$_1$ agonists are the most powerful compounds suppressing aggression in this model, the most effective ones being the mixed 5-HT$_1$ agonists. Selective 5-HT$_{1A}$ agonists marginally suppressed isolation-induced aggression, but it should be realized that in this model the mice are very experienced fighters with high levels of aggression. When aggression levels

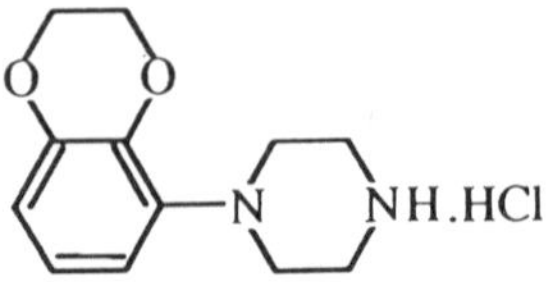

Figure 1   Eltoprazine hydrochloride.

Table 1 Median effective doses (ED$_{50}$) required to suppress aggression in isolated male mice

Compound*†	Effect on receptor	ED$_{50}$ (mg/kg)
Eltoprazine	1A/1B agonist (part)	0.3
TFMPP	1B/1C agonist (part)	1.0
RU24969	1A/1B agonist	0.7
8-OH-DPAT	1A agonist	> 21
Flesinoxan	1A agonist	1.1
Buspirone	1A agonist (part)	> 20
Ipsapirone	1A agonist (part)	> 20
DOI	2/1C agonist	> 10
Ketanserin	2 antagonist	3.2
Ritanserin	2/1C antagonist	4.4
Ondansetron	3 antagonist	> 4.6

*Administered p.o.
†Abbreviations: DOI, 1-(2,5-dimethoxy-4-iodophenyl)-2-aminopropane; 8-OH-DPAT, 8-hydroxy-2-(dipropylamino) tetralin; TFMPP, 1-[3-(trifluoromethyl) phenyl] piperazine.

are lower (see below), 5-HT$_{1A}$ agonists do reduce aggression. Sánchez et al. (1993) reported similar data for 5-HT$_1$ agonists in a recent paper, although 5-HT$_{1A}$ agonists were more potent in reducing aggression in their experiments. The 5-HT$_{2/1C}$ agonist 1-(2,5-dimethoxy-4-iodophenyl)-2-aminopropane (DOI) did not suppress aggression, whereas the 5-HT$_2$ and 5-HT$_{1C}$ antagonists ritanserin and ketanserin did suppress aggression, albeit it at higher doses. The 5-HT$_3$ antagonist ondansetron had no effect on isolation-induced aggression over a wide dose range.

In more ethologically based models of aggression in mice, we scored aggression as well as other behaviors displayed by mice in an aggression test (Olivier et al., 1989). Briefly, isolated mice are placed into a neutral test arena, where they fight a standard, group-housed opponent; mice then display intermediate levels of aggression. We showed that in this model it was difficult to differentiate selective 5-HT$_{1A}$ agonists from mixed 5-HT$_1$ agonists with regard to their specificity to reduce aggression. Although 5-HT$_{1A}$ agonists were slightly less specific in reducing aggression than mixed 5-HT$_1$ agonists, they were not as sedative as were, for example, neuroleptics (see Figure 2).

In contrast to mice, the suppressive effects of eltoprazine on rat aggression were far more specific than those of 5-HT$_{1A}$ receptor agonists. These compounds did reduce aggression, but at the expense of exploration, social interest, and an increase in inactivity. Mos et al. (1992a) have published the data for a wide range of different 5-HT$_1$ agonists in male and female rats. The model for aggression in male rats is the so-called resident–intruder paradigm, in which male rats defend a territory against an intruder-rat. The hormonal and situational factors governing male territorial aggression are

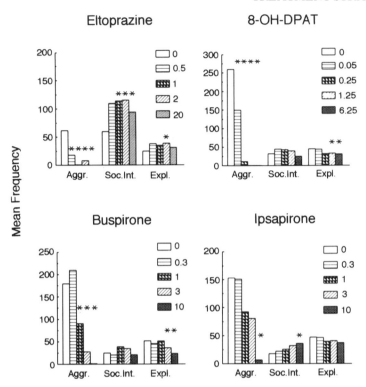

Figure 2 Effects of eltoprazine, a mixed 5-HT$_1$ agonist, and three 5-HT$_{1A}$ agonists on the behavior of male mice during an aggression test. The doses of the drugs used (mg/kg) are depicted in each figure. The main behavioral categories aggression (Aggr.), social interest (Soc.Int.), and exploration (Expl.) are expressed as frequencies of occurrence in a ten minute test ($*p < 0.05$, $**p < 0.01$, $***p < 0.001$, $****p < 0.0001$ against vehicle).

different from those governing aggression by female rats during the first postpartum weeks. Despite these profound differences, the effects of serotonergic compounds are quite similar in both models for aggression. An example for eltoprazine and buspirone is given in Figure 3. These data show that, in rats, eltoprazine is a far more specific suppressant of aggression than buspirone. The relative role of 5-HT$_{1A}$ and 5-HT$_{1B}$ receptors in the regulation of aggression will be dealt in more detail in the next section of this chapter. The important role for 5-HT$_1$ agonists is underlined by the lack of efficacy of many other serotonergic compounds in rat aggression models. The mixed 5-HT agonist quipazine only nonspecifically reduced aggression, and the 5-HT$_{1C/2}$ agonist DOI reduced aggression at the expense of an increased inactivity (Mos et al., 1992a). The specific 5-HT$_3$ antagonists ondansetron and MDL 72222 did not affect maternal aggression in lactating rats (Mos et al., 1990). Unpublished data on the 5-HT$_{2/1C}$ antagonist

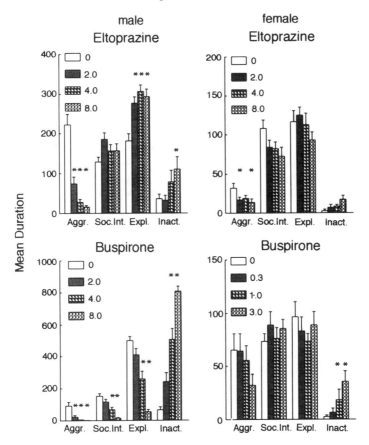

Figure 3 The effects of buspirone and eltoprazine on four behavioral categories are expressed as mean duration (seconds ± SEM). The doses of the drugs used (mg/kg) are depicted in each figure. The left column represents the data from resident–intruder aggression in male rats, the right column gives the data for maternal aggression by lactating female rats ($*p < 0.05$, $**p < 0.01$, $***p < 0.001$, $****p < 0.0001$ against vehicle). The behavioral categories are aggression (Aggr.), social interest (Soc.Int.), exploration (Expl.), and inactivity (Inact.).

ritanserine showed a lack of anti-aggressive actions for this compound. In summary, the most consistent as well as the most specific reduction of aggression in mice and rats is produced by 5-HT$_1$ agonists.

More restricted studies using neuroleptics as reference compounds showed the efficacy of eltoprazine in an aggression model in guinea pigs (unpublished data), in green vervet monkeys (M.T. McGuire et al., personal communication), and in pigs (Olivier et al., 1990). Only one study has been performed in pigs (unpublished data), in which eltoprazine and buspirone were directly compared. In the pig, a species which lacks the rodent 5-HT$_{1B}$

receptor but has the non-rodent homologue, the 5-HT$_{1D}$ receptor eltoprazine was an effective anti-aggressive compound. The same applied to buspirone which, in the pig, had a much more specific pattern of aggression reduction than in rats and mice.

In summary, in different animal species eltoprazine and other 5-HT$_1$ agonists had (specific) anti-aggressive effects, and these were much stronger and more consistent than the effects of most other serotonergic compounds tested. Data on 5-HT$_1$ antagonists are scarce. The nonspecific 5-HT$_1$ antagonist methysergide was ineffective in maternal aggression in rats. The 5-HT$_{1A}$ antagonists, like 1-(2-methoxyphenol)-4-(4-(2-phthalamido)butyl)-piperazine HBr (NAN-190), did reduce aggression (Sánchez et al., 1993), but there is also some evidence that NAN can exert (partial) agonistic activity. Our own preliminary data on more selective 5-HT$_{1A}$ antagonists do not indicate a major role for them in aggression in rodents.

MECHANISM OF ACTION

An important aspect of the regulation of aggression by serotonergic compounds is the precise mechanism of action. First it should be emphasized that some compounds are full agonists, i.e. they have the same intrinsic activity as the natural ligand. Independent of the tone of a given system, such compounds will mimic (part of) the action of the natural transmitter and this may result in a more activated system. Partial agonists, like buspirone and eltoprazine, have a lower intrinsic activity than the natural ligand. Thus, the functional effects may be less strong. If a system has a high tone, then administration of these compounds may reduce the output of the system because competition at the receptor site replaces the full agonist with a ligand exerting weaker effects. Thus, under certain conditions, partial agonists may act as antagonists. Under other conditions, however, partial agonists may act as full agonists. Such a situation is thought to apply to somatodendritic 5-HT$_{1A}$ autoreceptors in the raphe nuclei, where partial agonists act as full agonists. A comprehensive summary shows that the mechanism of action of serotonergic anti-aggressive compounds is quite complicated, and we do not know how to translate animal data to the human situation, i.e. it is unknown whether partial agonists act mainly as agonist or exert more antagonistic functions.

The studies aimed at uravelling this issue will be briefly summarized. Eltoprazine is a mixed 5-HT$_{1A/1B/1D}$ agonist and a (weak) antagonist at the 5-HT$_{1C}$ receptor. It is thus important to investigate which activity is responsible for the anti-aggressive activity. For eventual extrapolation to the human situation, the issue of 5-HT$_{1B}$ receptor affinity deserves special attention because this receptor is not present in human brain tissue, although a very homologous receptor, 5-HT$_{1D\beta}$, has been described. The

5-HT$_{1A}$ receptor is localized on postsynaptic neurons in the projection areas of the 5-HT system emanating from the raphe nuclei. The same receptor is also present at the cell bodies and dendrites of the serotonergic neurons in the raphe. Here it acts to reduce 5-HT cell firing, i.e. it reduces serotonergic neurotransmission. As well as occurring presynaptically, 5-HT$_{1B}$ receptors occur postsynaptically, where they act as autoreceptors and reduce 5-HT release from the nerve terminal. Lesions of the 5-HT cell bodies in the dorsal raphe of male rats, induced by the neurotoxin 5,7-dihyroxytryptamine (5,7-DHT) reduce the serotonergic innervation to many different brain areas. These lesions abolish not only almost all somatodendritic 5-HT$_{1A}$ autoreceptors but also most 5-HT$_{1B}$ presynaptic autoreceptors (Sijbesma et al., 1991). After such lesions, spontaneous resident–intruder aggression is only marginally affected, but eltoprazine still strongly and dose-dependently reduces aggression, even with a tendency to increased efficacy. These studies suggested important roles for postsynaptic 5-HT$_{1A}$ and/or 5-HT$_{1B}$ receptors in the modulation of aggression. Therefore another set of experiments was performed.

Mos et al. (1992b) injected eltoprazine or 8-hydroxy-2-(dipropylamino)tetralin (8-OH-DPAT; a prototypical potent and specific 5-HT$_{1A}$ agonist) into the lateral ventricle of male rats that were tested in a resident–intruder paradigm. Eltoprazine reduced aggression but 8-OH-DPAT did not, strongly suggesting that postsynaptic 5-HT$_{1A}$ receptors do not play a crucial role in the action of eltoprazine and perhaps play no role at all in the regulation of aggression. One of the mechanisms by which eltoprazine exerts its anti-aggressive action is thus by activation of postsynaptic 5-HT$_{1B}$ receptors. However, systemic administration of 8-OH-DPAT reduces aggression, albeit nonspecifically. Thus activation of 5-HT$_{1A}$ receptors directly or indirectly does affect aggression. A second series of experiments was performed in which 8-OH-DPAT was administered directly into the dorsal raphe (Mos et al., in press). This resulted in a nonspecific reduction of aggression, very much the same as after systemic administration. Similarly, administration of eltoprazine into the dorsal raphe led to a nonspecific reduction of aggression. Taken together, these data suggest that somatodendritic 5-HT$_{1A}$ autoreceptors on the one hand and postsynaptic 5-HT$_{1B}$ receptors on the other are involved in the control of aggression. This mechanism of action explains why eltoprazine is also an effective anti-aggressive compound in species without a 5-HT$_{1B}$ receptor, such as the pig. In these species, the most likely mechanism of action is via 5-HT$_{1A}$ receptors although the (weaker) agonistic effect of eltoprazine on the 5-HT$_{1D}$ receptor may contribute to the effect. Moreover, this may explain why in pigs the behavioral profiles of eltoprazine and buspirone are more alike than they are in the rat. In the rat, the 5-HT$_{1B}$ activity of eltoprazine adds considerably to the anti-aggressive efficacy, whereas buspirone presumably only acts by its (partial) agonistic activity at the 5-HT$_{1A}$ receptor. Whether the dopamine-D_2 (DA-D_2) antagonistic effects of buspirone interfere with buspirone's anti-aggressive effects is not clear.

Summarizing, the animal studies revealed that 5-HT_1 agonists, most notably the mixed 5-$HT_{1A/1B}$ agonists, are potent anti-aggressive compounds, at least in rodents. Studies on the mechanism of action support the role of both the 5-HT_{1A} and the 5-HT_{1B} receptor in reducing aggression in rodents. Studies of aggression in higher species also suggest anti-aggressive effects of eltoprazine, but these studies have so far been less detailed and extensive. Moreover, the difficulties in extrapolating from animal studies to human pathological aggression has been noted (Eichelman, 1992).

CLINICAL DATA

A search through the literature on the use of 5-HT agonists and antagonists in the treatment of aggressive behavior gives a limited and disappointing picture of the experience in the field. The articles and congress abstracts report clinical data on buspirone and eltoprazine only as representatives of 5-HT_1 agonists. No published data are available on other 5-HT_1 agonists, or on 5-HT_2 and 5-HT_3 antagonists in clinical aggression. From patent application lists, pharmacology papers and informal sources the impression arises that some clinical work has been performed with other 5-HT agonists or antagonists, but lack of formal publications prevents conclusions on such attempts. Results of other compounds acting on the 5-HT system (e.g. reuptake inhibitors) are reported in other chapters, hence this section will only deal with published buspirone data and on hitherto mainly unpublished clinical data from eltoprazine studies.

The rationale for the use of 5-HT_1 agonists has been explained in earlier chapters, and the first part of this chapter summarizes the preclinical pharmacological evidence of specific anti-aggressive effects observed with such compounds.

Studies using biological markers (Chapter 6) and challenge tests (Chapter 7) have clearly demonstrated a link between 5-HT and 5-HT receptors and (pathological) aggression. There is, however, no full agreement yet on the question as to whether the 5-HT–aggression link applies to aggressive behavior in general, to impulsivity, or to both (van Praag, 1991). Linnoila and Virkkunen (1992) heavily support a correlation between impulsivity and low 5-HT turnover in the brain. However, the criteria used to differentiate between impulsive and nonimpulsive aggressive offenders cannot be applied to different types of patients, for example demented elderly or severely mentally retarded.

Unfortunately our knowledge of the psychological aspects of aggression in individual patients is as yet inadequate for sorting patients into groups with similar abnormalities and testing different drugs according to their presumed main psychotropic activity on the different types of aggressive behavior, of which impulsive aggression is only one (De Koning and Mak, 1991).

BUSPIRONE

Since 1988 a number of case studies and a few uncontrolled or baseline controlled systematic studies in limited series of patients have been published. The published data apply to brain trauma (Levine, 1988; Gualtieri, 1991), dementia (Tiller, 1988; Yudofsky et al., 1990; Levy, 1992), mental retardation (Ratey et al., 1989, 1991; Ratey and O'Driscoll, 1989), children (Realmuto et al., 1989; Quiason et al., 1991), and attention deficit hyperactivity disorder in adults (Balon, 1990).

Critical inspection of the reported data reveals only scant information on aggressive behaviors. Agitation, akathisia, autistic symptoms, anxiety, or depression are often described as the major symptoms or syndromes to improve after buspirone. The instruments used to measure the aggressive behavior are rarely mentioned.

The use of buspirone in the relevant series of patients will be briefly summarized. Gualtieri (1991) reports on the use of buspirone in 13 mildly brain-injured patients with behavioral and emotional sequelae. Positive results were observed in two clusters of patients: three patients with extreme dysphoria and restlessness, and four patients with emotional lability, irritability induced by a depression, and angry outbursts related to temporal lobe lesions. The status of the patients was measured with a Neurobehavioral Rating Scale of 28 items. The dose in five out of the seven responders was low: 10–15 mg daily. The other six patients were failures; one did not respond and five discontinued buspirone due to adverse events.

Levy et al. (1992) performed a single-blind dose-escalation crossover study in 20 demented patients. These patients resided in the community and had behavioral problems. Treatment consisted of 2-week periods on different daily dosages of buspirone (15, 30, 45 and 60 mg). Results were measured using Reisberg's Brief Cognitive Rating Scale (BCRS) (1983) at the end of each dose-level period. Twelve patients completed the study. The dose of 30 mg buspirone was superior to baseline placebo on the behavior subscale of the BCRs in both the total score and subscales for aggression and anxiety.

Mentally retarded patients were extensively studied by Ratey and co-workers. Three series of patients were treated and the results published: a series of 14 mentally retarded patients who displayed anxiety and aggressive behaviors, another series of 14 retarded patients with dual diagnosis, and a variable placebo baseline dose-escalation study in six adult mentally retarded patients. In the first two studies positive changes were observed in nine out of 14 patients (64%), with improvements in a broad variety of symptoms related to hetero-aggressive and self-injurious behaviors. The results were interpreted as applicable to behaviors associated with hyper-arousal and anxiety (Ratey et al., 1989; Ratey and O'Driscoll, 1989).

In the third series a strict design was used, with a baseline period of variable length to reduce bias from the start of active medication (Ratey et al., 1991). During the subsequent treatment periods of 3 weeks each, step-up dose levels of 15, 30 and 45 mg were used, and at the end the dose was tapered off again over 2 weeks. Placebo was given over the remainder of the treatment period in the patients who started early on active medication. Aggression and anxiety were measured with the modified Overt Aggression scale and the Revised Conners Parent-Teacher Questionnaire (Conners, 1969). Cognitive effects of buspirone were also investigated. Six mildly to moderately demented patients who had at least one aggressive incident per week during the baseline period of 3 weeks were included in the study.

Aggression was decreased in five out of six patients, and the results seemed rapid and most favorable at the lower dose level of 15 mg daily, both at the beginning and during the taper-off phase. The effects on the Conners R scores were slower and better with the highest dose level of 45 mg daily. Only two out of six patients responded. During taper off a rebound in anxiety was noted. The effects on cognitive measures were not significant, but videotapes showed a reduction in agitation and excessive movements during buspirone treatment. Within the limitations of such a small study and in the absence of parallel placebo groups to control more rigorously for observer bias and for time effects, the results are interesting because they suggest a differential response of aggression and anxiety.

Although some of Ratey's adult patients had a co-diagnosis of pervasive developmental disorder, autistic children were the specific target group of Realmuto et al. (1989). They treated four children of 9 or 10 years old and compared the effects of buspirone 15 mg with those of methylphenidate 5–10 mg daily or fenfluramine 10–20 mg daily in 4-week periods separated by 1 week wash out. Extensive assessments were made weekly, including the Aberrant Behaviors Checklist, the Sensory Motor Behavior Checklist, the Social Awareness Inventory and the Conners Teacher's Questionnaire. Hyperactivity and aggression improved in two children on buspirone. Methylphenidate and fenfluramine had no effect or a negative effect on these problematic behaviors. The authors caution against generalization from these reports on short-term treatment and planned a double-blind study with buspirone in autistic adolescents.

The limited value of open and baseline-controlled studies will be further demonstrated by the results of double-blind placebo-controlled studies performed with eltoprazine.

Both (Ratey's and Realmoto's) groups of investigators were hesitant in their interpretation of the mechanism of action. Apart from possible involvement of the nonserotonergic effects of buspirone, for example dopamine antagonism, the agonistic action might enhance 5-HT function but also reduce activity, depending on the dose. Autism has been associated with increased 5-HT levels at least in whole blood, hence decreasing 5-HT activity may seem a logical therapeutic approach (Hanley et al., 1977; Chamberlain and Herman, 1990). Ratey et al., speculated that the low dose of buspirone, as found to be optimal in their aggressive patients, acts as an agonist and increases 5-HT function. However, as buspirone acts as a full agonist on 5-HT$_{1A}$ somatodendritic receptors and in this way shuts down 5-HT neurotransmission, decreased 5-HT function could be given as an alternative explanation for the anti-aggressive action.

ELTOPRAZINE

Models of aggression in volunteers

Models of aggression in volunteers have been promoted as tool for measuring the effects of 5-HT agonists in provoked human aggression under laboratory conditions (Bond, 1992). Although extrapolation of the results to patients with mental pathology and aggression remains a tremendous step, such models may bridge the even larger gap between animal models and patients in the clinic. Eltoprazine has been investigated in two models presumed to test aggressive behaviors in volunteers.

The first study employed a tentative model, proposed by O'Hanlon (Van Leeuwen et al., 1988). The provocative cue consisted of a movie showing a championship boxing match to young male volunteers interested in contact sports. As a control, a nature documentary was chosen, and to verify possible anxiolytic effects a horror movie was shown in the last session. The 48 volunteers were randomly distributed over four treatment groups, to receive eltoprazine 7 or 15 mg, diazepam 10 mg, or placebo. The neutral movie was shown during a baseline session, the aggression- and anxiety-provoking movies were presented at different sessions, always in that order.

The test battery was designed to measure psychomotor functions, mood and emotions (checklist and visual analog scale) and the Spielberger State/Trait Anxiety and Aggression inventories (Dutch versions; Van der Ploeg, 1980, 1982). Neuroendocrine arousal was measured by catecholamine excretions in urine, and sympathetic nervous system arousal was measured by electrodermal and electrocardiographic recordings. Diazepam, but not eltoprazine, induced the expected sedation in the objective psychometric assessments and subjective feelings. Eltoprazine only influenced the subjective experiences in comparison with placebo. Neither drug induced changes in feelings of aggression. With the lower dose of eltoprazine an increase in the Spielberger State Anxiety Score was found in comparison with placebo after the horror movie. Since the higher dose did not increase anxiety this may be a spurious finding. Norepinephrine and epinephrine (adrenaline) excretions were increased during the test sessions of active drug but not less so than with placebo. In the electrophysiological variables the only interesting finding was a decrease in skin conductance at both dose levels of eltoprazine. In total the results were disappointing.

It should be realized that in this model no actions were demanded, hence only changes in feeling, neuroendocrine, or electrophysiological variables could be detected. A drug that would primarily affect impulse control and block the aggressive acting out would not show efficacy in such a model. There may be other reasons, though, for the lack of results. In other centers movies were found inadequate as (eliciting) cues for aggression models (Professor P. Netter, personal communication).

The second study with eltoprazine, by D. Cherek (unpublished data), concerns a model developed and extensively validated by Cherek and co-workers (Cherek, 1981). The model employs a simple paradigm of two optional responses: a neutral one, to collect money, and an aggressive response to subtract money from a presumed competitor (in fact the computer). Psychometric tests were applied to test for selective effects. In sessions approximately 1 week apart, subjects were tested after a dose of placebo (baseline) and 5, 10, or 20 mg eltoprazine. Results showed a dose-related decrease in aggressive responses, but also in nonaggressive responses at doses of 10 and 20 mg. As the psychometric tests did not reveal sedation, the interpretation of the decrease in neutral responding remains difficult.

Pilot patient studies

We carried out initial studies with eltoprazine in several diagnostic groups with behavior disturbances: demented elderly patients, mentally retarded adults, chronic psychotic patients, and patients with a borderline personality disorder. These studies all followed a double-blind parallel-groups design with placebo run in. The active medication period lasted 3–4 weeks. Numbers of patients per study varied from 23 to 45, with a randomization of 2:1 or 3:1 in favor of eltoprazine. The primary aims of these studies were to verify safety and tolerance of eltoprazine alone or in combination with neuroleptics (the latter only in the psychotic and personality disordered patients).

Regular safety assessments, including laboratory tests, electrocardiograph (ECG) vital signs and neurological symptom checklists were performed in all studies.

The secondary aims of the pilot studies were to estimate adequate dose levels and explore methods of measuring aggressive behavior. The absence of good placebo-controlled, blind studies in clinical aggression forced us to build up experience in trial methodology along with studies concerning the possible therapeutic effects of eltoprazine.

As scales to measure aggression, an observer event scale—either the Staff Observation Aggression Scale (SOAS; Palmstierna and Wistedt, 1987) or the OAS (Yudofsky et al., 1986)—and a version of the Social Dysfunction and Aggression Scale (SDAS; Wistedt et al., 1990) were chosen. The Clinical Global Impression was used to estimate global changes (Guy, 1976). The safety and tolerance data from these pilot studies did not prevent further use of the dose levels tested. The study in psychotic patients, where combinations with neuroleptics were investigated, showed no negative influence of eltoprazine on the signs of dyskinesia. Withdrawal symptoms were rare.

In all studies, there were hints of therapeutic efficacy, particularly in the more severely aggressive patients. The largest study, of 45 psychotic and borderline patients, showed a statistically significant global improvement after 1 week (Table 2), suggesting an early onset of effect. No beneficial effect of any relevance was seen in the Brief Psychiatric Rating Scale (BPRS; Overall and Gorham, 1962). This suggested that the changes were mostly due to behavioral adaptations. The placebo-treated patients showed a more gradual improvement and at the end of the 3-week treatment period the groups were no longer significantly different.

This transient effect of eltoprazine could be due to initial sedation rather than actual serenic effects.

Further patient studies

In the second series of studies, we focused our attention on efficacy of eltoprazine in mentally retarded patients with hetero- or auto-aggressive behavior and, as second priority, on aggressive psychotic and personality disordered patients. The choice of mental retardation was primarily based on the medical need in this patient population. Another reason was a methodological one: aggressive mentally retarded patients usually remain institutionalized, which allows follow up under more or less stable conditions.

Mentally retarded patients

A large study was set up to measure effects in aggressive mentally retarded patients. A total of 19 centers spread over four European countries participated. The study followed a randomized parallel groups design with a 4-week baseline placebo followed by an 8-week double-blind period. After extensive screening, 205 patients with a diagnosis of mental retardation, some in combination with a pervasive developmental disorder, entered the baseline period. Of this cohort 160 patients who fulfilled further criteria were randomized to receive blind medication: 119 patients were assigned to

Table 2 Clinical Global Impression of change in chronic psychotic and borderline patients on eltoprazine (the basic regimen of neuroleptics was continued)

	Day 8		Day 15		Day 26	
Change	Eltoprazine (30 mg)	Placebo	Eltoprazine (30 or 40 mg)	Placebo	Post-eltoprazine	Placebo
Much improved	1	–	5	–	4	3
Minor improvement	10	–	8	3	11	2
No change	21	10	17	8	17	6
Minor worsening	1	1	3	–	–	–
Much worse	–	–	–	–	1	–
Total	33	11	33	11	33	11

the eltoprazine group and 41 to the placebo group. The dosage of eltopra-zine, after taper on, was 20 mg daily with an option to increase to 30 mg. At the end of the 8-week blind period the dose was tapered off. Three scales were used to measure aggression, the OAS, a 20-item version of the SDAS and a 0–10 point Global Aggression Scale (Bech, 1986). In addition, an overall clinical evaluation was determined at the end of the study. Six patients left the study prematurely.

When the total sample was analyzed, none of the major aggression variables showed a statistically significant difference between the groups. A decrease in scores of between 20 and 35% was observed between baseline and week 6, the last assessment on full-dose treatment in both groups. Of the separate symptoms in the SDAS, self-mutilation showed the most convincing improvement. The final clinical evaluation showed a surprising picture: 60% of patients in the eltoprazine group and 49% of the placebo-treated patients were reported to have displayed a significant improvement in behavior. Closer analyses revealed that the difference between the groups in favor of eltoprazine was due exclusively to the response rate in the severely aggressive patients, which was twice as high in that group as in the placebo group.

In the safety data, no unexpected or drug-related abnormalities were detected and tolerance was good. The data will be reported in detail elsewhere.

Psychotic and personality disordered patients

The relatively large pilot study of 45 patients in psychotic and borderline personality disordered patients had shown some early positive effects of eltoprazine, which was most evident in patients with a marked degree of aggressive behavior. The entry criteria for behavior were very loose in this study, hence a new study was set up, stratified for diagnosis and applying hard criteria of aggressive behavior, namely at least one episode of physical aggression during the 4-week baseline placebo period. In line with the study of mentally retarded patients, the double-blind period lasted 8 weeks, including taper on or off, with a maximum dose 40 mg daily. The set of aggression scales was the same as in the study of mentally retarded patients; to check for overall mental symptomatology the BPRS was added.

A total of 36 patients (mean age 34 years) entered the double-blind period, 18 chronic psychotic patients and 18 patients who had only a DSM-III-R Axis II diagnosis of antisocial or borderline personality disorder. Due to the unequal randomization, 23 patients received eltoprazine and 13 placebo. Three patients did not complete the study (two eltoprazine- and one placebo-treated).

Because of the small size of the study, statistically significant differences were hardly expected; indeed, we found no differences in the major efficacy parameters. There were, however, positive trends. Figure 4 shows the course of the total scores on the SDAS 20 items in the cohort of completers. Placebo responses were also considerable in this study. The scores of the Global Aggression Scale showed a decrease of 25% in the placebo group against 37% in the eltoprazine group. The OAS scores could not be evaluated. Periods of isolation due to behavioral problems had led to missing reports on essential days or weeks in the trial periods. The BPRS total scores differed markedly between the two strata of patients, as expected. Figure 5 shows the course of the BPRS scores in psychotic and personality disordered (mostly borderline) patients. There was a slight trend towards improvement during eltoprazine treatment in the psychotic patients.

There was no evidence of safety or tolerance problems. Withdrawal effects, increased anxiety, aggression, and nightmares were observed at taper off in one patient. With reinstitution of eltoprazine, these symptoms rapidly abated.

Long-term data were collected from patients in the two studies reported above, who responded well. Upon the investigators' request, patients entered a 6-month extension period because of deterioration when off medication after the original study. The treatment remained blind for the majority of patients in the extension treatment period. In addition, an open study was set up in the same categories of patients.

Compared with the first 8-week treatment period, re-entry (to the exten-

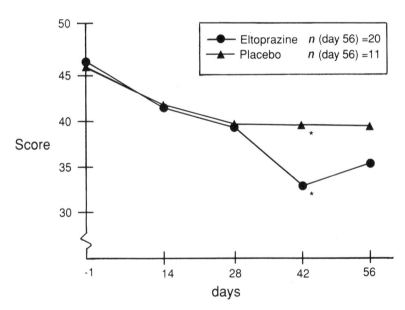

Figure 4 Mean Social Dysfunction and Aggression Scale 20-item total score in psychotic and personality disordered patients: comparison of eltoprazine with placebo.

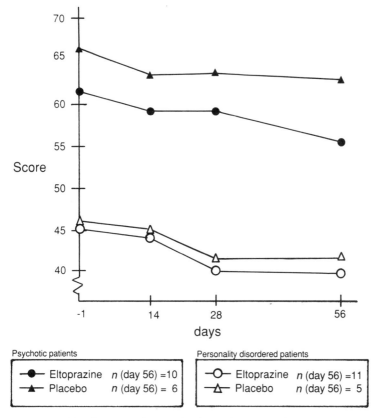

Figure 5 Mean BPRS scores in psychotic and personality disordered patients: comparison of eltoprazine with placebo.

sion study) produced in most patients similar responses in behavior, i.e. a slight trend in favor of eltoprazine. With continued treatment, however, placebo-treated patients fared at least as well as the eltoprazine group, and it was suspected that tolerance to eltoprazine developed. Similar experiences were reported by some, but not all, investigators in the open long-term study.

THE EFFICACY OF 5-HT$_1$ AGONISTS: FACT OR FICTION

The efficacy of 5-HT$_1$ agonists, with buspirone and eltoprazine as the best studied examples, has not been satisfactorily proven. This may be due to intrinsic lack of pharmacological effects on human aggressive behaviors. Alternatively, the matter of interspecies differences for some 5-HT receptors may play a role. Finally, the psychiatric patients may have abnormal receptor systems. It is clear that the preclinical data can not readily be translated to the human conditions of pathological aggressive behaviors.

Proof of specific anti-aggressive drug effects in patients is very hard to obtain. Heterogeneity of expression of behavior and basic pathology, the limited range of useful scales, strong placebo effects, multiple comedications, and problems in obtaining consent and Review Board approvals make the clinical aggression field a high-risk arena for any clinical investigator (and thus indirectly for the sponsoring industry as well). Recently, Eichelman (1992) has made a plea for more "individual-directed" research strategies in aggression and a more lenient attitude by the US Food and Drug Administration concerning proof of efficacy in aggressive behaviors. Taken together, the data from buspirone and eltoprazine studies yield questionable evidence of an improvement in impulse control. Improvements in aspects related to emotions and social behaviors may also play a role. This has been discussed by several investigators of buspirone and eltoprazine (Gualtieri, 1991; Realmuto et al., 1989; Verhoeven et al., 1992; Tiihonen et al., 1993).

The investigators of the larger series of patients treated with buspirone, Levy and Ratey, both report effects on aggressive behavior and anxiety (Levy et al., 1992; Ratey et al., 1991). In the study by Ratey et al., these effects seem to occur at a slightly different dose level and time schedule, the effect on aggressive behavior appearing earlier and at a lower dose (15 mg daily). Hence anxiolytic activity of 5-HT$_1$ agonists may not form the basis of possible anti-aggressive effects.

In the eltoprazine studies, positive effects on social attitude and communication were noted by several investigators (Verhoeven et al., 1992; Tiihonen et al., 1993; and unpublished data), leading to the suggestion that this drug might be useful in autistic patients. The hints of eltoprazine having different and more convincing effects on self-mutilation than on hetero-aggressive behavior, point to the need to separate auto- and hetero-aggressive behaviors in future studies of the effects of any compound on aggressive behaviors. Clear support is also given to this by the validation studies of the SDAS (Wistedt et al., 1990; European Aggression Rating Group, 1992).

Measurement of effects other than just pure reduction of the number of aggressive events per time unit is necessary to reveal the total spectrum of effects induced by a drug and to confirm the associations between symptoms of a psychiatric syndrome in individual patients for whom aggressive behavior may be only one of the intrinsic symptoms or may be a symptom of an incidental coexisting phenomenon.

ACKNOWLEDGMENTS

We thank Marijke Mulder for her dedicated secretarial support in preparing the manuscript.

REFERENCES

Adams, D.B. (1979). Brain mechanisms for offense, defense and submission. *Behav. Brain Sci.*, 2, 201–241.

Balon, R. (1990). Buspirone for attention deficit hyperactivity disorders. *J. Clin. Psychopharmacol.*, 10, 77.

Bech, P., Kastrup, M., and Rafaelson, O.J. (1986). Mini compendium of Rating Scales. *Acta Psychiatr. Scand.*, 73 (suppl. 326), 7–37.

Blanchard, R.J., Blanchard, D.C., Takahashi, T., and Kelley, M.J. (1977a). Attack and defensive behaviour in the albino rat. *Anim. Behav.*, 25, 622–634.

Blanchard, R.J., Takahashi, L.K., and Blanchard, D.C. (1977b). The development of intruder attack in colonies of laboratory rats. *Anim. Learn. Behav.*, 5, 365–369.

Bond, A.J. (1992). Pharmacologic manipulation of aggressiveness and impulsiveness in healthy volunteers. *Prog. Neuropsychopharmacol. Biol. Psychiatr.*, 16, 1–7.

Chamberlain, R.S., and Herman, B.H. (1990). A novel biochemical model linking dysfunction in brain melatonin, pro-opiomelanocortin peptides and serotonin in autism. *Biol. Psychiatry*, 28, 773–793.

Cherek, D.R. (1981). Effects of smoking different doses of nicotine on human aggressive behaviour. *Psychopharmacology*, 75, 339–345.

Conners, C.K. (1969). A teacher rating scale for use in drug studies with children. *Am. J. Psychiatry*, 126, 152–156.

Eichelman, B. (1992). Aggressive behavior: From laboratory to clinic. Quo vadit? *Arch. Gen. Psychiatry*, 49, 488–492.

European Aggression Rating Group (ERAG) (1992). Social Dysfunction and Aggression Scale (SDAS-21) in generalized aggression and in aggressive attacks. A validity and reliability study. *Int. J. Methods Psychiat. Res.*, 2, 15–29.

Gualtieri, C.T. (1991). Buspirone for the behavior problems of patients with organic brain disorders [letter]. *J. Clin. Psychopharmacol.*, 11, 280–281.

Guy, W. (ed.) (1976). *ECDEU Assessment Manual for Psychopharmacology*, revised, p. 218. U.S. Department of Health, Education and Welfare, Rockville, Maryland.

Hanley, H.G., Stahl, S.M., and Freedman, D.X. (1977). Hyperserotonemia and amine metabolites in autistic and retarded children. *Arch. Gen. Psychiatry*, 33, 323–329.

Huntingford, F.A., and Turner, A.K. (1987). *Animal Conflict*. Chapman and Hall, London.

Koning De, P., and Mak, M. (1991). Problems in human aggression research. *J. Neuropsychiatry*, 3 (suppl. 1), 61–65.

Levine, A.M. (1988). Buspirone and agitation in head injury. *Brain Inj.*, 2, 165–167.

Levy, M., Burgio, L., Davis, P., Sweet, R., and Janosky, J. (1992). Buspirone for disruptive behaviors in community dwelling patients with dementia. *J. Am. Geriatr. Soc.*, 40 (suppl. 10), 3.

Linnoila, V.M.J., and Virkkunen, M. (1992). Aggression, suicidality, and serotonin. *J. Clin. Psychiatry*, 53 (10, suppl.), 46–51.

Malmberg, T. (1980). *Human Territoriality: Survey of Behavioural Territories in Man with Preliminary Analysis of Meaning*. Mouton, The Hague.

Miczek, K.A. (1987). The psychopharmacology of aggression. In: *Handbook of Psychopharmacology*, vol. 19 (eds L.L. Iversen, S.D. Iversen, and S.H. Snyder) pp. 183–328. Plenum Press, New York.

Mos, J., Olivier, B., Van Oorschot, R., and Dijkstra, H. (1984). Different test situations for measuring offensive aggression in male rats do not result in the same wound patterns. *Physiol. Behav.*, 32, 453–456.

Mos, J., Olivier, B., and van Oorschot, R. (1990). Behavioural and neuropharmacological aspects of maternal aggression in rodents. *Aggressive Behav.*, 16, 145–163.

Mos, J., Olivier, B., and Tulp, M.Th.M., (1992a). Ethopharmacological studies differentiate the effects of various serotonergic compounds on aggression in rats. *Drug Dev. Res.*, 26, 343–360.

Mos, J., Olivier, B., Poth, M., and van Aken, H. (1992b). The effects of intra-ventricular administration of eltoprazine, 1-(3-trifluoromethylphenyl)piperazine hydrochloride and 8-hydroxy-2-(di-N-propylamino)tetralin on resident intruder aggression in the rat. *Eur. J. Pharmacol.*, 212, 295–298.

Mos, J., Olivier, B., Poth, M., Van Oorschot, R., and van Aken, H. (in press). The effects of dorsal raphe administration of eltoprazine, 1-(3-trifluoromethylphenyl) piperazine hydrochloride and 8-hydroxy-2-(di-N-propylamino)tetralin on resident intruder aggression in the rat. *Eur. J. Pharmacol.*

Moyer, K.E. (1968). Kinds of aggression and their physiological basis. *Communications Behav. Biol.*, 2, 65–87.

Olivier, B., Mos, J., Van der Heyden, J., and Hartog, J. (1989). Serotonergic modulation of social interactions in isolated male mice. *Psychopharmacology*, 97, 154–156.

Olivier, B., Mos, J., and Rasmussen, D.L. (1990). Behavioural pharmacology of the serenic, eltoprazine. *Drug Metab. Drug Interact.*, 8, 31–85.

Overall, J.E., and Gorham, D.R. (1962). The Brief Psychiatric Rating Scale. *Psychol. Rep.*, 10, 799–812.

Palmstierna, T., and Wistedt, B. (1987). Staff observation aggression scale. SOAS: Presentation and evaluation. *Acta Psychiatr. Scand.*, 76, 657–663.

Quiason, N., Ward, D., and Kitchen, T. (1991). Buspirone for aggression [letter]. *J. Am. Acad. Child Adolesc. Psychiatry*, 30, 1026.

Ratey, J.J., and O'Driscoll, G.A. (1989). Buspirone as a habilitative drug for patients with a dual diagnosis. *Fam. Pract. Recertification*, 11, 38–45.

Ratey, J.J., Sovner, R., Mikkelsen, E., and Chmielinsky, H.E. (1989). Buspirone treatment for maladaptive behaviour and anxiety in developmentally disabled persons. *J. Clin. Psychiatry*, 50, 382–384.

Ratey, J.J., Sovner, R., Parks, A., and Rogentine, K. (1991). Buspirone treatment of aggression and anxiety in mentally retarded patients: A multiple baseline, placebo lead-in study. *J. Clin. Psychiatry*, 52, 159–162.

Realmuto, G.M., August, G.I., and Garfinkel, B.D. (1989). Clinical effect of buspirone in autistic children. *J. Clin. Psychopharmacol.*, 9, 122–125.

Reisberg, B., London, E., Ferris, S.H., Borenstein, J., Scheier, L., and deLeon, M.J. (1983). The brief cognitive rating scale: language, motoric, and mood concomitants in primary degenerative dementia. *Psychopharmacol. Bull.*, 19, 702–708.

Sánchez, C., Arnt, J., Hyttel, J., and Moltzen, E.K. (1993). The role of serotonergic mechanisms in inhibition of isolation-induced aggression in male mice. *Psychopharmacology*, 110, 53–59.

Schipper, J., Tulp, M.Th.M., and Sijbesma, H. (1990). Neurochemical profile of eltoprazine. *Drug Metabol. Drug Interact.*, 8, 85–115.

Sijbesma, H., Schipper, J., De Kloet, E.R., Mos, J., Van Aken, H., and Olivier, B. (1991). Postsynaptic 5-HT$_1$ receptors and offensive aggression in rats: a combined behavioural and autoradiographic study with eltoprazine. *Pharmacol. Biochem. Behav.*, 38, 447–458.

Tiihonen, J., Hakola, P., Paanila, J., and Turtiainen, M. (1993). Eltoprazine for aggression in schizophrenia and mental retardation [letter]. *Lancet*, 341, 307.

Tiller, J.G. (1988). Short-term buspirone treatment in disinhibition with dementia [letter]. *Lancet*, 332, 510.

Van der Ploeg, H.M., Defares, P.B., and Spielberger, C.D. (1980). *Handleiding bij de Zelf-Beoordelings Vragenlijst.* Swets and Zeitlinger BV, Lisse, The Netherlands.

Van der Ploeg, H.M., Defares, P.B., and Spielberger, C.D. (1982). *Handleiding bij de Zelf-Analyse Vragenlijst.* Swets and Zeitlinger BV, Lisse, The Netherlands.

Van Leeuwen, C.J., Riedel, W.J., and O'Hanlon, J.F. (1988). Assessment of the antiaggressive effects of a putative anxiolytic, CGP 361A, versus those of diazepam and placebo in humans using a novel experimental approach. *Psychopharmacology,* 96 (suppl. 232), 358.

van Praag, H.M. (1991). Serotonergic dysfunction and aggression control [editorial]. *Psychol. Med.,* 21, 15–19.

Verhoeven, W.M.A., Tuinier, S., Sijben, N.A.S., et al. (1992). Eltoprazine in mentally retarded selfinjuring patients behaviours [letter]. *Lancet,* 340, 1037–1038.

Wistedt, B., Rassmussen, A., Pedersen, L., et al. (1990). The development of an observer scale for measuring social dysfunction and aggression. *Pharmacopsychiatry,* 23, 249–252.

Yudofsky, S.C., Silver, J.M., Jackson, W., Endicott, J., and Williams, D. (1986). The Overt Aggression Scale for Objective Rating of Verbal and Physical Aggression. *Am. J. Psychiatry,* 143, 35–39.

Yudofsky, S.C., Silver, J.M., and Hales, R.E. (1990). Pharmacologic management of aggression in the elderly. *J. Clin. Psychiatry,* 51 (suppl.), 22–28.

18 Psychotherapy in Patients with Impulsive Aggression

MICHAEL H STONE
Columbia College of Physicians and Surgeons, New York City, NY, USA

INTRODUCTION

The conceptual territory occupied by impulsive aggression* does not co-incide with an already standardized diagnostic entity, but instead overlaps with a number of psychiatric disorders described in the DSM-IV. There is more to impulsive aggression (IA), for example, than is covered by the term "intermittent explosive disorder" (No. 312,34 in the DSM-IV). The latter is based on "(a) several discrete episodes of loss of control of aggressive impulses resulting in serious assaultive acts or [in] destruction of property, and (b) the degree of aggressiveness . . . is grossly out of proportion to any precipitating stressors". There are in addition a number of exclusion criteria—such as borderline personality disorder (BPD) and attention deficit disorder/hyperactivity (ADD/H)—which would be *included* in the much broader concept of IA. Intermittent explosive disorder (IED) is similar to the diagnosis of "episodic dyscontrol", proposed by Andrulonis (1981), who noted that unpredictable aggressive outbursts were common in a group of adolescent males with BPD. Organic factors (head injury, birth trauma) seemed to play an important role in this patient population.

THE DIAGNOSTIC DOMAIN OF IMPULSIVE AGGRESSION

We may portray the diagnostic domain of IA by means of a Venn diagram, as in Figure 1. A number of important, and more tightly defined (i.e. by the DSM-IV criteria), conditions are shown, each of which overlaps to varying degrees with the concept of IA. Actually, to do justice to the multiplicity of overlappings would require a complex diagram in n-dimensional space ($n = 9$ in the present case), since each of the entities can co-occur with any or several of the others. Alternatively, one could devise a matrix showing the likelihood, given IA, of any of the possible comorbid conditions, and

---

*In speaking of "impulsive aggression", I am singling out that portion of the clinical domain in which *impulsivity* (which is not always accompanied by aggression) and *aggression* (which is sometimes cool and premeditated) overlap.

Impulsivity and Aggression. Edited by E. Hollander and D.J. Stein
© 1995 John Wiley & Sons Ltd

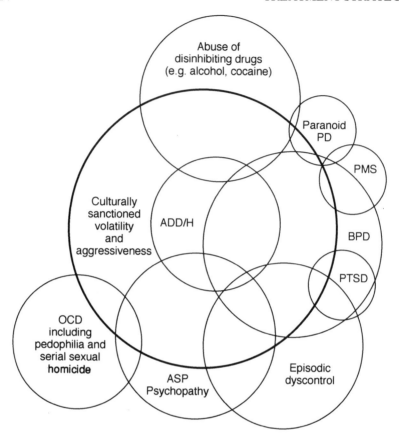

Figure 1   The domain of impulsive aggression.

also the likelihood, given one of the latter, that the patient also exhibited IA. At present we can only make educated guesses about the proportions we might encounter. Impulsive aggression constitutes a "fuzzy set" at this point (see Klir and Folger, 1988), and we have as yet little epidemiological data concerning the frequency with which borderline, paranoid, antisocial, and other patients may meaningfully be considered "impulsively aggressive". We do know, however, that abuse of disinhibiting drugs, most especially alcohol and cocaine, is quite common among those with BPD or antisocial personality disorder (ASPD). People with the conditions alluded to in Figure 1 are generally more likely to abuse substances, the effects of which then further fuel the engine of impulsive aggressivity. To take an extreme example, serial killers, many of whom exhibit obsessive compulsive disorder (OCD), often prime themselves with alcohol by way of catalyzing their transformation into the state where they feel emboldened to carry out their homicidal acts (unpublished data). At the other extreme, one may encounter, more in social than in psychiatric settings, people of a volatile nature, who periodically "fly off the handle", and do such things as crash a dish on the floor in a fit of pique, hurl an egg at a family member, etc., only to settle down immediately after the outburst—feelings calmer, and even a bit apologetic. Such behavior may be culturally syntonic, at least to the degree that this volatility may not trigger "caseness" (i.e. be of a sort that come to the attention of mental health professionals). This observation serves to highlight another important aspect of IA and its treatment, namely the intensity or degree to which aggressivity is present in the various related conditions or in any one patient with IA.

THE CONTINUUM OF SEVERITY RELATIVE TO THE DOMAIN OF IMPULSIVE AGGRESSION

Though one could discuss psychotherapy of impulsive aggression from the standpoint of diagnostic subtypes, as sketched in Figure 1, it is useful at first to view this clinical phenomenon from the perspective of severity.

Instances of culturally sanctioned outbursts of anger and mild aggression are "subclinical" with respect to treatment—or, at least, people given to such outbursts almost never present themselves to mental health professionals for therapy. In the continuum diagram shown in Figure 2, we might place such persons in Zone A—the zone of least severe examples. This zone blends in (as one of a series of overlapping "fuzzy" sets) to Zone B.

In Zone B we would place patients with IA, irrespective of their comorbidity pattern, whose outbursts of aggression are relatively infrequent and are rarely or never of such proportions as to get them into trouble with the authorities. Those in Zone B will generally have sought help voluntarily, if not for the impulsively aggressive acts themselves then for the predisposing underlying condition. The latter might be characterized by BPD, alcoholism, severe premenstrual syndrome (PMS), or any of the others, singly or in combination, mentioned in Figure 1. Those in Zone B, in other words, have indentified themselves as patients. They often feel some measure of bewilderment and remorse over their aggressive acts. To this extent they are more amenable to psychotherapy of one form or another than would those whose aggressivity is denied, is more habitual and severe, and who seldom

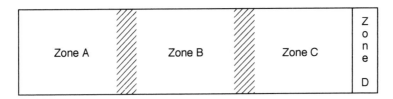

Figure 2 Impulsive aggression: the continuum of severity.

present themselves for help except at the insistence of family, friends, or co-workers.

Zone C may be said to contain persons of the last-mentioned type, i.e. those whose IA is habitual and severe and whose motivation for therapy is weak or absent. Many of the people in this zone show antisocial qualities, often enough to warrant a diagnosis of ASPD by the DSM-IV criteria (in addition to whatever other Axis I and II conditions they may have). The range of therapeutic interventions that have some chance of success for people in this zone is, as we shall see, narrower than for those in Zone B. Furthermore, the prognosis for amelioration and prosociality is poorer.

Zone D contains people in whom IA, besides being of great severity, has also led to the commission of felonies. Because I reserve this zone for those who are, in addition, beyond the realm of treatment, the line of demarcation between them and those in Zone C is sharp rather than blurred. As I have mentioned elsewhere (Stone, 1993), there does exist a realm of psychiatric-ally untreatable people: some, because they manifest to such an intense degree the psychopathic traits adumbrated by Cleckley (1972), and more recently by Hare et al. (1990), as to be totally contemptuous of and impervious to any therapeutic interventions; others, because the severity of their aggressive acts and the high likelihood of recidivism militate against their release from prison or secure forensic units.

From the standpoint of the DSM diagnostic categories, we cannot make a one-to-one mapping between the various relevant categories and the zones of the severity continuum, since most of these conditions themselves vary over a wide range of intensity. Menninger (1993) recently provided a fairly complete list of mental illnesses characterized by aggressive behavior, in-cluding many mentioned in Figure 1. Perhaps only one entity—sexual sadism—belongs to just one zone (D), though even here there are "milder" instances (to be placed in Zone C) of men who rape but without inflicting further physical damage upon their victims. Many instances of IA precipi-tated by alcohol or cocaine are comparatively mild (Zone B) and are amenable to treatment. The mechanisms involved in cocaine abuse are well outlined by Yudofsky et al. (1993), as is its treatment. The more severe cases (viz. habitual abuse of "crack") are much harder to treat, lie outside the realm of conventional psychotherapy, and often have forensic complica-tions.

In the section that follows we shall look at some clinical examples—some amenable to psychotherapy of one form or another, others less so or not at all.

CLINICAL EXAMPLES

Because of the rarity of IA-related conditions in "pure form" (where no other Axis I or II condition could be said to coexist), I prefer to present these cases in dimensional form. By way of illustration, I use a graph or grid in which the DSM diagnoses (including those related to personality) are arrayed along the x-axis. The y-axis consists of a 7-point scale, from 0 (the entity is not present at all) to 6 (entity maximally present). Numbers 4, 5, and 6 I reserve for conditions meeting the DSM criteria (4 = mildly, 5 = moderately, 6 = severely or maximally. Numbers 1, 2, and 3 represent subclinical degrees, where 3 is the most intense degree of the given condition, that still fails to meet the DSM criteria.

The resultant graph is shown in Figure 3. The diagnostic *profile* (with respect to both Axis I and Axis II) can then be represented for each patient of the following clinical vignettes via a shorthand, where the appropriate number is given for each of the 13 entities of Figure 3.

Example A

The patient in this example showed the following diagnostic pattern (see Figure 3 for abbreviations):

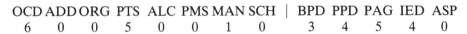

OCD ADD ORG PTS ALC PMS MAN SCH | BPD PPD PAG IED ASP
 6   0   0   5   0   0   1   0 | 3   4   5   4   0

A divorced lawyer in his early 50s, Thomas (all names are fictional)

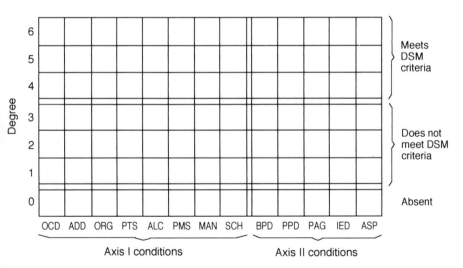

Figure 3 Conditions relevant to impulsive aggression × their degree: OCD, obsessive compulsive disorder; ADD, attention deficit disorder; ORG, organic syndrome, explosive; PTS, post-traumatic stress disorder; ALC, alcohol or cocaine abuse; PMS, premenstrual syndrome; MAN, mania; SCH, schizophrenia; BPD, borderline personality disorder (PD); PPD, paranoid PD; PAG, passive aggressive PD; IED, intermittent explosive PD; ASP, antisocial PD.

compulsively hoarded food and accumulated newspaper articles, photocopies of legal briefs, old letters etc., in such volume as to occupy almost all the living space in his apartment. Unable to throw anything away, he ended up sleeping on the floor. Abused sexually and physically as a child, he often experienced flashbacks, night terrors, and panic attacks. He had a hair-trigger sensitivity to any comment that could be construed as a slight, and would sometimes lash out physically at those whom he felt offended him—and once even struck a colleague at his firm. He knew he was "out of line" when he reacted this way, but he felt "something comes over me, and I can't control it". When a passionate affair several years after his divorce came to an abrupt end, he felt devastated, made a suicide attempt, and was briefly hospitalized. The people who "tripped his wire" were usually older men who resembled, in appearance or behavior, his abusive and much-hated father. This had become abundantly clear during the 5 years he had spent in four-times-a-week psychoanalysis, but his tendency to anger oubursts had not much abated. Various medications had been tried—including serotonin reuptake blockers—but he did not tolerate them well. When he transferred to my care, I saw that we had to rely on verbal means. He had a pretty fair grasp on his underlying psychodynamics, such that further exploration was not likely to yield major benefits vis-à-vis his irascibility. Counterbalancing Thomas' medication intolerance and the imperviousness of his symptoms to purely interpretive interventions was his high motivation to conquer his explosive tendencies. Over the course of a year he was able to reduce the frequency of his outbursts to near zero, via an eclectic therapy emphasizing exhortation to achieve self-control, followed by cognitive techniques ("count to ten, stifle your anger, wait till the wave of red-hot anger passes, call me if you need to, take notes on what got you so mad and let's you and I go over the scene as it unfolded, during our next session . . . "). The aim of the cognitive interventions was to get him to spell out in detail those aspects of the interpersonal situation that had ignited his anger, to recognize the similarities—but more importantly, the great differences—between the current situation and the (much more grievous) situations he had had to endure as a child. Thomas grew more able to realize, even when in the midst of an unpleasant encounter, that (a) the situation was not overwhelming, as had been the confrontations with his father, and (b) he was considerably less helpless now than he had been while still living at home.

Example B

The following pattern was relevant to the patient of this vignette:

OCD	ADD	ORG	PTS	ALC	PMS	MAN	SCH	BPD	PPD	PAG	IED	ASP
4	0	0	3	5	6	4	0	6	4	0	4	2

Helen was 36 years old when she sought help for depression and suicidal impulses, in the context of a deteriorating marriage. Having married once before when she was very young, she had one daughter, who had just left for college. Helen's second husband was a well-to-do member of a prominent European family. Despite, or perhaps because of, her several homes and many servants, she felt that she had nothing to do and had no sense of direction in her life. She had three first-degree relatives with manic depressive illness: her father was bipolar (he made and lost fortunes gambling), her mother had recurrent depression, and a sister had committed suicide. Helen herself was extremely moody, and became irritable to the point of combativeness the week before her period. This tendency was magnified considerably by abuse of alcohol. Though flirtatious and charming much of the time, her personality could "turn on a dime", becoming suspicious, vengeful and malicious (she would call her husband's relatives and fabricate embarrassing rumors about him, or else, in a fit of rage, break some of the antiques he collected). Once the mood passed, she would revert to her "normal" self as though nothing happened. With alcohol in her system she became pathologically jealous, and would often get into physical fights with her husband. A day later she would berate herself for having got so out of control, and would be genuinely mystified as to what had set her off.

Therapy progressed through a sequence of stages. At first it was important to foster a therapeutic alliance. Given the nature of her personality (borderline, with paranoid, explosive, and some antisocial features), it seemed most useful to adopt a sympathetic stance at the outset—paying more attention, for example, to her grievances (about her husband) and complaints (about having little to do that interested her) than to the role she played in accentuating these difficulties. She proved amenable to a combination of supportive and psychoanalytically oriented approaches. It became apparent, through her associations to her routinely primitive and frightening dreams, that she had been molested sexually by her father, beginning when she was 6 years old. She was afraid to tell her mother about this till after a suicide attempt at 15. Her mother then divorced her father. Helen married precipitously at 17, hoping to distance herself from the memories of her childhood. My sympathizing with Helen-as-victim—an easy task in the face of this history—helped us get to the next stage: one in which I could begin to hold her responsible for the many ways she contributed to her plight—by drinking, behaving abusively toward her husband, and pursuing no areas of artistic or other interests that might decrease her sense of boredom and futility. After about 4 months I felt I had enough leverage to suggest she join Alcoholics Anonymous (AA). Skittish at first, she became enthusiastic about AA, and achieved a steady sobriety. Meanwhile, a combination of anxiolytics and diuretics I had prescribed for her to take during the week before menses helped diminish the amplitude and frequency of her rage outbursts. Her marital relationship improved, since her husband no longer felt, in living with Helen, that he was (in his words) "walking through a sniper-infested jungle".

The success of the limit-setting interventions (in curbing the aggressive outbursts) ushered in a final phase of the therapy: here the focus was on her jealousy and its sources. Exploratory psychotherapy was the main modality. As Helen began to grasp more fully the connection between the original betrayal of trust (on the part of her father) and her lifelong assumption that men were "cheats", she could now sense that her husband's behavior was different from that of "all men" — as she had hitherto imagined them. She still felt jealousy on occasion, but was now more able to suppress the impulse toward aggressive "retaliation".

DISCUSSION

Crucial to any discussion of symptom or personality pathology is the role of action. Typically, patients with predominantly cluster C (anxious) personality disorders or who show phobic symptoms (e.g. social phobia and school avoidance) shy away from action, let alone aggressivity. Cluster B (dramatic) patients, especially those with borderline, histrionic or antisocial disorders, and also bipolar manic depressive patients, are action prone, customarily impulsive — and many are impulsively *aggressive* as well. Psychoanalysis developed, in part, out of a need to free up overly inhibited patients (hysterical, phobic, obsessive, depressive, masochistic) so that they could live richer lives by exercising their entitlement to sexual pleasure or to assertive actions — which they had hitherto denied themselves. There would appear to be on the face of it an inverse relationship between the degree (frequency/intensity/harmfulness) of impulsive aggressiveness and the efficacy of psychoanalytically oriented therapies, at least in their "unmodified" form.

A similar note was sounded by McGlashan (1992), in his commentary about prognostic factors in borderline patients. The ability to control aggression in significant relationships, for example, correlated in follow-up studies with a better outcome (McGlashan, 1992, p. 70). This is another way of saying that, in effect, the *least* impulsively aggressive borderlines do best (certainly with analytically oriented therapy; probably with any form of therapy). The same kind of equation emerges from the observations of Clarkin *et al.* (1992), in their recommendations concerning the psychoanalytical psychotherapy of borderlines. In their study, the "remainers" (who were also usually the positive "responders") tended to be those borderline patients who were highly motivated and able to work and to preserve a sense of structure and discipline in their lives (Clarkin *et al.* 1992, p. 285). Elsewhere, I have noted the poor long-term outcome in borderline patients (irrespective of whatever type of therapy they received) whose personality profile showed high degrees of hostility and irritability (Stone, 1990a, 1992).

There is unanimity of opinion regarding the importance of limit-setting techniques as a mainstay in the treatment of borderline patients, as an antidote specifically to their impulsivity. This is relevant to impulsive aggressivity, as well as to other forms of impulse dyscontrol (viz. promiscuity, shoplifting, or substance abuse). The main point here is this: therapists —to the extent that they do not become rigid adherents to one technique or school of thought, and thus to the extent that they permit themselves to be guided by the particularities of their patients—will, in working with the impulsive patient, inevitably find themselves steering in the direction of a behavioral–cognitive approach.

The "behavioral" aspects of this approach will include all the various forms of limit-setting interventions, such as (a) the utilization of therapist–patient contracts (where the patient may pledge not to indulge in suicidal or self-destructive acts, for example; Clarkin et al., 1992), (b) recommendation that the patient join a 12-step program, such as AA or Overeaters Anonymous (OA), or (c), in the case of hospitalized patients, the use of a token-economy system or other system of privilege gradations designed to curb maladaptive (including impulsive and aggressive) behaviors or to promote prosocial behaviors. Use of the "quiet room" or "seclusion room" represents the maximum degree of limit setting available in hospital settings as a control device for impulsive or aggressive behavior [and is often backed up by the use of "anti-impulsive" medications, such as the serotonin reuptake blockers, lithium, antiepileptics (carbamazepine or valproate), neuroleptics and β-adrenergic receptor antagonists]. Imipramine has been suggested in the case of a borderline patient with ADD and IA (Satel et al., 1988). The rationale for all such medications has been well discussed by Kavoussi and Coccaro (1993). To these more specific measures, one could add a whole host of spontaneous interventions therapists use in confronting impulsive aggressive aspects of their patients (of whatever diagnostic type), such as urging a patient to *refrain* from carrying out some intended destructive act and instead to *think about why* this act had such appeal, and in the ensuing dialogue with the therapist to fashion some more adaptive socially acceptable response. Examples of this were alluded to in my case examples, when I mentioned urging various patients to "count to ten" (or some higher number if necessary!), until a wave of anger had passed and they could begin to think reasonably and rationally about the solution to some interpersonal problem. Here again, one may speak of an "inverse relationship"—in this case, between the amenability of impulsive aggressive patients to limit-setting interventions and their "psychopathic-ness". The greater the latter (as manifested by callousness and contemptuous indifference to the feelings of others), the less one can hope to nip trouble in the bud via limit setting or via the calm discussion of possible consequences of one's actions (i.e. via cognitive dialogue).

If impulsive aggressivity pushes analytical therapy beyond its limits, summoning the need for a more cognitive–behavioral approach, psychopathy may be said to push cognitive–behavioral therapy beyond *its* limits. Up to what point, we may ask, can the constructive dialogue that is an important ingredient of cognitive therapy be useful in working with antisocial people? Here it is useful to bear in mind that significant differences exist between the DSM definition of ASPD and the definitions of "psychopathic personality". The former is defined mostly by antisocial *acts*; the latter, chiefly by particular *traits*, viz. callousness, glibness, lack of remorse, manipulative "conning", etc. Some antisocial people commit destructive acts, yet are not prominently psychopathic. Milder examples of this sort may prove amenable to the type of cognitive therapy outlined by Beck and Freeman (1990). These authors emphasize that cognitive therapy, " . . . rather than attempting to build a better moral structure through the induction of affect such as anxiety or shame", aims at "improving moral and social behavior through enhancement of cognitive functioning" (Beck and Freeman, 1990, p. 152). In practical terms, the therapy aims at getting the antisocial person to substitute for the knee-jerk lashing out at those who get in the way or bother one—the *weighing and measuring of the consequences* of the impulsive aggressive act one had been contemplating. The therapist might encourage the patient to participate in a kind of rehearsal of some unpleasant encounter:

THER.   What if your boss gives you another car to fix at 4:30 on a Friday, when you thought you were all through for the day?

PT.   I'd tell him to go to hell. I'd feel like punching him out!

THER.   And then what?

PT.   . . . probably fire me.

THER.   So how would that affect your trying to provide for your family?

PT.   It'd be a bum deal. But I got my pride. No one's going to push me around . . .

THER.   But you'd be better off holding on to that job.

PT.   Yeah, I guess.

THER.   So, all things considered, it might be better for you to . . .

PT.   . . . to say "shit!" under my breath and go fix the car and hang onto the job.

THER.   Yeah, sounds like that'd be the best thing.

Here we see the therapist nudging his patient into an examination of a *cost–benefit analysis* of two alternative coping strategies: the impulsive aggressive way (benefit: immediate gratification; cost: one's job) versus the prosocial way (gratification: preserving one's source of income; cost: a bit of pride, the stifling of a revenge fantasy). Mildly antisocial people showing very little psychopathy would presumably be amenable to this type of cognitive–behavioral approach; many such people improve either spontaneously or with the help of 12-step programs as they enter their 40s (Stone, 1990a; Robins et al., 1991). But if we were to be quite candid, we would have to acknowledge that people in the back of whose destructiveness is ruthlessness and contemptuousness do not respond to this or to any other form of treatment. These are the people who make up the Zone D of Figure 2. For the most part this region is occupied by felons commiting acts of violence against others (in such forms as rape, robbery, aggravated assault, murder, and the form of sexual sadism committed by serial killers). Not all offenders even of this degree of seriousness are beyond treatment. A percentage of rapists and pedophiles, for example, do experience remorse, and to this extent may be amenable to special types of behavioral therapy (especially in prison settings, where inmates are a "captive audience" to the efforts of specially trained experts in group and behavior therapy). That medications may also be helpful has been shown by Tupin et al. (1973), in their experience with lithium in aggressive prison inmates, and more recently by Kafka (1991), who achieved at least short-term success with fluoxetine in a man convicted of rape. Where impulsive aggression and psychopathy intersect, at all events, psychotherapy (of whatever sort) will usually fail. For this reason, I mention the topic here more for reasons of completeness. Elsewhere I discuss further the limits of therapy, especially when impulsive aggression has led to murder (Stone, 1993).

As for those impulsive aggressive patients who *are* within the realm of treatability, their growing number and the increasing attention they have received has led to a crossfertilization of ideas between traditional psycho-analytically oriented therapists and cognitive–behavioral therapists. It is not going too far to say that, until recently, proponents of these two disciplines were either antagonistic toward one another or at best content to inhabit separate spheres. Testimony to the crossfertilization that has finally begun to take place is to be found in the excellent discussion of the two disciplines by Stein (1992). Evidence for an openness to the cognitive–behavioral treatment philosophy is to be found, more implicitly than explicitly, in Kernberg's recent book on aggression in personality disorders (Kernberg, 1992). There, in dealing with a man whose personality combined borderline and paranoid configurations, Kernberg describes how this man once threatened him, having become convinced that Kernberg had "warned" a certain woman against him (a woman Kernberg had not spoken with, but knew by virtue of her having worked somewhere in the hospital where Kernberg was director). There was risk the patient was about to attack Kernberg physically. "Taking a deep breath," Kernberg (p. 170) relates, "I told Mr. M that I did not feel free to talk as openly as I wanted to because I was not sure whether he could control his feelings and not act on them. . . . He would therefore have to reassure me that our work would continue in the form of verbal discourse rather than physical action or else I would not be able to continue working with him . . . " Kernberg's intervention was successful, and the man did simmer down. Kernberg then commented to the patient: "you are absolutely convinced that I had warned the woman and am therefore lying to you, or else we are in a 'mad' situation where one of us is out of touch with reality, the other not". The man, growing more relaxed, could now acknowledge that Kernberg had been telling the truth. My point in reproducing this vignette is to show how an expert as solidly identified with psychoanalysis as is Otto Kernberg can, in dealing with a potentially aggressive borderline patient, shift gears, so to say, into a cognitive mode: exposing to the patient both arms of a "paradox" (as the patient experiences it), and in the ensuing dialogue, helping the patient resolve the paradox along more realistic lines. Later, in working with this patient, Kernberg was able to make a more "analytical" interpretation—to the effect that the patient had unwittingly recreated his childhood drama, of a sadistic father and terrified child . . . now with the tables reversed: the patient playing the sadistic father, forcing the therapist to play the frightened child. Here we see psychoanalytically oriented and cognitive–behavioral modalities being mixed and matched, with an impulsively aggressive patient, to suit the demands of the occasion, as the atmosphere changes from moment to moment, week to week, in the course of an ongoing therapy. In an earlier paper I advocated a synthetic/pragmatic approach to the therapy of border-line patients (including those with IA), embodying an "ABCD" of modal-ities: analytically oriented, behavioral, cognitive, and drug therapy (Stone, 1990b).

One might go a step further and state that impulsively *aggressive* patients [as opposed to the merely "acting-out"-prone patients commented on by Frosch (1977)], particularly those whom we encounter in the emergency room, *require* of us cognitive–behavioral techniques, along with some well-oiled empathic machinery, since in such extreme circumstances we do not know the patient well enough to (a) make relevant dynamic interpret-ations or (b) trust that such "deep" interpretations would be well received, let alone beneficial. I can think of no more poignant example in this context than the one provided by Harry Albert (1983), in describing his encounter with a paranoid and highly dangerous new father, apprehended in a hospital emergency room as he was trying to force his way to the obstetrics floor, there to murder his wife—whose baby, he was convinced, was by some other man. Their interchange (Albert, 1983, p. 281) is worth quoting *in extenso*:

PT. . . . and I know it's not my kid, so I have to kill her or I'm no kind of man.

HA Kill her? What do you mean?

PT. I shoot the fuck.

HA   Do you have a gun?
PT.   Here [*Points to his pocket*].
HA   That floor is full of women and babies. What if you hurt one of them — would you still feel like a man?
PT.   Women are all shit. All of them. No damn good!
HA   I see you are a strong man. Why not just beat the shit out of her? If you kill her, she can't apologize or make up for what she did.
PT.   It's not enough.
HA   Two men like us should be able to figure this out. The trouble is I'm afraid of guns ever since I was in the Army. Could you put the gun in the drawer while we talk so I can think straight?
PT.   No.
HA   How about just the bullets? It's hard for me to think straight when I'm scared.
PT.   You're a good guy. I don't want you to be scared, Doc. I'll put it in the drawer.

There is much to be said about the artful way in which Albert defuses the situation, complimenting the man, subtly questioning him whether it's all that "manly" to convert an obstetrics ward into a shooting gallery, admitting that he's scared of guns and that the patient has the upper hand, etc. Again, the main point is that the therapeutic interventions used in this life-threatening confrontation belong within the domain of the cognitive–behavioral. Dynamic interpretations about the man's low self-confidence, repressed homosexuality, envy of the attention about to be bestowed on the baby, etc., even if they were on target, would not have won the day.

Albert, who had analytical training but who considered himself primarily a "behaviorist", never developed a methodical exposition of his technique — which, as with many gifted therapists, was largely intuitive. Both Kernberg and Linehan, in contrast, carry their intuitions a step further and have made the theoretical foundation behind their intuitions *explicit*. Kernberg et al. (1989) have published guidelines for the psychodynamic psychotherapy for borderline patients. Their book contains some practical measures for dealing with aggressive patients, especially those who threaten the therapist during session time (Kernberg et al., 1989, p. 172). Linehan, in her recent book (1993) offers a methodical "strategies checklist" for dealing with many aspects of borderline-type psychopathology, particularly parasuicidal acts (viz. manipulative suicide gestures). The cognitive strategies outlined by Linehan focus more on aggression against the self (as suicidal behavior) than against others. Her recommendations, however, are applicable to the treatment of people with impulsive aggression as well. Interestingly, the checklist she provides (Linehan, 1993, p. 206) of basic strategies are similar in many particulars to those of dynamic psychotherapy, though the technical terms are different. Linehan numbers among the therapist's tasks, for example: T

(= therapist) gives developmental descriptions of change; T makes synthe-
sizing statements; T highlights *paradoxical* contradictions in the patient's
behavior, etc. These interventions closely resemble the clarifications, interpretations, and attention to paradoxical thinking that Kernberg underlines
as critical to his model of dynamic therapy with borderline patients. Since
impulsively aggressive patients in general "hug" the extremes of thought and
behavior ("I love my wife, but I could kill her if she even glances at another
man"), the ways which either Linehan or Kernberg suggest for dealing with
all-or-none thought and behavior are pertinent to IA as much as to BPD cf.
Lineham and Heard, 1992.

One's theoretical model of aggression and its role in our species is not
without relevance to one's therapeutic model *vis-à-vis* "impulsive aggression." The topic deserves some space here, necessarily brief, though it is
worthy under other circumstances of book-length discussion.

Tarnopolsky (1992), in his excellent critique of the Kernberg/Kohut
debate, draws attention to Kohut's strange dismissal of aggression as a topic
of central importance, and also to Kernberg's emphasis of aggression,
including "innate" aggression, as a core facet of borderline psychopathology. Tarnopolsky (1992, p. 198) mentions Winnicott's trenchant question:
"Does aggression come ultimately from anger aroused by frustration, or has
it a root of its own?" Previous attempts to answer this question, besides
taking on the air more of religion than of reason, have often been casuis-
tical, the "bottom line" being more a reflection of one's optimism or
pessimism about humankind. Thus, many psychoanalysts have clung to the
notion that aggression is "defensive", i.e. arising out of (postnatal) frustration, abandonment, abusive parenting, and the like. This is the optimist's
position, since it drags in its train the assumption that what is "merely"
environmental in origin can be fixed. Others, including Kernberg, posit the
existence of "innate" aggression as figuring prominently in the equation of
at least some forms of aggressive pathology, such as that noted in many
borderline patients. The neuropsychopharmacologist, Valzelli (1981), argues
for the preparedness of our genome to become programmed for a whole
catalog of aggressive variants: predatory, competitive, defensive, irritative,
territorial, maternal-protective, etc. Patterns are presumably laid down early
in life, via procedural (habit-)memory systems operating outside consciousness—within a brain already "wired" to fashion such programs. I find
Valzelli's model convincing, and have expanded on it, in relation to borderline and related disorders, in a commentary on Freud's "destructive instinct"
(Stone, 1991). A cursory glance at our history should convince all but the
most incurable optimist that territorial and irritative aggression, at the least,
are indelible parts, genetically based, of our behavioral repertoire. At the
same time, whether we develop prosocially or antisocially, whether we
become more like Mother Theresa or more like Hitler, depends a great deal
on family environment. But this is not an "either/or" matter. *Impulsive*

aggression may be seen as an expression primarily of what Valzelli meant by "irritative" aggression: the type of aggression that is associated with gross, and violent, over-reactions to other people who offend us for trivial reasons which we then blow out of proportion, or because they simply represent, symbolically, whatever or whoever it is that gets in our way. Bigotry, violently expressed, is one example. Impulsive aggression, as we have noted, may originate, in any given person, from genetic or constitutional (i.e. innate) sources, or from environmental sources, or from some unfortunate combination of both. This solves the old Nature/Nurture debate: it is not a question of either/or, but of how much of either.

As for the Nature side, genetic predisposition to psychosis (especially to bipolar manic depression) can enhance the likelihood of IA. This can occur even in predisposed persons raised by empathic and nurturing parents (see Spungen, 1983). Predisposition to epilepsy or to ADD/H can do likewise (Cadoret and Stewart, 1991). Perinatal brain injury from hypoxia, etc., may also conduce to an evolving IA. On the Nurture side, abusive parenting would figure most prominently, especially where physical or sexual abuse is of such magnitude as to cause an enkindled central nervous system, leading to heightened irritability or even to post-traumatic stress disorder (PTSD). But parental deprivation, abandonment, humiliation, gross favoring of one sibling over another, intrusiveness, or indifference also take their toll, and may contribute significantly to the eventual picture of IA. As Pittman (1993) has made plain, traumatic combat experiences, even in soldiers who have come from only mildly disturbing family environments, can lead to both PTSD and IA concomitantly.

Whatever the mix of contributory factors in any given case, the therapist will be confronting deeply entrenched patterns of stimulus–response, embedded, as mentioned above, in the habit-memory system—usually laid down within in the first 6 years of life, usually "ego-syntonic" as a result, and by no means easily dislodged. One speaks of these patterns as aggressive "schemata" (Huesmann, 1988; Stein and Young, 1992) or aggressive "inner scripts" (Gallwey, 1985; Stone, 1988). Huesmann (1988, p. 18) suggests that scripts are stored in memory through a two-component process: initial encoding of observed behaviors, followed by repeated rehearsals. Some children subjected to severe corporal punishment conceive a vivid hatred of the punitive parent. But others identify with the parent, assume the "correctness" of the abusiveness, and mete out similar flurries of bullying toward classmates; eventually, toward spouse and children. The ego-syntonicity of their aggressive script—if offended lash out; don't stop till you see blood—means that it is (at first) nonconflictual, and therefore scarcely modifiable by a therapeutic approach (viz. classical psychoanalysis) dependent primarily upon the resolution of conflict. The ego-syntonicity of impulsive aggression usually gets fortified by a vicious circle mechanism, as in Huesmann's example: "The aggressive boy's belief that everyone behaves aggressively is likely to be confirmed by the behavior of those around him, especially as his own aggressive actions incite aggression in others" (Huesmann, 1988; p. 19). It is this sort of vicious circle that the therapist of the impulsively aggressive patient strives to interrupt. The success of the attempt will usually rely upon a therapeutic strategy that incorporates—or may utilize exclusively—cognitive behavioral techniques. Maladaptive schemata need to be supplanted and overlain with adaptive schemata, the latter constituting a kind of inhibitory/over-ride mechanism [such that the earlier schema (wife burns toast: smash the plate, curse her out) is over-ridden by a new schema (wife burns toast: take it good-naturedly, remined her you prefer it a little lighter)]. Optimally, the newer, more adaptive schemata need to be reinforced by a more compassionate and (in the case of IA) less aggressive "philosophy" (the latter being one's superordinate schema controlling all subordinate schemata). Reprogrammed with such a philosophy, the patient might say to himself, instead of "the old man was right to hit up on mom when she didn't do as he said: a man's king in his own castle," something genuinely more human: "the old man musta' been nuts to treat mom that way! Treat people decent, they treat you decent . . . do what you want without your even having to ask".

A final comment on the treatment of impulsive aggression concerns factors in patients who cut across diagnostic lines and in therapists who cut across affiliations to this or that school of thought.

On the patient's side we look for adequate motivation for therapy, perseverance, taking one's condition seriously, and a capacity for remorse—especially in those whose aggressivity has caused bodily harm to others. Kernberg (1975) emphasized a similar set of positive factors in discussing prognosis in borderline patients. Psychopathy represents a 180° turn from this favorable picture and helps explain the inverse relationship between the degree of psychopathy and prognosis in IA, irrespective of the origins of the psychopathic personality traits. Those who argue that psychopathy stems from traumatic experiences and should be regarded as a brand of PTSD (Hodge, 1992) are not on solid ground, given the existence of psychopaths, including those committing serial sexual homicide, who come from nontraumatic backgrounds (Stone, 1994). The balance between *impulsivity* and *obsessionality/compulsivity* may be another factor affecting the prognostic equation in cases in which IA overlaps with OCD. As Stein et al. (1992) have suggested, people exhibiting sexual addictions and paraphilias respond less well to serotonin reuptake blockers than do people with sexual obsessions; i.e. those at the impulsive end of the spectrum seem less responsive. Because of the extreme action-proneness and probable meagerness of remorse in the severely *im*pulsive, their prognosis with respect to psychotherapy may well parallel their differential responsiveness to pharmacotherapy.

As for the qualities of the therapists who undertake to work with IA patients, a familiarity with a variety of techniques—including cognitive-behavioral—is highly desirable. Also desirable is compassion tempered with moral firmness: one must at the same time try to help IA patients gain control of their behavior, while making it clear that one holds them clearly responsible for the nature of their actions. Except in those situations where the etiological underpinnings of IA are almost exclusively (a) biological and (b) remediable by pharmacotherapy (as in certain cases of lithium-responsive bipolar disorder), there will usually be a serious personality disorder. As Costa and McCrae (1986, p. 421) mention: "Human nature is by no means easily changed; therapists would do better to think of effecting modest improvements rather than a 'cure'." Thus the virtue of patience is of crucial importance. One must think in terms of years, not weeks or months. Finally, I would add humility to the list. The therapist who works with IA patients is much in the position of the .300 hitter in baseball: lauded for his splendid success, but well aware this success involves failure seven times out of 10.

REFERENCES

Albert, H.D. (1983). Specific techniques with dangerous or armed patients. In: *Treating Schizophrenic Patients: A Clinical/Analytic Approach* (eds M.H. Stone, H.D. Albert, D.V. Forrest, and S. Arieti) pp. 275–288. McGraw-Hill, New York.

Andrulonis, P.A., Glueck, B.C., Stroebel, C.F., Vogel, N.G., Shapiro, A.L., and Aldridge, D.M. (1981). Organic brain dysfunction and the borderline syndrome. *Psychiatr. Clin. North Am.*, 4, 47–66.

Beck, A.T., and Freeman, A. (1990). *Cognitive Therapy of Personality Disorders*. Guilford Press, New York.

Cadoret, R.J., and Stewart, M.A. (1991). An Adoption study of attention deficit/hyperactivity/aggression and their relationship to adult antisocial personality. *Compr. Psychiatry*, 32, 73–82.

Clarkin, J.F., Koenigsberg, H., Yeomans, F., Selzer, M., Kernberg, P., and Kernberg, O.F. (1992). Psychodynamic psychotherapy of the borderline patient. In: *Borderline Personality Disorder* (eds J.F. Clarkin, E. Marziali, and H. Monroe-Blum) pp. 268–287. Guilford Press, New York.

Cleckley, H. (1972). *The Mask of Sanity*, 5th edn. C.V. Mosby, St. Louis.

Costa, P.T. Jr, and McCrae, R.R. (1986). Personality stability and its implications for clinical psychology. *Clin. Psychol. Rev.*, 6, 407–423.

Frosch, J. (1977). The relation between acting out and disorders of impulse control. *Psychiatry*, 40, 295–314.

Gallwey, P.L.G. (1985). The psychodynamics of borderline personality. In: *Aggression & Dangerousness* (eds D.P. Farrington and J. Gunn) pp. 127–152. John Wiley, New York.

Hare, R.D., Harpur, T.J., Hakstian, A.R., Forth, A.E., Hart, S.D., and Newman, J.P. (1990). The revised Psychopathy Checklist: Reliability and factor structure. *Psychol. Assess.*, 2, 338–341.

Hodge, J.E. (1992). Addiction to violence: A new model of psychopathy. *Criminal Behav. Ment. Health*, 2, 212–223.

Huesmann, L.R. (1988). An information processing model for the development of aggression. *Aggress. Behav.*, 14, 13–24.

Kafka, M.P. (1991). Successful treatment of paraphilic coercive disorder (a rapist) with fluoxetine hydrochloride. *Br. J. Psychiatry*, 158, 844–847.

Kavoussi, R.J., and Coccaro, E.F. (1993). Impulse personality disorders and disorders of impulse control. In: *Obsessive Compulsive-Related Disorders* (ed. E. Hollander) pp. 179–202. American Psychiatric Press, Washington, D.C.

Kernberg, O.F. (1975). *Borderline Conditions and Pathological Narcissism.* J. Aronson, New York.

Kernberg, O.F. (1992). *Aggression in Personality Disorders and Perversions.* New Haven: Yale University Press.

Kernberg, O.F., Selzer, M.A., Koenigsberg, H.W., Carr, A., and Appelbaum, A.H. (1989). *Psychodynamic Psychotherapy of Borderline Patients.* Basic Books, New York.

Klir, G.J., and Folger, T.A. (1988). *Fuzzy Sets, Uncertainty and Information.* Prentice-Hall, Englewood Cliffs, N.J.

Linehan, M.M. (1993). *Cognitive–Behavioral Treatment of Borderline Personality Disorder.* Guilford Press, New York.

Linehan, M.M., and Heard, H.L. (1992). Dialectical behavior therapy for borderline personality disorder. In: *Borderline Personality Disorder* (eds J.F. Clarkin, E. Marziali, and H. Monroe-Blum) pp. 248–267. Guilford Press, New York.

McGlashan, T.H. (1992). The longitudinal profile of borderline personality disorder: Contributions from the Chestnut-Lodge Follow-Up Study. In: *Handbook of Borderline Disorders* (eds D. Silver and M. Rosenbluth) pp. 53–83. International University Press, Madison, CT.

Menninger, W.W. (1993). Management of the aggressive and dangerous patient. *Bull. Menn. Clin.*, 57, 208–217.

Pittman, R.K. (1993). Posttraumatic obsessive–compulsive disorder: A case study. *Compr. Psychiatry*, 34, 102–107.

Robins, L.N., Tipp, J., and Przybeck, T. (1991). Antisocial personality. In: *Psychiatric Disorders in America* (eds L.N. Robins and D.A. Regier) pp. 258–290. Macmillan, New York.

Satel, S., Southwick, S., and Denton, C. (1988). Single case study: Use of imipramine for attention deficit disorder in a borderline patient. *J. Nerv. Ment. Dis.*, 176, 305–307.

Spungen, D. (1983). *And I Don't Want to Live this Life.* Random House, New York.

Stein, D.J. (1992). Psychoanalysis and cognitive science: Contrasting models of the mind. *J. Am. Acad. Psychoanal.*, 20, 543–560.

Stein, D.J., and Young, J.E. (1992). Schema approach to personality disorders. In: *Cognitive Science and Clinical Disorders* (eds. D.J. Stein and J.E. Young) pp. 271–288. Academic Press, New York.

Stein, D.J., Hollander, E., Anthony, D.T., Schneier, F.R., Fallon, B.A., Liebowitz, M.R., and Klein, D.F. (1992). Serotonergic medications for sexual obsessions, sexual addictions, and paraphilias. *J. Clin. Psychiatry*, 53, 267–271.

Stone, M.H. (1988). The borderline domain: The "inner script" and other common psychodynamics. In: *Modern Perspectives in Psychiatry*, vol. 11 (ed. J. Howell) pp. 200–230. Brunner/Mazel, New York.

Stone, M.H. (1990a). *The Fate of Borderline Patients.* Guilford Press, New York.

Stone, M.H. (1990b). Treatment of borderline patients. A pragmatic approach. *Psychiatr. Clin. North Am.*, 13, 265–283.

Stone, M.H. (1991). Aggression, rage and the destructive instinct reconsidered from a psychobiological point of view. *J. Am. Acad. Psychoanal.*, 19, 507–529.

Stone, M.H. (1992). Borderline anger and the border of treatability. *Psychiatr.*

Neurol. Jpn, 92, 824–830.

Stone, M.H. (1993). *Abnormalities of Personality: Within and Beyond the Realm of Treatment*. W.W. Norton, New York.

Stone, M.H. (1994). Early traumatic factors in the lives of serial murderers. *Amer. J. Forensic Psychiat.*, 15, 5–26.

Tarnopolsky, A. (1992). Borderline disorders: A British point of view. In: *Handbook of Borderline Disorders* (eds D. Silver and M. Rosenbluth) pp. 177–202. International University Press, Madison, CT.

Tupin, J.P., Smith, D.B., and Clanon, T.L. (1973). The long-term use of lithium in aggressive prisoners. *Compr. Psychiatry*, 14, 311–314.

Valzelli, L. (1981). *Psychobiology of Aggression and Violence*. Raven Press, New York.

Yudofsky, S.C., Silver, J.M., and Hales, R.E. (1993). Cocaine and aggressive behavior: Neurobiological and clinical perspectives. *Bull. Menn. Clin.*, 57, 219–226.

19 Legal and Ethical Issues*

ROBERT I SIMON
Program in Psychiatry and Law, Georgetown University School of
Medicine, Washington DC, USA

INTRODUCTION

A wide spectrum of psychiatric disorders may manifest impulsive and
aggressive symptomatology that presents serious legal problems for the
clinician. The malpractice risk in treating such patients is high, particularly
when they harm others or themselves. Suicide is the leading source of
lawsuits against psychiatrists. Moreover, in the USA, the Tarasoff case and
its progeny have effectively established a national standard of care to warn
and protect individuals endangered by our patients (Simon, 1992a, p. 306).

Involuntary hospitalization is a rather frequent intervention for patients
suffering from impulsivity and aggression disorders. One of the substantive
criteria in all jurisdictions for involuntary hospitalization is dangerousness to
others or self. Dangerousness, by itself, however, is insufficient. The patient
must also meet the mentally ill criteria.

The legal regulation of seclusion and restraint has burgeoned over the past
decade. Legislative as well as institutional regulation of seclusion and
restraint has proliferated. A substantial body of case law regarding seclusion
and restraint has developed.

Finally, criminal acts are the handmaiden of impulsivity and aggression
disorders. Arrests for assaultive behavior are common in individuals with
antisocial personalities and occur with some frequency in other personality
disorders as well. The insanity defense has been evoked not only for capital
crimes such as murder, but considerably less successfully for criminal acts
arising from impulse disorders such as kleptomania, pathological gambling,
pyromania, and intermittent explosive disorder. Additionally, the legal
problems of individuals who cannot control their spending are daunting. A
working knowledge of the law empowers the psychiatrist in the treatment
and management of these difficult patients. A number of legal interventions
have a medical jurisprudence dimension that can be utilized beneficially for
the patient (Wexler, 1990).

This chapter discusses the legal and ethical issues relating to psychiatric

---

*Portions of this chapter have been adapted from "The law in psychiatry", in: *American
Psychiatric Press Textbook in Psychiatry*, 2nd edn (eds R.E. Hales, S.C. Yudofsky, and
J.D. Talbott), American Psychiatric Press, Washington, D.C. (1994).

disorders in the context of US law. While the exact legal position varies from one country to another, many countries have broadly similar legislation, and the ethical principles of beneficence, nonmaleficence and social justice remain the same worldwide.

ETHICAL CONSIDERATIONS

During the first half of this century, the principle of patient autonomy was clearly recognized in the medical malpractice case *Schloendorff v. Society of New York Hospital* (1914). Justice Cardozo firmly enunciated the principal of patient self-determination by stating that "every human being of adult years and sound mind has a right to determine what shall be done with his own body, and a surgeon who performs an operation without his patient's consent commits an assault, for which he is liable in damages" (p. 126).

Since the late 1950s and early 1960s, the medical profession has moved away from an authoritarian, physician-oriented stance toward a more collaborative relationship with patients concerning their health-care decisions. This is especially reflected in contemporary ethical principles (American Psychiatric Association, 1992a). Thus, on ethical grounds, psychiatry endorses granting competent patients the legal right to autonomy in determining their medical care. Quite apart from any legal compulsion, most psychiatrists disclose truthful and pertinent medical information to their patients as a way of enhancing the therapeutic alliance (Simon, 1989; Simon, 1992a, p. 133).

The ethical principles of beneficence, nonmaleficence, and the respect for the dignity and autonomy of the patient provide the moral–ethical foundation for the doctor–patient relationship. Accordingly, patients with dementia or other brain disorders that significantly interfere with the capacity to make decisions require more active intervention by the psychiatrist. For example, the psychiatrist has a legal and ethical duty to obtain consent from substitute decision makers when a patient is incapable of making an informed decision. The rights of all patients are the same—only how these rights are exercised is different (Parry and Beck, 1990).

The ethics of social justice call for the fair allocation of medical resources in accord with medical need (Ruchs, 1984). Although seemingly a new development, the ethical concerns about equitable health care distribution are found in the Hippocratic Oath and in the tradition of medicine and psychiatry (Dyer, 1988). Thus, psychiatric patients are ethically entitled to have access to the same medical resources available to other patients. In a related example, it would be unethical to discriminate against patients with AIDS-related dementia by not providing adequate treatment and management resources (American Medical Association, 1988).

Individuals suffering from disorders of impulsivity and aggression often present the clinician with difficult ethical dilemmas. One instance that comes readily to mind concerns the patient threatening harm to another. The immediate ethical conflict involves the preservation of patient confidentiality (beneficence and nonmaleficence) versus the protection of others in society (social justice). *The Principles of Medical Ethics With Annotations Especially Applicable to Psychiatry* states, "Psychiatrists at times may find it necessary, in order to protect the patient or the community from imminent danger, to reveal confidential information disclosed by the patient" (American Psychiatric Association, 1992b, Section 4, Annotation 8). Moreover, in the majority of jurisdictions, the law requires warning or protecting endangered third parties. But except in the most obvious cases where violence appears to be imminent, the prediction of violent acts by psychiatrists is notoriously poor. Under these circumstances, does not ethical concern swing back to preserving the patient's confidentiality and protecting the treatment situation?

Another ethical situation involving the principle of justice occurs in the physician's response to domestic violence. The ethical principles of beneficence and nonmaleficence require the physician to respond to the social, spiritual and psychological aspects of domestic violence. Do no harm requires identifying domestic violence rather than prescribing inappropriate therapies as a result of making the wrong diagnosis (American Medical Association, 1992). But family life is regarded as private and sacrosanct. Identifying violence in the family invades the sanctuary of the family, violating norms of autonomy and self-determination. Nevertheless, Jecker (1993) asserts that such privacy beliefs interfere with the physician broadening his or her ethical duties to intercede on behalf of battered patients on the basis of the principle of justice. The principle of justice transcends the allocation of medical resources, encompassing issues of fundamental liberties, powers, and opportunities. Accordingly, justice forms a significant foundation for the physician's intervention in domestic violence. Mandatory steps that do not violate confidentiality and autonomy, such as medical education on domestic violence and training in the identification and treatment of abused patients, should be undertaken. Justice establishes conditions favorable to self-respect, carrying important implications for the physician's response in supporting the patient's self-respect and dignity.

PSYCHIATRIC MALPRACTICE

Psychiatric malpractice is medical malpractice. Malpractice is the provision of substandard professional care that causes a compensable injury to a person with whom a professional relationship existed. Although this concept may seem relatively clear and simple, it has its share of conditions and caveats. For example, the essential issue is *not* the existence of substandard care *per se* but whether there is actual compensable liability. In order for a psychiatrist to be found *liable* to a patient for malpractice, the four fundamental elements in Table 1 must be established by a preponderance of the evidence (e.g. more likely than not).

Medical malpractice is a tort or civil wrong—that is, a noncriminal or non-contract-related wrong—committed as a result of negligence by psychiatrists and causing injury to a patient in their care. Negligence, the fundamental concept underlying a malpractice lawsuit, is simply described as doing something that a person with a duty of care (to the patient) should not have done or failing to do something that a person with a duty of care should have done. The fact that a psychiatrist commits an act of negligence does not automatically make him or her liable to the patient bringing the lawsuit. Liability for malpractice is based on the plaintiff (e.g. patient) establishing by a preponderance of the evidence the four basic elements in Table 1.

Each of these four elements must be met or there can be no finding of liability, regardless of any finding of negligence. A psychiatrist may actually be negligent but still not be found liable. For example, if the patient suffered no real injuries because of the negligence or if there was an injury but it was not directly due to the psychiatrist's negligence, then a claim of malpractice will be defeated.

Critical to the establishment of a claim of professional negligence is the requirement that the defendant's conduct was substandard or was a deviation in the standard of care owed to the plaintiff. Except in the case of "specialists", the law presumes and holds all physicians to a standard of *ordinary care*, which is measured by its *reasonableness* according to the clinical circumstances in which it is provided.

THE SUICIDAL PATIENT

The most common legal action involving psychiatric care is the failure to reasonably protect patients from harming themselves. Table 2 provides an

Table 1   The four Ds of malpractice assessment*

A doctor–patient relationship creating a DUTY of care must be present

A DEVIATION from the standard of care must have occurred

DAMAGE to the patient must have occurred

The damage must have occurred DIRECTLY as a result of deviation from the standard of care

*From Simon (1992c) with permission.

Table 2 Civil liability for the suicide of a psychiatric patient: causes of action/ defense*

INPATIENT (HOSPITAL) LIABILITY
Diagnosis
1. Unforeseeable suicide: failure to properly assess
2. Foreseeable suicide:
   a. Failure to properly document
   b. Improper diagnosis or assessment

Treatment (foreseeable suicide)
1. Failure to properly supervise
2. Failure to restrain (high-risk patient)
3. Premature release (e.g. pass)
4. Negligent discharge
5. Unjustified freedom of movement

Defenses
1. Compliance with accepted medical practice
2. Lack of reasonable knowledge of suicidality
3. Justifiable allowance of freedom of movement (e.g. "open ward")
4. Reasonable physician's decision regarding diagnosis or course of treatment
5. Intervening acts or factors (e.g. third parties)
6. Extraordinary circumstances precluding or circumventing reasonable precautions or restraint

OUTPATIENT PSYCHOTHERAPIST LIABILITY
Diagnosis
1. Unforeseeable suicide: negligent diagnosis
2. Foreseeable suicide:
   a. Improper diagnosis

Treatment
1. Negligent treatment (e.g. supervision, abandonment, referral)
2. Failure to control (e.g. hospitalize)

Defenses
1. Compliance with standard of care
2. Diagnosis of suicidality not reasonable
3. Intervening acts
4. Extraordinary circumstances

---

*From Smith J, Bisbing S: *Suicide: Caselaw Summary and Analysis*, Legal Medicine Press, Potomac, MD, 1988, with permission.

overview of the most common areas of negligence for which an inpatient provider (psychiatrist or hospital) and an outpatient psychiatrist may be held liable if injuries or death result from a patient's suicide attempt.

In essence, theories of negligence involving suicide can be grouped into three broad categories: failure to properly diagnose (assess the potential for suicide); failure to treat (use reasonable treatment interventions and precautions); and failure to implement (treatment is negligently carried out).

These theories, each of which applies to inpatient and outpatient settings, are based on the practitioner's failure to act reasonably in exercising the appropriate duty of care owed to the patient. Patient suicides leading to wrongful death suits are based upon the legal concepts of foreseeability and causation. A typical lawsuit will argue that the potential for suicide was not diagnosed and treated properly, and that this resulted in the patient's death.

As a general rule, a psychiatrist who exercises reasonable care in compliance with accepted medical practice will not be held liable for any resulting injury. Normally, if a patient's suicide was not reasonably foreseeable or where the suicide occurred as a result of intervening factors, this rule will apply.

FORESEEABLE SUICIDAL PATIENTS

The evaluation of suicidal risk is one of the most complex, difficult and challenging clinical tasks in psychiatry. Suicide is a rare event with low specificity (high false-positive rates). A comprehensive assessment of a patient's suicide risk is critical to a sound clinical management plan. Using reasonable care in assessing suicidal risk can pre-empt the problem of predicting the actual occurrence of suicide, for which professional standards do not yet exist. Standard approaches to the assessments of suicide risk have been proposed (Blumenthal, 1990; Simon, 1992a). Short-term (24–48 h) suicide risk assessments are more reliable than long-term assessments.

As an accepted standard of care, an evaluation of suicidal risk should be made for all patients, regardless of whether they present overt suicidal complaints. A review of case law shows that reasonable care requires that a patient who is either suspected or confirmed to be suicidal must be the subject of certain affirmative precautions. A failure either to reasonably assess a patient's suicidality, or to implement an appropriate precautionary plan once the suicide potential becomes foreseeable, is likely to render a practitioner liable if the patient is harmed because of a suicide attempt. The law tends to assume that suicide is preventable if it is foreseeable. Foreseeability, however, should not be confused with preventability. In hindsight, many suicides seem preventable that were clearly not foreseeable.

INPATIENTS

Intervention in an inpatient setting usually requires:

1. Screening evaluations.
2. Case review by clinical staff.
3. Development of an appropriate treatment plan.
4. Implementation of that plan.

Careful documentation of assessments and management interventions with responsive changes to the patient's clinical situation should be considered clinically and legally sufficient psychiatric care. Assessing suicide risk is only half the equation. Documenting the benefits of a psychiatric intervention (e.g. ward change, pass, or discharge) against the risk of suicide permits an evenhanded approach to the clinical management of the patient. Consideration only of a patient's suicide risk is a manifestation of defensive psychiatry that interferes with good clinical care, possibly further exposing the psychiatrist to a malpractice suit. Psychiatrists are more likely to be sued when a psychiatric inpatient commits suicide. The law presumes that the opportunities to foresee (anticipate) and control (treat and manage) suicidal patients are greater in the hospital.

OUTPATIENTS

Outpatient therapists face a somewhat different situation. Psychiatrists are expected to assess the severity and imminence of a foreseeably suicidal act. The result of the assessment dictates the nature of the duty of care options. Courts have reasoned that when an outpatient commits suicide, the therapist will not necessarily be held to have breached a duty to safeguard the patient from foreseeable self-harm because of the difficulty in controlling the patient (*Speer v. United States*, 1981). Instead, the reasonableness of the psychiatrist's efforts will be determinative.

SUICIDE PREVENTION PACTS

Suicide prevention "contracts" created between the clinician and the patient attempt to develop an expressed understanding that the patient will call for help rather than act out suicidal thoughts or impulses. These "contracts" have no legal authority. Although possibly helpful in solidifying the therapeutic alliance, such "contracts" may falsely reassure the psychiatrist. Suicide prevention agreements between psychiatrists and patients must not be used in place of adequate suicide assessment (Simon, 1991).

LEGAL DEFENSES

One legal defense that has created a split in the courts involves the use of the "open door" policy in which patients are allowed freedom of movement, for therapeutic purposes. In these cases, the individual facts and reasonableness of the staff's application of the "open door" policy appears to be paramount. Nevertheless, courts have difficulty with abstract treatment notions such as personal growth when faced with a dead patient.

Another defense, the doctrine of sovereign or governmental immunity, may statutorily bar a finding of liability against a state or federal facility. An intervening cause of suicide over which the clinician has no control is another valid legal defense. For example, a court might find that the suicidal act of a borderline patient who experienced a significant rejection between therapy sessions, and then impulsively attempted suicide without trying to contact the therapist, was caused by the superseding intervening variable of an unforeseen rejection and not by the therapist's negligence. Finally, the best-judgment defense has been used successfully when the patient was properly assessed and treated for suicide risk but the patient committed suicide anyway (Robertson, 1991).

THE VIOLENT PATIENT

As a general rule, one person has no duty to control the conduct of a second person in order to prevent that person from physically harming a third person (Restatement [Second] of Torts 315(a) [1965]). Applying this rule to psychiatric care, psychiatrists traditionally have had only a limited duty to control hospitalized patients and to exercise due care upon discharge. Within the last two decades, this rule has changed. After *Tarasoff v. Regents of the University of California* (1976), the therapist's legal duty and potential liability have significantly expanded. In *Tarasoff*, the California Supreme Court first recognized that a duty to protect third parties was imposed only when a special relationship existed between the victim, the individual whose conduct created the danger, and the defendant. The court stated that "the single relationship of a doctor to his patient is sufficient to support the duty to exercise reasonable care to protect others" from the violent acts of patients.

A majority of courts have found no duty to protect without a foreseeable victim. Only a small minority of courts have held that a duty to protect exists for the population at large. Despite the fact that the duty to protect still is not law in a number of jurisdictions and is subject to different interpretations by individual courts, the duty to protect is, in effect, a national standard of practice.

In some jurisdictions, courts have held that the need to safeguard the public wellbeing over-rides all other considerations, including confidentiality. In certain states, a psychotherapist has a duty to act affirmatively to protect an endangered third party from a patient's violent or dangerous acts. While a few courts have declined to find a Tarasoff duty in a specific case, a growing number of courts have recognized some variation of the original Tarasoff duty. No court has rejected the duty outright as legally invalid.

A number of states have enacted immunity statutes that protect the therapist from legal liability from a patient's violent acts toward others (Appelbaum et al., 1989). The majority of these statutes define the therapist's duty in terms of warning the endangered third party and/or notifying the authorities. The phrasing of duty to protect in some statutes allows for a greater variety of clinical interventions.

RELEASE OF POTENTIALLY VIOLENT PATIENTS

Violent or potentially violent patients in an inpatient setting represent a unique and challenging situation for treating psychiatrists. In a hospital, there is more control over the patient than is available in an outpatient setting. Courts closely evaluate those decisions made by psychiatrists who treat inpatients that adversely affect the patient or a third party. Liability imposed on psychiatric facilities that had custody of patients who injured others outside the institution following escape or release are clearly distinguishable from the factual situation of *Tarasoff*. Duty-to-warn cases involve patients in outpatient treatment. Liability arises from the inaction of the therapists who fails to take affirmative measures to warn or protect endangered third persons. In negligent-release cases, however, liability may arise from the allegation that the institution's affirmative act in releasing the patient caused injury to the third party.

Lawsuits stemming from the release of a foreseeably dangerous patient who subsequently injures or kills himself or someone else are roughly five to six times more common than outpatient duty-to-warn litigation (Simon, 1992b).

Psychiatrists must not discharge patients and then forget about them. The patient's willingness to cooperate with the psychiatrist, however, is critical to maintaining follow-up treatment. The psychiatrist's obligation focuses upon structuring the follow-up visits in such a fashion as to encourage compliance. A study of Veteran's Administration (VA) outpatient referrals showed that of 24% of inpatients referred to a VA mental health clinic, approximately 50% failed to keep their first appointments (Zeldow and Taub, 1981). Nevertheless, limitations do exist on the extent of the psychiatrist's ability to ensure follow-up care. This must be acknowledged by both the psychiatric and legal communities (Simon, 1992a).

In either the outpatient or inpatient situation, psychiatrists will comply with the responsibility to warn and protect others from potentially violent patients if they reasonably assess a patient's *risk* for violence and act in a clinically appropriate manner based on their findings. Professional standards do exist for the assessment of the risk factors for violence (Simon, 1992c). No standard of care exists, however, for the prediction of violent behavior. The clinician should assess the risk of violence frequently, updating the risk assessment at significant clinical junctures (e.g., room and ward changes, passes, and discharge). A risk–benefit assessment should be conducted and recorded prior to issuing a pass or discharge.

INVOLUNTARY HOSPITALIZATION

A person may be involuntarily hospitalized only if certain statutorily mandated criteria are met. Three main substantive criteria serve as the foundation for all statutory commitment requirements. These substantive criteria are that the individual be (1) mentally ill, (2) dangerous to self or others, and/or (3) unable to provide for their own basic needs. Generally, each state spells out which criteria are required and what each means. Terms such as "mentally ill" are often loosely described, thus displacing the responsibility for proper definition onto the clinical judgment of the petitioner.

In addition to individuals with mental illness, certain states have enacted legislation that permits the involuntary hospitalization of three other distinct groups: developmentally disabled (mentally retarded), substance addicts (alcohol, drugs), and mentally disabled minors. Special commitment provisions may exist, governing requirements for the admission and discharge of mentally disabled minors as well as numerous due-process rights afforded these individuals (*Parham v. J.R.* 1979).

Involuntary hospitalization of psychiatric patients usually arises when violent behavior threatens to erupt and when patients become unable to care for themselves. These patients frequently manifest mental disorders and conditions that readily meet the substantive criteria for involuntary hospitalization.

Clinicians must remember that they do not commit patients. This is done solely under the jurisdiction of the court. The psychiatrist merely initiates a medical certification that brings the patient before the court, usually after a brief period of hospitalization for evaluation. Clinicians should not attempt to second-guess the court's ultimate decision concerning involuntary hospitalization. In seeking medical certification, the psychiatrist must be guided by the treatment needs of the patient.

Commitment statutes do not require involuntary hospitalization but are permissive (Appelbaum et al., 1989). The statutes enable mental health professionals and others to seek involuntary hospitalization for persons who meet certain substantive criteria. On the other hand, the duty to seek involuntary hospitalization is a standard-of-care issue. Patients who are mentally ill and pose an imminent, serious threat to themselves or others may require involuntary hospitalization as a primary psychiatric intervention.

LIABILITY

The most common cause of a malpractice action involving involuntary hospitalization occurs when a psychiatrist fails to adhere in good faith to statutory requirements and this leads to a wrongful commitment. Often these lawsuits are brought under the theory of false imprisonment. Other areas of liability that may arise from wrongful commitment include assault and battery, malicious prosecution, abuse of authority, and intentional infliction of emotional distress (Simon, 1992a, pp. 170–171).

SECLUSION AND RESTRAINT

The psychiatric legal issues surrounding seclusion and restraint are complex. Seclusion and restraint have both indications and contraindications as clinical management modalities (see Tables 3 and 4). The legal regulation of seclusion and restraint has become increasingly more stringent over the past decade.

Table 3 Indications for seclusion and restraint*

1. Prevent clear, imminent harm to the patient or others
2. Prevent significant disruption to treatment program or physical surroundings
3. Assist in treatment as part of ongoing behavior therapy
4. Decrease sensory overstimulation†
5. At patient's voluntary reasonable request

†Seclusion only

*From Simon (1992c) with permission.

Table 4 Contraindications to seclusion and restraint*

1. Extremely unstable medical and psychiatric conditions†
2. Delirious or demented patients unable to tolerate decreased stimulation†
3. Overtly suicidal patients†
4. Patients with severe drug reactions, overdoses or requiring close monitoring of drug dosages†
5. For punishment or convenience of staff

†Unless close supervision and direct observation provided

*From Simon (1992c) with permission.

Legal challenges to the use of restraints and seclusion have been made on behalf of the institutionalized mentally ill and the mentally retarded. Normally, these lawsuits do not stand alone, but are a part of a challenge to a wide range of alleged abuses within a hospital.

Generally, courts hold or consent decrees provide that restraints and seclusion can be implemented only when a patient presents a risk of harm to self or others and no less restrictive alternative is available. Additional considerations include:

1. Restraint and seclusion can only be implemented by a written order from an appropriate medical official.
2. Orders are to be confined to specific, time-limited periods.
3. A patient's condition must be regularly reviewed and documented.
4. Any extension of an original order must be reviewed and reauthorized.

In addition to these guidelines, some courts and state statutes outline certain due-process procedures that must be followed before a restraint or seclusion order can be implemented. Typical due-process considerations include some form of notice, a hearing, and the involvement of an impartial decision maker. Notably, patient due-process protections are only required in cases in which restraint and seclusion are used for disciplinary purposes. In the absence of language to the contrary, these procedures may be eased in cases of emergency.

The acceptability of restraint or seclusion for the purposes of training was recognized in the landmark case, *Youngberg v. Romeo* (1982). *Youngberg* involved a challenge to the "treatment" practices at the Pennhurst State School and Hospital in Pennsylvania. The Supreme Court held that patients could not be restrained except to ensure their safety or, in certain undefined circumstances, "to provide needed training" for patients. In *Youngberg*, the Court recognized that the defendant had a liberty interest in safety and freedom from bodily restraint. The Court added that these interests were not absolute and in conflict with the need to provide training. The Court also held that decisions made by appropriate professionals regarding restraining the patient would presumptively be considered correct. *Youngberg* is viewed as the first step in the right direction by advocates for the developmentally disabled. In addition, psychiatrists and other mental health professionals have lauded the decision because the Court recognized that professionals rather than the courts are best able to determine the needs of patients, including determining when restraint is appropriate.

Most states have enacted statutes regulating the use of restraints, normally specifying the circumstances when restraints can be used. Most often, those circumstances occur only when a risk of harm to self or danger to others is imminent. Statutory regulation of the use of seclusion is far less common. Only about one-half of the states have laws relating to seclusion. The majority of states with laws regarding seclusion and restraint require some type of documentation of their usage.

National guidelines for the proper use of seclusion and restraints have been established by the American Psychiatric Association Task Force on the Psychiatric Uses of Seclusion and Restraint (American Psychiatric Association, 1984). The Joint Commission on Accreditation of Healthcare Organizations (JCAHO) has promulgated detailed guidelines for hospitals regarding seclusion and restraint requirements (JCAHO, 1991, Sections 2.1–2.10, pp. 146–147). Professional opinion concerning the clinical use of physical restraints and seclusion varies considerably. Unless precluded by state freedom from restraint and seclusion statutes, a variety of uses for seclusion can be justified on both clinical and legal grounds (Simon, 1992b).

CRIMINAL PROCEEDINGS

Individuals charged with committing crimes frequently display significant psychiatric and neurological impairment. A history of severe head injury may be present. The possibility of a neuropsychiatric disorder must be thoroughly investigated. For example, Lewis et al. (1986) examined 15 death row inmates who were chosen for examination because of imminent execution rather than evidence of neuropathology. In each case, evidence of severe head injury and neurological impairment was found.

The causal connection between brain damage and violence remains frustratingly obscure. Violent behavior spans a wide spectrum from a normal response to a threatening situation to violence emanating directly from an organic brain disorder such as Klüver–Bucy syndrome, hypothalamic tumors, or temporal lobe epilepsy (Strub and Black, 1988). Moreover, violent behavior is usually the result of the interaction between a specific individual and situation. Brain damage and mental illness may or may not play a significant role in this equation. Psychiatrists must acknowledge limitations to their expertise concerning the possible connection between brain damage and violence.

CRIMINAL INTENT *(MENS REA)*

Under the common law, the basic elements of a crime are: (1) the mental state or level of intent to commit the act (known as the *mens rea* or guilty mind), (2) the act itself or conduct associated with committing the crime (known as *actus reus* or guilty act), and (3) a concurrence in time between the guilty act and the guilty mental state (*Bethea v. United States*, 1977). To convict a person of a particular crime, the state must prove beyond a reasonable doubt that the defendant committed the criminal act with the requisite intent. All three elements are necessary in order to satisfy the threshold requirements for the imposition of criminal sanctions.

The question of intent is a particularly vexing problem for the courts. For example, everyone would agree that killing another person is deplorable conduct. But should the death of a child in a car accident, the heat-of-passion shooting by a husband of his wife's lover, and the "cold-blooded" murder of a bank teller by a robber all be punished the same? The determination of the defendant's intent, or *mens rea*, at the time of the offense is the law's "equalizer" and trigger mechanism for deciding criminal culpability and the appropriate division of retribution. For instance, a person who deliberately plans to commit a crime is more culpable than one who accidentally commits one.

There are two classes of intent used to categorize *mens rea*: specific and general. Specific intent refers to the *mens rea* in those crimes in which a *further intention* is present, beyond that which is identified with the physical act associated with an offense. For instance, the courts will frequently state that the intent necessary for first-degree murder includes a "specific intent to kill" or a person might commit an assault "with the intent to rape" (Melton et al., 1987). Unlike general criminal intent, specific criminal intent cannot be presumed from the unlawful criminal act but must be proved independently.

General criminal intent is more elusive. General criminal intent may be presumed from commission of the criminal act. It usually is used by the law to explain criminal liability where a defendant was merely conscious or should have been conscious of his or her physical actions at the time of the offense (Melton et al., 1987). For example, proof that the owner of a boat sold it without first paying off the loan creates a presumption that the owner intended to defraud the lender. In order to deal with the vagueness of these two standards, many states have enacted their own definitions of intent.

Persons with certain mental handicaps or impairments represent an interesting challenge for prosecutors, defense counsel, and judges in determining what, if any, retribution is justifiable. Mental impairment often raises serious questions about the intent to commit a crime and the appreciation of its consequences.

In addition to *mens rea*, a person's mental status can play a deciding role in whether the defendant will be ordered to stand trial to face the criminal charges (*Dusky v. United States*, 1960), be acquitted of the alleged crime (*M'Naghten's Case*, 1843) (*United States v. Brawner*, 1972), be sent to prison, be hospitalized (*Commonwealth v. Robinson*, 1981; *Mental Aberration and Post Conviction Sanctions*, 1981; *State v. Hehman*, 1974), or, in some extreme cases, be sentenced to death (*The Eighth Amendment and the Execution of the Presently Incompetent*, 1980; *Ford v. Wainwright*, 1986). Before any defendant can be criminally prosecuted, the court must be satisfied that the accused is competent to stand trial: that is, understand the charges brought against him or her and to be capable of rationally assisting counsel with the defense.

COMPETENCY TO STAND TRIAL

In every situation in which competency is a question, the law seeks to reiterate a common theme: that only the acts of a rational individual are to be given recognition by society (*Neely v. United States*, 1945). In doing so, the law attempts to reaffirm the integrity of the individual and of society in general.

The legal standard for assessing pretrial competency was established by the United States Supreme Court in *Dusky v. United States* (1960). Throughout involvement with the trial process, the defendant must have "'sufficient present ability to consult with his lawyer with a reasonable degree of rational understanding and whether he has a rational as well as factual understanding of the proceedings against him" (*Dusky v. United States*, 1960).

Typically, the impairment that raises the question of the defendant's competence will be associated with a mental disease or defect. It is settled, however, that a person may be held to be incompetent to stand trial even if he or she does not suffer from a mental disease or defect as defined by the American Psychiatric Association (1993). For example, children under a certain age are ordinarily deemed incompetent to stand trial. Though the majority of impairments implicated in competency examinations are functional, rather than organic (Reich and Wells, 1985), various forms of psychiatric impairments will typically raise questions about a defendant's competency to stand trial.

Numerous commentators have sought to identify specific reality-based factors that could be used in assessing the general standards established in *Dusky*. One such attempt is the Competency to Stand Trial Instrument (CSTI), designed by the Laboratory of Community Psychiatry (McGarry, 1973). The CSTI involves the consideration of 13 functions "related to what is required of a defendant in criminal proceedings in order that he may adequately cope with and protect himself in such proceedings". The purpose of the CSTI was to standardize, objectify, and qualify relevant criteria for the determination of an individual's competency to stand trial. The presentation of these functions was written so it would be useful and acceptable to both the legal and medical professions.

The ultimate determination of incompetency is solely for the court to decide (*United States v. David*, 1975). Moreover, the impairment must be considered in the context of the particular case or proceeding. Mental impairment may render an individual incompetent to stand trial in a complicated tax fraud case but not incompetent for a misdemeanor trial.

Psychiatrists and psychologists who testify as expert witnesses regarding the effect of psychiatric problems on a defendant's competency to stand trial will be most effective if their findings are framed according to the degree to which the defendant is cognitively capable of meeting the standards enunciated in *Dusky*. Instruments such as the CSTI, for pragmatically illustrating actual functional conformity to competency standards, are especially useful.

INSANITY DEFENSE

In American jurisprudence, one of the most controversial issues is the insanity defense. Defendants with functional or organic mental disabilities who are found competent to stand trial may seek acquittal on the basis that they were not criminally responsible for their actions due to insanity at the time the offense was committed.

The vast majority of criminals commit crimes for a variety of reasons, but the law presumes that all of them do so rationally and of their own free will. As a result, the law concludes that they are deserving of some form of punishment. Some offenders, however, are so mentally disturbed in their thinking and behavior that they are thought to be incapable of acting rationally. Under these circumstances, civilized societies have deemed it unjust to punish a "crazy" or insane person (Coke, 1680; Blackstone, 1769). This is in part due to fundamental principles of fairness and morality. Additionally, the punishment of a person who cannot rationally appreciate the consequences of his or her actions thwarts the two major tenets of punishment—retribution and deterrence. Although the insanity defense is rarely used, a successful insanity defense is even rarer.

A generally accepted, precise definition of legal insanity does not exist. Over the years, tests of insanity have been subject to much controversy, modification and refinement (Brakel et al., 1985, p. 707). The development of the insanity defense standard in the USA has had four basic elements (see Table 5). The existence of a mental disorder has remained a consistent core of the insanity defense, while the three other elements have varied over time (Brakel et al., 1985, p. 709). Thus, there is variability in the insanity defense standard in the USA, depending upon which state or jurisdiction has control over the defendant raising the defense.

Following the acquittal by reason of insanity of John Hinckley Jr on charges of attempting to assassinate President Reagan and to murder others, an outraged public demanded changes in the insanity defense. Federal and state legislation to accomplish that result ensued. Between 1978 and 1985, approximately 75% of all states made some sort of substantive change in their insanity defense (Perlin, 1989). Nevertheless, a number of states continued to adhere to the American Law Institute (ALI) insanity defense standard or a version of it. The ALI test provides:

A person is not responsible for criminal conduct if at the time of such conduct

Table 5 Basic elements of insanity defense

- Presence of a mental disorder
- Presence of a defect of reason
- A lack of knowledge of the nature or wrongfulness of the act
- An incapacity to refrain from the act

From Simon RI: legal and ethical issues in traumatic brain injury, in: *Traumatic Brain Injury* (eds J.M. Silver, S.C. Yudofsky and R.E. Hales), American Psychiatric Press, Washington, D.C., 1994, with permission.

as a result of mental disease or defect he lacks substantial capacity either to appreciate the criminality (wrongfulness) of his conduct or to conform his conduct to the requirements of law. As used in this Article, the terms "mental disease or defect" do not include an abnormality manifested only by repeated criminal or otherwise anti-social conduct [Model Penal Code §4.01 (1962), U.L.A. 490-91 (1974)].

This standard contains both a cognitive and volitional prong. The cognitive prong derives from the 1843 M'Naghten rule exculpating the defendant who does not know the nature and quality of the alleged act or does not know that the act was wrong. The volitional prong is a vestige of the irresistible-impulse rule which states that the defendant who is overcome by an irresistible impulse that leads to an alleged act is not responsible for that act. It is on the volitional prong that experts disagree the most in individual cases.

By contrast, defendants tried in a federal court are governed by the standard enunciated in the Comprehensive Crime Control Act (CCCA) of 1984 (Pub L. No. 98-473, 98 Stat. 1837 (1984)). The CCCA provides that it is an affirmative defense to all federal crimes that, at the time of the offense, "the defendant, as a result of a severe mental disease or defect, was unable to appreciate the nature and quality or the wrongfulness of his acts. Mental disease or defect does not otherwise constitute a defense" (Model Penal Code §402, 98 Stat. at 2057). This codification eliminates the volitional or irresistible impulse portion of the insanity defense. That is, it does not allow an insanity defense based on a defendant's inability to conform his or her conduct to the requirements of the law. The defense is now limited to only those defendants who do not know what they are doing or who are unable to appreciate the wrongfulness of their acts (i.e. the *cognitive portion* of the defense).

The threshold issue in making an insanity determination is not the existence of a mental disease or defect *per se*, but the lack of substantial mental capacity because of it. Therefore, the lack of capacity due to mental defects other than mental illness may be sufficient. For instance, mental retardation may represent an adequate basis for the insanity defense under certain circumstances.

The impulse disorders of intermittent explosive disorder, kleptomania, pathological gambling, and pyromania generally have not fared well under the insanity defense. These conditions would not meet the cognitive prong of an insanity defense. Presumably, the volitional prong would be applicable but is usually insufficient by itself. Moreover, courts and juries tend to view criminal acts arising from impulse disorders as impulses not resisted rather than irresistible impulses. Pathological gambling no longer serves as a basis for an insanity defense (Rosenthal and Lorenz, 1992). McGarry (1983) points out that the lack of volitional control over the isolated act of gambling does not assume a lack of control over committing criminal acts in the service of the impulse to gamble. Compulsive gambling, however, is being raised as a mitigating factor at sentencing (Rosenthal and Lorenz, 1992). Less severe punishment is feasible, through a court's willingness to consider treatment, community service, restitution, and the possibility of probation.

Depending on the severity of the functional or organic mental disorder and its actual impact on an offender's cognitive and affective processes, a defense of insanity might be warranted. At the very least, however, the presence of a psychiatric disorder should be investigated as a *mitigating* factor that may have caused the offender to suffer from "diminished" capacity.

DIMINISHED CAPACITY

It is possible for a person to have the required *mens rea* and yet still be declared legally insane. For instance, a defendant's actions may be considered so "crazy" as to convince a jury that he or she was criminally insane and therefore not legally responsible. Yet his or her knowledge of the criminal act (e.g. committing a murder) was relatively intact. From this distinction, the law recognized that there are "shades" of mental impairment that obviously can affect *mens rea* but not necessarily to the extent of completely nullifying it. In recognition of this fact, the concept of "diminished capacity" was developed (Melton et al., 1987).

Broadly viewed, diminished capacity permits the accused to introduce medical and psychological evidence that relates directly to the *mens rea* for the crime charged, without having to assert a defense of insanity (Melton et al., 1987). For example, in the crime of assault with the intent to kill, a specific intent crime, psychiatric testimony would be permitted to address whether the offender acted with the purpose of committing homicide at the time of the assault. When a defendant's *mens rea* for the crime charged is nullified by psychiatric evidence, the defendant is acquitted only of that charge. In the above example, the prosecutor may still try to convict the defendant of another offense requiring a lesser *mens rea*, such as manslaughter (Melton et al., 1987). Patients suffering from psychiatric disorders who commit criminal acts may be eligible for a diminished capacity defense.

GUILTY BUT MENTALLY ILL

In a number of states, an alternative verdict of guilty but mentally ill (GBMI) has been established. Under GBMI statutes, if the defendant pleads not guilty by reason of insanity, this alternative verdict is available to the jury (Slovenko, 1982). Under an insanity plea, the verdict may be:

1. Not guilty.
2. Not guilty by reason of insanity.
3. Guilty but mentally ill.
4. Guilty.

The problem with GBMI is that it is an alternative verdict without a difference from finding the defendant plain guilty. The court must still impose a sentence upon the convicted person. Although the convicted person will receive special treatment if necessary, this treatment provision also is available to any other prisoner. Moreover, the frequent unavailability of appropriate psychiatric treatment for prisoners adds an additional element of spuriousness to the GBMI verdict.

EXCULPATORY AND MITIGATING DISORDERS

Psychotic disorders of differing etiology form the most common basis for an insanity defense. But in addition to the major psychiatric and organic brain disorders, a number of other conditions may provide a foundation for an insanity or diminished capacity defense.

Automatisms

For conviction for a crime, there must be not only a criminal state of mind (*mens rea*) but also the commission of a prohibited act (*actus reus*). The physical movement necessary to satisfy the *actus reus* requirement must be conscious and volitional. In addition to statutory and common law in many jurisdictions, Section 2.01(2) of the Model Penal Code (1962) specifically excludes from the *actus reus* the following:

(a) a reflex or convulsion; (b) a bodily movement during unconsciousness or sleep; (c) conduct during hypnosis or resulting from hypnotic suggestion; [and] (d) a bodily movement that otherwise is not the product of the effort or determination of the actor . . .

A defense claiming that the commission of a crime was an involuntary act is usually referred to as an automatism defense.

The classic, though rare, example is the person who commits an offense while "sleep walking". Courts have held that such an individual does not have conscious control of his or her physical actions and therefore acts involuntarily (*Fain v. Commonwealth*, 1879; *H.M. Advocate v. Fraser*, 1878). A conscious, reflexive action carried out under stressful circumstances may qualify for an automatism defense. For example, a driver who is being attacked in his car by a bee loses control in attempting to swat the insect. The car strikes a pedestrian who is killed. An automatism defense may exist to a charge of vehicular homicide. Other situations relevant to psychiatry, in which the defense might be used, arise when a crime is committed during a state of altered consciousness caused by a concussion following a head injury, involuntary ingestion of drugs or alcohol, hypoxia, metabolic disorders such hypoglycemia, or epileptic seizures (Low et al., 1982).

There are, however, limitations to the automatism defense. Most notably, some courts hold that if the person asserting the automatism defense was aware of the condition prior to the offense and failed to take reasonable steps to prevent the criminal occurrence, then the defense is not available. For example, if a defendant with a known history of uncontrolled epileptic seizures loses control of a car during a seizure and kills someone, that defendant will not be permitted to assert the defense of automatism.

Intoxication

Ordinarily, intoxication is not a defense against a criminal charge. Because intoxication, unlike mental illness, mental retardation, and most neuro-psychiatric conditions, is usually the product of a person's own actions, the law is naturally cautious about viewing it as a complete defense or mitigating factor. Most states view voluntary alcoholism as relevant to the issue of whether the defendant possessed the *mens rea* necessary to commit a specific intent crime or whether there was premeditation in a crime of murder. Generally, however, the mere fact that the defendant was voluntarily intoxicated will not justify a finding of automatism or insanity. A distinct difference does arise when, because of chronic heavy use of alcohol, the defendant suffers from an alcohol-induced organic mental disorder, such as alcohol hallucinosis, withdrawal delirium, amnestic disorder, or dementia associated with alcoholism. If competent psychiatric evidence is presented that an alcohol-related neuropsychiatric disorder caused significant cognitive or volitional impairment, a defense of insanity or diminished capacity could be upheld.

Temporal lobe seizures

Another "mental state" defense occasionally raised by defendants regarding assault-related crimes is that the assaultive behavior was involuntarily precipitated by abnormal electrical patterns in their brain. This condition is frequently diagnosed as temporal lobe epilepsy (Devinsky and Bear, 1984). Episodic dyscontrol syndrome (Elliot, 1978; Monroe, 1978) has also been advanced as a neuropsychiatric condition causing involuntary aggression. Studies have hypothesized that there are "centers of aggression" in the temporal lobe or limbic system—primarily the amygdala. This hypothesis has promoted the idea that sustained aggressive behavior by these persons may be primarily the product of an uncontrollable, randomly occurring, abnormal brain dysrhythmia. Hence, the legal argument is raised that these individuals should not be held accountable for their actions. Despite its simplicity and occasional success in the courts, there is little in the way of empirically significant data to support this theory at this time (Blumer, 1984).

METABOLIC DISORDERS

Defenses based on metabolic disorders have also been tried. The so-called "Twinkle Defense" was used as part of a successful diminished capacity defense of Dan White in the murders of San Francisco Mayor George Mosconi and Supervisor Harvey Milk. This defense was based on the theory that the ingestion of large amounts of sugar contributed to a state of temporary insanity (*People v. White*, 1981). The forensic psychiatric report stated that the defendant had been "filling himself up with Twinkies and Coca-Cola" (Blinder 1981–82, p. 16). After specifying a number of factors that contributed to the murders, the forensic examiner concluded with his opinion concerning Dan White's ingestion of certain food (Blinder 1981–82, pp. 21–22):

> Finally, there is much evidence to suggest recently recognized physiological aberrations consequent to consumption of noxious edibles by susceptibles. There are cases in the literature challenged with large quantities of refined sugar. Furthermore, there are studies of cerebral allergic reactions to the chemicals in highly processed foods; some studies have documented a marked reduction in violent and antisocial behavior in "career criminals" upon the elimination of these substances from their diet, as well as the production of rage reactions in susceptible individuals when challenged by the offending food substances. For these reasons, I would suggest a repeat electroencephalogram preceded by a glucose-tolerance test, as well as a clinical challenge of Mr. White's mental functions with known food antigens, in a controlled setting.

Hypoglycemic states also may be associated with significant psychiatric impairment (Kaplan and Sadock, 1989). When a substantial blood glucose depletion occurs, a wide variety of responses may occur, including episodic and repetitive dyscontrol, temporary amnesia, depression, and hostility with spontaneous recovery (quick recovery following the consumption of appropriate nutrients) (Wilson, Braunwal and Isselbacher, 1991). The degree of mental abnormality associated with hypoglycemic states varies from mild to severe according to the blood glucose level. It is the degree of disturbance, not the mere presence of an etiological metabolic component, that is determinative in a mental state defense. This principle also applies to mental dysfunctions produced by disorders originating in the hepatic, renal, adrenal, and neuroendocrine systems (e.g. premenstrual syndrome) (Parry and Berga, 1991).

CONCLUSION

Psychiatrists are increasingly called upon by the courts to provide expert advice and testimony concerning violent behavior. The causal connection between mental illness and violent behavior is murky at best. Psychiatrists must acknowledge limitations in their expertise about the etiology of violent behavior and in the assessment of violent individuals. Most violent individuals are not mentally ill as mental illness is currently understood. As such, they are the appropriate responsibility of society's law enforcement agencies.

REFERENCES

American Medical Association Council on Ethical and Judicial Affairs (1988). Ethical issues involved in the growing AIDS crisis. *JAMA*, 259, 1360–1361.

American Medical Association Council on Ethical and Judicial Affairs (1992). Physicians and domestic violence. *JAMA*, 267, 3190–3193.

American Psychiatric Association (1984). *American Psychiatric Association Task Force Report 22: The Psychiatric Uses of Seclusion and Restraint*. American Psychiatric Association, Washington, D.C.

American Psychiatric Association (1992a). *Opinions of the Ethics Committee on the Principles of Medical Ethics with Annotations Especially Applicable to Psychiatry*. American Psychiatric Press, Washington, D.C.

American Psychiatric Association (1992b). *The Principles of Medical Ethics With Annotations Especially Applicable to Psychiatry*. American Psychiatric Association, Washington, D.C.

American Psychiatric Association (1994). *Diagnostic and Statistical Manual of Mental Disorders*, 4th edn. American Psychiatric Association Press, Washington, D.C.

Appelbaum, P.S., Zonana, H., Bonnie, R., et al. (1989). Statutory approaches to limiting psychiatrists' liability for their patients' violent acts. *Am. J. Psychiatry*, 146, 821–828.

Blackstone, W. (1769). *Commentaries*, vol. 4, pp. 24–25.

Blinder, M. (1981–82). My examination of Dan White. *Am. J. Forensic Psychiatry*, II, 12–22.

Blumenthal, S.J. (1990). An overview and synopsis of risk factors, assessment and treatment of suicidal patients over the life cycle. In: *Suicide Over the Life Cycle* (eds S.J. Blumenthal, and D.J. Kupfer) pp. 685–733. American Psychiatric Press, Washington, D.C.

Blumer, D. (1984). *Psychiatric Aspects of Epilepsy*. American Psychiatric Press, Washington, D.C.

Brakel, S.J., Parry, J., and Weiner, B.A. (1985). *The Mentally Disabled and the Law*, 3rd edn. American Bar Foundation, Chicago.

Coke, E. (1680). *Third Institute*, 6th edn, p. 6.

Devinsky, P., and Bear, D.M. (1984). Varieties of aggressive behavior in patients with temporal lobe epilepsy. *Am. J. Psychiatry*, 141, 651–655.

Dyer, A.R. (1988). *Ethics and Psychiatry. Toward Professional Definition*, p. 34. American Psychiatric Press, Washington, D.C.

Elliot, E.A. (1978). Neurological aspects of antisocial behavior. In: *The Psychopath* (ed. W.H. Reid). Brunner/Mazel, New York.

Jecker, N.S. (1993). Privacy beliefs and the violent family: Extending the ethical argument for physician intervention. *JAMA*, 269, 776–780.

Kaplan, H.I., and Sadock, B.J. (1989). *Comprehensive Textbook of Psychiatry*, 5th edn, vol. 2, pp. 1219–1220. Williams & Wilkins, Baltimore.

Lewis, D.O., Pincus, J.H., Feldman, M., et al. (1986). Psychiatric, neurological and psychoeducational characteristics of 15 death row inmates in the United States. *Am. J. Psychiatry*, 143, 838–845.

Low, P., Jeffries, J., and Bonnie, R. (1982). *Criminal Law: Cases and Materials*, pp. 152–154. The Foundation Press, Mineola.

McGarry, A.L. (1973). *Competency to Stand Trial and Mental Illness. Crime and Delinquency Issues Series*, DHEW pub. no. HSM 73-9105. Rockville, MD.

McGarry, A.L. (1983). Pathological gambling: A new insanity defense. *Bull. Am. Acad. Psychiatry Law*, 11, 301–308.

Melton, G.B., Petrila, J., Poythress, N.G., et al. (1987). *Psychological Evaluation for the Courts*. Guilford Press, New York.

Monroe, R.R. (1978). *Brain Dysfunction in Aggressive Criminals*. Lexington Books, Lexington, MA.

Parry, J.W., and Beck, J.C. (1990). Revisiting the civil commitment/involuntary treatment stalemate using limited guardianship, substituted judgment and different due process considerations: A work in progress. *Med. Phys. Disabil. Law Rep.*, 14, 102–114.

Parry, B.L., and Berga, S.L. (1991). Neuroendocrine correlates of behavior during the menstrual cycle. In: *Psychiatry*, vol. 3 (ed. J.O. Cavenar) pp. 1–22. J.B. Lippincott, Philadelphia.

Perlin, M.L. (1989). *Mental Disability Law: Civil and Criminal*, vol. 3. Michie, Charlottesville.

Reich, J., and Wells, J. (1985). Psychiatric diagnosis and competency to stand trial. *Compr. Psychiatry*, 26, 421–432.

Robertson, J.D. (1991). The trial of a suicide case. In: *American Psychiatric Press Review of Clinical Psychiatry and the Law*, vol. 2 (ed. R.I. Simon) pp. 423–441. American Psychiatric Press, Washington, D.C.

Rosenthal, R.J., and Lorenz, V.C. (1992). The pathological gambler as criminal offender: Comments on evaluation and treatment. *Psychiatr. Clin. North Am.*, 15, 647–660.

Ruchs, V.R. (1984). The "rationing" of medical care. *N. Engl. J. Med.*, 311, 1572–1573.

Simon, R.I. (1989). Beyond the doctrine of informed consent—A clinician's perspective. *J. Expert Witness Trial Attorney Trial Judge*, 4, Fall, 23–25.

Simon, R.I. (1991). The suicide prevention pact: Clinical and legal considerations. In: *American Psychiatric Press Review of Clinical Psychiatry and the Law*, vol. 2 (ed. R.I. Simon) pp. 441–451. American Psychiatric Press, Washington, D.C.

Simon, R.I. (1992a). *Clinical Psychiatry and the Law*, 2nd ed. American Psychiatric Press, Washington, D.C.

Simon, R.I. (1992b). Clinical risk management of suicidal patients: Assessing the unpredictable. In: *American Psychiatric Press Review of Clinical Psychiatry and the Law*, vol. 3 (ed. R.I. Simon) pp. 3–63. American Psychiatric Press, Washington, D.C.

Simon, R.I. (1992c). *Concise Guide to Psychiatry and Law for Clinicians*, pp. 147–148. American Psychiatric Press, Washington, D.C.

Slovenko, R. (1982). Commentaries on psychiatry and law: "Guilty but mentally ill". *J. Psychiatry Law*, 10(4), 541–555.

Strub, R.L., and Black, F.W. (1988). *Neurobehavioral Disorders: A Clinical Approach*, p. 456. Davis, Philadelphia.

Wexler, D.B. (1990). *Therapeutic Jurisprudence: The Law as a Therapeutic Agent*. Carolina Academic Press, Durham.

Wilson, J.D., Braunwald, E., and Isselbacher, K.J. (1991). *Harrison's Principles of Internal Medicine*, 12th edn, vol. 2, p. 1759. McGraw-Hill, New York.

Zeldow, P.B., and Taub, H.A. (1981). Evaluating psychiatric discharge and aftercare in a VA medical center. *Hosp. Community Psychiatry*, 32, 57–58.

LEGAL CITATIONS

Bethea v. United States, 365 A2d 64, (D.C. 1976) *cert. denied*, 433 U.S. 911 (1977).

Commonwealth v. Robinson, 494 Pa 372, 431 A2d 901 (1981).

Dusky v. United States, 362 U.S. 402 (1960).

Fain v. Commonwealth, 78 Ky 183 (1879).

Ford v. Wainwright, 477 U.S. 399 (1986).

H.M. Advocate v. Fraser, 4 Couper 70 (1878).

Mental Aberration and Post Conviction Sanctions, 15 Suffolk UL Rev:1219 (1981).

M'Naghten's Case, 10 Cl. F. 200, 8 Eng. Rep. 718 (H.L. 1843).

Neely v. United States, 150 F2d 977 (D.C. Cir), *cert. denied*, 326 U.S. 768 (1945).

Parham v. J.R., 442 U.S. 584 (1979).

People v. White, 117 Cal. App. 3d 270, 172 Cal. Rptr 612 (1981).

Schloendorff v. Society of New York Hospital, 211 NY 125, 126, 105 NE 92, 93 (1914).

Speer v. United States, 512 F Supp. 670 (ND Tex. 1981), affd, Speer v. United States, 675 F2d 100 (5th Cir. 1982).

State v. Hehman, 110 Ariz. 459, 520 P2d 507 (1974).

Tarasoff v. Regents of the University of California, 17 Cal. 3d 425, 551 P2d 334, 131 Cal. Rptr 14 (1976).

The Eighth Amendment and the Execution of the Presently Incompetent, 32 Stan L Rev:765 (1980).

United States v. Brawner, 471 F.2d 969 (D.C. Cir. 1972).

United States v. David, 511 F2d 355 (D.C. Cir. 1975).

Youngberg v. Romeo, 457 U.S. 307 (1982), on remand, *Romeo v. Youngberg*, 687 F2d 33 (3rd Cir. 1982).

Index

nb – page numbers in *italics* refer to figures and tables

Compiled by Jill Halliday